Exporting the
American Gospel

Exporting the American Gospel:
Global Christian Fundamentalism

STEVE BROUWER

PAUL GIFFORD

SUSAN D. ROSE

Routledge
New York and London

Published in 1996 by

Routledge
29 West 35th Street
New York, NY 10001

Published in Great Britain by

Routledge
11 New Fetter Lane
London EC4P 4EE

Printed in the United States of America on acid-free paper.

Library of Congress Cataloging-in-Publication Data

Brouwer, Steve, 1947–
     Exporting the American gospel: global Christian fundamentalism / by Steve
Brouwer, Paul Gifford, Susan D. Rose.
        p. cm.
     Includes bibliographical references.
     ISBN 0-415-91711-5 (alk. paper). — ISBN 0-415-91712-3 (pbk. alk. paper)
     1. Fundamentalist churches.   2. Fundamentalism   3. Church history—20th
century.   I. Gifford, Paul, 1944–   .   II. Rose, Susan D., 1955–   .   III. Title.
BX7800.F863B76   1996
270.8'2—dc20
                                                                    96-8439
                                                                    CIP

Acknowledgments

We would like to thank the Fundamentalism Project, the Academy of Arts & Sciences, and Dickinson College for their support of this research. In particular we want to thank Professor Scott Appleby, co-director with Martin Marty of the Fundamentalism Project, for his encouragement and insightful critiques.

Contents

ONE

Introduction:
Global Christian Fundamentalism

> It's a release. I come here after working hard and getting dirty and hungry, and here...I can feel good, free for a while. I don't have to think about anything else but Jesus.
>
> —a follower of Brother Almeda's
> Miracle Crusade in the Philippines

A new kind of Christian fundamentalism, once thought to be unique to the United States, is spreading across the globe. A transnational religious culture is meeting a common need in the mega-cities of the developing world, in the slums that surround them, and in the outlying agricultural districts as well. In tiny brick and mud tabernacles with metal roofs and dirt floors, and in huge downtown auditoriums seating five thousand or twenty thousand, pastors are delivering the same message to their congregations: beseech God for your individual salvation, attend to the literal word of the Bible as the basis of truth, and spread the good news in preparation for the miraculous end of history and the beginning of Christ's millennium.

As the year 2000 approaches, there is considerable international receptivity to a fundamentalist Christian message and a sophisticated and powerful network for spreading the Word. Pat Robertson, for example, launched "Proyecto Luz" (or "Project Light"), a television revival aimed at all of Central America, in 1990. Broadcasting on Guatemalan TV with a program designed at the Christian Broadcasting Network in Virginia, the campaign reached over 60 percent of the Guatemalan audience, a record for any kind of programming. In the next six months, the revival engaged thousands of evangelical and Pentecostal churches throughout Central America.

Not all such activity starts in the U.S. heartland. The healing revivals of German evangelist Reinhard Bonnke, the most popular preacher in Africa, draw the largest crowds in the world: daily attendance of over two hundred thousand has been recorded in Nigeria, Kenya, and the tribal homelands of South Africa. And Paul Yonggi Cho, a Korean Pentecostal minister, has pioneered a fruitful combination of theology and organization to promote the growth of independent mega-churches. Cho is the pastor of the world's largest church, the Yoido Full Gospel Central Church in Seoul, South Korea, which claimed to have over eight hundred thousand members in 1994.

While the leaders of the new Christian faith come from various nations, the message is predominantly American. When believers enter a church in Africa, Asia, or Latin America, they participate in a form of worship that can be found in Memphis or Portland or New York City. Perhaps it will be Pentecostal, or Southern Baptist, or a ubiquitous charismatic product marketed by Bible schools in places such as Tulsa and Pasadena. These Protestants disseminate beliefs that can comfort middle-class businessmen at a prayer breakfast in Rio de Janeiro and inspire the poorest of the world's would-be consumers at a Bonnke crusade in Lagos. They proclaim, in a multitude of languages, new kinds of Christian powers and entitlements, such as those enumerated by Kenneth Copeland's "Voice of Victory," from Fort Worth, Texas:

> You are entitled to reign in life like a king...there are certain rights, certain liberties which you have as a son of God...you have the right to use each one of the things God has.

We are clearly in a new era of religion. Spiritual fervor is burning in many parts of the world, and it has become fashionable to label the believers—be they Muslim, Hindu, Jewish, or Christian—as "fundamentalists" who are somehow in conflict with the secular processes of modernization and global development. To many Westerners, the forces of "Islamic renewal" seem frightening and dangerous because they are rejecting and resisting many of the premises of "Westernization," and because Islam is a growing religion of 1.2 billion adherents. There are, of course, many currents within Islam, and some with genuinely fundamentalist traits, such as the Shi'ites in Iran, who attract so much attention because of their willingness to defy the United States in sociopolitical conflicts in the Middle East.

This book, however, focuses on the new Christian fundamentalism, a form that rivals Islamic radicalism in its global scope and is very likely more potent in its cultural influence, precisely because Christianity is a core element of "Western civilization." Christianity has been, historically, the modernizing and Westernizing religion that has spread over the globe in concert with the mercantile and industrial expansion of capitalism and the establishment of colonial empires. Today Christian countries (with Japan being the single exception) overwhelmingly control the world's productive resources and manufacturing, banking, and commercial institutions, as well as the dissemination of culture generated by scientific, academic, and commercial sources. This position of cultural and socioeconomic hegemony is reinforced by numbers: the world's 1.7 billion Christians are spread over a greater proportion of the globe than Muslims.[1]

Some recent interpretations of world events have tended to separate the processes of modernization and religious change into different camps, suggesting that economic globalization (the modern phenomenon) is opposed by cultural tribalism (a reversion to more primitive modes of association). This picture of conflict, McWorld versus Jihad,[2] gives appropriate credit to the aggressive spread of American business and media culture, but neglects the ways in which religious cultures are also enmeshed in the process of modernizing and globalizing themselves. For Christian fundamentalism in particular, the universalizing of the faith is intertwined with the homogenizing influences of consumerism, mass communication, and production in ways that are compatible with the creation of an international market culture by global capitalist institutions.

Christian fundamentalists represent only one part of the widespread European and North American cultural framework that has roots in a common Christian heritage, yet they are wielding a great deal of influence because their message and their powerful evangelization machinery generally have their origins in the United States. These fundamentalists are "Bible-believing" Protestants with a specific mission to win souls for Jesus in every country on earth. They have emerged from the broad ranks of socially conservative evangelical Protestantism, and include members of various denominations and independent churches, encompassing Pentecostals and Baptists, charismatics and Calvinists, and many other traditions. Born-again evangelical Christians comprise about 25 percent of the U.S. population, or sixty-five million people, and probably number more than four hundred million people worldwide, where their ranks are multiplying at phenomenal rates. A substantial portion of these constitute the fundamentalist base within the United States and abroad.[3] And some significant religious groups outside fundamentalist evangelical circles such as the Mormons and Jehovah's Witnesses share many beliefs and orientations.

Since Protestant Christianity, especially in the United States, has had a history of producing doctrinal disputes, splitting into rival denominations, and even creating individualized independent churches, it is important to note the common attributes that define the new fundamentalist Christianity (see Appendix). First, there is a personal, "born again" relationship between the believer and Jesus; this should lead the believer to convert others as part of the global evangelical mission. Secondly, God's sacred words are available to each believer in the text of the Bible, which is sufficient for an understanding of the world and as a guide to righteous living; usually this message is considered literally inerrant. Strict standards for personal behavior are usually mandated, such as abstention from alcohol and the prohibition of sexual activity outside of marriage, and a socially conservative view of human activity is strongly encouraged: that is, personal belief and piety are necessary for salvation, whereas social reforms to redress human inequalities are either peripheral or discouraged altogether. Religious historian William G. McLoughlin described the social conservativism of Christian fundamentalists and neo-evangelicals this way in the 1970s: "Neo-Evangelicalism justifies turning one's back on worldly affairs so complex that only God can cope with them. It argues that we can change the world only when God has changed the hearts of everyone in it."[4] Today their approach is not so passive. Heartened by their evangelistic and political successes, fundamentalists are still opposed to egalitarian social reforms but more active in demanding that their prescriptions for godly behavior be adopted by the society as a whole.

The final defining element of fundamentalist belief is the tendency to look for miraculous, God-centered interpretations of history, usually under the banner of Biblical millennialism and dispensationalism. Millennialist belief revolves around the certainty that the Second Coming of Christ is imminent and that His thousand-year rule over Earth will soon follow (the timing and degree of divine punishment meted out to non-believers vary according to premillennial and postmillennial versions). Dispensationalism, a rather complex form of alternative historical study that is derived solely from a closed and intricate system of Biblical sources and references, has been developed over the past two hundred years in order to support millennialist belief and predictions. In most versions there are dispensational ages of human history (coinciding, in creationist fashion, with the history of Earth and the universe) that culminate in the age of Christ's rule over the entire globe.

The broad segment of evangelicals who ascribe to this kind of fundamentalism should not be defined as narrowly as those who labeled themselves "the Fundamentalists" in the early part of the twentieth century in order to distinguish themselves from more liberal Protestants. Those conservatives, mostly Presbyterians and Baptists, were fairly exclusive, and particularly wary of associating with the new Pentecostal churches, the "wild sects" whose converts were mostly poor and marginalized people. Today, the new Christian fundamentalists are best defined by the more inclusive criteria of belief listed above. In the globalizing evangelical culture, little is to be gained from a sectarian, interior point of view, the kind that certain elements of Protestant culture once used to maintain their doctrinal purity and distinctive identities.

Within the traditions that support the new fundamentalism, many differences remain. However, they have been less troubling and divisive to the overall evangelical movement in the past twenty-five years. For instance, Pentecostal Christians, who believe in the Baptism of the Holy Spirit, emphasize miraculous experiences for the individual believer, such as prophecy, healing, and speaking in tongues. They have emerged from the shadow of the old Christian fundamentalism, but they have not rejected its broad tenets; rather they have transformed and energized the experience of worship while also adopting strong fundamentalist loyalties to Biblical inerrancy, creationism, and millennialist dispensationalism. Other fundamentalists of the "old style," including many in the Southern Baptist denomination and independent Baptists such as Jerry Falwell, disagree with Pentecostal practice and think that genuine miraculous "gifts" were endowed only in Biblical times, not in the present.

The key point is that such differences among fundamentalist Christians have receded in importance and provoked less conflict in recent years. This happened in part because fundamentalism has become a more dynamic social and political movement in the United States, exemplified by Jerry Falwell's Moral Majority, Pat Robertson's candidacy for the U.S. presidency in 1988, and the emergence of the Christian Coalition as a major force in the 1994 and 1996 elections. The conservative evangelical Christians who provide the energy for such activism generally fall within our definitions of the new fundamentalism. As they became aware of their increasing power within the Republican Party over the past fifteen years, and of the possibility of pushing for a conservative social agenda at local, state, and national levels, they began to concentrate on building alliances and relying on simpler, less doctrinaire definitions of acceptable Christianity. As Pat Robertson declared in his 1986 book, *America's Dates with Destiny*: "Evangelicals are finding themselves more and more united...they are committed to a speedy and wholehearted return by America to her Judeo-Christian heritage."[5]

The second reason for more inclusiveness among new Christian fundamentalists is, we believe, even more compelling. It arises from the dominance of Pentecostalism in evangelizing efforts around the world—it is the main force generating conversion to Christianity, and the conversion of Catholics to Protestantism. Pentecostals describe their churches as "full Gospel," meaning that believers are "filled with the Holy Spirit" in a way that was promised to the early Christians in the Gospels and other books of the New Testament; that is, they have access to miraculous powers, "the gifts of the Spirit," including rites of healing and driving out demons that have immense appeal in various cultures. Paul Yonggi Cho asserts that the unique spiritual power of Pentecostalism and neo-Pentecostalism has propelled the growth of Christianity over the past sixty years:

> Eighty percent of all the converts to Christianity have come, not from the vast majority of Christians who have not been filled with the Holy Spirit, but from those who have the Holy Spirit dwelling in them.[6]

As is the practice of many evangelists, Cho may be inflating the figure, but it does correlate with the fact that most new Protestants have been recruited outside of North America and Europe; in Latin America two thirds to three quarters of all Protestants are now Pentecostal.[7]

Although the new Christian fundamentalism possesses a theological doctrine and a religious practice that are American, it is in the process of becoming an international religious culture generated by enthusiastic, broad-based movements in dozens of countries. While U.S. missionaries and their resources are still very strong players (most Protestant missionaries are from the United States[8]), indigenous fundamentalist churches have become partners in propagating and deepening the faith. The existence of thousands of denominations and independent churches may seem chaotic, but they have little time for serious doctrinal dispute as they compete to fill the vacuum created by massive social dislocation and economic transformation. Harvey Cox has even suggested that "Pentecostalism...is actually a kind of ecumenical movement."[8] Moreover, the Pentecostal churches are engendering similar religious practices in non-Pentecostal traditions, even within "mainline" denominations connected to more liberal, distinctly non-fundamentalist Protestant and Catholic churches. A number of religious scholars have attested to the effectiveness of the "enthusiasm" and "power" generated by the Pentecostals. In their latest, more middle-class manifestations, the new fundamentalists are referred to as neo-Pentecostals and charismatics (see Appendix), depending on where they are located in the world; their churches are pursuing their own programs of innovative growth and political influence.

Why Does Christian Fundamentalism Work and Where Is It Going?

In the course of this book, we shall attempt to describe some of the characteristics of the new Christian fundamentalism. First we look briefly at its theological origins and permutations in the United States, where it combined and simplified many of the attributes already developed within nineteenth- and twentieth-century conservative Protestantism. Then we offer case studies from our research abroad: in-depth examples of its implementation in countries as diverse as Liberia, the Philippines, Guatemala, and South Korea, and a broad outline of its diffusion on one continent, Africa. Since the subject and field of study are so vast and uncharted, we emphasize some trends at the expense of others, selecting examples that illuminate the innovative ways in which a global religious culture is being formed. We give attention to the recent U.S. export of "faith" theology (or "prosperity" theology) because it is booming almost everywhere, especially in large urban areas with middle-class constituencies. This quintessentially American faith, which promises material "blessings" and spiritual "power encounters" to all, is rapidly shaping the content of the evangelical message that is spread among the lower classes.

This leads us to inquire about the relationship of new fundamentalist Christianity to the transformation and globalization of the world's cultures in general. How is it possible that people in the rest of the world are adapting their beliefs to precepts developed in Oklahoma, Texas, and California? And conversely, how can Protestant practice adapt so quickly to the requirements and peculiarities of a changing world? We note that rapid religious change is occurring simultaneously with the industrialization of many parts of the developing world and the concomitant commodification of everyday life. Is there, in a way analogous to the connection between evangelical Protestantism and industrial development on a national scale in the nineteenth century, now a fledgling connection between worldwide capitalist expansion and a new form of internationalized Christianity?

The United States, in spite of its uneven economic performance of recent years, still possesses powers that can shape the world. The proliferation of its popular media culture is unchallenged; its military might is unmatched; its dedication to the spread of corporate capitalism and international finance is still unwavering. In a world where old political and social entities are straining under the pressure of globalization, American-led economic development seems to offer access to a smoothly running and well-integrated world system. At the same time, American evangelists and their foreign brethren are marketing a supra-national and supernatural solution to religious uncertainties. Astute Christian entrepreneurs are successfully selling a new international belief system.

Within Christianity new organizational structures have evolved that are much more nimble than the old forms of denominational Protestantism in the United States or the tradition-bound hierarchies of the Roman Catholic Church. The mega-church of Paul Yonggi Cho, the broadcasting network of Robertson, the Campus Crusade directed by Bill Bright, and even the unique business/religious empire of Reverend Sun Young Moon are essentially corporate transnational religious entities under the control of entrepreneurial authority figures. They can and do speedily ally with each other and a plethora of smaller independent churches on both practical business matters and matters of the faith. These connections are facilitated by parachurch support groups such as the Full Gospel Business Men's Fellowship International with its nearly one million members. The influence of these entities already threatens to outstrip the dwindling older Protestant denominations in the United States, and in some parts of the developing world the new churches and parachurches are simply obliterating old denominational lines.

This late-twentieth-century religious culture is reproducing itself rapidly within or, some might say, on top of vastly different cultures in Latin America, the Caribbean, Africa, and Asia; even, over the last few years, in Eastern Europe and the former Soviet Union. Some of these countries are very poor and struggling to develop and modernize themselves; others have already been, or are rapidly becoming, industrialized. Everywhere local cultures are disintegrating, traditional family structures and mores are collapsing, and urban areas are awash with people who are already detached from their traditions. They may be impoverished wage earners, anxious secretaries, ambitious young businessmen, struggling shopkeepers, or highly trained engineers. The new fundamentalist Christianity offers them a variation of the disciplined faith that helped sustain daily life in previous periods of industrialization and urbanization.

The world economic picture, especially in most places where fundamentalist Christianity is spreading, is rather bleak. Economic growth stagnated in the highly industrialized countries between 1970 and 1995, and in most parts of Latin America and Africa (and some places in Asia) there was a precipitous decline in the already meager living standards of most people. Although a second round of industrialization and modernization is taking place worldwide, it has not yet proved itself to be beneficial to more than a handful of nations. Harsh political realities have often accompanied the dire state of economic affairs. Despite the democratic institutions that are appearing in some countries (many of them as yet superficial), many developing nations have been saddled with repressive governments and social austerity measures dictated by the International Monetary Fund. Christian fundamentalists often appear to prosper in the presence of political authoritarianism and economic misery. Some governments, such as those in the Philippines and El Salvador, have even introduced evangelical religious indoctrination of their armed forces as one component of Low Intensity Conflict initiatives prescribed by the United States.

Fundamentalist notions of spiritual warfare and social orderliness are aggressively marketed by the new evangelizing forces because they are intent on competing with a cast of spiritual enemies. They are seeking a final confrontation between Good and Evil. They see this Evil, depending on the particular local circumstances, embodied in the false religions of socialism, Islam, humanism, feminism, and even Catholicism.

Catholicism is at times treated gently and simply dismissed as an insufficiently developed or weak form of Christianity. At other times fundamentalists perceive communistic, satanic qualities within Catholicism, especially in places where liberation theology is prevalent. Because of the demise of communist governments in the Soviet Union and Eastern Europe, the threat of socialistic governments is somewhat diminished in the eyes of fundamentalist Christians. In its place another false religion fomented by the AntiChrist is gaining recognition: Islam. According to one Christian writer in Africa, now that God has demolished the Iron Curtain, "the wall of the Islamic world is also going to crumble very soon."[10]

Although it is beyond the scope of this book to adequately describe changes taking place in various Islamic cultures, we are intrigued by developments that are common to both Islam and Christianity. The modern fundamentalist trends that form a part of both religions are well-suited for transnational growth and distribution, with simplified messages of the Word that can be transferred and translated easily in globalizing societies. Both have a mixture of egalitarian and authoritarian impulses that are imbedded in absolutist belief systems. Significantly, both Islamic and Christian fundamentalism have reacted to the emerging freedom of women with anti-feminist programs that reinforce their patriarchal roots: they restrict female roles, teach the submission of women to men, glorify motherhood, control sexuality, and re-establish the dominance of males in positions of social authority. The new Christian fundamentalism is a reconfiguration of patriarchal power; it may welcome female participation and celebrate womanly qualities, but only when it can subordinate women to male control.

The simultaneous appearance of Islamic and Christian fundamentalism also has implications within the larger social and political sphere. Political scientist Samuel Huntington has warned about the impending "clash of civilizations" and the disruptive role of religion. Huntington is clearly most concerned about the threat of the Islamic revival to the orderly governance of the capitalist world system, and he is openly in favor of a conservative, elitist view of Western civilization (of the kind that used to dominate mainstream, upper-class Protestant circles.) However, his description of the international influence of Islam also pertains to the fundamentalist revival that has usurped the global role within Protestant Christianity: "The renewal of religion," he writes, "provides a basis for identity and commitment that transcends national boundaries and unites civilizations."[11] The irony (which Huntington misses) is that Christian fundamentalism, not Islam, may have the potential to create more conflict internationally, for it can avail itself of all the advantages and power generated by a Western-dominated economic system and its invasive message of consumption.

For instance, the "prosperity theology" of neo-Pentecostal Christians projects the notion that faith can instantly gratify material wants. This concept improves upon the American "gospel of wealth" that was preached to middle-class congregations a century ago, for it makes the religious culture compatible with the worldwide commodity culture. Even the poorest people in the poorest lands see daily images of consumer goods and want to buy articles with globally recognizable names, often American ones. The president of the

Radio Corporation of America (RCA) once succinctly summed up this universal identification with commodities (as he tried to explain why his company was closing television factories in the United States and expanding in areas of cheap labor abroad): "We live in a global village," he said. "The girls of Taiwan want their Mickey Mouse T-shirts, too."

By making the connection with a global culture of consumption, we do not want to suggest that the American roots of the new fundamentalism are superficial or that the powerful imagery of Christianity is being reduced to the level of the Disney corporation, which has its own standards of hegemony.[12] Nor should one conclude that the success of Christian evangelists depends on temporary political phenomena in the United States, such as the rhetoric employed by the Reagan administration in the 1980s and by the Christian Coalition in the 1990s. Rather we are suggesting that the new faith is inclusive, so powerful and widespread that it is easily adapting to a number of modern contingencies. It would be a mistake to think that the emphasis on material considerations necessarily shortchanges spirituality, for above all the new fundamentalism is expansionary, ambitiously extending its reach over more and more phenomena—natural and spiritual, material and psychological.

Although the spiritual nature of Christian fundamentalism is undeniable, this does not necessarily imbue it with the rational spirit once attributed to Protestantism by Max Weber. Its intellectual inventiveness has been concentrated on reformulating the old fundamentalist message while articulating new forms of active spiritualism. A classic example is Pat Robertson's reaction to Hurricane Gloria in 1985. He ordered Gloria, which was devastating the East Coast of the United States, to bypass Virginia Beach and his Christian Broadcasting Network: "In the name of Jesus, we command you to stop where you are and move northeast, away from land, and away from harm. In the name of Jesus of Nazareth, we command it." The hurricane missed Virginia Beach. Robertson later declared that this demonstration of his spiritual power should convince Americans that he had corresponding political powers: "It was extremely important because I felt, interestingly enough, that if I couldn't move a hurricane, I could hardly move a nation…it was very important to the faith of many people."[13]

This kind of Christian fundamentalism sees itself as the only avenue to divine power, the only true religion qualified to "move a nation." This would not be any more disquieting than similar convictions among some contemporary Muslims and Hindus, were it not closely connected to other firmly held American beliefs. Christian fundamentalists in the United States, in common with many other social and political conservatives, also believe in the Manifest Destiny of their country, in the God-given right to get rich, and in the necessary preeminence of U.S. military power. Perhaps the dissemination of their religious beliefs is not imperialistic in the old colonial sense, just as the spread of multinational corporations cannot be ascribed to capitalistic plotting on Wall Street. However, even as Christian fundamentalism is purveyed by an aggressive international sales force—Koreans, Nigerians, Germans, Filipinos, Brazilians, Australians, and Guatemalans—the social product that they distribute so successfully around the world is clearly stamped "Made in the U.S.A."

> Those Americans are the Franciscans and the Dominicans of our time. They may not see it that way, but they are the religious arm of an economic, political, and cultural system.
>
> —Salomon Nahmad,
> National Indigenist Institute of Mexico[14]

TWO

Fundamentalist Americanism and Christian Fundamentalism

To comprehend the global diffusion of the new forms of Christian fundamentalism it is necessary to understand the forces that generate the faith and its accompanying theology within the United States. Among the many strengths of the belief system, something we will call "fundamentalist Americanism" stands out: the belief peculiar to U.S. Christianity that simultaneously sanctifies American nationalism and the American gospel of success, wealth, and prosperity.

Belief in fundamentalist Americanism—the faith that God's plan for the United States and its individual citizens is one of superiority, unending growth, and prosperity—has been strong and dynamic throughout U.S. history. It is by no means unique to Christian fundamentalists, yet recently they have embraced this faith more passionately than other religious and secular groups. This gives them a militant legitimacy that commands respect outside their ranks and helps inspire fundamentalists to evangelize outside the United States, for they are convinced that Americans have something superior to offer the rest of the world. And the people who are the object of their evangelization are impressed, too, not just by U.S. wealth but also by the self-confidence and practical "can-do" spirit of missionary and parachurch organizations.

It would be tempting to equate this kind of Americanism with the various modes of civil religion that are practiced elsewhere in the world, whether they emphasize the role of the nation and institutionalize nationalistic rites, or celebrate ethnocentric values that seem particularly salient to their peoples' identity. But fundamentalist Americanism has always incorporated civil religious values within a larger schematic of faith, making it particularly distinct at this moment in history from other forms of nationalism. It is so inextricably mixed with U.S. Christianity that it cannot be called a secular religion. It has a tendency to celebrate the expansionary economic and political power of the United States, now the only global superpower, in other parts of the world.

Americans still believe, unlike the citizens of other advanced industrialized countries that once tried to imbue colonies with their special cultures, that other peoples of the globe can and ought to be made over in their image. This religious preoccupation is fueled by the fact that the United States presently has the world's dominant culture. "Americanization" is promoted through the proliferation of American media and commodities, through adherence to American-led programs of economic development, and through the adoption of English as the international language. Fundamentalist Christian Americanism pushes this globalization and simplification of culture more intensely, on the religious plane, because its believers have more than something to sell. They have a particular Biblical truth to share and billions of unsaved souls to rescue.

More than a few empires and nations, both ancient and modern, have developed the notion that God, or some other form of Providence, smiles upon their expansionary efforts and the prosperity that economic and territorial expansion can fulfill. In the United States this imperialistic zeal was bred into the national psyche from the beginning and has been repeatedly renewed in pursuits of "Manifest Destiny" and historical mission. Today, however, as intellectual and even geopolitical justifications for expanding the American presence in the world are weakly stated or on the wane, a resurgent kind of Protestantism is finding powerful theological justifications for saving the world. More than ever before, this faith in America is based in the supernatural, the apocalyptic, and the miraculous—thus giving rise to a dispensationalist, millenarian, and Pentecostal theological framework that supports the new fundamentalism.

Belief in America

Christian fundamentalists in the United States could not have appealed to a broad spectrum of conservative Americans without re-establishing a belief in America's special place among nations. Furthermore, the United States could not have projected its faith to a large part of the world without a conviction that other peoples ought to be guided and ruled by American principles, both civil and religious. Since the time of the Puritans, Protestantism has served as the civil religion of the colonies and the United States. Concepts of participatory government and national purpose were not a substitute for religion, for they were embedded in practices and experiments that were directly connected to the religious Europeans who settled the country. As the nation expanded, it grew confident of a more global mission, so that there was little public doubt that God's objectives and American policy were one and the same. Cotton Mather, preaching in 1692 in Massachusetts, spoke about the role of America's chosen people in a manner that was adopted by U.S. missionaries and statesmen for the next three centuries:

> The New Englanders are a People of God Settled in those which were once the Devil's territories…a People here accomplishing the promise of old made unto our Blessed Jesus, that He should have the Utmost parts of the Earth for His possession.[1]

By the mid-nineteenth century, the American equation—that the United States equals the Christian good—had become more specifically identified with a Manifest Destiny and the expansion of capitalism. Thus William Gilpin, the governor of the Colorado Territory in 1846, described this creed in his report to the U.S. Senate:

> The destiny of the American people is to subdue the continent.
> Unite the world in one social family.
> Divine task! Immortal mission!
> America leads the host of nations as they ascend to this order of civilization…the industrial conquest of the world.[2]

When the twentieth century arrived, Woodrow Wilson was a staunch Presbyterian and the progressively minded president of both Princeton University and the United States. Although his kind of mainstream Protestantism was becoming secularized, liberalized, and modernized, Wilson based his vision, the noble task of "making the world free for democracy," on the premise that the United States was uniquely qualified for its divine calling. Thus he stated confidently that:

> America was born a Christian nation. America was born to exemplify that devotion to the elements of righteousness which are derived from the revelations of Holy Scripture.[3]

At the end of the twentieth century evangelical leaders Jerry Falwell and Pat Robertson remain faithful to this tradition. They join conservative Republicans in criticizing the old mainline Protestant denominations for abandoning, or at least being half-hearted about, the celebration of the United States' supernatural status as a nation. When Falwell began building the reputation of the Moral Majority in 1976, he visited the fifty-one most important shrines of American civil religion—the fifty state capitols and the U.S. Capitol in Washington—in order to stage his patriotic-religious "I Love America" rallies. The first chapter of his 1980 book calling for a moral reawakening, *Listen America,* does not talk about sin and redemption, but rather about free enterprise and the battle against global communism and the Soviet Satan. He certainly wrote about what he believed, but also tailored it to a nationalistic audience that was hearing a similar message from Ronald Reagan. Falwell quoted some of the lesser-known lyrics from the U.S. National Anthem to define and bolster his argument:

> Praise the Power that hath made and preserved us a nation
> Then conquer we must when our cause is just
> And this be our motto: "In God is our Trust."[4]

Between the beginning and the end of the twentieth century, the fundamentalists realized an important victory over the more moderate and liberal forms of the Protestant tradition. How, we might ask, had they become the foremost spokespeople for Americanism?

The process began in the 1940s and 1950s rather improbably with the ultra-conservative harangues of anti-communist fundamentalist-separatists Carl McIntire and Billy James Hargis. As their message was reinforced by the somewhat milder and popular evangelistic anti-communist message of Billy Graham, the broadening ranks of Christian fundamentalists began to take control of a strong pro-Americanist position that was being vacated by liberals. Some leaders in the historic churches began to hedge on total commitment to America First. An important capitulation was their frequent reluctance to identify the nuclear muscle of the U.S. with Christ and the nuclear dangers of the USSR with Satan. Many liberal churchmen only compounded this problem: their flirtation with the politics of disarmament, which was construed as lack of Americanism and patriotism by religious ultra-conservatives, was followed by their discomfort with, and opposition to, the Vietnam War. Their conservative critics alleged that the relativistic philosophy and secular compromises favored by mainstream theologians and intellectuals had harmed the nation and damaged the fortunes of the older Protestant denominations. By the end of the 1970s, most conservative and fundamentalist Christians had thrown in their lot with Ronald Reagan, who wanted God's chosen country to redress the humiliation of Vietnam and again stand tallest and best among all nations.

These sentiments had their roots, for both Reagan personally and the conservative and religious right generally, in the days of McCarthyism, and more broadly from 1945 until the late 1950s. There had been a general resurgence of conservative evangelical revivalism (which included, but was not dominated by Pentecostal healing revivals), and its most famous proponent was Billy Graham. In the late 1940s, Graham helped redefine the "old-time" fundamentalist message (which dated back only to the end of the nineteenth century) as he staged revivals for the Youth for Christ organization. He, like many other preachers, had taken notice of the peculiar resurgence of American nationalism; more than ever before Americans were regularly exhorted to believe in their country as it engaged in the battle of good against evil. Christian good was equated with anti-communist Americanism; as for evil, Graham once said: "My own theory about communism is that it is masterminded by Satan."[5]

This kind of evil not only threatened American interests in all parts of the world; it also had the insidious power, according to Graham, of attacking the very fabric of American life: "One of the great goals of Communism is to destroy the American home and cause moral deterioration in this country."[6]

Geopolitical concerns were merged with the evangelical defense of the patriarchal family, as red-blooded American men were asked to protect the honor of their country and their women.

In these beliefs, Graham found support far beyond the bounds of the older generation of fundamentalists. For instance, William Randolph Hearst, the newspaper tycoon, had been struck by Graham's all-American appearance and anti-communism, and so transmitted a two-word message to his editors across the country, instructing them to "Puff Graham."[7] In 1946 and 1947, John Foster Dulles, who would later become Eisenhower's secretary of state, wrote a series of articles for *LIFE* magazine stating that: "What America needs now is a spiritual revival."[8] By the time of the Korean War, he believed that the United States embodied the qualities of heroic crusader in Korea: "We have borne a Christian witness...we have acted as God gave us to see the right."[9] Dulles was completely reversing the opinion of nationalism he held before World War II, when he condemned it "as the form of patriotism which personifies the nation as a living being endowed with heroic qualities."[10] Without believing in the kinds of Biblical inerrancy that motivated evangelicals like Billy Graham, conservative establishment representatives like Dulles formulated a Manichean, more or less fundamentalist view of the saved and the unsaved. According to Dulles:

> The world is divided into two groups of people: the Christian anti-communists, and the others.[11]

Conservative Baptists, Pentecostals, and other fundamentalists readily accepted this global-political mission as part of their own program of intense religious evangelization. Their congregations, which were often composed of people of modest means, were rich when compared to the lost souls who inhabited the rest of the globe. Through devoted tithing they could afford to send out a steady stream of missionaries and Biblical literature. Appeals in the name of anti-communism were particularly effective in the money-raising efforts of successful independent evangelists and revivalists who started their own foreign mission programs.

At this time the fundamentalist Christian understanding of Biblical prophecy began to reshape the role of fundamentalist Americanism in world politics. The nuclear standoff between the Soviet Union and the United States terrified most people in those years, but for fundamentalists the threat of atomic war was also fraught with promise. The imminent Second Coming of Christ was associated with Armageddon, so it was imperative that evangelicals complete the "Great Commission," which was Christ's injunction to spread the Word to all nations. There was an urgency about completing this task as quickly as possible before the "end times" arrived. In some versions of dispensationalist theology, the dissemination of The Word would hasten the arrival of the end: when all nations had been evangelized, Jesus would make his return and "rapture" true Christians up from the Earth just as it was being destroyed. Cameron Townsend, a missionary to Guatemala and the founder of the Wycliffe Bible Translators (later the Summer Institute of Linguistics), interpreted the fulfillment of Matthew 24:14 to be:

> Good news of the Kingdom will be proclaimed to men all over the world…and then the end will come.[12]

In the minds of fundamentalists, endless connections existed between current world events and the Biblical prerequisites for the Second Coming. Among these, none seemed more significant to many Christians than the special status of Israel and the restoration of Zion, another sign of end-time activity:

> Whoever stands against Israel, stands against God.
> —Jerry Falwell

> God will bless those who bless Israel, but He will bring low those who would harm the Jews.
> —Lester Sumrall[13]

The conflict between Israel and its Arab neighbors seemed to provide the site for the final conflagration, in which their respective superpower supporters, the United States and the Soviet Union, would engage in the ultimate battle between good and evil. According to dispensationalist theology, it would be advantageous for Christians to convert the Jews immediately before the end. Frequently evangelistic organizations, such as Gordon Lindsay's Christ for the Nations, gave special attention to Israel, though with little success in winning Israelis to Jesus. Later, in the early 1980s, Pat Robertson operated according to the same rationale when he bought a powerful television station in Southern

Lebanon near the Israeli border, the only foreign affiliate of his Christian Broadcasting Network. This location retains its importance in the apocalyptic Biblical vision today, since Muslim countries have now assumed the mantle of evil from the departed Soviet Union. Not only are leaders like Gaddafi and Saddam Hussein demonized by Christians (and the Western press, for that matter), but Muslim peoples in general are labeled by evangelists as "spiritually oppressed" and in "Satan's bondage."[14]

The insistence of American Christians on the special status of the United States is not completely unique; in fact, it is mirrored in the beliefs of Calvinist fundamentalists who settled in South Africa and Northern Ireland. They felt, like the Puritans in America, that God had made a special covenant with them that guaranteed their special, elevated status compared to the heathen, whether indigenous Africans or Irish Catholics. Political scientist Steve Bruce, writing about the Scottish Presbyterian tradition that informs Northern Irish Protestants, notes that:

> there has always been a strong tendency for Calvinists to see themselves, in images drawn from the history of the children of Israel, as an elect "collectivity," a tendency exaggerated when threatened by a large mass of "heathens."[15]

Bruce suggests that intense nationalism is the reason that many contemporary Northern Irish Protestants vote for people like Ian Paisley, the fundamentalist preacher who made a successful career in British Parliament by representing the extreme right and excoriating Irish Catholics. The fundamentalist candidates are perceived as extreme but exemplary by the more moderate Protestants who admire them for their stalwart nationalism and defense of Protestant values.[16]

Christian fundamentalism in the United States no doubt draws upon similar sympathies. However, American religious nationalism is unique because of its peculiar global character. Christian fundamentalists in other countries find common cause with American evangelists because the United States is the well-spring of anti-communism and a host of other cultural ideologies and values that have become transnational. Halfway around the world, religious leaders have managed to link the destinies of their countries to that of the United States. This has led to interesting hypotheses about supernatural intentions in history, among them the Rev. Sun Myung Moon's justification of the elimination of American Indians by white settlers in North America:

> America's existence was according to God's providence. God needed to build one powerful Christian nation on earth for his future work. After all, America belonged to God first, and only after that to the Indians. This is the only reason that can justify the position of the Pilgrim settlers.[17]

If such Biblical interpretation sometimes helps foreign Christians justify the questionable activities of the founders of the United States, it also can lead them to discover the divine purpose prophesied for their own nation. Reverend Moon, who considers himself a Christian, has stated that "Korea has replaced Israel as 'the land of the Messiah,'"[18] even hinting that he might be the one to fill the role. However heretical they may find such a comment, many other Protestant Koreans, whose theology remains more firmly in line with conventional fundamentalist views, share Moon's view about Korea's special place in contemporary history.[19] They, too, see Korea as the Holy Land of the East, sharing with the United States the task of evangelizing the world, maybe even superseding the U.S. in God's plans for Asia. An official at the Yoido Full Gospel Church described the process this way: "Americans are the generation who planted the seeds. We [Koreans] will harvest them."[20]

The propensity of Korean Christians for millenarian doctrines originated with fundamentalist Presbyterian evangelists in the early twentieth century; but it is also connected to their precarious geopolitical position during the Cold War. If the nuclear battle with Satanic forces began on their own territory, then their connection to American godliness would lead to their redemption.[21]

During the Central American wars of the 1980s, there was an evangelical boom that had complex links to the ideology of spiritual conquest and the diffusion of U.S. political and economic influence. A host of U.S. missionaries found a variety of ways to assist the Nicaraguan Contras, as well as the military regimes in El Salvador, Honduras, and Guatemala. Pat Robertson was among them in 1982 when he launched "Operation Lovelift," his multimillion dollar airlift of aid in support to the born-again Christian dictator of Guatemala, General Rios Montt, who had identified the enemy: "the rottenness has a name, communism or the Antichrist."[22] When Robertson returned to Guatemala in 1990 to inaugurate the evangelizing extravaganza known as Proyecto Luz, one of his auxiliary purposes was to portray Rios Montt as an eminent and responsible civilian, a man who once nobly served his country and his faith and was now prepared to be elected president of the country. To Robertson and his cohorts, this extension of evangelicalism and Americanism was the most natural thing in the world.

The Gospel of Wealth and Prosperity

Another indispensable part of the American faith has also been appropriated by the fundamentalists: the gospel of wealth. This fixation with material gain had early roots, for even in the seventeenth century Calvinists were establishing religious precedence for unequal property relations in America. Governor Winthrop of the Plymouth colony provided clear sanction for class divisions among settlers as well as a rationale for taking land away from the indigenous people:

> God Almighty in his most holy and wise providence hath disposed of the con-
> dition of mankind, as in all times some must be rich some poor, some high and
> eminent in power and dignity; others mean and in subjection.[23]

By the first half of the nineteenth century, American Protestants anticipat-
ed a limitless bounty of goods created both by extending the boundaries of
the nation and by means of manufacturing. As part of this process, the earliest industrialists were evangelizing their workers in the small towns where
water-powered mills were developed. By their very proximity to their mill
operatives, the owners were led to work directly through the main Protestant
churches—Episcopal, Presbyterian, Congregational, Baptist, and Methodist—
in order to inculcate Christian discipline and respect for the processes of early
capitalism. The owners and their families often became personally engaged in
founding Sunday schools and evangelical "mission" churches that taught
proper Christian deportment and work habits to their employees. They were
sadly disappointed when the workers did not measure up to their expectations. For instance, Clementina Smith, the daughter of a cotton manufacturer
who was active in evangelization efforts, explained why her father's mill
operatives went on strike to protest falling wages in 1842:

> It would seem that the Spirit of Evil has been abroad among this people...many
> have made shipwreck of their faith.[24]

Satan, as in this case, apparently won small battles in the religious struggle
to "improve" the masses. But the Protestant faith would not be deterred from
continually adapting to the changing requirements of capital and social relations in a rapidly industrializing country. The expansion of economic opportunities and the U.S. territory afforded room for an evangelicalism tinted by
Arminian optimism; Protestantism could help some of the faithful realize the
generosity of God right here on Earth. The owners of capital and founders of
fledgling industries took a direct and paternalistic interest in the affairs of their
workers. They attempted to demonstrate their own probity and enlightenment, which not only reflected their good fortune, but also demonstrated the
good Christian life that the lesser classes, who often shared the same villages
with them, should emulate. The strivers among the working people might be
rewarded someday with chances to be foremen; it was even possible, if they
were able mechanics and organizers among them, for a few to start their own
little manufacturing operations. Historical anthropologist A. F. C. Wallace,
who studied this convergence of evangelicalism and capitalism in *Rockdale*,

noted that such towns set an example for the continuing cultural and economic development of the United States:

> It was in Rockdale, and in dozens of other industrial communities like
> Rockdale, that an American world view developed which pervades the pre-
> sent—with a sense of superior Christian virtue, a sense of global mission, a
> sense of responsibility and capability of bringing enlightenment to a dark and
> superstitious world, for overthrowing ancient and new tyrannies, and for mak-
> ing backward infidels into Christian men of enterprise.[25]

After the Civil War, the relationship between teaching Christianity and
reaching for prosperity gained a new dimension. As industrialization allowed
personal fortunes to multiply extravagantly, and as government and the rich
worked hand in hand to guarantee the ascension of a new corporate and
banking structure, the idea of pure wealth—sometimes rather distant from
notions of hard work and moral probity—became the American Dream. The
reverence for riches was sanctified by both secular and religious beliefs,
although sometimes the churchmen and the "realist" entrepreneurs seemed to
be switching roles. The millionaire industrialist Andrew Carnegie, a confirmed atheist, wrote a book titled *The Gospel of Wealth*, which legitimatized
his own vast accumulations of capital and did much to convince well-placed
Protestants of the merits of the philosophy of Social Darwinism. About the
same time, the eminent Protestant magazine, *The Congregationalist,* offered its
ruthless solution to popular protests about the increasing disparity in wealth,
an alternative to the reforms sought by striking workers:

> a Gatling gun or two, swiftly brought into position and well served, offers, on
> the whole, the merciful as well as effectual remedy.[26]

There was a different message to those who were benefiting from the increasing disparity between the social classes. Russell H. Conwell, the Baptist
preacher who built the biggest church in America in Philadelphia during the
Gilded Age, preached his famous "Acre of Diamonds" sermon over 6,000
times across the United States. He congratulated the wealthy stratum of society for doing their job and encouraged others to do God's will as well:

> I say that you ought to get rich, it's your duty to get rich.[27]

As the main Protestant denominations and the class of industrialists cooperated in incorporating this gospel of wealth into the American civil religion,
there was an important nineteenth century development in evangelical practice that would give form to fundamentalist Christianity in the twentieth century. This was the invention of the urban Bible College by Dwight D. Moody
of Chicago, the most influential evangelist of the late nineteenth century.

Moody managed to devise a combination of simple theology, business boos-terism, and enthusiastic Christian witness that appealed to working- and lower-middle-class people in the cities, especially to displaced rural white Americans struggling to keep their heads above water. Moody appealed directly to the industrialists for help in financing his efforts:

> I say to the richest men in Chicago, their money will not be worth much if communism and infidelity sweep the land...there can be no better investment for the capitalists of Chicago than to put the saving salt of the Gospel into these dark homes and desperate centers.[28]

When Moody took his revivals from city to city, the richest Americans openly supported him and served on his welcoming committees: Cyrus McCormick and George Armour in Chicago, John Wanamaker in Philadel-phia, Cornelius Vanderbilt and J. P. Morgan in New York. But his talent did not lie in convincing the elite of their moral rectitude, but rather in inspiring the average American, who was suffering from declining earnings, to believe in a conservative social message and his own financial success:

> I have heard reform, reform, until I am tired and sick of the whole thing. It is the regeneration by the power of the Holy Ghost that we need.[29]
> I never saw the man who put Christ first in his life that wasn't successful.[30]

Moody helped fuse the American civil religion, with its beliefs in the supe-riority of the United States and the importance of the individual pursuit of wealth, with what would become the basis of fundamentalist Christian the-ology: individual salvation and evangelization, Biblical inerrancy, and an anti-historical and anti-scientific use of premillenial dispensationalism. When this particular fusion was reborn in late twentieth-century fundamentalism, more liberal, mainstream Protestant institutions were failing to preach the gospel of wealth as faithfully as their nineteenth century Protestant predecessors, just as they were a little laggard in their patriotism and nationalism.

The heyday of American liberalism, in economics, politics, and religion, occurred between 1945 and 1975. Among other things, it depended upon two social phenomena, the growing prosperity of average Americans and the increasing economic and social equality in the United States.[31] Steady eco-nomic growth and the fact that prosperity was shared across classes con-tributed to a sense of magnanimity, an acceptance of the idea that the American Dream might one day include everyone. Liberals recognized that many poor and non-white Americans did not share in the new prosperity of the working class, and they convinced a good part of the general population that universal social programs were an acceptable way to share the nation's bounty.

This democratization of the gospel of wealth, which tapped into older feelings of Arminian benevolence and shared civic duty, was dependent on the status of Americans as the world's richest citizens. The practical application of liberal ideas became more problematic as the United States began to decline from its position of overwhelming dominance in the world economy. The process of gradual disenchantment with mid-twentieth-century liberalism was accelerated when average American wages began a continuous slide downward (about 1973),[32] while inequalities in the income and wealth of different social classes began to increase significantly. Many liberals in the older Protestant traditions were not ready to mount a spirited defense of money and property, in fact, some Protestants and Catholics were exploring the radical implications of liberation theology and the Biblically supportable idea that Christ had come for the poor, not the rich.

This meant the door was open for new Christian fundamentalists to resurrect the old gospel of wealth and reshape the adoration of material blessings into a new gospel of prosperity. The audacious tent evangelist, A. A. Allen, who previously had gained attention for his healing miracles, was one of the first to add promises of wealth. In Philadelphia in 1962, he announced he would "lay hands on believers who gave $100 toward the support of our missionary outreach and bestow upon each of them THE POWER TO GET WEALTH." By the late 1960s, the testimonials in his *Miracle Magazine* emphasized financial blessings more than divine healing,[33] a tactic that was soon to be incorporated into the messages of many television evangelists.

From the beginning the beacon of the prosperity message was Tulsa, Oklahoma, the home of Oral Roberts and a number of other Pentecostal evangelists. One of these, T. L. Osborn, was perhaps the first Pentecostal preacher to live in openly lavish style as proof of God's benevolence. In 1970, he had established his "Pact of Plenty" concept with the readers of his magazine, *Faith Digest*, and relied on the simple Biblical message: "Give and it shall be given unto you."[34]

Osborn was credited by one of his fellow evangelists, David Nunn, as "providing one of the greatest leaderships in a hundred years" and propelling the world Pentecostal revival when he evangelized in the Third World. Osborn's enthusiasm and certainty of financial success rubbed off on indigenous preachers, instilling "confidence in them that they've got the ability and that they can carry out the work of evangelizing their own countries."[35]

Oral Roberts, the premier televangelist in the United States for many years, used the proceeds of his ministry to build an accredited university, which he named after himself. His success, and the spread of the charismatic movement in the 1960s, led him into the mainstream of American Protantism. In 1966 Billy Graham invited Roberts to join him at the World

Congress on Evangelism in Berlin, and in 1967 Roberts left the Pentecostal Holiness Church and joined the much more liberal United Methodist denomination. His slogan, "Expect a Miracle," still held promise of divine healing, but he had incorporated the neo-Pentecostal faith in prosperity into his preaching. He popularized the notion of "seed faith," which suggested that the TV viewer, by planting a "seed" (a donation to the evangelist), would later be rewarded by a large financial return. One of Roberts's slogans was: You Sow It, Then God Will Grow It.[36]

Variations on this theme were developed by many, from well known media stars Pat Robertson and Jim Bakker to lesser known ministers Kenneth Copeland and Kenneth Hagin, who developed "faith" theology (this is known by its detractors as the "name it and claim it" theology).[37]

Thousands were committed to "seed-faith" and "Blessing Pacts" with Roberts's ministry. Readers of his magazine *Abundant Life* contributed their stories, which often related how mundane and pleasing events in the life of a middle-class employee or businessman were transformed into interventions of the Holy Spirit: "A Raise, Plus a Bonus," "New Job as A General Manager," and "Sales Have Tripled" were typical testimonials to the power of the Lord in 1970.[38]

The supernatural power of the Pentecostals may seem trivialized by such worldly pronouncements, but it is worth remembering that the powers of the Spirit, even for the poorest of the poor in the "unworldly" denominations that gave birth to Pentecostalism, were thought to be effective in meeting "felt needs." The poor not only rejoiced in the process of receiving the Holy Ghost, but they hoped He would intervene to throw out the demon of alcoholism, heal chronic sicknesses, and dissipate the devilish lust that broke up families. In the U.S., the land of plenty, workers lived like the middle class, and advertising and television turned everyone into a consumer, conspicuous or otherwise. Perhaps a new chapter in "felt needs" was needed to allay the anxiety about catching up with the problems of easy credit and earning enough to meet one's debts. In any case, anxiety over money had become a most pressing American preoccupation, as can be illustrated by the experience of Oral Roberts at the end of the 1970s.

At that time Roberts and his university were pushed to the brink of bankruptcy by the combination of his ambitions, which included the construction of a City of Faith medical center, and the faltering U.S. economy. His biographer, David Edwin Harrell, notes that Roberts's version of prosperity theology had functioned up until that point: "Seed-faith theology was the financial message which allowed the huge expansion of the Roberts ministry in the late 1970s."[39] However, by 1979, a dispirited Oral Roberts, "in the midst of his deepest financial trials," attended the Tulsa camp meeting of Kenneth Hagin at the Rhema Bible Training Center. Hagin, whose "faith formula" taught neo-Pentecostal and charismatic believers that their good fortunes were guaranteed by God, proceeded to call Roberts to the podium and dedicated that night's collection to him. Roberts, reduced to tears, tried to refuse, but Hagin intoned, "sit down and just accept what the Lord is doing." The response of the huge crowd—about $400,000 was raised that night—overwhelmed Roberts, who recollected:

> It was a moment of drama such as I have not witnessed in my entire Christian experience…I sat with my head in my hands, tears flowing down my cheeks, realizing that nothing like this had ever happened in my behalf.[40]

Roberts' experience is indicative of the way that the neo-Pentecostal movement had transformed the old gospel of success and wealth. Nineteenth-century proponents such as Dwight Moody and Russell H. Conwell had both assumed that the Bible would enable the hardworking Christian to reach his individual goals and get rich in the process. The new gospel of prosperity cranked up the equation of faith another notch, and taught that the Christian, if he truly believed, was entitled to receive the material blessings of the Lord on the basis of faith alone. It was probably still presumed that Christians ought to dutifully apply themselves to their work, but the connection between diligence and providence became very blurred. The primary proponents of the Faith Movement were also products of the Tulsa evangelical boom: the evangelist Kenneth Hagin, who had been forced out of the Assemblies of God, had founded his Living Waters Church in suburban Tulsa, and through his Rhema Bible School was exporting the faith to all parts of the world. Kenneth Copeland, a former student of Roberts's and his airplane pilot, founded a ministry with his wife, Gloria, and promoted the same message on nationwide television from Fort Worth.

The Faith Movement expressed a simple theology: that Christians received good fortune and good health because they had a right to expect such things from God. Prosperity had been won for all by Christ, if only they knew how to ask for it. The proof is found in such Biblical verses as:

> Mark 11: 23-24 "Whatever you shall ask in prayer, believe that you receive it, and you will."
>
> Matthew 9: 29 "ACCORDING TO YOUR FAITH be it unto you"
>
> Philippians 4: 19 "My God will supply every need of yours according to his riches in glory in Christ Jesus."[41]

On the one hand this theology teaches that one has a right to demand material satisfaction, that God has entered into a contract with the believer and therefore will deliver the goods. On the other hand, the presumption is that if one does not receive what one prays for, some deficiency in faith is the cause. This includes health as well as wealth. Illness, according to Hagin, may be a sign of insufficient faith: "I believe that it is the plan of God our Father that no believer should ever be sick."[42] This emphasis in faith healing goes beyond what Oral Roberts had been preaching; Roberts believed in miracles through the benevolence of a good God, but did not think that illness was proof of bad faith. The Faith Movement and other charismatics and neo-Pentecostals think otherwise; Pat Robertson wrote in his book *The Secret Kingdom* that he was certain that "if a person is continuously in sickness, poverty, or other physical or mental straits, then he is missing the truths of the Kingdom."[43]

The experience of Oral Roberts, personally overwhelmed by the material manifestations of Hagin's divine intervention, led him closer and closer to the Faith Movement. He drifted away from his alliance with the Methodist Church (the core of the theology department at Oral Roberts University, made up of Methodists, was dismissed between 1984 and 1986.) This may have been due to theological schism, but surely Roberts was also aware of the market trends. The independent ministries and their attendant parachurch organizations of neo-Pentecostals had become the powerful growth area of Protestant Christianity in the United States and much of the rest of the world; meanwhile almost all of the old denominations were shrinking in numbers.

The kind of faith practiced in the neo-Pentecostal churches represents a new kind of fundamentalism that only a short time ago was considered to be on the lunatic fringe of religious practice. In order to demonstrate such extreme materialistic basis of American religion, detractors could once point to obscure little sects, such as the Church of Hakeem in Los Angeles, whose African-American leader exhorted his poor followers to shout: "Richer faster! Richer faster! Richer faster!"[44]

But by the early 1980s, more prosperous adherents of a similar faith were moving into the mainstream, whether they were white, black, or brown. For instance, the Crenshaw Christian Center of Fred Price, also an African-American minister in Los Angeles and a fervent proponent of prosperity theology, had grown into one of the largest churches in the United States and served a multiracial, middle-class constituency. He spoke often in predominantly white domains such as Oral Roberts University, and in fact was a major donor to Roberts's City of Faith. Pentecostal churches of the poor have always been notable for attracting Americans of all races and immigrants from different cultures. Some of the same openness seems to be present in the new middle-class neo-Pentecostal/charismatic churches, which have made this extension of the efficacy of the faith more respectable. This inclination was once noted by anthropologist Marvin Harris, in a way that many religious people understood as disparagement:

Humankind's religious impulses are more often than not as much instrumen-
talities in the struggle for worldly wealth, power, and physical well-being as
manifestations of the search for spiritual salvation.[45]

Today this might be taken as more of a compliment, suggesting that no doors
are shut to those who believe, that nothing can stop the true and determined
Christian. So widespread did this kind of practice become that even television evangelists with strong roots in Baptist fundamentalism, such as Jerry
Falwell, could suggest there was a monetary return. In spite of his premillennial gloom about the future and his disapprovals of the Pentecostal "gifts" promoted by other evangelists, Falwell was able to say on his "Old Time Gospel
Hour":

> Maybe your financial situation seems impossible. Put Jesus first in your stew-
> ardship and allow him to bless you financially.[46]

Falwell's Baptist faith, which once would have been representative of "old-
style," separatist fundamentalism, was being transformed into a "new style"
fundamentalism that was comfortable with the accumulation of material
goods in suburban America. Falwell, like the others, not only continued to
sanction the old gospel of wealth, accumulation of capital by the rich, but also
reached out with the new variation for the middle class and those who
aspired to the middle class. Through the new adaptations of the faith introduced by neo-Pentecostal or charismatic Protestantism, many Christians
came to understand that they are "entitled," through divine intervention in
their lives, to material rewards on earth.

No one defined this sense of entitlement better than Pat Robertson in the
late 1970s in his book *The Secret Kingdom.* According to Robertson, the Secret
Kingdom is unlocked by a faith in God that will reveal the Secret of Wealth,
the Secret of Success, the Secret of Greatness, and the Secret of Miracles, all
of which are gifts of God to true believers; once faith has let the believers see
or feel the Secrets, said Robertson, they merely have to invoke "Kingdom
Power" and ask for what they want:

> We have a title deed to what God has promised. Our role is to believe in our
> hearts that it has been accomplished, according to what God has given us the
> deed to, and then speak it.[47]

Pentecostalism goes Middle Class

In the 1950s the Pentecostal healing revivalists appropriated the religious
Americanism of Billy Graham, but other evangelicals remained wary of the
gifts of the Spirit. In the 1960s, a general charismatic renewal spread the
Pentecostal practices of speaking in tongues and the laying on of hands

throughout a wide variety of Protestant and Catholic congregations, both liberal and conservative. At first this development was disconcerting to fundamentalistic evangelicals such as Graham, for this kind of Spirit was theologically suspect to them. More to the point, it was very threatening to their social conservatism because the spiritual powers unleashed seemed so unpredictable. Pentecostalism required years to expand and demonstrate that it generally had a conservative and fundamentalist Christian orientation.

The development of strong parachurch organizations, often representing those who had achieved the proper badge of material success, helped the Pentecostals gain acceptance. One of the most influential new parachurches was the Full Gospel Business Men's Fellowship International, which developed dynamic chapters in the United States and abroad that represented hundreds of thousands of respectable businesspeople. It helped unify the perspective of Pentecostal churches and, perhaps more importantly, its respectability and strength helped persuade non-Pentecostal evangelicals to be more tolerant and supportive. Bill Bright of the Campus Crusade for Christ, for example, began allowing Pentecostal believers to serve as missionaries in his organization in 1983.

No doubt the exponential growth of Pentecostal and neo-Pentecostal Protestant churches also facilitated this kind of acceptance. But also important was the growing conservatism and middle-class orientation of those who believed in the full Gospel; by the 1980s most had decisively moved rightward in concert with messages of Ronald Reagan and Pat Robertson, the latter being accepted as a spokesperson by fundamentalists of all persuasions even though he referred to himself as a "charismatic." In this milieu, the nature of the "blessings" of the Holy Ghost began to change, at least in their relative emphasis, so that the promise of material rewards for true believers became more and more prominent. This belief in the divine provision of worldly goods, a gospel of prosperity, has sometimes been labeled neo-Pentecostal or charismatic because it seems quite distinct—in fact, altogether foreign—to the theology of the traditional Pentecostal churches (although it has by now found its way into the beliefs of some of them as they have become more prosperous).

Today the dividing lines between the traditional Pentecostals and the neo-Pentecostals is ambiguous. The egalitarian spiritualism of the former has allowed for direct self-selection of ministers based on their experience with the Heavenly Spirit. Yet these Pentecostals, who were once at the bottom of the Protestant heap, are not now (if they ever were) uniformly poor and meek. They have always expected divine power to assist them in matters of their health, and some may be attracted by neo-Pentecostal access to material security. When urban or rural Pentecostals see their social status improve, they may not so clearly distinguish themselves from middle class suburban neo-Pentecostals; more importantly they see that the neo-Pentecostals have complimented them by assuming their style of worship and projecting their spiritual force toward achieving a number of goals. This kind of demonstration of faith can promote alliances.

Fundamentalists have often been unfairly branded as "anti-modern" and uneducated, as if they were a bizarre anomaly that did not fit in with secular American society. But American Protestantism has displayed its ability to adapt itself to modern contingencies and cultural realities while preserving its dedication to the twin civic doctrines of Americanism, extreme nationalism and unapologetic pro-capitalism.

We have emphasized Pat Robertson, not because we want to give inordinate credit to one televangelist among many, nor because we feel his Christian Coalition is more important than a number of organized fundamentalist forces. Robertson should be understood as but one suitable example of the modern fundamentalist Christian, prominent because of his worldly successes: he made a respectable attempt to gain the Republican nomination for president (against a formidable establishment candidate who was forced to adopt many of Robertson's views); he operates a very large and successful television network, the Christian Broadcasting Network; he leads a fundamentalist university called Regent University; he appears regularly on his television show, the *700 Club;* and he has numerous contacts with evangelicals around the world. Robertson is a representive hybrid of the various strands that make up the new Christian fundamentalism: evangelicals, Pentecostals, and old-time fundamentalist Baptists. He is educated, middle class, Southern Baptist, political and social conservative, charismatic (or neo-Pentecostal), born again. He is also a creationist, a premillennial dispensationalist, and a Biblical literalist. The modernity of Robertson's faith is represented by the power of his "charismatic" Protestantism, an addition to the U.S. evangelical faith that is rather easy to comprehend, according to Robertson biographer David Edwin Harrell:

> Charismatics simply added an overtly miraculous dimension to the body of positive thinking and success theology already present in American evangelicalism. As Jesus said, "Ask, and it will be given to you."[48]

Pat Robertson, as already noted, was not the first preacher to popularize the Pentecostal gifts and the accessible "charisma" of Christ among broad sectors of the American middle class. In the 1960s, all kinds of Christians were looking for a direct spiritual connection, a definitive and powerful experience of the Holy Ghost in their lives. Oral Roberts, with his roots in hardscrabble

Oklahoma, exemplified the origins of Pentecostal practice as it had evolved among the dispossessed, that is, the rural and urban poor of the United States in the first half of the twentieth century. His genius lay in his ability to extend much the same experience of the Holy Spirit into the new blend of charismatic Pentecostalism, meeting the needs and desires of better off, "more respectable" worshipers.[49]

Despite the neo-Pentecostal emphasis on material gifts from God, it should not be implied that Robertson, Roberts, or others merely borrowed a convenient and powerful "trick" or tool for manipulating the lower classes, and then redirected that "power" toward the needs of the middle classes. What impressed Robertson, a graduate of Yale Law School who chose to study divinity at a fundamentalist Bible college in New York City, was the intensity of worship he saw in little storefront Pentecostal churches in poor sections of New York.[50] Robertson and other middle-class evangelicals were impressed by the strength of belief among the poor, and by the miraculous events that accompanied the outpouring of religious emotion. Whether the middle-class adoption of such religious experience—speaking in tongues, the laying on of hands for healing, the driving out of evil demons, or the gift of prophecy—is as intense, or "real," can hardly be judged.

New fundamentalist Christians such as Pat Robertson were able to adopt some of the spiritual power and mechanisms of the Pentecostals and successfully weld them onto the other fundamentalist components, including the civil religious belief in America that they had appropriated from more liberal Christians. Robertson's own background as the son of a conservative U.S. senator from Virginia (a state's rights Democrat) prepared him to identify with the "dominionists," who expect that Christians should come to power by using direct political means as well as through evangelical conversions. Their goal is to turn the United States into a more Christian country and the Earth into a more Christian world. The expansion of Pentecostal powers, which can be trivialized if the discussion is limited to "prosperity," begins to look much more substantial as the Spirit embraces active engagement with the social and political world. The middle-class orientation projects a sort of Pentecostal Calvinist covenant with America, a path to Christian victory at a time when contenders are few.

In his book, *The End of Victory Culture,* Tom Engelhardt ably demonstrates that between 1945 and 1975, liberal mainstream America lost its ability to believe in a glorious "war story" that can sustain U.S. hegemony, and he also asks:

> Do Americans then, have the capacity, the resources, or the need to create a new national narrative of any sort, and if so, how would such a narrative be linked to a war story?[51]

A sizable minority of Americans are already reworking a new Christian fundamentalist narrative that resurrects that urgent sense of national mission. The majority of U.S. citizens may never accept this story, but in the absence of another one, its adherents have demonstrated that their spiritual power is indeed potent, for they have overhauled the assumptions of fundamentalist Americanism and substantially redirected the political process in the United States. Some have hypothesized that the new Christian fundamentalism is merely a temporary coalition of Protestant fragments (some of which even appeal to Catholic charismatics) that will soon fall apart, since it is the tradition of Protestants to endlessly split and reconstitute themselves. However, the political and social history of the 1980s demonstrated the uncanny ability of Ronald Reagan's Republican Party and the New Christian Right to work together on both domestic and foreign policy issues, and in ways that could not be reduced to the cynical operations of right-wing opportunists. Then, in the 1990s, the Christian Coalition took over control of many state Republican Party machines, starting with South Carolina and Virginia in 1993, and began to be the major player in defining the agenda of the national party. Their success is not due to Robertson's "charismatic" leadership, but to the grass-roots dedication of one and a half million believers who have the organizational contacts with millions of other Americans, whether they be in James Dobson's "Focus on the Family," the Full Gospel Business Men's Fellowship, the Southern Baptist Convention, or the hundreds of independent megachurches that have sprung up in the suburban American landscape.

The fact that a new Christian fundamentalism is emerging worldwide allows the American model of spiritual power new kinds of access to other countries. Pentecostal accessibility allows evangelists the opportunity to keep refashioning their Christian nationalism and faith in prosperity into something with a global character.

THREE

The Changing Theology and Practice of Fundamentalism in the Twentieth Century

Notice that the Beast, rising out of the sea in Revelation 13, has the feet of the bear!...The fact that the Beast of Revelation 13 has the feet of the bear, infers the Beast Power in its rise is associated with Russia and Communism.

—Gordon Lindsay[1]

*D*uring the time when the Soviet Union was the major impediment to American hegemony in the world, it was natural that fundamentalist preachers would add their particular interpretations of history to the anticommunist chorus that enveloped the land. Their outlook, however, was basically ahistorical and dependent upon mysterious divinations of God's intent, which could not be discerned by rational human analysis. Moreover, it was God's will that human history, which was temporary and impure, was about to come to an end.

Gordon Lindsay, like many conservative and liberal U.S. preachers who were active during the time of the Cold War, laced his writings and talks with Biblical references to the Soviet Union. Through his magazine, *Voice of Healing,* he represented the mainstream of the Pentecostal healing revivals in the 1950s in the United States, and in the 1960s was an important advocate of widening this evangelical effort, especially through neo-Pentecostal and charismatic appeals to people outside the old Pentecostal networks. He expanded his operations into the international arena and, in 1967, changed the name of his magazine to *Christ for the Nations.* Lindsay was neither as flamboyant as such Pentecostal evangelists as A. A. Allen and T. L. Osborn, nor as prominent and influential as televangelist Oral Roberts and his university in Tulsa. Still he managed, by the time of his death in 1973, to build up an entrepreneurial, family-run religious business that operated a thirty-acre office park in Dallas, Texas. He had helped fund over three thousand church building programs in eighty-three nations; his books, fifteen million of them, had been distributed worldwide in forty-six different languages; and his Bible school and audio teaching tapes were educating a whole new generation of neo-

Pentecostal and charismatic groups.[2]

When Lindsay spoke of "the Beast" and "the Bear," he was not cooking up his own corny homemade theology or borrowing from some other evangelist's obscure and bizarre recipe. His references came straight from the established theological heart of the U.S. fundamentalist tradition, the Scofield Reference Bible, which was published in 1909. Since that time, this Bible and a host of imitators have provided the central authority of Biblical inerrancy for a wide range of Christian fundamentalist interpretation, whether Baptist or Pentecostal, conservative Presbyterian or charismatic. The copious notes and allusions arranged by C. I. Scofield are codified references that enliven, directly and indirectly, a great deal of conservative evangelical literature. They are based on a nineteenth-century doctrine of dispensationalism, which claims to explain all of history through Biblical prophecy. Over time many of these interpretations have entered the everyday social discourse of many Americans; for example, the best-selling book in America in the 1970s, by a large margin, was *The Late Great Planet Earth* by Hal Lindsey. This thoroughly dispensational volume of prophecy explained everything from youth rebellion to drug addiction, from the threat of nuclear war to the coming of the "end times."

Non-evangelical social and political conservatives often found these Biblical interpretations helpful, too. President Ronald Reagan, for instance, was known to mention the evil Magog in reference to his plans for defeating the Soviet Union. Magog, a demonic representation appearing in the Book of Ezekial, chapters 38–39, was originally identified with Russia by Scofield, whose notation read:

> Magog: the primary reference is to the northern [European] powers, headed up by Russia, all agree.[3]

The publication of the Scofield Bible was part of a flurry of fundamentalist intellectual activity at the beginning of the twentieth century. It was closely followed, from 1910 to 1915, by *The Fundamentals*, the twelve volumes that served as theological primers on conservative Protestant Christianity and gave "Fundamentalism" its name. They were not isolated intellectual creations but rather the culmination of a fifty-year process of division between conservative and liberal elements in U.S. Protestant denominations.[4] The conservative Protestants thought of themselves as traditionalists, since liberals were associated with a growing accommodation to "modernism," that is, the acceptance of secular and naturalistic explanations of the universe and humankind. Yet, conservative evangelicals in the late nineteenth century were themselves making a number of creative adaptations to theological training and belief in order to produce the kind of fundamentalism that developed in the twentieth century. In part this was due to the fact that liberals, whether religious or not, had captured much of the intellectual territory represented in universities, which were beginning to sever their ties to religious denominations and doctrines. Not only did theology departments and divinity schools become liberalized, but the study of the natural sciences, history, politics, and the new social sciences became less and less amenable to Biblical interjection or interpretation.

Thus the art of Biblical interpretation, once the province of American intellectuals, became hardened into the doctrine of Biblical inerrancy and strict interpretation of the Word. In these circumstances, the Bible became more than a piece of divinely inspired writing; it was transformed into a mystical source book for systematic divination, especially in the milieu of the Bible Colleges and the Bible Conferences that arose between 1870 and 1925. As academic history, geology, and biology became irreconcilable with their literalist Bible explication, conservative Protestants created an anti-history that was strictly codified. In effect, "God's history" was to be interpreted by reference to the sacred text, but was not to be diluted or sullied by the new kinds of human or natural history.

The Scofield Bible wrapped the original Biblical text in a cocoon of interpretation that derived from a number of Biblical conservatives, the most important of whom was an Englishman named John Nelson Darby. In the mid-nineteenth century Darby taught a doctrine called Dispensationalism, which divided all of history into specific time periods that were supposedly spelled out in the Bible.[5] At this time, many interpreters were devising their own chronology of dispensations or Biblical periodizations, but Darby chose seven distinct eras as his basis of history and contended that the world was now in the sixth dispensation, The Age of the Church. At the heart of this reading of history was the notion that in all six ages from most ancient times to the present, humankind had refused to accept God's law and the teaching of Christ. Hence, the corrective was at hand: the seventh dispensation, the Second Coming of Christ and the thousand-year Age of Christ were imminent and would come at some undisclosed moment. At that moment, all the saved souls on Earth would be gathered up into heaven with Christ—The Secret Rapture—and the rest of the people on Earth would be damned and consumed by the catastrophes prophesied in the book of Revelation. This was a premillennialist version of history; only afterward would Christ return to Earth with his faithful to establish his thousand-year reign.

Although Darby had founded a small and splintered denomination in England, called the Plymouth Brethren,[6] his influence was only substantial in North America, where he traveled extensively on seven lecture tours between 1862 and 1877.[7] His doctrines were eagerly assimilated, not always in the way he intended, by an American public that was hungry for prophecy and the millennium of Jesus. Before the Civil War, most American millennialists had been the optimistic sort, often called postmillennialists, who believed that America was actually the culmination of the thousand-year process of perfection that would end in Christ's return to earth. After the carnage of the Civil War and amidst the massive social disruption caused by the industrialization of the United States, the more pessimistic premillennialist position gained favor: it taught that the ways of the world were evil and fraught with damnation, so that believers should concentrate on saving their souls, not their society. Darby's conservative dispensationalism fit in nicely with the doctrines of Biblical inerrancy formulated by Dwight Moody and a host of urban revivalists.

At Bible conferences at Niagara and Northfield, Massachusetts (where C. I. Scofield was pastor at the Moody Church), the leading conservative evangelists met for many summers to discuss the proper use of the Holy Book.[8] By the beginning of the twentieth century, Bible Colleges were being established in all of the major U.S. cities: the Moody Institute in Chicago in 1886, the Bible Institute of Los Angeles in 1907, and the Philadelphia College of the Bible in 1914; the Dallas Theological Seminary was founded in 1924 in the tradition of C. I. Scofield. These institutes combined Bible memorization with the dispensationalist reading of history, thus providing a quick education for untrained ministers and the "Gap Men," Moody's name for the lay preachers and street evangelists who were going to save souls as quickly as possible. Their job was to fulfill the Great Commission, bringing the Biblical Word to all the Earth's people, before the imminent Second Coming of Christ. Given the grim promise of sudden damnation for the unsaved that pervaded the premillennialist message, Moody (and all the evangelists who have followed the pattern of his aggressive campaigns up until the present time) put a premium on "body counts"; that is, they actually counted and wrote down the number of individual souls who were saved on any particular day or night of a revival.

If the universities had the leisure to educate the sons of the elite and the middle class in a liberal theology that permitted human dabbling in the "historical" nature of the Bible, Moody and the conservative evangelists performed another function (whether consciously or not) in stressing the inerrancy and "anti-historical" limits of the Bible. They were able to convince their major sponsors, often the leading capitalists of the day,[9] that their version of the Bible and premillennial prophecy was very appropriate for the working classes. The laboring poor were being tempted by something much more dangerous than liberal Christianity—the spectres of communism, anarchism, democratic socialism, and labor unionism that had drifted across the Atlantic from Europe. This new, egalitarian reading of history was not only "Satanic" in influence (according to both corporate owners and conservative evangelists), it was also appealing enough to make men and women want to become literate. People were learning to read by poring over radical tracts instead of the Bible. At the end of the nineteenth century, the fact that capitalism delivered very few rewards to the mass of working people was already apparent to the lower classes; all they needed was some historical and social explication that such a social order was both unfair and unnecessary.

The various doctrines of socialism and utopianism, whether they originated with Karl Marx, Eugene Debs, or Henry George, had a millennialist factor of their own, for they promised a secular promised land somewhere in the future to those who believed. These ideas were not so contrary to the optimistic vision of Biblical postmillennialism that had dominated American thought in the early nineteenth century:

> Allow me to say that, in America, the state of society is without parallel in universal history. With all our mixtures, there is a leaven of heaven; there is goodness there; there is excellent principle there. I really believe that God has got America within anchorage, and that upon that arena, He intends to display his prodigies for the millennium.
>
> —Samuel H. Cox, moderator of the General
> Assembly of the Presbyterian Church, 1846[10]

For Moody and those who have followed him unto the present day, the task was not really the pessimistic eradication of this sunny, pro-American millennialism. The evangelists often have had strong optimistic natures themselves, and have tended to act as cheerleaders for the status quo and the American Way. Historian William G. McLoughlin described Moody's function:

> He was brought to the cities in times of unemployment by middle class churchgoers and businessmen precisely to tell the workers that the American Dream was true, that the system was fundamentally sound.[11]

Moody, like many preachers who would follow him, both fundamentalist and liberal, shaped the positive millenarian or Arminian outlook into a purely individualistic form in which the believer could feel bound to profit from adhering to a gospel of success and wealth. On the other hand, the postmillenarian message was mixed with the proper doses of premillenarian pessimism that stressed that salvation must be immediate and individual. Moody and others needed to persuade the would-be believers of the desperateness of their sinful situations, which had to be neatly and quickly resolved before the Second Coming:

> I look on this world as a wrecked vessel. God has given me a lifeboat and said, "Moody, save all you can."[12]

Fundamentalism and Liberalism

While it is fair to say that liberal Protestantism broke with tradition at the turn of the century, it would be a mistake to confuse most theological liberalism in the early twentieth century with economic egalitarianism or leftist politics. Liberal Protestantism was a vehicle controlled by and for the educated classes, who were, of course, the elite who could afford university educations. For this reason it should be recognized that the radical nature of the Social Gospel affected only a minority of theologians, ministers, and congregations. The Social Gospel did have influence on the Protestant mainstream by making them aware of reform efforts, and helped push them toward some degree of business regulation and acknowledgment of poverty. However, it must be remembered that most establishment church members were profoundly anti-socialist; Progressive Era reforms were by and large capitalist adjustments to laissez-faire excesses instituted by confident and contented members of the middle and upper classes.[13] Theological liberalism was often compatible with economic conservatism, since it arose between 1870 and 1929, an era when economic and social inequalities reached historic highs in the United States. The distinctions between the upper classes and the working classes were immense, not least because the workers were so often non-Protestant immigrants or the sons and daughters of immigrants.[14]

In associating the liberalization of mainstream Protestantism with the advent of scientific education, it must be remembered that this education was the realm of the privileged in American society, most of whom in the early twentieth century were white Anglo-Saxon Protestants. Hence, in embracing Social Darwinism and an evolutionary point of view contrary to Biblical inerrancy, there was a strong tendency (maybe the majority tendency), to twist emerging scientific study into pseudo-scientific belief.[15] Between 1900 and 1930 American universities were not overflowing with wide-eyed radical professors and anti-establishment students; much more prevalent were the distinguished professors and university presidents who pursued or condoned the transfer of Darwinian biological logic into the spheres of psychology, political science, eugenics, and economics. At times it seemed as if the "elect," who had once defended their elevated status with Calvinist doctrine, were now content to use science to confer superiority on themselves. The whole purpose of IQ tests was twisted in order to demonstrate racial, ethnic, and gender inferiorities.[16] Geopolitics was reduced to (or commended as) the aggressive struggles of superior nations (or races) to reach the next step in human evolution. Colonialism was justified as a system that offered magnanimous care and/or strict punishment to the newly conquered, "childlike" races, who still had to evolve into a species capable of enjoying Western civilization. The so-called science of eugenics, heavily endowed by philanthropists, promised to produce a more satisfactory (and presumably more Anglo-Saxon) race of people in the future.

The liberal ascendancy in American Protestantism at the turn of the twentieth century quite possibly never represented the thoughts of most Protestant congregations, which probably held onto more traditional beliefs. However, the process of secularization, of accommodation with scientific and historical modes of investigation (whether or not their political implications were conservative or radical), was comfortable and reassuring to the upper classes: scientific progress, industrial progress, and spiritual progress seemed to go hand in hand.[17]

Secularization was incorporated into religious belief (or vice versa), according to sociologist Peter Berger, because it was so compatible with:

> the infrastructural foundation of Protestant liberalism—the period of capitalist triumphs in economy and technology, of Western expansion, and of bourgeois cultural dominance—in sum, the "golden age" of bourgeois capitalism. This was a period of profound confidence in the cultural, political, and economic values of Western civilization, a confidence fully reflected in the optimistic Weltanschauung of Protestant liberalism. The compromises of the theologian, consequently, were not negotiated under duress, but in the confrontation with a secular culture deemed entirely attractive and praiseworthy, not just materially but in its values. Put crudely, it paid to sell out on certain features of the tradition. It should not surprise us that the dominance of Protestant liberalism coincided with the period during which this bourgeois world retained its attractiveness and, indeed, its credibility.[18]

This liberal worldview began to self-destruct in Europe with the advent of World War I and economic turmoil of the 1920s. But in the United States, the bourgeois era continued almost undisturbed throughout the 1920s, precisely the time when religious conservatives, wrapping themselves in "fundamentalism," were forced to retreat from the main stage of American Protestantism. What should be emphasized, however, is that this occurred precisely at the time when upper-class control of wealth, political power, and industrial production were at their zenith. Theological liberalism, though it had allowed versions of the Social Gospel to emerge in the radical views of Walter Rauschenbusch and others before the 1920s, had little room for populist egalitarianism. It is in this light that we can understand the association, so prevalent among the American population even today, of liberalism with elitism. In the 1920s, when the Presbyterian Church was splitting up over doctrines of Biblical "inerrancy," it was often upper-class, economic conservatives—John Foster Dulles is one example—who became great supporters of liberal theologians such as Henry Emerson Fosdick. Dulles, a graduate of Princeton and the Sorbonne, later became very active in the National Federation of Churches (the forerunner of the National Council of Churches), directing its Committee on Peace during World War II.

On the other hand, political luminaries such as William Jennings Bryan, long associated with populism and the progressive wing of the Democratic Party, associated themselves with "old-time religion" and the fundamentalists. One of the major reasons Bryan enlisted himself in prosecuting the "creationist" case against evolution in the Scopes trial in 1926 was that he gravely distrusted the use of evolutionary theory in the social and political realms. He rightly saw that elitist social theory had appropriated Darwinism through the agency of Herbert Spencer, William Graham Sumner, and a host of others; Social Darwinism was the sworn enemy of populism, for it presumed that equalization of opportunities and means for the different social classes was both unscientific and against the laws of economic progress. Furthermore, Bryan was appalled at the slaughter that civilized nations inflicted upon themselves in World War I, and felt that the theory of "survival of the fittest" among nations was a sure recipe for even more bloodshed and war.[19]

Pentecostalism: Reviving Fundamentalism

As some Protestant denominations split into separate liberal and conservative churches over Biblical inerrancy and creationism, the old fundamentalists seemed to withdraw from view just as an important new kind of Christianity was emerging at the lowest levels of American society. Pentecostalism, a true religion of the dispossessed, was spreading rapidly among poor people of all races, both urban and rural. The year of 1906, marked by the Azusa Street revivals in Los Angeles led by the black evangelist William J. Seymour, is often credited as the beginning of American Pentecostalism. The largest Pentecostal denomination, the Assemblies of God, was formed in 1912. The Pentecostals pursued a vigorous religion that they felt would sanctify the lives of the poor; in many ways they followed the path of the more established fundamentalists and the holiness movement that preceded them. They embraced very strict rules of personal comportment to show that they indeed practiced a Christian lifestyle; they accepted Biblical inerrancy as God's way of defining the world; and they believed in dispensationalism and the Second Coming of Christ as the supernatural determination of history.

Pentecostals had little interest in a gospel of wealth, whether the "success" doctrine of evangelists in the Moody tradition or the less blatant Sunday self-satisfaction of liberal, middle-class worshipers in mainstream churches. In order to achieve their goals, Pentecostals immersed themselves in the "Full Gospel." At one level, as their preachers were the first to admit, the power of

Jesus and the Holy Spirit worked within the boundaries of their communities of worship to meet "felt needs" in practical ways. That is, it helped them overcome immediate suffering due to human failings (or sin) and fight off the demons of alcoholism, mental anguish, sexual temptation, and family discord. Secondly, the discipline and frugality and honesty emphasized in all daily activities helped these Protestant families survive amid a rapidly changing social order. Third, their religious experience was energetic, fervent, and emotionally satisfying. Pentecostal gatherings served to bond the devotional group together with shared intensity of worship at the same time they offered each participant an opportunity for enthusiastic release from daily cares and anxieties.

But Pentecostal beliefs in the supernatural went much farther: practicing the Full Gospel meant having access to the power of Jesus in its entirety, living as the first New Testament Christians had lived, poor in material terms but rich in the full appreciation of Christ's supernatural powers. In fact, the faithful can be granted one or all of nine Biblical gifts of the Spirit: the word of wisdom, the word of knowledge, the gift of faith, the gift of healing, the gift of miracles, the gift of prophecy, the gift of discerning spirits, the gift of tongues, and the gift of interpretation of tongues.[20]

There is, of course, no lack of Biblical justification for these gifts:

Acts 2: 4—And they were all filled with the Holy Ghost, and began to speak with other tongues, as the Spirit gave them utterance.

Acts 19: 6—And when Paul had laid his hands upon them, the Holy Ghost came on them; and they spake with tongues, and prophesied.

Pentecostals were shunned by other, more prosperous Protestants, not because of their art of Biblical interpretation, but because the enthusiasm, wildness, and even sensuousness of their worship were rather frightening. The bias of more staid evangelical Protestants attributed a certain irrationality and lack of self-control to the lower-class Pentecostals. Speaking in tongues, the most common gift bestowed on the believers during church services, sounded like pure gibberish to the uninitiated, whether they were fundamentalist Baptists or liberals. But for Pentecostals, their total immersion in church life and the emotional release of their worship signified genuine religious expression. Religious historian George M. Marsden has noted how liberal Protestant and Pentecostal belief systems have been correlated with the intensity of their religious expression:

Pentecostals accentuated the supernatural just at the point where liberals stressed the divine elements in the natural. So while modernists might speak of a gentle "religion of the heart," Pentecostals insisted that true heart religion be evidenced by unmistakable signs of the Spirit's transforming power....[21]

Given their lack of material resources, perhaps it was appropriate that Pentecostal ministers did not need extensive training for the ministry, since the direct "calling" from God and the presence of the Holy Ghost were the compelling proofs of one's fitness for preaching. In the early part of the twentieth century, the egalitarian nature of this religious calling was evidenced by the participation of poor people of all races. Most distinct compared to other Protestant traditions was the Pentecostal acceptance of women preachers. The most famous Pentecostal evangelist in the United States between 1920 and 1945 was Aimee Semple McPherson, who began as a healing revivalist and then built her own temple in Los Angeles in 1923. McPherson issued her own monthly magazine, *The Bridal Call*, and founded her own Pentecostal tradition, the Foursquare Gospel Church. Whether because of her proximity to Hollywood, or because healing miracles attracted people of all social classes, McPherson was one of the first Pentecostals to demonstrate that this kind of Protestantism might move beyond its constituencies among the poor.[22]

Immediately after World War II, divine healing propelled Pentecostalism into the mainstream of conservative American Protestantism. The evangelists came directly from the Pentecostal tradition; Oral Roberts, for instance, was brought up in the Pentecostal Holiness Church and A. A. Allen was ordained in the Assemblies of God in 1936. These preachers found Biblical justification for spiritual healing in the example of Jesus and his early followers; the Holy Spirit was available to cure disease, make tumors and deformities disappear, cast out demons who caused affliction, and even bring back the dead. The revivalists practiced their craft in giant tents where thousands of excited believers joined them in four- to five-hour services. Each Pentecostal tent meeting culminated in "the Miracle":

> All the gifts of the Holy Spirit, including speaking in tongues and prophesying, and all the expressions of joy so common in Pentecostal worship were present in the early revivals, but they were not the central theme. The common heartbeat of every service was the miracle—the hypnotic moment when the Spirit moved to heal the sick and raise the dead.[23]

The nationwide healing revival, which lasted for approximately a decade, ended because it came into conflict with the organized Pentecostal churches like the Assemblies of God. The churches were often embarrassed by false claims or outright fakery performed in public. They did not appreciate the overestimation of healing at the expense of other powers of the Spirit, including the more mundane faith that helped believers deal with the pressures of daily life and the temptations of sin. A. A. Allen, who was suspected of perpetrating flagrant frauds of the miraculous, was dismissed from the Assemblies of God and went on to found his own independent charismatic ministry and community in Arizona, which he named Miracle Valley.[24]

After 1958, divine healing retained its place in the traditional Pentecostal churches, and would become even more influential in the new charismatic and neo-Pentecostal movements that were inspired by the Pentecostal revival. By this time Pentecostals were sharing in the post-war prosperity that lifted the fortunes of most Americans amid a social atmosphere of significantly more economic and racial equality. As Pentecostals moved into the decently paid sectors of the working class and the middle class, they, like devout Protestants of other eras, put significant amounts of their savings into missionary efforts. The Assemblies of God, the various Churches of God, and a vast array of independent ministries spawned by the revivalists and evangelists became engaged in planting churches all over the world. Pentecostalism began to take hold in various foreign cultures, perhaps because its supernatural methods matched or exceeded those of indigenous practices, but also because its intense, egalitarian religious culture offered solace and a participatory community to poor and dislocated sectors of the population, just as it had in the United States. The stage was set for a worldwide boom in evangelical, fundamentalist culture with a new Pentecostal emphasis.

Pentecostals are not generally, as some writers have claimed,[25] averse to Biblical fundamentalism. The nature of their experiential worship has not precluded attentive devotion to Biblical strictures and legalisms. They now have the resources to support Bible schools, foreign missions, and involvement in fundamentalist social and political movements, which allows them to explicate their faithfulness to the Biblical text and pursue their own innovations in dispensational eschatology. This is having a profound effect on conservative evangelicalism, in part because Pentecostals are having remarkable success in evangelizing the world.

Church Growth and the Theology of the "Third Wave"

In the early twentieth century and after World War II, U.S. Protestant evangelists operating abroad were repeatedly thwarted in their attempts to create permanent, self-sufficient and self-propagating congregations. One American missionary to India, Donald McGavran, noted that Indian missions were usually failures and reasoned that this was because foreigners failed to recognize the homogeneous castes, groups, or tribes that were capable of adhering to both a common identity and a new religion. In 1965, McGavran began to teach his theories of church growth, based on the "homogeneous unit" principle, at the Fuller School of World Mission, a part of the Fuller Theological

Seminary in Pasadena, California.[26] He connected his theories to his analysis of another factor: that Protestant missionaries who neglected the "full Gospel" were not very successful in most parts of the world. Sociologist David Stoll has pointed out how this failure, this lack of understanding of religious motivation, applied to Latin America.

> Pentecostal churches dealt directly with beliefs in magic, more generally with the complex, influential networks of sorcery and healing in Latin American society, through ecstatic forms of worship. Missionaries who derided such beliefs as superstitious and condemned Pentecostal methods for dealing with them were not equipped to deal with Latin American religious life.[27]

Such Christian feedback from the rest of the world began to affect the very core of evangelical belief and practice in the United States. By 1984, the Fuller School of World Mission began offering courses that linked the proper methods of evangelization with the message of neo-Pentecostalism; one such course was called "Signs, Wonders, and Church Growth," which featured a workshop in miracles.[28] This development signified the inevitable point at which non-Americans would simultaneously borrow from the new fundamentalist religious ideology and contribute to the new strategies and structures that would spread the Word.

Probably no single minister has been more representative in this regard than Paul Yonggi Cho of Korea, the Christian admired worldwide for his success in church growth. He believes a new intervention of the Holy Spirit on Earth began approximately one hundred years ago with the advent of Pentecostalism, then was followed by the charismatic movement, and now has culminated in a Third Wave (a concept also introduced at the Fuller Theological Seminary). The Third Wave has less emphasis on speaking in tongues and gives more attention to "signs, wonders, miracles, and healings." Cho says that this methodology allows him and other pastors to provide "power encounters" to believers in order to prepare them for "spiritual warfare," because the moment has come when "God is marching forward and attacking the realm of the devil."

Paul Yonggi Cho and many other foreign evangelicals are not particularly worried by the old distinctions that were once made among fundamentalists, Pentecostals, and conservative Protestants in the United States. Although he is associated with the Assemblies of God, Cho preaches the gospel of prosperity as vigorously as any televangelist in the United States. He has conducted his workshops on church growth for conservative Presbyterians and Baptists in Korea, and has introduced Oral Roberts at conferences as his "spiritual father." Within his organization Church Growth International, Cho has cultivated a following of aggressive neo-Pentecostal ministers in many big cities around the world, from Singapore to Lagos. Among them is Dick Bernal, the pastor of the large Jubilee Church and Bible School in San Jose, California, and a product of the Rhema Bible Training Center and the Lester Sumrall Evangelistic Association.

Cho commends Bernal for his contributions to demonology and the arts of spiritual warfare, especially his book, *Come Down Dark Prince*, which "offers a clear strategy for dismantling demonic strongholds and making a lasting impact for God in our cities."[29] Bernal's book also has clear implications for the other religions of the world: "God demands that the 'high places' of idol worship be totally torn down."[30] His description of this kind of idolatry specifically includes important elements of Islam, Hinduism, Judaism, and Catholicism.

Cho is not a Messiah figure in Korea, any more than Pat Robertson is in the United States. Both are highlighted here as representative of the kind of successful Christian entrepreneur who helps to reinvent Christian fundamentalism and then proceeds to sell it as effectively and rapidly as possible. The appeal of Paul Yonggi Cho is undoubtedly tied to the need of many people in the world's industrializing cities to identify with success and find a powerful new set of values. But success is not tied only to the values of a globalized capitalist culture; it has meanings related to the deep, underlying traditions of folk religion in almost all of the world's societies, traditions that have always sought magical assistance in guaranteeing health, prosperity, and the destruction of personal demons. Korean sociologist Kim Kyong Suh notes that:

> The Korean church has a shamanistic tendency, following the indigenous belief system—totemism, shamanistic fetishism, and other kinds of nature worship. Korean shamanism is a belief system of this-worldly blessings—material wealth, good health, and other personal and familial well-being. The emphasis on worldly personal blessing became a significant part of the Christian congregational life.[31]

Undoubtedly, the ability of humans to ask for direct supernatural intervention in their lives is rather exciting, whether it concerns bringing in the positive, such as personal prosperity, or carrying away the negative, such as demons. Increasingly, the power of this faith—and perhaps its superiority over the old folk religions—can be demonstrated by the size of the demons to be exorcised. Although personal lust and alcoholism are still worthy adversaries, the Christian faith warriors are now pursuing social scourges, among them drugs and urban decay, and ultimately, the political and religious heresies planted by Satan in the hearts of socialists and Muslims. The globalizing forces of Christian fundamentalism have not yet produced mass organizations comparable to those generated by the Christian right in the United

States, such as Focus on the Family and the Christian Coalition, but they are certainly capable of harnessing spiritual power on behalf of social and political causes. The new Christians have focused their "power encounters" on the incredibly rapid process of conversion. As their energies and resources multiply, who knows where they will apply these powers.

FOUR

Guatemala:

Protestant Modernization or Evangelical Apocalypse?

*I*n an Indian village on the shores of Lake Atitlan, beneath the towering volcanos that dominate the horizon of Guatemala, five young women in traditional, multicolored skirts and blouses are invoking a religious chant with powerful gestures and loud voices. The listener who does not understand their language might first suspect that this is an ancient indigenous rite, but then would notice that the women are all waving Bibles rhythmically with their right hands. They are street evangelists, intent on spreading the Word of Jesus and saving the souls of their neighbors.

The year is 1987. Offshore, a passenger boat carries a cargo of sixty people: half are indigenous residents of various lakeside villages, the others are North American missionary families of several evangelical persuasions. Twenty years earlier, half of the passengers would likely have been foreign visitors, but they would have been long-haired young people sporting backpacks. The shift to clean-cut Christian missionaries reflects a major change in the cultural influences exported from the United States. And more important for Guatemala, this change correlates with a rather astounding transformation of the religious landscape. A country that was somewhere between 1.5 percent and 3.5 percent Protestant in the early 1960s became, by 1990, nearly 35 percent Protestant.[1]

Guatemala is one of many small nations that is being forced to adapt to a global economy and culture, albeit under circumstances that have been especially violent and abrupt. Guatemala's own upper classes and military rulers have been eager to join the globalizing trend. Whether this transformation is viewed as an inevitable result of the diffusion of superior Western principles and rational organizations or the imposition of an invasive dominant system, the Guatemalan version of "modernization" has been brutal. Amid cultural disruption and suffering so enormous that it can genuinely be called apocalyptic, Guatemala has also been transformed in the past thirty years from one of Latin America's most secular nations to one of its most religious.

The Protestant churches that thrive in poor urban barrios, highland Indian villages, and middle-class city neighborhoods, whether connected to U.S. denominations or to a plethora of new groups founded by Guatemalans themselves, follow the patterns of theology and practice found in the broad new culture of evangelicalism, fundamentalism, and Pentecostalism in the United States. How is it that developing, so-called "backward" societies are being made over by economic, social, political, and even religious influences emanating from the United States?[2]

Secularism, Modernization, and the Apocalypse

Undoubtedly there are many social factors that have induced Guatemalans to convert so rapidly to the predominantly fundamentalist brands of Pentecostal Christianity. We cannot pretend to explicate the many mechanisms at work in Guatemala, and can only remind the reader that this country, about as big as Tennessee and home to almost ten million people, is as complex as many societies that are far larger. The nation contains a mixture of persistent cultures and languages including Mayan, Spanish, and Catholic elements that have interacted for almost five hundred years. In fact, the distinctiveness of Guatemalan culture, and the tenacity in various eras of its Indian and mixed-race Ladino populations in the face of domination by elite landowning and business classes, might make one wonder how North American Protestantism could engage much attention at all. For almost one hundred years, in fact, Protestants were present in Guatemala but had very little impact.[3]

When U.S. Protestants were invited into Guatemala by the liberal, pro-development government that took power in 1871, they enjoyed the distinct advantage of knowing the Catholic Church was losing power. In their struggles to promote foreign investment in export agriculture and railroads, significant numbers of middle- and upper-class citizens of Guatemala were battling successfully to deprive the Catholic Church of all its property; not only were its vast land holdings nationalized and resold to investors, but even its church buildings were taken over by the state. Although Protestant missionaries were noted for some educational accomplishments among their limited constituencies, their presence did not ignite a religious transformation of the country. Quite the contrary. Guatemala became one of the most secularized countries in the Western Hemisphere. By 1940, the population had grown significantly, but the number of Catholic priests had scarcely changed since 1872, when an inventory counted only 119 in the whole country.[4] The Protestant conversion rate remained minuscule.[5]

Protestant missionaries arrived at the end of the nineteenth century from historic denominations in the United States such as the Presbyterians and the Episcopalians. They were followed by the Central American Mission, the evangelizing agency of fundamentalist C. I. Scofield, in the early 1900s; but neither the older Protestants nor the rival fundamentalist presence did much to directly alter a landscape where formal Christian institutions were not prominent.

In the industrializing world of the West in the nineteenth and early twentieth centuries, nations seemed to take certain concurrent steps, mostly forward, toward democratization and increasing economic well-being for all. But in Guatemala and many other Latin American countries, modernization in the late nineteenth century was synonymous with capitalist agricultural or mining development, with ever increasing confiscation of very productive land formerly held by peasants, communal indigenous groups, and ecclesiastic orders of the Catholic Church. The new private owners concentrated their production on exports to Europe and the United States. Accompanying this process was investment in the construction of railroads, port facilities, and communication systems. Democracy was limited to small sectors of the middle and upper classes; therefore, the vast majority, including Ladino peasants and all Indian groups, were subject to repressive legal measures, uncompensated confiscation of their land, and programs of forced labor on the plantations.[6] Jose Miguez Bonino describes the process of modernization in Latin America over the past century:

> The leaders of emancipation and modernization had their faces turned toward Europe and the U.S.A. and their backs to the interiors of their countries. There, Indians and peasants were simply incorporated as cheap labor for production.... A free press, free trade, education, politics—all the "achievements" of liberalism—were the privilege of the elite. For the growing Latin American masses, undernourishment, slavery, illiteracy, and later on, forced migration, exploitation, crowding and finally repression when they claim their rights—these are the harvest of one century of "liberal democracy."[7]

In Guatemala, modernization did not become synonymous with democratization until 1944 with the election of a social democratic government that dedicated itself to severely limiting the power of the landed oligarchy and foreign corporate interests while promoting substantial social reform. It led to the institution of universal public education and rural health clinics,[8] land reform and full democratic participation, all with the aim of giving the large majority of citizens—Ladino workers and peasants as well as indigenous villagers—full citizenship and a decent livelihood. By most measures the social reform government worked rather well for ten years: one million acres of farmland were purchased from absentee owners and redistributed to one hundred thousand peasant farmers;[9] half of all agricultural and industrial workers were organized into unions; literacy rates increased and infant mortality steadily declined.[10] Because Guatemala was blessed with a diligent people, an almost perfect climate in the highlands, very rich volcanic soils and an abundance of other natural resources, the goal of providing a modest but decent standard of living for all working people was very attainable.[11]

Unfortunately, in 1954, the United Fruit Company, the United States, and a sizable portion of the Guatemalan landowning elite chose to end this successful experiment in democracy by means of a CIA-backed military coup. As expropriated land was returned to large landowners and to United Fruit, a repressive regime was installed that quickly rounded up, jailed, and executed progressive political and labor leaders. A succession of ever more barbarous governments, either directly controlled or else immensely intimidated by the powerful Guatemalan Army, pushed the great majority of the population further and further into poverty. Living standards fell to such depths that in 1992 only 13 percent of the population lived above the poverty line.[12]

The government sustained this level of inequality by using terroristic violence to stem the rising levels of popular dissatisfaction. Political leaders seeking redress at the ballot box, Indians who resisted further takeover of their land, and urban workers who sought to unionize were systematically eliminated or "disappeared." In the 1960s, as an alternative to the futility of peaceful protest, a small faction of military dissidents joined displaced Ladino farmers to form a guerrilla insurgency against the government in the relatively underpopulated eastern section of the country; this was largely subdued in the name of anti-communism by a beefed-up Guatemalan Army that enjoyed the assistance of U.S. Green Beret advisors.[13]

In the 1970s, as repressive measures continued to stifle any kind of peaceful dissent, urban young people and many of the increasingly marginalized Indian settlements in the highlands were deciding to take up arms against the government. Three separate guerrilla armies were formed to fight against an army that had become by far the largest and most professional in the region. Just as this conflict was breaking out, Guatemala was struck by an enormous earthquake in 1976 that killed twenty thousand, caused extensive damage in urban zones and rural villages alike, and displaced hundreds of thousands from their homes. At this point, La Violencia began, the period of death and devastation that was worse than all the other savagery in the Central American region, including the prolonged conflicts that raged in neighboring El Salvador, Nicaragua, and Honduras. In what was, for the most part, a large-scale government extermination program rather than a military engagement of guerrilla forces: 150,000 people were killed, 440 Indian towns and villages were wiped off the map, hundreds of thousands of civilians fled into exile in Mexico and the United States, and one million people left their homes to take up internal exile in some other area of Guatemala.[14]

The worst levels of La Violencia subsided in 1984, but since then the level of violent repression implemented by the state has remained high, military and business corruption has become more rampant, and the economy has fallen into depression-like circumstances that have continued to erode living standards and social services for 90 percent of Guatemalan citizens. Now 72 percent of Guatemalans can no longer afford a minimum diet, up from 52 percent in 1980. The purchasing power of the average citizen is now only 22 percent of what it was more than twenty years ago.[15]

Health-care delivery, as demonstrated by increasing infant-mortality rates and child malnutrition, became worse than anywhere in the Western Hemisphere, including Haiti. Guatemala's expenditure on public education declined to the second-lowest in Latin America, 1.8 percent of GDP per capita.[16] The tax structure, continually retailored since the years of reform, reduced the overall percentage of taxation to only 5.3 percent of national income, the lowest in Latin America and the second-lowest in the world.[17]

Was it unreasonable for Guatemalans to believe that this was the apocalypse, and to find solace in an apocalyptic religion?

Catholics and Pentecostals and Social Change

Violence and the threat of death were not the main reasons Guatemalans moved toward Christian fundamentalism, but they certainly accelerated the process. Like much of the developing world, Guatemalan society was undergoing profound structural change that undermined traditional culture and modes of living. Many poor and uprooted Guatemalans sought spiritual certainties that could help them survive and adjust to the hardships of new social and economic conditions. One of the survival mechanisms was provided by the small, insular communities in the Pentecostal churches, but it was not the only spiritual option available.

Although the Catholic Church had been weakened substantially, it had the potential of remaining a major social force if it could change. In the past it acted as one of the three institutional pillars that supported a Latin American model of internal domination, along with the oligarchy, which consolidated economic ownership and political power in the hands of a few families, and the military, which used any means at its disposal to maintain social order. The Catholic Church's lessons in conservative hierarchical hegemony taught the people to obey the oligarchical and military powers. The Catholic Church in Guatemala had already been stripped of much of this kind of repressive

power, and the changes in worldwide Catholicism, especially those engen-
dered by Vatican II, were pushing the Church toward reform.

In the 1950s and 1960s, the Catholic Church was rejuvenated to a certain
extent; in the cities it expanded schools and institutions that served the upper
and middle classes; in the countryside, a new cadre of religious workers, most
of them foreigners because of the exceptional dearth of ordained
Guatemalans in the past, began to transform religious life. The number of
priests, 531, had more than quadrupled from its 1940 level; the number of
nuns had increased eightfold to 805.[18] Catholic Action, a neoconservative
movement promoted internationally by the Vatican to purify the Church of
popular accretions and to resist secular, "communist" influences, was more or
less sustained in its mission in urban Guatemala, but in the countryside,
Catholic Action priorities were most often redirected toward various kinds of
progressive reform. Priests and nuns often engaged in practical projects in the
community—to promote public health, start primary schools, and organize
cooperative stores and agricultural entities—and they also trained thousands
of lay catechists to help them deliver the sacraments and teach the Gospel.

Among the communities in rural areas, old patterns of syncretic Mayan-
Catholic worship and "cofradia" associations among village elders were
beginning to break down; they were simultaneously challenged by younger
generations in the newly energized Catholic Church. At the grass-roots level
far from the direction of the church hierarchy, priests and lay people began
combining their religious energy with social analysis and activity.[19] As in
many parts of Latin America, this spiritual social awareness originated before
ideas of liberation theology were developed and before secular, guerrilla rebellion manifested itself. Given that the popular reform movement of the 1944-
1954 Arevelo-Arbenz years had been thoroughly suppressed, it was perhaps
natural for some of the reformist zeal of the following decade to be channeled
through the Catholic Church, where it met less government opposition than
in openly political forums.

At the same time, the social forces that pushed people out of their old cultures and into the urban slums were creating opportunities for Protestant
evangelizing, particularly on the part of small Pentecostal churches.
Pentecostals tied to North American denominations exercised a small but significant influence on religious life by the 1960s because they offered intense
worship and new community to poor Guatemalans who had left their traditional roots behind. In 1968 Bryan R. Roberts described some typical congregations in Guatemala City and noted the precariousness of poor Protestants'
existence compared to their poor Catholic neighbors. Although representatives of each religion had almost identical literacy rates and incomes, the Pentecostals were much more likely to be in engaged in some kind of marginal

self-employment (but eager to get factory jobs like many of their Catholic neighbors had), were newer arrivals from the countryside and had many fewer relatives in the capital, voted much less, and would not take part in voluntary civic improvement efforts.[20] In fact, they concentrated their voluntary efforts and financial donations solely within their churches and spread rumors "actively sabotaging community-wide organizations."[21] Roberts noted that their attraction to dispensational dogma seemed to match their life experiences, in which material security was tenuous and disaster lurked nearby. Their Bible readings stressed that the world must pass through a series of disasters, a pattern that "fits Guatemala's political and economic misfortunes."[22]

Catholicism among the working poor of Guatemala City, according to Roberts, was more of a comfortable reference point than an active pursuit. Most Catholics did not attend church services regularly and had no access to a priest and did not formally marry. Their Catholicism was a matter of baptism and custom in the form of personal devotions that individuals made to the Virgin or an appropriate saint.[23] When Guatemala's social fabric, full of inequalities already, began to disintegrate, Pentecostal churches were prepared to offer a special kind of shelter and could multiply themselves quickly, especially where Catholic structures were not changing or expanding to meet such needs.

Pentecostalism kept filling the cracks of social and spiritual dislocation in a modest way until the mid-1970s, when the world seemed to face destruction on all fronts. The earthquake of 1976, the military violence of the period, and the displacement of the poor from the land as a result of agro-export capitalism created fertile conditions for conversion. With their apolitical and fundamentalist outlook based on Biblical dispensationalism, the Pentecostals empowered individuals to concentrate on survival without having to tackle the larger socio-political issues that loomed so far beyond their control.[24] The small, intimate Pentecostal church groups welcomed people into a personally supportive community and laid out strict guidelines for daily behavior. Like the fledgling Catholic base communities, which were often criticized or ignored by the Catholic hierarchy, Pentecostal churches offered individual believers full participation while providing community support.

Given the country's oppressive political climate, however, the new wave of evangelicalism acted as both comforter and silent conspirator. Neither the government nor the military looked kindly upon religious organizations that were openly or even implicitly political. Like North American Protestant fundamentalism in the 1930s and 1940s, Pentecostalism in Central America remained largely separatist, often otherworldly and strongly pietistic. In the 1970s and '80s, the rise of publicly reported, politically inspired violence fueled the pietistic impulse. An individualistic religious faith was safer than a collective and political one, which elicited terrorism from the state and the right-wing elite.[25]

As Jose Miguez Bonino has argued, Latin American Protestantism tended either to defend the existing oligarchies or to alienate people from the real concerns of society.[26] The disintegration of community life, then, provided opportunities for Guatemalan evangelicals to establish successful congregations that were inclusive, disciplined, and fraternal.[27]

From the beginning North American missionaries had taken advantage of the situation. Historian Virginia Garrard-Burnett suggests that Guatemalans' acceptance of Protestantism was partly "due to the impact of large-scale evangelism efforts orchestrated by the United States." The Latin American Mission (LAM) launched a massive evangelical crusade called Evangelism in Depth. Its arrival in Guatemala in 1962 coincided with the imposition of martial law by President Miguel Ydigoras Fuentes. According to Garrard-Burnett, "The timing of the Evangelization in Depth crusade was no coincidence…for the LAM was the flagship of a movement among conservative fundamentalists in the United States who sought to offer a 'spiritual alternative to communism'" in the Third World.[28]

Combining old-style revivalism with modern marketing techniques, LAM launched the first successful large-scale "crusade" by Protestants in Guatemala. Evangelism in Depth converted 15,000 Guatemalans in its first year, and Protestant growth rates increased steadily until the middle of the decade. Stressing numerical growth over doctrinal differences, the effort also spawned scores of new denominations in Guatemala, many of which had little or no affiliation with churches, groups, or monies from the United States.[29] As Dennis Smith has suggested, such evangelistic efforts clearly imported the kind of religious individualism characteristic of North American evangelicalism.[30] Apolitical positions were the safest for missionaries who wanted access to the country since any type of Social Gospel could offend Guatemalan authorities and might jeopardize the missionary enterprise.

It is not surprising, then, that Pentecostals and the North American evangelistic support network were poised to act in Guatemala when the 1976 earthquake devastated the country. North American and Western European aid (money, supplies, and personnel) poured in from churches, denominations, and Protestant parachurch agencies. Local church groups and enthusiastic young pastors mobilized their existing members for the task of saving more souls for Christ. Soon, evangelical membership leapt forward by a dramatic 13 percent annually, double the rate of conversion in 1970.[31] When destruction by natural causes was followed by years of military devastation, the prospects for evangelizing kept multiplying. By 1982, Protestants constituted 22 percent of the population.

New elements in the Catholic Church were not so lucky. Priests and lay workers in rural areas, even though they seldom supported the guerrilla movements, were assumed by the army to be part of the bulwark of peasant resistance. In rural and city areas alike, religious participation in such things as labor organizing, health provision for the poor, cooperative stores and food production was easily equated with "communism" by the ultra-right forces of the state. Generally the Catholic bishops did not openly support liberation theology and the kinds of Christian base communities that had spread with a degree of hierarchical blessing in such countries as Brazil.

In rural areas in 1980 and 1981, twenty Catholic priests and nuns were assassinated or kidnapped. Ninety-one priests and seventy-eight nuns left the country under threat of death. Hundreds of lay catechists were murdered, and churches and church schools were closed. Seventy parishes no longer had priests, and in the province of Quiche not one Catholic church remained open. Catholic attempts to support peaceful resistance in the cities were also suppressed with a heavy hand. For instance, after twenty-seven union leaders were abducted in Guatemala City in 1980, religious workers decided to offer a Catholic retreat house as refuge for another union meeting two months later. The army promptly broke in and kidnapped seventeen more union officials, none of whom was ever seen again.[32]

Evangelicalism and Politics

Many Catholics were actively political at the grass-roots level, on a continuum ranging from mild reformism to explicit liberation theology. The huge majority of evangelicals, on the other hand, were decidedly apolitical, but nevertheless benefited from the extermination plans put into effect by the right-wing elements. In Guatemala, the right included members of the landed elite, the military, and upper-class business and professional groups united to oppose the advances of Mayans, small-scale ladino farmers, and all sectors of private and public wage earners.

In 1982, a military coup brought to power an outspoken neo-Pentecostal evangelical, General Efrain Rios Montt. The event signaled an end to apolitical pietism among many Protestants. Montt's open expression of his evangelical faith led a growing number of Pentecostals, especially middle-class neo-Pentecostals, to consider the implications of their faith for the nation's political situation. Rios Montt was on the outside of elite political circles, including the top generals who conspired with the oligarchy, and so gained the support of junior officers in the army who believed he would fight corruption and impose authoritarian solutions to La Violencia.

A Catholic turned born-again fundamentalist, Rios Montt was a member of the California-based Church of the Word (El Verbo), whose theology helped shape the content of the Sunday afternoon radio talks he delivered after he assumed power. He identified the enemy: "communism, or the Antichrist, and all means must be used to exterminate it."[33] Some evangelicals in North America considered Rios Montt to be "the embodiment of a modern Christian soldier in the Central American Cold War."[34] Pat Robertson flew to Guatemala and embraced Rios Montt five days after he seized power. In an introduction to the general's biography, Robertson extolled his virtues:

> In a country that had been noted for corruption, oppression and violence, there was now joy and hope. A corrupt regime had been overthrown and a born-again Christian had been installed as president of the junta. I knew in my heart that Rios Montt offered the people of his country—indeed the people of all of Latin America—a true alternative between the oppression of corrupt oligarchies and the tyranny of Russian-backed communist totalitarianism.... I enlisted the prayers of tens of thousands of evangelicals across America.[35]

In 1982 Robertson raised millions of dollars for the general's military dictatorship in a "humanitarian aid" project, Operation Lovelift. The money helped support Rios Montt's pacification plan, which forced the relocation of Indians in the highlands after his soldiers effectively carried out his "guns-and-beans" campaign (*fusiles y frijoles*).[36] With the stated goal of "wiping out communism in the highlands," the general's regime massacred thousands of people and destroyed hundreds of villages, forcing up to one million Indians to flee their homes.[37] As one army official explained, the military and civil efforts to purge insurgents had a clear motto: "If you are with us, we'll feed you; if you're against us, we'll kill you."[38]

By the summer of 1983, the guns-and-beans campaign had brought an enforced peace to the region and the government began establishing "model villages" (*polo de desarollo*) for displaced Indians. Evangelicals played an active role in the resettlement villages, which provided food, shelter, and work in a tightly controlled, highly monitored environment.

According to Virginia Garrard-Burnett, the evangelical churches as "apolitical entities" became "an ideal foil for the politicized Catholic church in the highlands during Rios Montt's era. With government support, evangelicals could co-opt the social efforts of Catholic catechists" by organizing literacy training, health care, and relief aid projects.[39] Many Indian catechists had to flee the country; one was Nobel Peace Prize winner Rigoberta Menchu, who survived after other members of her activist Catholic family had been killed by the military.

Some people who stayed behind made a pragmatic decision to convert to Protestantism. With many evangelical groups offering handouts, as well as a seemingly "depoliticized" message of salvation, turning to Protestantism was a reasonable course of action. Moreover, some Guatemalans found that the guerrilla forces with whom many had sympathized were unable to protect them, and as Protestants they might be better protected from the ravages of the Army. National Assembly member Claudio Coxaj, a Mayan Catholic and a member of the ruling Christian Democrats, claimed that "the principle reason so many people converted to evangelical faiths is that they didn't want to die."[40]

David Stoll describes the case of an evangelical pastor turned army informant, Pastor Nicholas, an Ixil pastor of the Pentecostal Complete Gospel Church of God. In 1982, Pastor Nicholas decided to inform the army of the whereabouts of the Guerrilla Army of the Poor (EGP), enabling the army to sweep the guerrillas out of the immediate area. His decision came after his brother and brother-in-law and sixty-two other townsmen were hauled out of their houses and butchered by the army in reprisal for a July 1980 EGP raid on the Cotzal barracks. "The guerrillas only provoke the army and then they go," Nicholas told Stoll. "We are the ones who suffer the consequences."[41]

The flight to evangelicalism was often an expression of powerlessness. Juan Cedillo, pastor of the fast-growing Prince of Peace church in Nebaj, suggests that:

> Many left the Catholic church because of the trauma of war that taught them that man couldn't create heaven on earth. We found that the earthly battle doesn't change anything. We must accept the suffering of this world in order to be saved by Jesus Christ in the world to come.[42]

Many Guatemalan evangelical leaders, like their counterparts throughout the world, publicly advocate that it is God's will for His people to obey civil authorities (citing Romans 13) and to refrain from all political action that challenges the status quo.

Montt's annihilation of families and villages, and the cohesive body of language, customs, and values peculiar to Catholic/Mayan culture and religious practice, was probably more influential in turning people toward Protestantism than Montt's own religious views or the influence of North American evangelicals.[43] The terrifying reality of the displaced Indians more or less matched the worldview offered by fundamentalist evangelicals. Impending doom and the Second Coming of Christ offered both an explanation for their devastated society and a promise of a new and better world in heaven.

The simplicity of the evangelical message offered a clear and orderly future and compelling lifestyles for self-improvement. The emphasis on the family and clean living attracted many people—especially women, who then attempted to include their husbands in the church.[44] In 1978 Julian Lloret enumerated three major motivations for the conversion of 112 Indian families whom he interviewed in highland villages: 1) desire for healing and restored health, 2) deliverance from drink or other vices, 3) deliverance from magic or witchcraft.[45]

Guatemalan Evangelicalism Today

Contemporary evangelical fundamentalism in Guatemala is a popular, fragmented, and adaptable movement that is flourishing among the rural and urban poor as well among middle- and upper-middle-class city dwellers. Whether in the countryside or the city, Protestant churches in Guatemala are essentially fundamentalistic: they tend to be dispensationalist, anti-intellectual, anti-ecumenical, and culturally separatist. While all Protestants are referred to as evangelicals in Central America, the majority of Protestants in Guatemala would be considered fundamentalist by North American standards. A small minority of Protestant churches tend toward their own version of liberation theology and are amenable to working with Catholics.

Consistent with patterns of Protestantism in other cultural contexts, Protestant churches in Guatemala proliferate as splinter groups break away from the "mother" church, both as a result of conflict and of deliberate church "planting." According to Everett Wilson, the emphasis on evangelism means that "rarely does a church not have [extension] congregations, missions or preaching points (*campos blancos*)."[46] Radiating out from a "parent" church, lay leaders or newly trained pastors are likely to establish a new congregation in a neighboring locale. As Wilson documents, the formation of congregations tends to follow a pattern whereby:

> National evangelists, sometimes but not generally accompanied by a missionary, visited a series of villages and towns to identify interested persons in whose homes meetings could be held. The more enthusiastic members radiated out to neighboring villages and plantations.... Many new congregations were patronized by a family that donated land for a *temple* or otherwise supported a nuclear church.[47]

The rapid proliferation of new evangelical groups has been staggering.[48] Wilson distinquishes sixty-eight groups among Guatemalan evangelicals, the two largest denominations being the Assemblies of God and the Church of God. Most other churches, whether independent or belonging to recently organized local denominations, also belong to the Pentecostal or holiness traditions which account for 70 percent to 80 percent of all Guatemalan Protestants.[49] Although these groups essentially operate independently, their efforts are often reinforced by transnational evangelical organizations from the U.S., such as Christ for the Nations, Campus Crusade, Full Gospel

Business Men's Fellowship International, OC Ministries, and Youth With A Mission.

For many of the large urban churches that cater to the small but influential middle and upper-middle classes, the evangelical message tends to legitimate wealth and prosperity. These churches have embraced "prosperity theology" (sometimes called the "name-it-and-claim-it" school of thought or the "health-and-wealth" gospel) that has filtered down from the North. The neo-Pentecostal churches thrive on practical ministries designed to help the middle class cope with widespread personal and family problems. Like North American "megachurches," they offer educational and worship experiences for the entire family. Sermons and courses address topics such as raising children, building strong marriages, managing households, avoiding work-related stress and establishing relationships with God through prayer, fellowship, and, especially, Bible study. Most of their members were lapsed or unhappy Catholics, or increasingly, members of other Protestant churches. For example, one upper-class woman indicated that she left the Presbyterian church for one of Guatemala City's large neo-Pentecostal churches because the latter "gives power" (*da poder*) in a way that the old denominations do not.

Preaching and Teaching to the Poor: the Assemblies of God

Up until the end of the 1980s, the most popular TV evangelist was not Pat Robertson but Jimmy Swaggart. His highly emotional Pentecostal performances, translated very convincingly into Spanish, resonated with the kind of intense religiosity practiced in most Guatemalan Protestant churches. Since Swaggart was at the time associated with the Assemblies of God, the largest Protestant denomination in Guatemala, he gained influence by channeling millions of dollars in annual donations to their churches. When we first visited Assembly of God church schools in 1987, we found they relied heavily on funding from Swaggart. This changed after 1988, when Swaggart was exposed in a sexual scandal in the U.S.; he lost his denominational ties to the worldwide Assemblies of God network, and his television ministry in the U.S. and abroad declined.

As in many other developing countries, television plays an important role in Guatemalan life. Even in the *barrios* many Guatemalans own television sets. Communal viewing, particularly among neighbors and extended families, is common, building the potential national television audience to over 70 percent of the population and approximately 80 percent of church goers.[50] Most religious television in Central America is evangelical programming produced in the United States.[51] Television is the embodiment of North American Pentecostalism and neo-Pentecostalism. The same economic factors that make Central America heavily dependent upon all types of North American television make Guatemalan evangelicals dependent upon the productions of their media-rich neighbors to the North.

Swaggart's popularity in Guatemala in the middle-to-late 1980s far exceeded his televisual appeal in the United States. At his heyday, Swaggart's weekly program reached an estimated two million to three million adult viewers in the United States—roughly 2–3 percent of the population. In Guatemala, Swaggart's show was seen regularly by one-fourth to over half of the nation.[52] Roughly three-quarters of the country's active church goers had seen his program—more than any other media evangelist.[53] Moreover, Swaggart's appeal largely transcended the divisions and animosities among Guatemala's religious groups, including the Catholic-Protestant split.[54]

Swaggart's popularity can be attributed to a number of things. First, his program was simply one of the most engaging religious broadcasts on Guatemalan television. Like Pentecostal expressiveness generally, Swaggart communicated in an aural and visual style that conveyed great spiritual anticipation and displayed dramatic flair. In spite of the technical effort behind every one of his broadcasts, especially the taped crusades, the programs created the illusion of being live, unrehearsed, unplanned events.[55]

Second, Swaggart's Pentecostalism matched the growing style of evangelicalism already present in Guatemalan culture. The televangelist seemed to resonate with the Spirit-led Protestantism gaining popularity across the country, especially in the Spanish-speaking regions. Even Swaggart's Spanish translator, used extensively at revivals taped in Latin America, effectively duplicated the televangelist's kinesics and vocal style and habits. Swaggart's popularity in the region reflected a natural communicative affinity between the oral cultures of Pentecostal Guatemala and the Pentecostal Southern United States.[56]

Third, Swaggart's outspoken attacks on liberal social and personal mores resonated with Latin American cultural prohibitions and taboos. He attacked many of the very things that plagued the region's families and neighborhoods: alcohol abuse, drug use, infidelity, and so forth.

In Guatemala, as in many parts of the world, Pentecostal churches are poor congregations served by equally indigent ministers. Although the Jimmy Swaggart Ministry kept a few staff members in posh offices on the upper floors of the Sheraton "Conquistador" Hotel, most Swaggart funds that reached Guatemala went directly to the poor. Money was funneled to construct churches, feed children, provide basic health clinics, and give scholarships to Assemblies of God elementary schools. Thus Swaggart had it both ways: he was the media star who drew attention to powerful Christian witness, and he represented the true Christian involved in moral uplift and the alleviation of suffering.

Many non-Pentecostal missionary groups had been in Guatemala for years before Swaggart arrived on TV, but without the success generated by Spirit-filled worship. Pure effort, in terms of numbers of missionaries and total years labored, does not mean that a certain kind of fundamentalism is bound to triumph. Two of the largest evangelizing agencies in Guatemala are the Central American Mission (CAM) and the Southern Baptist Foreign Mission, which each support forty-six full-time, long-term missionaries (those who give more than four years' service) from the United States. They are closely identified with an old-style fundamentalism that was first made available to Guatemalans almost a century ago. CAM was established by the famous dispensationalist C. I. Scofield and three Texas businessmen, and it first sent missionaries to Guatemala in 1899. One of the early CAM preachers was Cameron Townsend, founder of the Wycliffe Bible Translators.

Although numerous small Baptist and CAM churches are scattered around Guatemala, they are vastly outnumbered by the later arrivals, the Pentecostals who added the key ingredient of Spirit-filled worship to the strict moral codes and dispensational outlook of their predecessors. Arriving in the 1920s, the North American Pentecostal denominations have thrived since the late 1960s. The two largest, the Assemblies of God and the Church of God, each represent 12 percent of the evangelical population and thousands of small congregations. There are now thousands of independent and self-generating Guatemalan churches (representing almost 50 percent of all Protestants), and their Pentecostal characteristics are very much indebted to the traditions of both the Assemblies of God and the Church of God.

The Church of God and the Assemblies of God, in the words of one minister and educator, "do not serve the poor, they are the poor."[57] Those who teach in their Christian schools are happy to have any kind of job in a society characterized by very high unemployment and poverty rates. They generally settle for salaries that are less than half the very low salaries paid to public school teachers. These evangelical teachers[58] are dedicated people who teach without textbooks and other materials when, as is often the case, they cannot afford them. They are proud that their students have escaped the *humanismo* that pervades the public schools and can partake of an education that is thoroughly *creacionista*. The teachers do not get training in any specific North American curriculum. Their educational philosophy is supplied mainly through the consistent messages coming from their pastors and the evangelical radio and television programs of Swaggart, the *700 Club,* and others.

Evangelical schools offer a basic education to students who might not otherwise receive one. They help relieve the overcrowding of the public schools, which are often severely limited in terms of space, desks, teachers, and basic resources. One extremely dedicated principal, who operated a fundamentalistic school for working-class children in Quetzaltenango, indicated why her very low budget was adequate for the needs of her students. When she compared them to students at a much more prestigious school, she was very frank about social class: "Because we are lower class, we have to move more slowly; because they are ministering to a higher class of people, they can grasp more complicated ideas and make faster spiritual progress."[59]

We visited the largest of the Assembly of God schools, Liceo Bethesda, which is in Zone 19, one of the very poor colonies on the outskirts of Guatemala City. The first Assembly of God school in Guatemala, Bethesda saw its enrollments grow from eighty students in 1973 to nine hundred students in 1987 to thirteen hundred students in 1990. Between 1983 and 1988, Swaggart's ministries helped support Bethesda and fifteen other Assembly of God schools in Guatemala, distributing some $9,000-10,000 per month.[60]

With Swaggart's fall from grace in 1988, the money flow to overseas missions dried up, and a number of schools and programs were forced to close. (Swaggart at one time was providing over $15 million a year for various overseas missions; these funds once supported a school system serving over thirteen thousand children in El Salvador, and almost as many in Honduras.)[61] Guatemala appears to be the only country in which no school had to close. Ministerio Piedad, a local Guatemalan organization created through the Assemblies of God, was operating thirteen schools throughout the country, with a total enrollment of some seven thousand to eight thousand students in 1990. A number of health clinics and lunch programs the schools were sponsoring, however, had to be discontinued.

On our first encounter with Bethesda School in July 1987, we found a crowded school of nine hundred students with a student-teacher ratio of 48:1, a health clinic for students and their families, and a free lunch program. Bethesda had few curricular materials other than a desk for every student. In March 1990, the school operated with four hundred more students but fewer teachers, none of whom had received a salary increase since 1987. The free lunch program was no longer available, and the clinic, which had been closed for months, had just reopened on a part-time basis. It occupied three rooms: a waiting room, a room with a couple of beds for those who needed to rest, and a little room that stored drugs that had been shipped from a German mission. Although church members had begun to dig a well in 1987, little progress had been made by 1990, so that the Bethesda school and clinic had no potable water.

Neo-Pentecostalism for the Upper-Middle Class

Although the huge majority of Guatemalans and Guatemalan Protestants are poor, new fundamentalist churches have had significant growth among more prosperous and educated people, ranging from shopkeepers to middle managers to professionals. These churches are generally called neo-Pentecostal (in the United States these would also be labeled charismatic, a term reserved in Guatemala for certain Catholic believers and worship groups). Like neo-Pentecostal and charismatic churches in the United States, the neo-Pentecostal Guatemalans are less concerned with strict behavioral limits of the sort imposed in fundamentalist churches of the poor (both non-Pentecostal and Pentecostal), and are more interested in gifts of the Spirit that favor health and wealth. For the most part these churches are independent. Some are on the brink of becoming megachurches, and they have usually been founded by Guatemalans themselves without direct missionary aid.

These congregations are beginning to have influence in the political sphere, using religious broadcasting to express their ideas of piety and morality to the society at large. This trend in Guatemalan fundamentalism is at an early stage, perhaps equivalent to the New Religious Right in the United States in the late 1970s when it was struggling to set its agenda. The large churches de-emphasize sinfulness and offer a message more palatable to those who are more satisfied with their lives, and who want personal, comforting, and practical advice mixed with an emotional and professional worship service.

At the Fraternidad Cristiana, Pastor Jorge Lopez preached to as many as 3,100 on Sunday mornings in 1987 (he began with thirty-five members in 1979). His sermons stress family issues, focusing on such things as financial stewardship, raising children, and building strong marriages. His recruiting slogan is *una iglesia para la toda familia* (one church for the whole family). At present, many Guatemalan families are split not only between Catholicism and Protestantism but also among various Protestant churches. In trying to attract new families or new members from families who already belong, Fraternidad Cristiana organizes bimonthly breakfast meetings at the elegant Camino Real or Sheraton "Conquistador" Hotels. The cost of an average breakfast for a family of four is approximately 75 quetzales, the monthly income of many Guatemalan families. Most of the members are former Catholics who visited the church for the first time at the invitation of friends, out of curiosity, or because they had witnessed Lopez's television or radio programs. Lopez is a former radio and TV personality who first joined one Protestant denomination, then split to form his own church.[62] He writes editorial columns regularly in *La Prensa,* a conservative daily that is the nation's largest newspaper, and his Sunday services are often rebroadcast on television and radio. As in the United States, conservative evangelicals have been immensely successful in capturing a huge percentage of the broadcast market. In Guatemala City, the Protestants broadcast about 5,900 minutes of TV and radio programming each week, compared to just three hundred minutes by

Catholic stations.[63]

Lopez is not afraid to preach on the necessity of personal political involvement as he offers the congregation Biblical principles for selecting the right candidates for political office. Privately he advises people how to vote in upcoming elections. Many church members have been associated with the MLN,[64] the ultra right-wing National Liberation Movement, which in turn has been linked with the military death squads that have kidnapped and murdered thousands of moderate and progressive leaders for the past twenty years. The MLN, which helped form several governments after the coup of 1954, has sought to ban labor unions and keep Guatemalan taxes as low as possible.

Lopez's sermons are meticulously tailored to the expectations of his congregation. In one homily concerning management,[65] Lopez referred to "a study from an eminent North American university" that argued that 80 percent of the people cannot work adequately without constant supervision and direction, that 16 percent can work on their own with just a little direct supervision, and that only 4 percent of the population has what it takes to be self-sufficient, give orders, and effectively manage enterprises and the work of others. Lopez went on to say that God wants those who are in authority, the managers, to be good stewards of various kinds of property. Because their responsibilities are great, their compensation should be great. They have earned it.

Lopez explained that the attitude of good management will be passed down through the ranks so that the lower echelons will appreciate their duty in keeping things orderly. In the same way, he noted, the wife will learn from the husband how to communicate appropriate orders on cleanliness to her maid, for it would be silly for her to attempt to do everything herself just because she has not learned to effectively manage the work of her servants.

As the sermon returned to the general task of running society efficiently, the pastor interjected the Biblical story of Joseph and his brothers to remind his listeners that the position of leadership and managing others can provoke jealousy; leadership demands faith in God, who will provide one with the strength to persevere. Joseph, who was bestowed with his coat of many colors because of his qualities of intelligence and leadership, had to overcome the hostility of his older siblings and learn to lead wisely.

Fraternidad Cristiana is a not a U.S. transplant, that is, it was not started under the aegis of a North American denomination or mission. Some might argue that this makes it more purely "Guatemalan." A counterargument might be that middle- and upper-middle-class Guatemalans are much more similar to U.S. citizens than to the majority of Guatemalans who live in rural poverty or city slum areas. The Guatemalan upper-middle class is very much

dependent on the United States for cultural guidelines. They are the only citizens, aside from the very rich, likely to have had some educational experience in the United States (often college level, occasionally Bible school training). Like their counterparts in many countries (Mexican social scientist
Rudolfo Saberhagen would call them part of an international comprador
class), they are thoroughly linked into the international network of consumer
tastes and goods dominated by the United States, and usually will take their
theological guidance, in terms of books and tapes and movies, from U.S.
sources. Certainly by their cars, electronics equipment, home appliances, and
even some of the products they select at their supermarkets, they would be
indistinguishable from North America suburbanites. Furthermore, many of
these church members might work directly for U.S. or multinational companies as corporate managers and sales representatives, or indirectly in other
professional capacities.

Churches such as Fraternidad Cristiana, influenced by education and relative prosperity, openly address the personal problems faced by tens of thousands of former Roman Catholics in urban areas. Among evangelicals, Lopez's
message is probably the least doctrinaire and the most compatible with the
sentiments and ideas of charismatic Catholics. As the neo-Pentecostal/charis-
matic message has become more familiar in upper-middle-class and business
circles, the distinction between Protestant and Catholic may not seem that
important to many. David Stoll reported that some Protestants were angry
when the Full Gospel Businessmen's Fellowship in Guatemala City elected a
Catholic leader, an occurrence that is unusual but probably compatible with
the goals of this very large and influential U.S.-based parachurch multinational.[66] The megachurch and parachurch networks are reaching out for relevance
and control over the world around them, rather than looking for proscriptive
controls over personal daily habits or perfect individual sanctity. These neo-
Pentecostal believers typically embrace conservative political values, which in
Guatemala usually translates into support for the government and military;
such sympathies allow Pastor Lopez to air his religious broadcasts free on the
government channel.

The neo-Pentecostals' interest in good government in no way implies
interest in social justice or the redistribution of wealth. Their primary interest
is public order and tranquility. Carlos Ramirez, the head pastor at El Verbo
(The Word Church attended by Rios Montt), once emphasized on three successive Sundays that what Guatemalans needed was "discipline, obedience,
and authority." Although this might seem like the rhetoric of a ruling class
that has trouble keeping its population in line, the true upper class is not
represented. The few hundred families who make up the Guatemalan oligarchy and control the country's economy do not usually go to El Verbo or

any other neo-Pentecostal church. They have remained comfortably Catholic, at least in nominal terms, even as the country's economic and social situation has deteriorated. Thus Ramirez was speaking for those one or two steps below, who are frustrated by the growing inability of the oligarchy and the military to provide the kind of "order" that was once sufficient to subdue restless citizens and criminal elements. They may even be seen as "reformist," an up-and-coming class of professionals and business representatives with ties to efficient multinational bureaucracies, who are sincerely appalled at the corruption in the highest ranks of power. The disintegration of Guatemalan society, which leads poor Guatemalans to submit themselves to fundamentalist self-discipline in order to survive, makes neo-Pentecostals long for discipline of another kind, the kind once promised by a former dictator:

> At times God chooses to unite the religious world and the political world as He did when he chose King David to lead the nation of Israel. Similarly He picked General Rios Montt to temporarily lead Guatemala as prophet and king in 1982–1983 and he may choose to do so again.[67]

Politics is not always the focus of El Verbo and other upper-middle-class constituencies, however. Much energy is expended on the mundane miracles needed to provide for the growing expectations of the average church member. Testimonies regularly are voiced or appear in church publications attesting to the fact that the Lord does not forget those who ask Him to meet their needs. They tend to sound exactly like the endorsements of "seed faith" found in Oral Roberts's *Abundant Life* magazine in the 1970s, in articles with titles such as "A Raise Plus a Bonus" and "New Job as General Manager."[68] For instance, one of El Verbo's Sunday bulletins read as follows:

> A year ago my wife and I were looking for a house to buy. With patience and prayers we sought the house that suited us best, but realized that we could afford only two thirds of the price. We, my wife and I, prayed for three days intensely and then felt at peace in buying it even though we still did not have the extra money. I gave the owner my down payment. Three weeks later my boss called me to say that I, as a manager, was responsible for the positive results in my factory. The bonus which I received covered the remaining third of the cost of the house with just enough left over to cover the other expenses of moving. Glory to God! Alleluia!

This sort of modest magic catches the imagination of neo-Pentecostal worshipers in general, and is useful for pointing out the special attributes of their churches and the special calling of their leaders. One independent and increasingly influential church, El Shaddai, is led by Pastor Cabelleros, a young urban professional who felt the divine call to open a ministry in his mother-in-law's garage in 1982. One of his staff people explained that the Lord had led him to study abroad in the United States, yet Cabelleros arrived there knowing not a word of English. This problem was solved "supernaturally"—that is, he began comprehending and speaking English immediately, a kind of practical derivative of the ability to speak in tongues.

El Shaddai, like Fraternidad Cristiana, offers bilingual private school education at the primary level, a considerable drawing card for families who want their children to succeed professionally. In contrast to El Verbo, whose private school gives the same strong emphasis to *disciplina* that is offered in Sunday sermons, El Shaddai stresses the power of love and caring emanating from its teachers, all of whom are members of the church. The children are expected to learn Christian behavior by following the example of their teachers. Students, often at a young age, are also assumed to be "open to the Holy Spirit"; thus teachers encourage other students to gather together when another child is feeling sick and perform a "laying on of hands" in order to cast out any demons before a pill is administered.

The neo-Pentecostal churches, while often positioning themselves to meet various middle-class expectations, also keep abreast of the latest trends in theological fashion emanating from the United States and elsewhere. By the early 1990s, most large neo-Pentecostal churches were well aware of the various ways to practice "spiritual warfare" against large and small principalities and emissaries of Satan; they knew about the successes of Paul Yonggi Cho,[69] and many were hoping to become true megachurches through the implementation of the cell system of the church growth movement. Pastor Cabelleros and his congregation at El Shaddai embarked on their own "prayer warfare" campaign; using the analogy of casting demons out of a person, they decided to cast demons out of their country.[70] The goal is to chase out the satanic creatures that have inhabited Guatemala for centuries, some of them brought by the Spanish Catholic conquistadors, others dwelling within Mayan culture since pre-Columbian times.

El Shaddai was recently home church to Guatemalan President Serrano, who in 1991 became the first Protestant to be elected chief of state. Serrano was deposed in 1993 when he attempted an "auto-golpe" akin to the one executed by Fujimora in Peru.[71] He had previously belonged to one of the first churches to achieve a real megachurch presence, the ELIM church in Guatemala City; it bridges the class divide by creating strong cell groups and subchurch networks in different neighborhoods, and was founded by a Guatemalan minister who calls himself a prophet. ELIM's congregation is unusual for mixing working-class Ladinos and Indians, lower-class peddlers, middle-class shopkeepers, and upper-middle-class professionals and managers.[72]

Agua Viva: Intense American Religion with Intensive American Presence

Although Guatemalans actively promote the new Christian fundamentalism and keep abreast of developments around the world, one of the most intense religious experiments is being carried out by Americans. There is an unusual concentration of missionaries, calling themselves Agua Viva,[73] in the city of Quetzaltenango in the western highlands. Agua Viva has the largest number of long-term Protestant missionary personnel in Guatemala, forty-seven Americans, outranking even the long-established Central American Mission and the Southern Baptist missionary apparatus, the world's largest Protestant sending agency. Agua Viva represents a new kind of multi-purpose para-church organization that has been directly spawned by the "faith" tradition of the Rhema Bible College in Tulsa and a large charismatic, neo-Pentecostal church in Broken Arrow, Oklahoma, called Living Waters.

Agua Viva has built a new church on the edge of the Quetzaltenango that can hold a congregation of thousands under a wide-spanning roof supported by huge steel beams. More impressive still is Agua Viva's Bible School complex about a mile away. The complex features a multitude of new, handsome buildings including a large Bible Study Center, a dining hall, numerous apartments, separate smaller study buildings, a school for missionary children, a medical center, construction headquarters, and orphanage houses. One reason Agua Viva can support so much building activity is that a Guatemalan construction laborer earns at most a dollar a day, and a skilled craftsman such as a mason or carpenter, about two dollars.[74] A little guard house by the main gate is manned by uniformed Guatemalan guards, ex-military men who carry submachine guns. One must speak to them upon entering because the rest of the multi-acre compound is surrounded with a tall concrete wall topped with barbed wire and broken glass.

Agua Viva was founded in 1979 by Jim Zirkle, once a housing contractor and cabinet maker, then a graduate of Rhema Bible School, now the proud father figure who is duplicating Rhema's educational and evangelical function in the middle of Central America. The church claims to be self-supporting on the basis of contributions from Guatemalans, while the Bible School receives over one and a half million dollars a year from Living Water Teaching International, its fund-raising affiliate in Oklahoma. In addition, all of Agua Viva's missionary personnel, most of them graduates of Rhema, are self-supporting, meaning that they raise funds to support themselves and their families by returning each year to a home base or mission circuit and requesting donations. Reverend Zirkle requires missionaries to raise about twenty thousand dollars a year or more for their living expenses; on this they can live very well, like the Guatemalan upper-middle class, and can help demonstrate that the church's prosperity theology really does work—according to Zirkle, "God does not want us living in a pigsty." In addition, missionaries must contribute additional funds of their own (an undisclosed amount) toward the operating expenses of the Bible School.

Agua Viva considers its church to be secondary to its educational mission at the Bible School, which recruits ministers from small churches all over the country. These ministers must pay fees for their classes, attend regularly for almost a year, and complete twelve courses ranging from preaching to healing to tithing. Teaching poor ministers how to get their congregations to tithe regularly is considered a central part of the mission; it will encourage the minister to aggressively increase his flock, and may one day lift up his income to the level where it provides full-time employment. A kind of neo-Pentecostal positive thinking merges with the prosperity theology to convince the Guatemalan pastor that he is capable of overcoming local poverty. The school does not provide information on the success rate of the graduating ministers, who number about two hundred each year.

Central to the recruitment of ministers into the school, especially pastors from remote areas, is something called the "campaign," a three-day tent revival and traveling medical clinic that reach remote Mayan villages in the mountains of Huehuetenango, or plantations in the Pacific lowlands. An expedition of five Mitsubishi vans and five Suzuki and Toyota jeeps sets out with tents, medical supplies, preachers, and one to three doctors (the latter usually Guatemalan evangelicals, or an occasional Christian physician on a short-term visit from the States.) The jeeps often have to drag the vans through deep mudholes and jungle before reaching a piece of open land, usually donated by a plantation owner, where the huge revival tent can be erected. The plantation owners are seldom evangelical Protestants but appreciate the free medical care dispensed, feeling that they will get partial credit and that the revival might do some good for their undisciplined workers. (The very first missionaries of Scofield's Central American Mission were brought to Central America by Canadian plantation owners in 1890.) The doctors treat cuts, dispense medicines, and pull teeth each morning, and religious services are held in the afternoon and evening. The revival tent can hold from one thousand to three thousand people; according to one missionary "in Huehuetenango in the North we got three thousand Indians, they're so small you can really pack them in." The yield in that particular location, he added, "was thirteen hundred people saved, ten blind people restored to sight, five cripples enabled to walk, and two dead babies brought back to life."[75]

Not only does the high-impact campaign serve as an instrument that impresses any local ministers with its spiritual power, but also it ranks as the

favorite event for U.S. visitors who have come with the intention of making
large donations to Agua Viva. Often these patrons are flown to the plantation
site of the revival for one day in an Agua Viva plane; or they may share in the
tropical adventure, riding in jeeps and camping throughout the whole campaign—"something people pay a lot of money for in the States, like a safari or
a rafting trip." Agua Viva's two airplanes and all their campaign vehicles were
donated to them by the Kenneth Copeland ministries. Copeland, before he
became an advocate of prosperity theology and a TV evangelist, had been the
pilot of Oral Roberts's private plane.

Among the missionaries a majority of the men come from military backgrounds, few have been college educated, and a large number have significant
experience in construction and agriculture. The ex-military men feel their
experience following orders and practicing a strict regimen was necessary for
uniting a group of ambitious people and working under an authority figure
such as Reverend Zirkle. The military connections have helped develop their
very friendly relationship with the Guatemalan Army, which regularly gives
its permission for the missionary excursions into remote areas and gives landing rights to Agua Viva aircraft at secluded military airstrips. The missionaries
take pride in having a "can-do" mentality. In the first place, the attitude
derives from their experience in building, farming, and actually making things;
secondly they feel they have been disciplined to carry out successful "missions," military or otherwise.

Agua Viva thus exudes some of the "muscular" Christianity common to
other missionary eras, especially that described by Jean and John Comoroff in
their book about nineteenth-century non-conformist missionaries sent from
Britain to Africa. They note the common lower-middle-class backgrounds of
Livingstone and most who followed him—they were from "the dominated
fraction of the dominant class"[76]—and that their experiences as mechanics or
farmers prepared them better than others for the rigors and adaptations
required in primitive lands.

> The Nonconformist evangelical societies concurred. For a long time they
> stressed the need for men with practical skills, humble horticulturalists and
> craftsmen rather than elevated scholar-priests.[77]

Also, as ministers they moved up into the lower ranks of "respectability," even
though their education was limited. These men had taken a safe step forward
in the changing British society, leaving behind the artisan and rural classes
whose future existence was already doomed. Finally, the missionaries saw
themselves as emissaries of God and ambassadors of Britain, representing
everything that was properly British at the far reaches of the Empire:

"Their ideological categories and symbolic practices, born of the refashioned culture of industrializing Britain, were to direct their civilizing mission."[78]

The Agua Viva missionaries are not refugees from the kind of brutal industrialization that reshaped nineteenth-century Britain, but some of them were definitely influenced by the reindustrialization and economic swings that reshaped the United States, particularly the Midwest, in the 1980s. Some had escaped the boom-and-bust oil economies of Oklahoma and Texas; one was an Iowa farmer who leased his acreage and barns before heading to Central America; another had been a construction foreman in taconite mills and lumber camps in Minnesota and had found fewer and fewer opportunities to employ his skills. The ten-year-old son of this construction veteran described life in Guatemala, "At home my dad says we'd be practically poor, down here we've got a maid and we live like kings."[79]

Like the British upholders of empire, the Agua Viva missionaries are enthusiastic believers in their own nationalism and a whole range of American values and habits they think they must inculcate. Americanism and Christianity are interchangeable in their thinking and indispensable for people who must be rescued from a life of laziness and vice. Agua Viva missionaries take a fairly disdainful view of the life of the average Guatemalan, who is thought to be too afraid to stand up straight and make a success of himself:

> Catholic teaching has turned men into groveling worms who believe they are weak, incompetent, and loaded down with sin. They don't realize that Jesus has taken away the burdens of their sin so that they can stand upright like real men. Their weakness is proven by the fact that women control the money in this country.

They make this conclusion (an erroneous one) because so many Indian and ladino women are busy selling their wares in the outdoor markets and small stores; it contributes to the missionaries' overall view of Catholicism as a warped feminine version of Christianity:

> They worship Mary as a holy mother, Jesus is not important because he was a criminal who got punished at the crucifixion.... They've become so convinced by the Catholics that they are sinful scum that they do not believe they can be righteous and do not know that once they are saved in Christ that they really are righteous![80]

Agua Viva prides itself on offering a faith that guarantees this righteousness and the exercise of mighty powers. In addition to the usual Pentecostal gifts of speaking in tongues, prophecy, and healing, the faith tradition of Hagin and Copeland promises Christlike status to the believer who is born again. One pamphlet handed out at services offers the Spanish version of Kenneth Copeland's message:

> When a man accepts Jesus as Lord...he enters the kingdom of God as a son himself and co-heir with Jesus Christ....You are entitled to to each one of the things that God has.

Agua Viva, like its progenitors in Tulsa and Fort Worth (home to Kenneth and Gloria Copeland's ministry), guarantees explicitly that by exercising the power of God's Word one can have "unlimited blessings and gifts" of a material nature, including both wealth and health; moreover, one is equipped with "a force of powerful security which will enable you to confront Satan face to face and triumph over him and his torments." Reverend Zirkle and his lieutenants recount many examples of how their faith preserved them when they were surrounded by "communists" while conducting tent campaigns, and how the Holy Spirit guided and hid their movements so they could avoid certain confrontations with guerrillas.

Because Agua Viva is still in its first stages of development, it is impossible to know whether it will continue to grow and prosper, or whether its impressive buildings and lavish spending will amount to no more than a decade or two of miscalculated overinvestment by ambitious, entrepreneurial missionaries. Their church, formally called Ensenanza de Agua Viva to connote its connection and secondary standing in relation to the "teaching" of the Bible School, initially drew almost one thousand worshipers and seems to have potential to develop into a megachurch. It developed a membership that ranged from professionals and the near-rich (one doctor's wife had a truckload of hotdogs brought in from her brother's meat factory in Guatemala City to serve at a giant picnic) to the poorest indigenous people living homeless on the city streets, who were recruited and transported regularly to services in church buses and were fed afterwards. Poor people were subjected to "prosperity sermons" and induced to part with any coins they had, since the notion of tithing and trusting in the Lord's willingness to pay back a believer "one hundredfold" is central to the Agua Viva teaching.

Agua Viva originally had no intentions of setting up its own network of independent, neo-Pentecostal churches, but the particulars of its theology had the effect of alienating some of its graduating ministers from their denominational associations or leading to doctrinal schisms within their congregations. By presenting itself as a non-denominational teaching institution with the newest techniques that the U.S. had to offer, Agua Viva for several years avoided threatening other existing church structures. After a while, however, Agua Viva's youthful and ambitious legal director created new procedures for registering and licensing ministers; in this way he provided some legal status for three ministers who wanted to expand their independent churches and also offered institutional backup to two ministers who were threatened with dismissal from the Presbyterian Church if they did not temper their prosperity message and Pentecostal fervor.

Agua Viva also sees itself as a training arena for missionaries who have joined the Zirkle team, showing them how to launch similar efforts elsewhere. A number of the missionaries have specifically chosen Agua Viva because they are ambitious and eager to move on to new challenges; they feel that the money they have raised personally to support Agua Viva has been well spent on their own training for expanding evangelization. Direct offshoots of Agua Viva have been set up in such places as Costa Rica, Honduras, and Nicaragua, the latter operating a radio station even during the Contra War in the late 1980s. Other experienced missionaries were preparing for ministries further afield: one military veteran had been trained in a Japanese language program and was ready to return to Japan; an air force veteran, Agua Viva's chief pilot, was planning to join the newly expanding field of evangelizing East Germany.

In a small, developing nation where most citizens have been getting poorer for decades, Agua Viva's substantial funds and aggressive personnel are able to create a significant presence. With the exception of teaching its missionaries rudimentary Spanish language skills, Agua Viva makes little concession to Guatemalan culture. In a sense the Bible School is as unapologetic as any conquering military force; a small part of the U.S. Bible Belt has descended upon a segment of another society and is vigorously starting to make things over in the image of the U.S.A. Armed with the faith theology from Tulsa, and the economic means and practical skills needed to produce a semblance of prosperity in a very poor country, the new teachers are certain they have answers that will work anywhere. They would see their particular kind of Christian fundamentalism as universally applicable; moreover, they believe deeply that it is destined to succeed as a new and truly global culture.

FIVE

Spiritual Warfare: The Case of the Philippines

> God is preparing the Church for the greatest spiritual battle we have
> ever seen—the bringing down of the strongholds of the devil on our
> land—and will require the most concerted effort by the people of God
> at waging war against the real enemy, Satan....
>
> —Ramon Orosa, president of Oro International
> Ministries, former president of City Bank, Manila [1]

Pastor Orosa is calling upon the faithful to battle against the
encroachments of The Evil One—not an unusual rallying cry among born-
again believers. He promotes power evangelism, using "spiritual warfare" to
both strengthen believers and confront enemies. What he more boldly suggests, in the context of this still overwhelmingly Catholic country, is that
much of the Filipino Christian heritage is associated with the forces of darkness: "What is in store for us is a spiritual victory of such proportions as to
undo the devil's works of the last 450 years which have obscured and veiled
the glory of the Lord in the Land."[2]

Like Orosa, the new wave of Christians refer to themselves simply as
"Christians," consciously excluding Catholics and liberal Protestants. In a
sense, they are attempting to fulfill both the Great Commission and the
mandate proposed by U.S. President William McKinley in his Benevolent
Assimilation Proclamation of December 21, 1898. McKinley conveniently
overlooked the Catholic faith of the Filipinos as he justified his program of
war and annexation to a delegation of U.S. Methodists: "I went down on my
knees and prayed Almighty God...it came to me in this way...there was
nothing left for us to do but take them all, and to educate the Filipinos, and
uplift and civilize, and Christianize them, and by God's grace do the very best
we could by them, as our fellow-men for whom Christ also died."[3]

This is "spiritual warfare" in its most literal sense, for a new religious
movement is trying to push out the spiritual tradition that preceded it. The
direct attacks of the new fundamentalists upon Catholicism represent only
one battle in the war that saves lost souls and prepares the way for the Second
Coming of Christ. Demonic forces are everywhere to be confronted. While

fundamentalists still deal with fighting off the personal demons that cause illness, alcoholism, and marital discord, they increasingly engage themselves in
struggles to exorcise "territorial demons" and "satanic influences" in the larger confrontations between good and evil. In the Philippines they continue to
fight against communism, both on the ideological plane (which would include
the heresies of liberation theology) and on the real battlefields where government forces pursue the guerrilla bands of the New People's Army. They attack
false idols, including the Virgin Mary and the saints, which they argue have
weakened the Catholic variety of Christianity, and the "satanic" religion of
Islam, which flourishes especially on the island of Mindanao.

Power evangelism is ready to take on economic underdevelopment, too;
the Philippines are seen as the poor sister of Asia, underperforming in comparison with almost all their Asian neighbors because of the sinfulness, laziness, and territorial demons that support all the things that undermine productive activity and civil rectitude. One of the most interesting examples of
spiritual warfare is its connection to the training of the Armed Forces, the
national-security doctrine of Low Intensity Conflict, and the need to pacify
elements who are hostile to modern capitalist development of the islands.

Protestants versus Catholics

Pastor Orosa, like many Protestant evangelists in other lands, sees his mission
as one of national salvation: "I believe in all my heart that it is God's purpose
that our nation be the spiritual *burning bush*, the beacon light of all of Asia, the
last frontier of evangelism."[4]

Many Catholics interpret this as a hostile invasion by outside forces, for
there is no question that the Philippines is one of the major sites for U.S. evangelical missionary activity: in 1992 it had 1,961 missionaries serving for four
years or more, a number surpassed only by the 2,229 who served in Brazil. At
the same time, only 276 Catholic missionaries from the U.S. and Canada were
serving in the Philippines.[5]

The relationship forged between U.S. evangelicalism and Filipino culture is
related to U.S. colonization in the first half of the twentieth century and its
continued military presence after World War II. Many U.S. Army and Navy
chaplains, and enlisted men as well, functioned as de facto missionaries and
engaged in evangelism, charitable endeavors, and the distribution of Scriptural
tracts. In 1947 representatives from the GI Gospel Crusade in the Philippines
and Japan met in Denver, Colorado, to form the Far Eastern Gospel Crusade
(now SEND International). This rapidly became one of the major interdenominational evangelical mission agencies working in East Asia. The U.S. fundamentalists and evangelicals moved with relative ease in Filipino society
because of strong cultural connections: English is spoken and written by a

large portion of population; many Filipinos immigrated to the United States; and U.S. military personnel frequently married and settled in the Philippines. Nonetheless, a significant growth in Protestantism did not occur until recently.

Fundamentalist groups (as referred to by Catholic researchers) or the new wave of Christian groups (as referred to by Protestant researchers) have multiplied significantly since 1980. A study conducted by Monsignor Bayani Valenzuela for the Archdiocese of Manila indicates that between 1980 and 1988 there was more than a 500 percent increase in the number of non-Catholic Christian religious groups that were registered with the national government.[6]

Evangelical Protestants also claim that church growth has been significant. By October 1991, the Philippine Crusades Research team for DAWN 2000 (Discipling A Whole Nation),[9] reported that they had located just over twenty-three thousand evangelical churches operating throughout the Philippines (this would include all Protestant denominations and independent churches). Of these twenty-three thousand, approximately nine thousand four hundred had been founded between 1900 and 1980, but the majority, thirteen thousand six hundred churches, came into being between 1980 and 1990.[8] This reflects growth of 145 percent in the number of individual churches.

In response to the growth and influence of the new Christian groups, the Catholic Bishops Council of the Philippines published a pastoral letter in January 1989 that launched a furious debate about "the fundamentalists." Warning about the recent influx of fundamentalist sects, the council's Pastoral Statement fueled religious contention that was publicly fought out in the mainstream press. The council then set up "Guidelines for Dealing with Fundamentalists":

> We ask our people not to endanger their faith through a false sense of ecumenism which often serves as the entry point of many of these sects....We must regretfully say that the fundamentalist sects, with their aggressive and sometimes vicious attacks on the Catholic Church, do not practice an ecumenism which we can trustingly reciprocate.... For now, preachers and members of fundamentalist groups should not be allowed to teach in Catholic meetings even under the guise of giving witness. We also ask our faithful not to join so-called ecumenical prayer or study groups, or other meetings organized by fundamentalist groups. Our faithful must also be aware of financial enticements to join the fundamentalists.[9]

The Catholic guidelines distinguished between the fundamentalists and the National Council of Churches of the Philippines (NCCP), with whom the Catholics declared they had "cordial relations." The National Council of Churches, in fact, had misgivings about the fundamentalists that paralleled

Catholic concerns. In a 1988 report on "New Religious Movements in the Philippines," the NCCP warned against "the application of religion as a campaign to preserve American interests and maintain U.S. hegemony that has spread from Latin America to Asia, particularly the Philippines."[10] This concern, echoed by Protestant and Catholic leaders, is linked to apprehensions about conservative religious support of Low Intensity Conflict and a civil war that has been going on for over forty years.

Few conservative Filipino Protestants, even those clearly aligned with fundamentalist traditions and associations, want to lay claim to the term "fundamentalist." Mainstream and evangelical Protestants have an immediate aversion to the term and are very cautious about "definitions of fundamentalism." Most Catholics are quite ready to use the term, usually in a pejorative sense. But as a result of the media skirmish, increasing numbers of Catholic leaders are careful to distinguish between types of Protestants, fundamentalist and non-fundamentalist. By 1992 a shift in both understanding and strategy occurred, as many Catholic leaders decided to quit "fueling the fire" and consciously de-emphasized the power that they thought fundamentalists had or potentially might have in the Philippines.

Clearly religious semantics were a very important, and politically sensitive, subject at the beginning of the 1990s. In the daily newspapers, accusations and counteraccusations about the political role and agenda of the fundamentalists and Catholic Church took center stage, at least for a while. In fact, fundamentalists, who are still a small minority of Filipinos (80–85 percent of whom are Catholic), probably received a disproportionate amount of attention. Why?

Reasons that immediately surface are the tremendous growth of "fundamentalist" groups, the threat they pose to the Catholic Church from whom recruits are drawn, and the suspicions about the political as well as the religious role of the new wave of Christians pouring into the Philippines, especially U.S.-affiliated ones.

Historical Background

The Philippines were originally Christianized by Spanish invaders who arrived "with cross and sword" in 1521 and remained for almost four hundred years. Different Catholic orders spread out among the many islands and quickly converted the indigenous peoples; by 1591 they counted six hundred sixty thousand Christians. While the people converted to Catholicism, many retained part or all of their pre-colonial religious beliefs and practices.[11]

The Philippine Revolution of 1898 ended the rule of Spain, but ushered in the United States. After a mock battle at Manila Bay, the Spaniards surrendered to American troops.[12] The bloody war that followed was between the

U.S. and Filipino nationalists; when it finally ended in 1902, six hundred thousand Filipinos had died, and the Philippines became a U.S. colony. It was then that the first American missionaries entered under the banner of "Manifest Destiny."

From the beginning U.S. Protestants helped set the stage for conquest. Methodist Bishop James M. Thoburn, having spent three weeks in the Philippines, advised the U.S. Senate Committee on the Philippines that Filipinos were "a cut above North American Indians, but regrettably ranked below the Chinese and far below the Anglo-Saxons."[13] The belief in racial superiority bolstered America's certainty of its divine mission, which for the first time legitimized imperialist expansion outside the Western Hemisphere. Only two weeks after Commodore Dewey's victory at Manila Bay in 1898, the Presbyterian General Assembly pronounced:

> God has given into our hands, that is, unto the hands of American Christians, the Philippine Islands.... By the very guns of our battleships God summoned us to go up and possess the land.[14]

Just as Filipinos resisted U.S. colonization from 1899 to 1902, so did they conduct a fierce guerrilla campaign against three years of Japanese occupation during World War II. The most powerful guerrilla group to emerge was the *Hukbalahap* (Huks for short). In March 1942, left-wing labor, peasant, and intellectual leaders developed a People's Anti-Japanese Army which at its peak numbered some ten thousand members with a mass base many times larger.[15] The Huks became strong in Central Luzon, an area of intense peasant resistance to the landlord/plantation economy before the war. When the U.S. Armed Forces returned to Central Luzon in early 1945, the Huks helped them fight the Japanese forces. But as the Japanese surrendered, the U.S. disarmed the Huks, arrested their leaders, and dismantled the local governments they had established. In their place, the U.S. installed reliably pro-American officials from the pre-war elite, some of whom had served the Japanese.[16]

Though the Philippines were granted independence on July 4, 1946, the political apparatus was kept in the hands of those who had benefited from the colonialist plantation economy. By 1949, the Huks had openly rebelled against repressive landlords. Although the revolt was wholly indigenous, the U.S. undertook a massive counterinsurgency effort, involving military operations and covert actions, similar to those later used in Vietnam but without directly employing U.S. troops. The Huks threatened U.S. interests because they were opposed to the Military Bases Agreement; they favored a radical restructuring of Philippine society; and they were led by the communists.[17]

The defeat of the Huk insurgency in the early 1950s enabled the new era of elite democracy and neocolonialism to move ahead, but with little economic progress. By the end of the 1980s, the per capita annual income was $590 in the Philippines, a major U.S. Pacific ally in World War II, while in Japan, which lost the war, it was $15,000.[18] In other rapidly developing East Asian countries, incomes were anywhere from three to fifteen times greater than in the Philippines.

Although the Philippines formally achieved political independence in 1946, and finally closed the large U.S. military facilities (Clark Air Force Base and Subic Naval Base) in 1993, it has not been able to regain economic sovereignty. It remains captive to a system of neocolonialism, in which a tiny landlord class dominates the economy in league with transnational corporations. Two percent of the population owns 75 percent of the land and capital. The problem of foreign control of the economy intensified during the martial-law years (1972–1986). In order to secure loans from the World Bank and the International Monetary Fund (IMF) to pay off its foreign obligations, estimated at some $25 billion – $30 billion, agreements were forged with transnational corporations, which have exploited inexpensive Philippine labor and raw materials.[19]

With worsening economic and labor conditions, dissatisfaction grew, and peasants and workers became increasingly radicalized. By 1972, the country was accurately described by one newspaper as a "seething volcano."[20] In that year Ferdinand Marcos declared martial law, a form of dictatorship that lasted until 1986. The Huks re-emerged in the form of the New People's Army, the military arm of the Communist Party of the Philippines, after imposition of martial law and grew rapidly. The National Democratic Front formed in April 1973 and established a broad coalition of groups on the left. The Catholic Church, especially among the lower ranks, became progressively more radicalized. Many priests and nuns began working on behalf of the poor, establishing Christian base communities; some even joined guerrillas in the rural areas.

In August 1983, Senator Benigno Aquino Jr., the most prominent leader of the opposition, was killed while in the custody of the Marcos military. His assassination fueled even wider protest, often peaceful mass rallies, that finally led to the EDSA (Epifanio de los Santos Avenue) People's Revolt of 1986 that ousted Ferdinand Marcos from power and installed Benigno Aquino's widow, Cory Aquino, as president.

Claimed as a victory by the Catholic Church, the so-called EDSA Revolution was seen as a religious event inspired and initiated by religious groups. Liberal representatives of the NCCP were also enthusiastic and hopeful about the peaceful revolt.[21] Among evangelicals, according to Lorenzo Bautista's study, an apolitical stance and conservative views were dominant.[22] The Philippines Council of Evangelical Churches, the largest association of born-again Protestant churches, took no definite policy position in relation to EDSA. Indecisive to the end, it vacillated between stressing Romans 13:1-7, wherein Christians are called upon to obey the ruling authorities, and a caution that civil obedience may sometimes be an option but only after one had exhausted the judicial and constitutional processes.[23] While a number of fundamentalist organizations and churches did actively participate in the mass demonstrations, every account of positive evangelical involvement could find its negative counterpart.[24]

The New Fundamentalists

Depending upon one's predilections, the growth of the new Christian groups since 1980, which accelerated after 1986, is a cause for concern or celebration. Among the newcomers, much rejoicing is made over the statistics on church growth, even though Protestants remain a small minority (under ten percent). In the Catholic camp, there is grave concern over the successes of the evangelicals.

According to a study of New Religious Movements in the Philippines, the martial law period was a time of "steady and marked increase in the influx of evangelists both in person and (in) electronic media. There [was] no government restriction of any kind to their operations."[25] And, according to interviews with over thirty Protestant and Catholic leaders in the spring of 1992, the new Christian groups experienced even more vigorous growth after Cory Aquino came to power. Many raised questions about a possible connection between the "invasion of the fundamentalists" and the number of attempted military coups between 1986 and 1989, though they noted the lack of concrete evidence and the need for more research.

After the 1986 overthrow of Marcos and the election of Aquino, non-Catholic Christian groups poured into the country. From 1980 to 1986, an average of twelve of these groups registered every month; in 1987 and 1988 this rate doubled to twenty-four per month. Before 1980, only 228 of these groups were part of the religious landscape of the Philippines; by 1988, there were 1,676 of them.[26]

Consistent with the rise of fundamentalism in other politically and economically unstable places, fundamentalists in the Philippines join the cacophony of religious voices that compete with one another in the attempt to claim authority in the midst of social chaos. These groups are proliferating in the very places where Christian base communities have been active and liberation theology has been embraced.

While the new fundamentalists tend to be loosely organized, most often in non-denominational, independent churches, many do belong to the umbrella organization of the Philippine Council of Evangelical Churches. The council is the largest organizing body of evangelical churches, with a membership of 1.6 million individual members and seven thousand member churches. Established in 1965, it joined the World Evangelical Fellowship in 1974. In 1980 PHILRADS, its relief and development arm, was organized and it became a charter member of the fellowship's Development and Relief Alliance. The Philippine Council of Evangelical Churches, organized to present a distinctly evangelical voice and presence, publishes a magazine, *Evangelicals Today*, which claims to "provides a prophetic forum" for its member churches. Through the National Ecumenical Consultative Committee, the council represents evangelical concerns about national issues to the president of the Philippines; through its membership in the Church and Defense National Committee, it "maintains constant dialogue with the Armed Forces of the Philippines on matters concerning peace and order, as well as Human Rights."[27] The former general secretary of the council, Rev. Agustin (Jun) Vencer, was recently appointed as head of the World Evangelical Fellowship (the first non-Westerner to be so appointed). At virtually the same time, newly elected President Fidel Ramos appointed Vencer head of intelligence for the Armed Forces of the Philippines. As an organization, the council serves as a counterpoint to the liberal National Council of Churches. A study conducted for the Catholic Archdiocesan Office for Ecumenical and Interfaith Affairs reports that while there is doctrinal similarity among the new fundamentalists, two distinct groups emerge: "'homegrown fundamentalists' and 'U.S.-affiliated fundamentalists.' The former are considered generally, though not always, to be relatively apolitical, though more nationalistic, and primarily concerned about conversion, individual salvation, and spiritualistic practices such as healing. The latter group is considered by many to have more of a political agenda."[28]

The new Protestants also acknowledge differences among themselves, but shun the "fundamentalist" label. While "apolitical" positions are still espoused, a number of born-again groups have become increasingly politicized as a result of the political and economic turmoil of the 1980s. Such politicization has led to greater social involvement, mostly conservative, but with some evangelical representation on the progressive end of the continuum.

Filipino writings on liberation theology, the debt crisis, and alternatives to capitalist development are both numerous and sophisticated. Social activism is well-coordinated, and progressive Christian thought as articulated by both Catholics and liberal Protestants carries a great deal of weight in religious and political circles in the Philippines. In this context, the "new Christians" have fashioned a conservative theological response that emphasizes the old standards of individual piety while also stressing the importance of "spiritual warfare" in solving sociopolitical issues.

Like their counterparts throughout the world, the new fundamentalist Protestant groups in the Philippines emphasize individual salvation rather than social reform, attributing poverty and national calamities to sin and laziness. According to them, both individual and social problems are rooted in God's revenge for man's disobedience; the solution, therefore, lies in greater obedience and faithfulness to God.

Jun Vencer argues that evangelicals need to seek solutions by dealing with root causes; referring to the book of Joel, he writes: "Firstly, the sins of the people against God were the real reason for the calamity. The locusts, the drought and the fires were the tragic effects of the real cause which is rebellion against God. Secondly, the economic collapse is a sign of national sin. Because God is justly in control, and because the tragedy is due to sin, then the prophet is calling for fasting and prayer 'to spare Thy people' (Joel 2:17).[29] "We should pray for suffering....difficult times are transcendental times," he elaborated. "In the face of national calamities, ordinary human means will no longer work."[30]

Ramon Orosa echoes Vencer's sentiments: "The problems in the Philippines have resulted because people turned their back on God."[31] In an article in the *Ministry Digest*, he writes: "The ills of our nation are primarily spiritual in character, meaning that sin abounds and rules in the nation....We are a nation under judgment by God.... In the Old Testament, when the nation of Israel came under judgment, there were generally three major sins prevalent. Idolatry, occultism, and great social injustice. (Religious) leaders are invited to make their own determination as to the prevalence of these issues."[32]

Given the strength and legitimacy of liberation theology within Filipino society, the severe economic and political conditions, and the relatively open political space in which such rhetoric is voiced, evangelicals often mention "structural injustice" even if they concern themselves primarily with individual salvation and sinfulness. Given this definition of the problem, their energies and resources go into organizing spiritual crusades and relief organizations.[33] The new fundamentalists would agree that one obligation of the church-going Christian is a "concern for and duty to the poor"; however, this is not to be confused with the liberationist requirement that the church is obligated to a thoroughgoing "preference or option for the poor." The new fundamentalists have another answer to overcoming poverty; they invoke spiritual powers to gain prosperity.

In some parts of the Philippines, the message of prosperity theology is as boldly and crudely proclaimed as elsewhere in the world—the many churches associated with such neo-Pentecostals as Don Stewart, Lester Sumrall, the Rhema School, and Kenneth and Gloria Copeland instruct the faithful to pray for financial salvation. A more interesting innovation is a variation of prosperity theology that transcends the individual's desires and addresses the national context of economic development, emphasizing the power of collective prayer and the need for careful stewardship of capital. Butch Conde, pastor of the megachurch Bread of Life Ministries, which established the first prayer mountain in the Philippines, refers to the prayer power of the Koreans and the rewards it has brought:

> But the intense prayer life of the Koreans has not only resulted in their miraculous church growth; it has also brought miraculous advancement to the whole nation as well. Devastated by two major wars, Korea gradually rose from the economic shambles to become one of the most prosperous nations in the world today—a leading manufacturer of cars, ships, electronics and other products.[34]

Vencer likewise advocates prosperity theology quite explicitly for both individuals and the nation as a whole: "National recovery may include the following blessings. God gives each one power to make wealth. He will grant the wisdom to men and women in the wheels of industry.... God promises economic prosperity.[35]

Such theology can serve as a pro-capitalist antidote to the Christian (Catholic) base communities and liberation theology. Critics of the new fundamentalists argue that promises that God will grant riches, if only the individual (or his nation) believes, is a distortion of the Christian message. In such articles as "Kulturang Coke at Relihiyong 'Born-Again,'" the late Father Jeremias Aguino, priest of the Philippine Independent Church, explicitly drew the connections between the global consumerist culture and fundamentalist expansion.[36]

Believers themselves may question why they are not receiving the blessings that are preached to be forthcoming. In his sermon, U.S. Pastor Tom O'Dowd of the Word of the World Church in Bacolod City, Negros, tells his poor congregation that God indeed promises financial prosperity, citing Matthew 21:22. "But," he says, "God is testing the congregation—there is time between the promise and fulfillment." The "lag time" is attributed to interruption by evil forces who are waging spiritual warfare upon the nation.

Spiritual Warfare and Geopolitical Territories

The focus on spiritual warfare permeates the message of the new wave of Christian groups in the Philippines. It weaves its way into sermons, TV and radio broadcasts, and Christian publications. For instance, in August 1991 the Christian Journal in Manila recommended two books by Youth With A Mission (YWAM) leaders: *Spiritual Warfare* by Dean Sherman (the dean of the College of Christian Ministries at YWAM's University of the Nations in Kona,

Hawaii) and *Taking Our Cities For God,* by John Dawson (the YWAM director in California). The editor of the *Journal* noted with approval that the Philippine publisher of the books, the Overseas Missionary Fellowship, had clearly gone "charismatic" and given up its "monotonously pietistic diet" of the past. That is, this older fundamentalist parachurch organization (with decidedly non-Pentecostal origins) was changing to accommodate the new-wave fundamentalists.

The 1989 issue of the Filipino evangelical magazine *Ministry Digest* is titled "The Church at War: Assaulting the Gates of Hell." The special feature "Christians and the Coup" focused on the sixth and most violent coup that took place after Aquino came to power. Referring to the December 1989, coup, which claimed at least 113 lives and almost toppled Aquino's government, the issue included numerous articles on spiritual warfare, including: "Prepare War! The Spirit's Call to Spiritual Warfare" by Daniel Tappeiner; "Are You Covered? Know Your Place of Protection in Times of War!" by Gilario Romero; and "Territorial Spirits: Identifying Demonic Spirits over Geographical Domains."

In his article on "Territorial Spirits," C. Peter Wagner writes: "I have come to believe that Satan does indeed assign a demon or corps of demons to every geopolitical unit in the world, and they are among the principalities and powers with whom we wrestle."[37] Wagner reports that "former Secretary of the Interior, James Watt, through sensitivities acquired in his past association with the occult, perceives specific dark angels assigned to the White House," as well as various places in the Third World. He cites the example of Lester Sumrall in the Philippines, who "cast out a spirit of an inmate in Bilibid Prison" which was "followed by dramatic change in the receptivity of Filipinos to the Gospel."[38] Although enthusiastic about preparing for spiritual battle, Wagner cautions that "dealing with territorial spirits is major league warfare. It should not be undertaken casually. If you do not know what you are doing, and few whom I am aware of have the necessary expertise, Satan will eat you for breakfast."[39]

Brother Eddie Villanueva, the spiritual director of the Jesus Is Lord (JIL) Fellowship and national chairman of the Philippines Jesus Movement, argued that the coup was a punishment sent by God because of Filipinos' disobedience and Catholic idolatry: "In 1986, God gave us the miracle of EDSA but look at what our countrymen have done. Instead of attributing the miracle to God, they have chosen to honor a so-called lady of peace and erected a statue and shrine for her, at the behest of Catholic religious leaders, supported by our top government officials. This is pure and simple idolatry and because of it our whole nation suffers."[40]

In "This Will Not Be the Last Coup...," Rev. Fred Magbanua, managing editor of the Far Eastern Broadcasting Corporation in 1989, relayed a dream he had in which God talked to him and said: "Ramos, Enrile, and people power…you have not given me the glory for what I have done for you. Thus, I have allowed this coup to happen. And this will not be the last. Unless you as a people will learn to give me the glory and honor, there will be more coups and problems that will come upon you as a nation."[41]

The vivid and pervasive use of military imagery in religious rhetoric is characteristic of the new wave of Christian groups and echoes the most influential global evangelizing agencies. Bill Bright, founder of Campus Crusade for Christ, which is very active in the Philippines, is quoted as saying that: "Proclaiming the gospel is like a military offensive, with the mass media serving as the Air Force—softening up the objective—so that the ground forces can come in and capture an area."[42]

The new Christians repeatedly argue that the enemy—communists, Muslim fundamentalists, idolatrous Catholics—must be struck down. In order for this to happen, Christians have to ready themselves for war. Tappeiner (a Filipino who earned his Ph.D. from Fuller Theological Seminary) writes: "The warfare Christian…recognizes that the Lord is mustering His warriors for end-time warfare with the enemy." To further make his point, he cites Joel 3:9-10:

> Declare this to nations: Prepare war, stir up the mighty men. Let all the men of war draw near, let them come up. Beat your plowshares into swords, and your pruning hooks into spears; let the weakling say, "I am a warrior."[43]

On the Island of Negros: Putting Spiritual Warfare to Work

Negros is the epitomy of the plantation island. Once nicknamed Sugarlandia, it was a new frontier totally developed by capitalist export agriculture after 1850, and particularly after the U.S. conquest in 1898. The elite Negrense landowners have been renowned throughout the twentieth century for their lavish lifestyles, their open collaboration with U.S. investors, and their exploitation of the impoverished sugar workers. Negros is one of the important sites of labor unrest and government-rebel conflict,[44] as well as increasing religious hostility. An Irish-born Columban priest in Bacolod City, Father Niall O'Brien (incarcerated in 1983 for over a year for his involvement in organizing basic Christian communities and later exiled by Marcos) talked about Capalit, a town in Negros that was attacked by government planes:

> After the bombing hundreds of people took refuge in a public school in the town where there was no water or toilet facilties. Local politicians handed out tiny bars of soap with their name and picture on them. The people lay around exhausted in the sweltering GI-roofed classrooms because they had been

driven out of their homes. Meanwhile two guys with bullhorns and their Bibles were haranging them and asking them to: 'give up your riches for God.' I asked the preachers what possible riches they were referring to as the people were destitute. They pointed to some hens and a pig. At the same time they were selling religious pamphlets. The scene was grotesque and unreal.[45]

Among the new fundamentalist churches contesting the terrain is Word for the World, a charismatic Christian fellowship in Bacolod City. In 1992, it was able to "bring eight hundred souls to the Lord in six months," according to its pastor, Tom O'Dowd.[46] He reported that "some 256 members began to attend our services, afraid of the New People's Army and the uprising."[47] They began to plant churches and run crusades in the countryside and on haciendas. Their religious rhetoric is unashamedly militaristic; it is difficult to determine cause and effect, but there appears to be a curious interaction at work. The message frames the context of legitimacy or illegitimacy of particular actions.

In one of its English-speaking Sunday morning services, Pastor Tom , as he is known, read from the Scriptures: "As Moses said to Joshua, taking an army of eight million over the mountain, 'don't be afraid of the enemy, be strong and of good courage and the Lord will go before you'" (Deuteronomy 31:5-8, 23; and Psalms 27). On this particular morning in June 1992, the band warmed up the congregation to sing: "Sound the trumpet in Zion, Sound the alarm on the Holy Mountain," and "Rush the walls of the city." Then Pastor Tom began preaching, addressing his formerly Catholic congregation by talking about Mary as an unwed mother, one who was scorned. "Mary was a fine Christian, we'll see her in heaven. There's no need to worship her, she was a real person." He then warned against idolatry: "Don't burn candles or incense, don't engage in rituals. Read the Bible."

O'Dowd continued to preach about the need to be strong, to take the offensive: "You kick the devil. The devil comes to kill, steal, and destroy—you must be strong. I know you're hurting. What should I do? Cry? NO, I should teach you to be strong—protect and teach you."

He also emphasized the need for obedience and moderation: "The path of freedom is the middle road, the balanced path....You are commanded to read the Bible; it doesn't mean you'll understand it.... (Furthermore) God's not on our side—He's on His side. You have to follow Him and then you'll win! You are commanded to be strong in the Lord. We are part of God's Army."

The slightly veiled references to Catholic "idolatry" and the military metaphors hit close to home because the Christian base communities are already successful in Negros, and because the civil war is being actively waged between the Armed Forces of the Philippines and the New People's Army in the mountainous areas around Bacolod City. In Negros Occidental, no one escapes the conflict—the only thing to be determined is whose side you are on—and those boundaries seldom are left to individual choice or definition.

In fundamentalist circles, spiritual warfare and the "enemy" are defined by only the most spiritually informed Christian leaders, who in terms of influence hail largely from the U.S. The average rank-and-file church members must be very careful; they are cautioned that in spiritual warfare one is playing with fire, and only those who are trained to use their special powers will survive. Thus, while stressing the need for each individual to fight the good fight and be prepared as Christian soldiers in God's army, the majority of members is relegated to the status of foot soldiers who must conform to the regulations and commands of the officers. While this hierarchy is distinct from the church bureaucracies of historic Catholicism and denominational Protestantism, the new fundamentalists—sometimes identified with the "third wave" of Pentecostals—can nonetheless encourage a paternalistic system of spirituality. The average member is expected to conform to collective goals as defined by the spiritual elite.

A sign, hanging out from the back of a series of office buildings in Bacolod City, reads: REACH OUT: EQUIP AN ARMY. Here a charismatic group of some seventy members reaches out to a larger group of two hundred people, primarily students, through small cell groups devoted to Bible studies. Its director, Joberto Ramos, a young man in his twenties and a native to the area, describes their mission:

> We believe we are an army equipped to fight against the demons. We witness to former NPA (New People's Army) people....The Social Gospel and liberation theology are promoted by communist sympathizers and priests. I sympathize with them because they helped people organize themselves but I can't work with them; I can only work through Jesus.[48]

In the struggle for the minds and the faith of the people, the Protestant pastor is following a well-established tradition. A representative of Campus Crusades for Christ put it this way: "Christians are the best foes of communism. Therefore, evangelism helps to create a bulwark against communism."[49]

But a Roman Catholic priest sees something quite different: "Of particular and growing concern to many of us in the Philippines is the evident, intense and highly orchestrated fear of communism being engineered and promoted. Among the groups promoting such paranoia are the Unification Church, its political arm, CAUSA International, the World Anti-Communist League... along with its Philippine affiliates, such as the Philippine Anti-Communist Movement, as well as by several fundamentalist religious sects who are making inroads into the Philippine society."[50]

How literal is the new Christians' "spiritual war" against "communism"? While suspicions abound about fundamentalist subservience to the Armed Forces of the Philippines, concrete evidence of direct complicity in military activity is difficult to find. Peter Brock, formerly with the NCCP and now on staff at the World Council of Churches, argues: "The reality is that the U.S., including the CIA…will cooperate with anyone who will advance U.S. interests. This will include religious groups of any tradition. Fundamentalist groups that already have a pro-U.S. orientation will be more easily co-opted, misled or even convinced to assist their cause, whilst they are also highly susceptible to the lurid U.S./CIA propaganda against "Godless communism." But the burden of proof remains with the accuser who alleges an "imperialist conspiracy."[51]

Born-again Christians and opposing camps acknowledge, however, that ideological warfare against communism is being waged by the new wave of fundamentalists. Pastor Tom uses the threat of communism to rally support and donations in the United States. In his summer 1991 missions letter, he writes: "In bondage to alcoholism, loan sharks, gambling, superstition, and ignorance, (Filipinos) have little hope for a better life in this world or the next. Various communist groups have been successful in infiltrating these communities resulting in the current insurgency problems. But is this the answer? We believe there is a better one—Jesus."

He then offers news about "Hacienda Harvest," specifying which haciendas have allowed Christian revivals on their premises, how many people came, and examples of faith healing. There is no information indicating that hacienda owners are being influenced to offer better wages, medical care, or education for the children and workers who are trapped within a feudal system of economic exploitation. Pastor Tom does acknowledge the maltreatment and low pay of workers and low wages: "It's almost a master-slave relationship here (Negros)—workers get maybe $2.50 a day," but he goes on to argue that one "has to understand the planters, too—they need good workers."

As in other societies where exploitative agro-export industry is based on large haciendas (Guatemala, for example), the plantation owners (who are largely Catholic) are willing, at times even eager, to have the evangelists hold camp meetings on the plantation. They preach the same messages of obedience, loyalty, sobriety, and industry that Pastor Tom Dowd emphasizes:

> The Gospel teaches them (workers) not to steal, to raise self-esteem. They can become happy through redemption from God.…The Gospel lifts people out of poverty and ignorance. It can help them physically and spiritually.…We have to lift people up culturally.…to stop them from gambling and drinking.… Finally, through the Gospel they will find financial prosperity.[52]

Plantation owners as well as evangelists argue that the converted become better workers with the evangelical emphasis on hard work, "clean living," and individual worker responsibility; moreover it supplies an antidote to the successful Christian base communities where liberation theology has helped develop an informed analysis of socioeconomic exploitation.

Pastor Jose Rivera of Maranatha in Bacolod City argued that the Christian base communities of the Catholics were communist inspired. "The Bible tells us we should oppose labor unions, modernism, liberalism, communism—they are all false religions." The pastor, who at times seemed uneasy in his interview, added in a tired voice: "One day Christians will rule, but not now. When Christ comes back, he'll find most Christians poor.... During the long drought of 1983 and the sugar-cane crisis, people in Negros became very responsive to the Word of God. God sends them earthquakes and typhoons time and time again to tell them that what is important is the salvation of the soul. Let the body suffer."[53]

Both Father Niall O'Brien and Father Romeo Empestan, who have been involved in Christian base communities, argue that the dramatic entry and growth of Protestant fundamentalist groups in Negros occurred after Operation Thunderbolt.[54] In 1988–1989, the Armed Forces launched the operation in Negros, bombing people out of the mountains so that they could not support the New People's Army. Official documents report eight hundred dead, though others argue that thousands died. Thunderbolt was intended to avenge the killing of five soldiers and one civilian by the New People's Army. The bomber attacks were followed by Sikorsky helicopter gunships that targeted some rebel hideouts but also hit numerous towns and villages populated by civilians. By May 1989, thirty-five thousand Negros refugees had fled their homes, the largest single evacuation on the island since World War II. Lacking even rudimentary health-care facilities, the refugee sites became centers of disease and starvation. Epidemics of measles spread through the crowded and unsanitary quarters, and children died. This is when, according to Father O'Brien, the fundamentalists arrived, "carrying their Bibles and preaching in the streets and on buses: 'give up your riches for the kingdom of heaven.'"

Miguel Colonel, a senior officer who instructed Counter Subversion and Insurgency for the Armed Forces and co-presided over Operation Thunderbolt with General Jarque, wrote explicitly about the goals and roles of the military's "Hearts and Soul Campaign." Arguing that the major reason for the Philippines' underdevelopment is communist insurgency, Colonel describes the Pro-Democracy People's War (also the title of his 768-page book) that he helped devise for the Philippine Army. To combat insurgency, specifically in Negros Occidental, the Army used a multipronged approach:

Civil Government, the police, and the military will wage warfare...to mobilize the pro-democracy non-governmental organizations, civic groups, and individuals into counter-National Democratic Front organizations.[55] All these (military) efforts will be reinforced by public information, education, spiritual, and propaganda campaigns.[56]

National Security Doctrine and Low Intensity Conflict

The convergence of military and religious messages and methods makes many Filipinos suspicious of the new Christian groups. Father Tom Marti, a Maryknoll priest who has researched the politics of the religious right in the U.S. and the phenomenon of fundamentalism in the Philippines, expresses concerns about the relationship of these groups to the counterinsurgency program: "The growing intrusion of fundamentalist organizations into the Philippines fits in very well with the doctrine and strategy of the U.S. Government's Low Intensity Conflict (LIC). Their strong anti-communist line can lend support to military efforts to define communism as the most serious problem confronting the Philippines."[57]

The LIC doctrine involves "political, economic, and psychological warfare, with the military being a distant fourth in many cases," according to Col. John Waghelstein, commander of the U.S. Army's Seventh Special Forces. "It is total war at the grassroots level."[58] To left-leaning Christians in the Philippines, this promise of "psychological warfare" suggests a role for right-wing fundamentalists, one that would be conducive to "strategies of LIC put into use in Central America and elsewhere in the Third World."[59]

Reflecting upon the 4,500 missionaries who flooded the country in the spring of 1990 for the Campus Crusade for Christ New Life campaign, Bishop Erme Camba, general secretary of the United Church of Christ in the Philippines, expressed the concern of both Catholics and mainline Protestants in the Philippines: "We are concerned about the issue of timing. We are wondering about the possible connection between the (U.S. military) bases talks and the arrival of these missionaries. Though we have no positive proof linking the two, fundamentalist groups are traditionally conservative and perhaps they are being used without their knowledge."[60]

Other critics of the new Christian groups have pointed to the fundamentalistic origins of such vigilante groups like as Alsa Masa and Kaming Kristiyano Kontra Komunismo (KKKK: We Christians Against Communism).[61] For the most part, however, it appears that most vigilante groups with a religious orientation involve a syncretic mix of indigenous and folk-Catholic elements. For instance, many wear anting-antings (amulets) and carry various oils on their bodies for protection, believing they will make them invisible.

Such anti-communist vigilante groups have been responsible for creating terror in areas suspected of being sympathetic to the New People's Army and in many cases are encouraged and supported by the military.[62]

Commander Bagyo of a Pulihan vigilante group operating in the mountains of southern Negros Occidental indicated that his group formed in 1989 to "defend the oppressed and what is right." The Pulihans organized "after we realized that most people are evil and act as if there is no God in this world." Dualistic in his thinking, he talked about two Gods—the God of light and the god of dark, gods of good and evil. Commander Bagyo (whose self-chosen name means "lightning") said he had no opinions about politics—"I am not concerned with political things, only spiritual ones"—but admitted: "I'd rather choose war—you can hide from your enemies, but you can't hide from hunger." While at first he insisted that he did not side with either the military or the New People's Amry (NPA), Bagyo later indicated that his group scouted for the military. When asked if they were supported by the military, he responded: "We don't get paid by them—They give us donations, but they don't pay us. And we're out in front, and they say, 'We'll back you up,' but when the fighting gets tough, and we look around, they're not anywhere—and they get paid! A lot of people have died—NPA, military, civilians—but most of those salvaged [executed on the spot] are by the military. They are the ones who have more guns."[63]

While many Catholic bishops and priests have protested the abuses committed by vigilante groups, Cardinal Sin has allied with the government and advocated the organization of armed vigilante groups, arguing that helpless citizens need to defend themselves against the abuses of both leftist and rightist elements in society: "the service of the armed vigilante groups will complement the efforts of the military and policeman who remain the constitutional protectors of the people."[64] One Catholic critic indicated that the Cardinal's motivations were not apolitical at all:

> This endorsement by the most influential cleric in the country baptized the policy of Low Intensity Conflict which aimed at militarizing Filipinos through formation in vigilante groups to fight communist insurgents. This endorsement was met with disbelief and anger from many church workers who were targets for vigilante...abuse."[65]

A similar endorsement was provided by President Aquino in a speech given to the Philippines Military Academy, where she stated her tolerance of vigilante groups and her policy versus the insurgent rebels, "the unsheathed sword of Total War."[66]

Filipino intellectuals, within academia and the established churches, have offered a variety of analyses. Professor Alice Guillermo of the University of the Philippines in Diliman has questioned the intentions of the Philippine government and those who provide nonprofit aid. She cites the Ford Foundation's willingness to sponsor programs that claim to revive traditional religions, but then are reoriented along conservative lines in order to safeguard U.S. interests. "There is one right-wing sect in Mindanao, for instance, which flies the U.S. flag side by side with the Philippine flag because according to them, the U.S. is a holy country like the Philippines."[67]

To another scholar, Suzara, the complexity and volatility of the politicoreligious situation in the early 1990s made it difficult to decipher exactly what the alliances were: "the volatile configurations of a church-blessed Aquino government, a Philippine military supported by the United States, Aquino-endorsed vigilantes, and military-assisted cultist vigilantes pose formidable theoretical and methodological challenges."[68]

However, the liberal Protestant Bishop Camba felt the connections were rather clear, and based upon a sympathetic relationship between U.S. evangelical and foreign policy interests:

> The U.S. has given substantial amounts of military aid to help quell the rising sentiments of our people for national sovereignty. It has used the media to portray freedom-loving Filipinos as godless ideologues who are out to grab power....The sacred Scriptures are being used by certain evangelists to reduce our arguments for change into the terms of an other-worldly battle between good and evil.[69]

New Christians, the Military, and Value Formation

The Armed Forces of the Philippines expanded, from fifty thousand in 1972 to two hundred seventy-five thousand in 1990, to include such paramilitary forces as the Citizens Armed Forces Geographical Units (seventy thousand men) and numerous vigilante squads. As the military grew stronger, it assumed greater power in relation to Corazon Aquino's civilian government, which weakened steadily between 1986 and 1992. After each of the six failed coup attempts during her presidency, Aquino made fresh concessions to the army. Surveys of officers and enlisted men indicated that as many as 50 percent of the military supported a takeover by coup.[70]

During this time military and paramilitary groups harassed priests, pastors, and lay people who promoted land reform and opposed counterinsurgency programs. An investigation into violence against the Church in Pagadian came to a typical conclusion: "The Church has protected our forests and seas so the fisherman and farmers can have livelihoods. And because of the Church's stand, many who serve the Church have been killed."[71]

The conflict with progressive Christian groups led the army to consider how it would appeal to "the heart of the masses." In 1987, an article appearing in the military journal *Ang Tala*, "Will Taiwan's Anti-Communist Strategy Be As Effective in the Philippines?," had already noted:

> The striking resemblance between the communists' strategies in Taiwan and the Philippines and in the rest of the non-communist countries...makes "POLITICAL WARFARE" or simply "POLWAR"...a very effective strategy alternative to counter the ever increasing communist threat.... (Its) main function is to stir up, win over, rally, organize and lead the masses behind the enemy line, to fight under one's banner...The battlefield of the army is the land, that of the air force is the sky, and that of the navy is the sea; the battlefield of political warfare is the heart of the masses.[72]

At the 1989 Military Christian Fellowship Conference held in Seoul, Korea, Brig. Gen. Honesto Isleta (formerly the official spokesman for the Philippine Armed Forces) reported on the focus of the "Spiritual Readiness Seminar," which included such subjects as Self-Image, Developing Convictions, Spiritual Growth, and Spiritual Warfare.[73] Increasingly the Protestant chaplaincies of the army were filled by fundamentalists, and the military was meeting with born-again Christian groups. In March 1989, the National Association for Democracy was formed. It brought together conservative Christians, vigilante groups, and army officers in order to generate nationalist religious support for the Philippine state, something thought to be lacking among the ranks of the Catholic and mainstream Protestant churches.[74]

In 1991, at the South Asia Pacific Conference of the Association of Christian Military Fellowships held in Manila,[75] Col. Ernesto Sacro gave the welcoming address. Using Psalm 23 as a basis for his remarks, he reminded the military men of their responsibility to shepherd the people: "The people we are shepherding are sheep. The sheep have to be led by a shepherd, they can't by themselves exist without a shepherd."[76] The fundamentalist language of spiritual warfare was well-established and central to the conference; Ephesians (6:10-12) was a favorite scriptural reference:

> Our battle is not against flesh and blood, but against the rulers, against the power of this dark world, and against the spiritual forces of evil in the heavenly realms.

The National Association of Democracy, whose stated objective is "to fight the communist insurgency," claims a mass base that runs into the millions. Father O'Brien estimates that 30 percent to 40 percent of the association's members are fundamentalists, and they are closely allied with the Army and vigilantes in the Citizens Armed Forces Geographical Units.[77] An organizational pamphlet for the association lists member organizations which include Gavino Tica's Alliance for Democracy and Morality (ADAM). ADAM, an association of over 100 groups, often publishes "press releases that are true copies of military disinformation campaigns,"[78] according to one study. The 1987 U.S.-Philippine Fact-Finding Mission found that ADAM had associations with the Philippine Defense Ministry and with John Whitehall, a U.S.-based Australian who serves as vice-president of the World Anti-Communist League (WACL).[79]

Rev. Gavino Tica, president of International Baptist Ministries (mother church for some 487 fundamentalist Baptist churches in the Philippines),[80] helped to organize ADAM. According to Rev. Tica: "ADAM represents all shades of Protestant belief and even some Catholics....We don't discuss doctrinal details...(like) baptism. Whether we sprinkle or immerse, we are both marching and we stay together. We're united against communism."[81]

ADAM holds rallies that draw crowds of 35,000 to 100,000 "regular" people, from farmers to fisherman to planters. Tica describes their purpose: "We use our influence to lobby against pornography and the liberalization of the divorce law and abortion laws....We're concerned with morality. Our primary concern, however, is communism—not Marxist but Maoist communism....Our people are deceived—[they] think communism is falling apart when they look at Eastern Europe and Russia, but communism is a threat as long as China exists—and China's only two hours away. Pretty soon, China will be so strong we won't be able to resist....We need a big battle."[82]

A protege and friend of Jerry Falwell, Tica is willing to promote more theological compromise than Falwell in creating a Moral Majority-like organization. Describing himself as both "a 100 percent Full Gospel preacher" and a "fundamentalist Baptist"—labels that would be difficult to combine in the United States—Tica has been very effective in bringing together various strands of conservative Protestantism. In addition to a large network of churches, Tica credits his ministry with sponsoring: a training camp for soldiers; nineteen Christian schools (nursery to high school) enrolling some eight thousand students; 822 extension Bible schools; 178 feeding centers; an International Christian Relief Program serving forty-two thousand children; and livelihood training programs in urban areas and among various tribes (including the Balooga, Tiboli, Mangans, and Magots), training some fifty thousand people at all educational levels.[83] "I believe," he says, "that we can turn this country around....We have a country to win."[84]

Tica, who has a Ph.D. in psychology from Temple University in Philadelphia and received seminary training in Chattanooga, Tennessee, talks about using behavioral modification techniques in seminars given for the military. "The best way to change society is to change people's minds," he says. In this

capacity, Tica and ADAM have been quite active in organizing Value Formation Courses in the Armed Forces of the Philippines (AFP).

President Fidel Ramos, a Protestant elected in 1992 and formerly the chief
of the Armed Forces, defended the Value Formation Courses in 1987 as the
"major new component of civil military operations" because they would promote the "development, interiorization and enrichment of spiritual, moral and
nationalistic values in the professional soldier in order to transform him into
a God-centered, people-dedicated and nation-oriented individual....The scope
of Value Formation is moral and spiritual development, socio-cultural integration, and command value orientation, information, and education....One of
the specific objectives of the program is to promote acceptance by the people
in insurgency-affected areas that the AFP works for their welfare."[85]

In 1987 Value Formation Courses were under way in all AFP camps and
installations.[86] According to Tica, the military is not only willing but eager for
such seminars. "One of the top military leaders has asked me for Bibles....We
don't have enough time for all the requests." Graduates of the Value Formation courses are called "Soldiers of God," and "those who are potential leaders will be tasked to organize a Basic Military Cell (BMC) in different areas."[87]
Once 40 percent of the military is born again, Tica believes that evangelicals
will be able to wield power.[88]

A number of new Christian groups are active in the Value Formation
Courses, including: Word of Life International, Living Waters Fellowship
(Rhema origins), Heaven's Magic, the Christian Life Fellowship, El Shaddai,
and Joshua for Christ. Rev. Norma Tinio, president of the Word of Life, specifically thanked the Kenneth Copeland Ministries, the Flying Medical Samari-
tans, and Women's AGLOW Fellowship (the female associate group of the
Full Gospel Business Men's Fellowship) for their support.[89] Word of Life distributed a report in which they described the three-day seminar that Tinio
conducted at WESCOM, Palawan Island, "where more Officers, and soldiers
received Jesus into their hearts. Likewise, bundles of KENNETH COPELAND
BELIEVER'S VOICE OF VICTORY MAGAZINES AND OTHER TRACTS
WERE HANDED OUT WITH LOVE" [capitals in the original].

In the maiden issue of "Joshua for Christ: Bringing the Good News to the
Military," this ministry proudly proclaims it has conducted "weekly Bible
studies and devotions since December 22, barely 10 days after the termination
of the last coup attempt." The organization uses Campus Crusade's Four
Spiritual Laws in its training programs and is exuberant about the miraculous
changes taking place within the ranks of the military: "Soldiers...keep themselves fit for physical battle as they beat their bodies too for the spiritual
warfare."[90]

Soldiers for Christ, the Christ Mighty Warriors Christian Fellowship, and the Christian Military Fellowship are Christian organizations internal to the Armed Forces. The Christian Military Fellowship describes itself as "an association of Believers in the Armed Forces of the Philippines who are committed to follow the teaching of Jesus Christ." Like a number of the other groups, they hold Bible studies, prayer groups, conferences, and seminars, and they cooperate with local Christian fellowships, churches, worldwide Christian military fellowships and ministries.

Another highly visible group in the Philippines is Wilde Almeda's Jesus Miracle Crusade International Ministry, which holds anti-communist rallies throughout the country in the name of Christ. Claiming millions of followers throughout the Philippines, Almeda regularly packs in people in a large stadium in Manila. A huge banner flanking the stage reads: "Communism is Satanism," and another refers to the international embrace of Almeda's organization and its alliance with Jubilee Crusades. A charismatic group that believes in faith healing and speaks in tongues, the Jesus Miracle Crusade has cadres of young volunteers who live, pray, and work together. It appears to be a very patriarchal, authoritarian community where believers are required to fast for long periods of time.[91]

There are interesting examples of other charismatic Christians who come from elite groups but transcend former religious and class barriers in the interest of forming political and social alliances. Celia Diaz-Laurel, the famous Filipino movie star and wife of Aquino's vice president, was instrumental in holding anti-communist rallies and seminars as part of the military training. She was president of CAUSA Philippines, the political arm of the Unification Church. (CAUSA's name in the Philippines was changed to the Spiritual Action Movement Foundation.) Diaz-Laurel used a slide show produced by Sun Myung Moon's operation and explained why: "His materials on communism are so complete, you can't afford to do it on your own....What do they have against Rev. Moon? There's resistance from Cardinal Sin; there's resistance from all over the place. But his [Rev. Moon's] members are very devoted, very enterprising—he does so much business."[92]

In addition to holding government seminars for the Bureau of Labor and Health, Diaz-Laurel initiated groups for poor people held at the Senate building:

> I tell them, "There is no reason why you should not prosper. The Lord has showed you all his tricks. If you are not prosperous, then you haven't followed his instructions...or you don't understand...."

> I tell them, "If someone strikes you on the right cheek, then give them the left cheek. If you retaliate, you'll get slapped one thousand times. Vengeance belongs to God."

Diaz Laurel did not use labels to describe her faith. A baptized Catholic, she spoke in charismatic terms of intercession ("through Sun Myung Moon's intercession Gorbachev received South Korea's head of state") and of spiritual healing that mixes elements of charismatic faith healing and Indian mysticism (Raj Yoga). "Everybody," she concludes, "serves the Lord in their own way."[93]

The Politics of Religious Rivalry

The new fundamentalists put much pride in the numbers of souls who come to Christ and the number of churches planted. In fact, church planting is perhaps the major structural preoccupation of the new fundamentalists. International church growth agencies such as Philippine Crusades, an affiliate of U.S.-based Overseas Crusades, and "Disciplining A Whole Nation" (DAWN) International, financed by American church growth experts, seek to coordinate efforts among various groups by holding seminars, pastoral conferences, and crusades. They support a well-financed structure of Bible schools, mission agencies, research centers, publishing houses, and broadcast ministries. DAWN actively collects data on geographical regions, specifying where there are no Protestant churches, and what kinds of competition and socioeconomic conditions exist. Jim Montgomery, president of DAWN International, reported that in 1986 twenty-two nations had a DAWN project under way; by 1989 the nations numbered forty-three. That doubled to eighty-nine by the end of 1990, and "There are now (1991) at least 116 countries involved in some measurable form!" The goal of DAWN 2000 Philippines is "to plant a viable and reproducing local church in every Barangay by the year 2000 A.D."

According to Jun Vencer, the tremendous amount of church growth in the Philippines has been aided in large part by the coordination of international church planting efforts. Vencer reports that by December 1990 there were 23,200 congregations in 32 percent of the *barangays*; 54 percent of them were planted during 1981–1990, and 22 percent were planted in the period 1971-1980. "These may be correlated to the fact that the first Church Growth Seminar took place in Baguio City in 1974 and the (National Church Growth) Strategy Congress that led to the formal organization of DAWN Philippines was held in 1985.... It is evident that DAWN as a catalytic movement is a significant factor."[94] Although most of the new churches are "independent" (nondenominational and non-centralized), they tend to interact with other groups that are supported by highly coordinated national and international evangelistic crusades, rallies, Bible schools, missions, and media.

About 85 percent of Filipinos, roughly fifty million people, were Catholic as of 1990, but there were only 5,319 priests and 7,908 nuns in the entire country. This translates into one priest for every 9,400 people.[95] In contrast,

Villanueva's Jesus is Lord Fellowship, with some three hundred thousand members, had five thousand pastoral workers; Sumrall's Cathedral of Praise had eight hundred workers for Metro Manila alone. The new Christian churches specialize in creating a community of believers who are trained to evangelize. The Cathedral of Praise holds some one thousand Bible studies a week for its neighborhood cells, which are composed of 10–20 people each; and the staff conducts some seven thousand home visits every month, so that each member of the church is assured a home visit once every other month. Sumrall also keeps a computer data base that includes an entry on each of the fourteen thousand members of his flock.

Unlike other religious groups, these new Christians have maximized the use of both radio and television. A survey of the weekly TV guide indicated that in Metro Manila alone, a total of twenty-seven religious shows were aired on fifty-one spots for a total of forty-six hours every week, with "fundamentalists" filling the most time, approximately thirty hours of air time a week.[96] TV evangelists regularly aired in the Philippines included Rex Hubbard, Jimmy Swaggart, and the PTL Club.

The Philippine Christian Service Directory of 1990–1991 listed some 220 Protestant schools, Bible schools, and seminaries throughout the Philippines. A number of groups, including Campus Crusade for Christ, Maranatha, Inter-Varsity Christian Fellowship,[97] and the Navigators are active on college and high school campuses. Bishop Ben Dominquez, a priest of the Philippine Independent Church of the Risen Lord at the University of the Philippines, estimates that twelve "fundamentalist" groups are active on the campus. They probably have an outreach to two thousand of some twelve thousand students.[98]

As Protestants move vigorously into previously held Catholic territory, a good deal of friction and suspicion has been generated. The militaristic rhetoric used by the new Christian groups is echoed by descriptions of "onslaught" and "attack" from the Catholics. In "Two Letters on Fundamentalism" taken from *Catholic Answers to "Bible" Christians,* such concerns are laid out by one Catholic priest:

> Protestant fundamentalism is, literally, on the march. Its special object of hate and fear is the Catholic Church. Fundamentalist bookshops are full of anti-Catholic propaganda that is as out of date as witchhunts and the tired old lie that priests charge penitents for forgiving their sins, or that the Pope is the Beast of the Apocalypse....

> In the face of a resurgent and militant anti-Catholicism calling itself "Evangelicalism" and "Fundamentalist Christianity," one has been obliged, finally, to come out of the corner and start fighting back.

The new Christian groups are often blatantly anti-Catholic. Although Gavino Tica is willing to work with Catholics against communism, he blames the Catholic Church for the economic and spiritual poverty of the nation:

> Why are we (Filipinos) poor? What is the source? Number 1 is religion—the fiestas. Our farmers will save all year in order to give an offering to an idol.... They learn to offer bribes to the saints, to bribe God through the saints. These are the values they learn and then they try and bribe the police. Lots of strings are attached....[99]

Tica also accuses the Catholic Church of being hypocritical, and exposes the wedge between different factions of the Church: "Here they are (liberation priests) marching for land reform, while the Catholic Church is one of the largest landowners in the Philippines. Let them give up their land first."

Catholics are accused of being both too radical and too fatalistic. According to Tica, the Number 2 problem in the Philippines is also religion:

> Religion: the non-involvement of Christians, the fatalism in Catholicism—that you should just fold your arms and wait for Jesus, that you shouldn't be worldly. Therefore, our first remedy must be massive evangelization.[100]

Indeed, the Catholic Church is concerned because the new Christian groups are effectively evangelizing and successfully recruiting Catholics as members. In "Catholic Guidelines on Fundamentalism," the Philippine bishops write: "A growing fear is that young people who have been raised Catholic are becoming Fundamentalists. This takes place in a rather big scale in high schools and college organizations such as Long Life, Youth for Christ, Campus Crusade for Christ, InterVarsity, Teen Challenge, the Navigators."[101]

The established Catholic Church in the Philippines, as well as many places in the Third World, is being challenged both from within—as priests and people "opt for the poor" and organize Christian base communities along the lines of liberation theology—and from without. The bishops suggest that the Catholic Church should: 1) focus more on the Bible; they named 1989 as the year of the Bible; 2) provide catechesis that will enable Catholics to better defend their positions; 3) devise pastoral approaches that will better reach out to all, to make people feel as though they belong, and to establish smaller, more personal communities within the church; 4) make the liturgies and prayer meetings "fraternally warm gatherings. Preparation of biblically based homilies delivered with conviction and the power of the Spirit will go a long way towards enlivening our liturgies"; 5) recruit and train lay evangelizers.[102]

In a section on various pastoral actions, the Catholic Bishops of the Philippines write: "Authentic charismatic prayer meetings as well as Basic Christian Communities (BCCs) have proven to be a good antidote against

Catholics joining the Fundamentalist groups. Priests, therefore, should look at them more positively and encourage them in their parishes."[103] On the other hand, some Catholics blame the BCCs for the success of the evangelical movement. Father O'Brien reported visiting a woman on a large hacienda who whipped out a copy of *Time* magazine with an article on Christian base communities, saying: "There! This (Roman Catholic) Church of the poor— these BCCs—that's why we're losing people." O'Brien and others have argued that the rebirth of Protestant fundamentalism in the Philippines in the late 1970s has encouraged a corresponding conservative response or "fundamentalism" among some Catholics. Thus forces within the Church work at cross purposes, offering the egalitarian grass roots movement of the BCCs on one side, and exclusive, ultra-conservative organizations such as Opus Dei on the other.

The Catholic bishops are becoming aware that the primary challenge is that of spiritual renewal and revitalization. The new fundamentalist churches are growing in large part because of the spiritual vitality and emotional fervor of their services, the emphasis on the individual expression of religious faith, and the tight network of support provided by the communities of believers. The bishops are realizing that official Catholic responses, such as printed attacks on fundamentalists or the production of Catholic television programs, are only defensive replications of the strategies of the fundamentalists. Certainly Catholics and the older Protestant traditions in the Philippines have reacted to the aggressiveness of the new Christian groups, which have assailed their churches with an onslaught of media power and coercive conversion strategies. But a more pressing challenge is the positive appeal of intense religious experience that these groups provide on a daily basis.

Conclusion

In the Philippines, as elsewhere, the new Christian groups do not represent a monolithic movement, although they generally share a fundamentalist belief system. A few born-again evangelicals have even embraced something they call "transformation" theology, allying themselves with progressive Catholics, liberal Protestants, and secular forces who are concerned with human rights violations and environmental well-being. But the vast majority of new evangelicals are fundamentalistic, especially in their approach to spiritual warfare on the social and political planes. Their thinking is framed in dualistic terms of good and evil forces, with the "insurgents" identified as being the major satanic force.

The issues are complex and the stakes high. All Filipinos are aware of their crippling national debt and the political and economic instability of their society. The majority of Filipinos, of any religious persuasion, would claim that

they resent dependency on foreign powers. However, the new fundamentalists, if pressed, will tend to support the status quo and link their future with
the United States. Gavino Tica is clear about why he and other ADAM associates have supported the pro-American "Value Formation" courses:

> We (the Philippines) are in bondage economically—but I am a very pragmatic
> person.... Being in bondage to America is preferable to being in bondage to
> China.[104]

Given the status of the Philippines as a colony or semi-colony of the U.S.
throughout most of the twentieth century, and the frequent state of internal
rebellion against U.S. domination, it is not surprising that evangelicalism
keeps using military metaphors to maintain its sense of sociopolitical order.
Melba Maggay, general director of the Institute for the Study of Asian Church
and Culture, argues that on this level the appeal of fundamentalism is not so
much about "salvation" as power: "Many of our people respond not to
abstract social analysis but persons of power....The charismatics have grown
because they are speaking to that part of the population that is not much
interested in salvation but on issues of power. We must understand that in
this culture anyone who speaks for God is automatically assumed as having
some kind of power."[105] She points out that, as in many other places and
times, the charismatic personality can draw people to join all sorts of groups
and causes. "If you have come to know genuine spiritual experience given to
you by a missionary who has a right-wing agenda, it will be very difficult for
you to distinguish your faith from its political baggage."[106]

Maggay quite willingly acknowledges the strong religious dimensions of
the new faith, but she adds: "A political agenda seems to be exported to us
along with the charismatic faith."[107] She notes that foreign evangelists, who
know little about the cultural and political context they have entered, were
very quick to push political compromise and acquiescence along with their
Gospel preaching:

> We saw in evangelicalism in the Philippines for the last 20 years under Marcos
> a reluctance to speak out against human rights violations because it wants its
> freedom to preach assured.... (There is) a very brutal pragmatism which will
> prop up dictators for the sake of American-style democracy. I would like some
> answers to that because the evangelical church in the Philippines is perhaps the
> most deeply colonized and dependent on American values.[108]

In fact, now that U.S. military bases have been voted out of the Philippines
and the U.S. government may no longer have the will to maintain military or
economic commitments, the new fundamentalist Christians see an even more
vital role for themselves. This may demonstrate how a faith born in the

U.S.A. and exported into diverse cultural settings of neocolonialism can take on transnational characteristics. The faith develops new ways of giving sacred support to secular concerns of political economy. Certainly, in the early 1990s, most Filipino fundamentalists still supported a continued U.S. military presence. But a few, like Butch Conde, head of the megachurch Bread of Life, took independent positions and favored closing the U.S. bases. Perhaps this simply shows that neo-Pentecostals can adapt very quickly to changing realities. In his admiration of the Koreans, and his emulation of their custom of building "prayer mountain" retreats, Conde may be signaling other Filipino evangelicals that they must be aware of the various paths to Christian success that now circulate in the Far East.

One does not hear much talk about the kind of Christian theocracy that has circulated in Guatemalan evangelical circles. This is not so much because it is unappealing (in fact, many of the contributors to Philippine evangelical magazines are dominion theologists), but because it is not pragmatic. Protestants represent less than 10 percent of the population, and in spite of their growing influence in the Armed Forces and elsewhere, the Catholics control a much more powerful range of institutions. Nonetheless, fundamentalists are wildly optimistic about the power of Christ to transform not only individuals but whole countries. They are unlikely to give up their attachment to U.S. values and missionary establishments, but they undoubtedly will be open to more contacts with the new model nation of global evangelism, South Korea. There were 3,272 Korean missionaries serving worldwide in 1994 (as opposed to just ninety-three fifteen years earlier), and 401 of them were in the Philippines. This was second only to the 454 missionaries dispatched to the states of the former Soviet Union.[109] The Korean presence augments rather than replaces the U.S. faith, and thus gives added inspiration to Filipino fundamentalists as they try to reshape the destiny of their country.

SIX

South Korea:

Modernization with a Vengeance, Evangelization with the Modern Edge

> An art collector will naturally be drawn to Florence, a mountain climber to the Himalayas. In much the same way a social scientist interested in modernization will have his attention fixed on East Asia.
> —Peter L. Berger[1]

*I*f one visits with Protestants in Central America, Africa, South America, or the Philippines, the dominant influence of the U.S. church and parachurch groups and their particular kind of conservative evangelicalism is obvious. In spite of this, believers in many regions of the world are often most excited by an evangelist who is neither an American nor a fellow countryman, but a Korean. They talk of Paul Yonggi Cho, the neo-Pentecostal leader who purposefully chose a first name that signifies that he is following in the shoes of the universal evangelizer of the first century of Christianity.[2]

Another strong Korean presence has for at least fifteen years spent millions of dollars to bring scholars, journalists, and religious leaders by the thousands to educational conferences in Japan, Europe, the United States, and Korea. This sponsor—under auspices of the New Ecumenical Research Association, the International Religious Foundation, the Parliament of World Religions, International Christians for Unity and Social Action, the World Media Conferences, The Washington Institute for Values in Public Policy, and a host of other organizations—has invited intellectuals and writers from around the world to look at the globalization of religions, communications, and social relations. The sponsor is the Korean-based Holy Spirit Association for the Unification of World Christianity, better known as The Unification Church of Reverend Sun Myung Moon.[3]

Koreans have become prominent in endeavors that twenty or thirty years ago would have been controlled by evangelical representatives of the United States. Yonggi Cho has become the foremost practitioner of Pentecostalism and church growth evangelism; the Reverend Moon has availed himself of the resources and opportunities to start transforming the conservative American civil religion into a global anticommunist civil religion. Those attracted by instrumentalist conspiracy theories might make a facile correlation: South Korea, sitting on the front lines of the Cold War, has been occupied by the United States military forces for almost fifty years and has been required to perform certain tasks dictated by conservative U.S. religious/political ideology. Such a superficial dismissal of religious belief would fail to give credit to the character of Korean Christianity, and it would also miss the depth of the historical transformation of Korea during this century. South Korea (and North Korea, too, but in different ways) has undergone a one-hundred-year period of modernization—culturally, economically, and politically—that has been as complete, and maybe as ruthless, as anywhere on earth. South Korea, a completely industrialized country, borders on First World status; it is much closer to the development levels of the West and Japan than to the Third World status of many other areas where the new fundamentalist Christianity is growing most rapidly.

Japanese Domination, Korean Authoritarianism

In 1884, just as Japan was about to take over the destiny of Korea, the first Protestant missionary, the American Dr. Allen, arrived to be the physician of the Korean royal family. Only three years later the monarchs were forced by the competing interests of Japanese, Chinese, Russian, and Western nations to dismantle the laws and structures that supported their totally intact, ancient feudal society. Korea had been socially and productively backward, dominated by a small Yangban or landlord class that lived off the labor and goods produced by an impoverished peasantry and an auxiliary slave system. As Japan won out over its rivals and established a subservient colony, Korea began a steady transition from the poor, completely agricultural, and feudal institutions of the old Yi dynasty to the prosperous, modern, capitalist, urbanized, and bureaucratized society of the present day. During most of this hundred-year period, the Korean people were forced to live under political conditions as repressive and authoritarian as those imposed by the old feudal regime, though different sectors of society have mounted strong rebellions and resistance at various times.

The Japanese imperialistic control of Korea, begun in 1895 and turned into formal colonial ownership from 1910 to 1945, was as harsh as any fascist regime imposed in Europe; the exploitation of Korean farmers, miners, workers and women was totally directed toward feeding the Japanese and their war machine. After Japan was defeated in World War II, the authoritarian government that grew up in South Korea under American supervision from 1945 to 1987 (giving up any pretense of democracy in 1960) was not as grim; it allowed for economic expansion under Korean ownership, although at the

price of severe repression of the Korean laboring classes and dissenting political groups.[4]

The South Korean people, having already been subjected to the brutal
work ethic of the Japanese occupation, were prepared (dare we say modernized?) in spirit to adapt to the regimen that would produce great industrial
growth from the 1960s through the 1980s. The economic miracle that has
transformed the country and dazzled economists worldwide has come at a
stiff price: at the end of the 1980s the South Koreans worked the longest
workweek in the industrialized world. Their average workweek was fifty-five
hours in 1987. At this point they had outstripped their erstwhile developmental rivals, Singapore and Taiwan, the two other "Asian tigers" who also
achieved spectacular industrial growth by applying highly authoritarian
discipline; by 1987 those two countries had backslid a bit, requiring only
forty-seven and forty-eight hours per week, respectively, from the average
worker.[5] South Korea's rate of industrial accidents, the highest in the world for
many years, has even jumped dramatically in recent years, by about 33 percent between 1986 and 1990.[6]

Consequently, South Korea has grown and modernized itself significantly
by imposing draconian measures upon the majority of Koreans and by leaving many workers in a state of relative deprivation. The Korea National Bank
wrote that in 1991:

> 88 percent of the GNP comes from unearned income...the worst obstacle to the
> healthy development of the Korean economy is the concentration of econom-
> ic wealth in several big companies and the monopolistic possession of these
> properties and management by individual families.[7]

The level of political repression required to usher in modern capitalism
was severe and steady, but did not usually degenerate into "apocalyptic"
destruction of the kind employed in such Central American countries as
Guatemala, where terroristic military regimes had neither prospects nor ability for creating economic growth or a modern state. (Although one should not
forget that apocalyptic events immediately preceded Korean development:
the Korean War, 1950-53, which left one million civilians dead and two-thirds
of the nation's industrial capacity destroyed.) An exception in recent years
was the military terror imposed in the Kwangju massacre in May 1980, when
the Korean Army attacked the civilian population of the city of Kwangju and
killed as many as two thousand people.[8] More generally the Korean state
employed steadier intimidation through large networks of spies, police, and
enforcers employed by the Army, the Korean CIA, the municipal and national governments, and the large employers.

The Korean government encouraged a highly "planned economy" and worked closely with the giant companies, called "chaebol," to make their manufacturing production for export the centerpiece of Korean industrial production. These chaebol, usually under single-family ownership, have been allowed to expand horizontally into innumerable industries with the approval of the state: as of 1990 the four biggest chaebols—Hyundai, Samsung, Lucky Kumsung, Saewoo—had achieved total sales that were equal to 60 percent of the gross national product.[9]

The fact that the chaebol system has made a few families very rich has been perceived as something akin to robbery: "Many working-class people think of rich people as 'thieves.' A certain wealthy district in Seoul is called Thieves Village."[10] Korean political scientist Hang Yul Rhee asserts that most Koreans are much more egalitarian-minded than North Americans, and that U.S.-style income inequality is a prescription for political havoc in Korea.[11]

Popular outrage finally plunged South Korea into political turmoil. In 1987, fed by general resentment that Korean prosperity had not trickled down to the majority, the Korean people rebelled and forced an opening for both political democracy and free labor unions. Growing democratic, labor, and student movements combined forces in the "Grand Labor Struggles" of the summer of that year, which initiated a wave of seven thousand labor strikes that would last from 1987 to 1990. [12]

Although new unions succeeded in establishing themselves in many companies and made some gains in wage bargaining, the force unleashed against them was fierce. Not only did police and Army units help to suppress working people, but many companies hired their own private squads, called Kusadae, to intimidate employees. Long, staged battles took place in the Hyundai and Daewoo chaebols. In 1987, fifteen thousand troops and police attacked workers barricaded within the Hyundai shipbuilding yards—"by helicopter, land, and sea"; the following year the same battle was fought again, this time with nineteen thousand government troops.[13] Some multinational firms such as the ICC Corporation, a Japanese-owned company that is one of the largest shoemakers in the world (twenty thousand workers), employed the Kusadae in the customary Korean fashion. Thugs hired off the street, management personnel, and some male workers armed themselves with clubs and iron bars and attacked about one thousand low-paid female workers who were conducting a sit-down strike.[14] Among other foreign employers who used Kusadae to terrorize young women employees was a subsidiary of the U.S. Tandy Corporation (Radio Shack products). In both cases many victims were beaten, sexually abused, and later fired by the companies.[15]

The democratic movement and the violence it evoked from the corporate sector and the state were disruptive enough to force the military dictator, Chun, out of power in favor of the more conciliatory Roh Tae Woo, another

Army general chosen in the semi-democratic election of 1988. Roh, in turn, was replaced by a democratically elected civilian, Kim Young Sam, in December 1992. Kim Young Sam, until the previous year, had been an important leader of the democratic political opposition; his thirty-year career of defying the authoritarian state was made possible by his ability to operate safely within the structures of the Protestant churches of South Korea. Kim Dae Jung, the other perennial opposition figure, had survived over the same period of time through his ties to the Catholic Church.[16]

Although politically and theologically liberal Protestants and Catholics make up a small percentage of Korean Christians, the major churches—particularly the National Council of Churches in Korea, the liberal Presbyterian Church in the Republic of Korea, and the Catholic Church—have offered a haven for the oppressed and an outspoken voice when others were silenced. This narrow political refuge gave voice to students who otherwise would have been tracked down by the very large and efficient state security forces; to labor activists who otherwise would have been beaten or jailed or thrown out of their jobs; and to teachers and journalists who might likely have joined tens of thousands of others from their professions in Armed Forces' sponsored re-education camps.[17] This egalitarian, democratic, left-leaning element in Christianity is found most clearly in "minjung," or people's theology, the Korean version of liberation theology that finds support from both Protestants and Catholics.

Catholic theology, on its original entry into feudal Korean society via Jesuits and others in the eighteenth century, was seen as particularly subversive to the complex, extremely inegalitarian "yangban" structure. Carter J. Eckert and other historians have argued that "it is clear what attracted Koreans to Catholicism was above all its creed of equality, its tenet that the whole of humankind are alike the children of God.... It must have been a moving experience for...commoners to...worship Him on a basis of equality with the yangban." "Catholicism was in itself a grave and growing indictment of yangban society," hence the severe "Persecution of 1801" and "Persecution of 1839" were meant to eradicate Catholics and Catholicism in Korea.[18]

Anti-democratic rule has evoked spirited and very constant resistance in South Korea, and one portion of the large Christian presence in the country has done a great deal to keep the democratic spirit alive. Surprisingly, perhaps, this progressive tendency has not grown rapidly with the successes of the democracy movement in recent years. The large majority of Korean Christians, in particular within the dominant and quickly growing Protestant branch, are very conservative and either opposed to or uninterested in political opposition. They are generally characterized as right-wing and fundamentalist by their more liberal brethren. Song Kon-ho, a Christian and former editor of a large Korean newspaper, describes them this way:

> Conservative churches, however, still boast nearly ninety-five per cent of the
> Christian followers and continue to expand their influence at a rapid pace
> through the Pentecostal movement, as for example, the Full Gospel Church.
> These churches invariably lack any social or political concern.[19]

A Tradition of Religious Opposition

Lest we think that Christianity is the only faith that has found an opposition-
al role to the ways in which modernization, Japanization, Westernization,
and capital formation have been achieved in South Korea, it is worth noting
that Koreans have experimented with various new religious influences. They
have sought an antidote to their distress in divine solace, restitution, legitimation, and deliverance. Throughout the past century, Koreans have repeatedly resisted and rebelled against their subordination in religious terms, beginning with the Tonghak Peasant Rebellion of 1894.

The Tonghak movement was based on a new syncretic religion—Tonghak
means "Eastern learning"—that drew on elements of Taoism, Buddhism,
Confucianism, and even some parts of Catholicism (even though the last influence was emblematic of the evil "Western Learning" that supposedly accompanied imperialism). Tonghak taught that Mankind is God and all people are
equal. Its adherents probably would have overthrown the Korean monarchy if
both China and Japan had not sent troops in to quell the peasant armies.[20]

Tonghak not only helped inspire later rebellions, but also a whole stream
of new Korean religions that have thrived in the twentieth century. For many
people, as their social structure was being made over for "the economic miracle" by Western and Japanese influences, the new religions offered a way to
save Korean values, keep faith in the face of extreme adversity, and wait for
the transformation of Korea into the "promised land." One study done in 1971
estimated that these religious sects numbered about two hundred and forty,
variously associated with the traditions of shamanism, Chungsan, Taoism,
Buddhism, Christianity, "Eastern Learning," and Confucianism. Most of these
sects were syncretic, drawing on other religious traditions, and so held some
beliefs in common: 1) that the chosen people were the Koreans; 2) that they
were awaiting the imminent advent of a perfect world; 3) that they would
found a universalistic faith that other nations could also accept; 4) that they
would be led by a Savior or leader with special powers who would bring
them together; 5) that this would occur at the proper apocalyptic moment; 6)
that in the meantime, believers should accept the shamanistic magic of the
leader as the appropriate way to drive off evil influences and gain worldly
success.[21]

These new religions have attracted about ten percent of the South Korean population and constitute one of the two expanding sectors in religious life, the other being Protestant Christianity, which now represents more than 25 percent of all South Koreans.[22] The tendencies listed above describe not only the new religions, but also the beliefs of the Protestant fundamentalists and Pentecostals.

Up until World War II, the numbers of Protestants, led by Presbyterians, grew modestly but represented less than 2 percent of the population.[23] In the early part of the century, however, the influence of Protestants exceeded their numbers because many middle-class believers, most of them educated in Presbyterian and Methodist schools, were able to pursue careers in education, medicine, and other emerging professions (sometimes even studying in the United States). The mission-run hospitals, schools, and universities were often the best in the country and gained a reputation for Christian service to the poor. Protestants had the opportunity to modernize Korea in a way that would counteract Japanese influence and promote democratic reforms.

Some Korean writers contend that the Protestant churches might have grown larger in the early 1900s if they had not imitated the quietistic performance of the Americans who controlled the direction of the Korean denominations. (Presbyterians, followed by Methodists, completely dominated early Korean evangelization.) The U.S. missionaries chose not to offend the Japanese rulers (and perhaps bring on their own expulsion), during nationalistic revolts of 1907–1911 and the March 1st Movement that began in 1919. This was more than a tactical decision, for the most important missionary figures deplored the political activities of some of their new converts. The Presbyterian influence derived directly from the fundamentalist side of the church and the new conservative theology emanating from Princeton; it taught a dispensational faith that cautioned waiting for the coming of Christ rather than political rebellion.[24]

Many young Korean Christians felt torn between different Biblical interpretations of their fate. One convert, An Ch'angho, in keeping with his American teachers, saw his nation's suffering and sinfulness in acquiescent terms: "Christ told the Jews that it was because they were full of evil deeds and devoid of all goodness that God took the rights from them and handed them over to others, and this surely applies to Korea today."[25] Other new Christians found national hope in millenarian beliefs; Yang Yusan, a Korean evangelist who moved to San Francisco in 1907, wrote to a Korean Nationalist newspaper "not to forget that Christianity is expected to rescue Korea from Japan just as the Israelites were delivered from the Egyptians."[26]

It is within this ambivalent context that the entry of Protestantism into Korea must be understood. On the one hand, it was appealing as a creed

supporting nationalism and the possibility of a more benign kind of modernization, particularly since it had no connection to the Japanese modernizers
who were so efficiently crushing and reordering the traditional Korean social
structure. The faith grew very quickly between 1887 and 1907 and emboldened young Christian patriots to join other nationalists, including the
Choundo-gyo (Heavenly Way) descendants of the Tonghak movement, in
opposing Japanese imperialism.

Missionaries, on the other hand, attributed their rapid early growth to the
giant nationwide revival of 1907, "an outpouring of the Holy Spirit." David
Kwang-sun Suh explains that the orientation of the Americans put a fundamentalistic stamp on Korean religion that has lasted until the present day:
"The revival meetings...set the tone of Korean Protestantism: emotional, conservative, Pentecostal, individualistic, and other-worldly."[27]

The revivals initially did recruit more believers, but they also stressed fundamentalist and dispensationalist avoidance of the sinful world. Since the
revivals were intentionally inaugurated by the missionaries to counteract specific nationalist uprisings, including the Righteous Armies of 1907–11 and the
March 1st Movement of 1919, many Koreans wondered whether the
Americans had conspired with the colonizers or were just avoiding the over-
lords' wrath. Later, in 1938, many Korean pastors humiliated themselves (or
humbled themselves, depending on one's point of view), by agreeing to
engage in Shinto ceremonies imposed by the militaristic Pan-Japanese
regime.[28]

When Americans appeared again in Korea as liberators in 1945, their religion did not appear as passive as it once had. Syngman Rhee, a Christian
nationalist in exile, returned to head the government, and U.S. missionaries
and Korean pastors alike resumed preaching their conservative message, but
they added very direct nationalist sentiments, inextricably mixed with anti-
communism, that had been missing before the war.[29] The Protestant churches began growing rapidly: six hundred thousand members in 1950, 1.14 million in 1960, 2.2 million in 1970. Then, in the next decade the faith exploded,
more than tripling in numbers as it added five million new adherents. As
in many parts of the world, Pentecostalism spearheaded the remarkable
increase.[30]

With the Pentecostal dimension added, and the nationalist longing no
longer denied, fundamentalist Protestantism in Korea now had a great deal in
common with the new Korean religions. The powerful spiritual connection
that is evidenced in the miracle cure of the Pentecostal and charismatic revival
meeting is also central to the shamanistic traditon in Korea. According to a
study on new religious movements, "Most new religions in Korea accomplish
their missionary work by way of faith healing." [31]

The healing miracle involves more than just applying "good" hands and personal magical powers upon "bad" bodily sickness; it requires the good spirit—in Pentecostalism, the one and only Holy Spirit—to drive out the demons or evil spirits that are causing the affliction. In the Korean new religions, the healer follows the shamanist tradition of allowing oneself to be possessed by the good spirit: "most universal in shamanism is the relation between its believers and shamans through the latter's personal experience and exorcist rites called *kut*. A shaman is regarded as a professional officiant of exorcism who can display his special function of experiencing a state of self-effacing ecstasy." [32]

The Korean Pentecostal pastor is just such a powerful officiant. Through the processes of speaking in tongues, prophecy, and other gifts of the Spirit, he allows his body, given up to ecstatic experience, to be the conduit of the Holy Ghost's overwhelming power. Such shamanistic power, added to the other considerable attributes of the Christian faith, allows the Pentecostal to emulate and possibly outperform the spirit power evoked in the other new religions: for example, "Ch'oe Che-u's 'ardor to get in touch with spirits'; the 'incantation of the divine general' of Nuryang Ch'ondo-gyo: the 'spell to chase the devils away' of the Pongnam-gyo; and the 'art of moving spirits and attaining a godly spirit' of the Ch'on'gyo-do."[33]

The new religions have also emphasized a Korean-centered world, at least in the future, where the Korean example would inspire other nations of Asia and the rest of the globe toward a faith of universal understanding. The spirit and destiny of the nation are tied into the sense of religious triumphalism. The Chongdo-gyo religion, which has headquarters on Mount Kyeryong (the concept of a prayer mountain is important to many, including Korean Pentecostals in Yoido Full Gospel Church), teaches that "Korean will become an international language and the Korean people the messiah for all the peoples of the world." Another sect, the Ch'onji Taean-gyo, has an understanding that "Korea is the land of the Five Elements and the center of the world." In the Segye Ilka Konghoe religion, preachers assert that the Koreans are "the newly chosen people." T'ongil-gyo prophesies that "Korea is the country which will witness the advent of Christ."[34]

The last mentioned, T'ongil-gyo, is the Korean name for the Unification Church. Reverend Moon's assertion that the Second Coming will take place in Korea may seem extreme by Christian standards of the West (especially if Moon himself is taken to be a Messiah figure; at times he has depicted his own role as more akin to a second John the Baptist); however, his belief in Korea's role as a leading evangelizing nation is shared by a good many more orthodox Protestants.[35]

Lee Daniel Soonjung has traced the history of the National Evangelization

Movement, which has "challenged the church to accept God's special commission of the Han-race (Korean people)."[36] The Protestant pastor who led the
movement, Shin Hyun Gyoon, was as adamant as the non-Christian new religions about the central role of his people: "We are the priesthood nation to all
the world...the role of the Western church is at an end." Shin's enthusiasm for
Korea's special role was not only acceptable in mainstream denominations,
but was encouraged by Korean President Park during the 1960s and 1970s.[37]
Naturally, Shin provided Biblical justification for injecting this strong nationalism into the faith, and emphasized the nation's direct connection to Israel:

> God chooses his people from the Semitic line. We Koreans are in the line of
> Shem, the first-born of Noah, a nation from the East, a single-race people, and
> a small and weak nation. Korea is a nation divinely chosen for tomorrow.[38]

The sense of great national mission is shared by a great many South
Korean Protestants; it has been encouraged as well by post-World War II governments in order to generate patriotic, anti-communist fervor and include the
masses, otherwise disenfranchised, in the mission of building up the Korean
economy. Park, president from 1961 to 1979, is credited both with backing the
leader of the Korean Campus Crusade for Christ, Billy Kim, and injecting
evangelical crusades into the ranks of the South Korean Army. A U.S. missionary who collects data on Christian conversions estimates that 50 percent
of the Army are evangelical believers.[39]

Since they had been associating with U.S. post-war missionaries who carried the Christian/nationalist germ themselves, South Koreans understand-
ably felt a touch of Manifest Destiny coursing through their veins. This kind
of religious nationalism might be competitive, or it might end up being com-
plementary to the U.S. Christian purpose. The most far-reaching applications
of Christian nationalism/anti-communism, as transformed into an international anti-communism, were engineered through the complex religious/busi-
ness apparatuses constructed by Sun Young Moon, which will be detailed
later in this chapter.

Religious Modernization: The Leading Edge, Cho and Moon

Even though the new Christian fundamentalism usually has deep roots in the
United States, it can develop specific characteristics within different national
contexts. Sometimes very large churches have emerged with strong indigenous attributes, charismatic leadership, and nationalistic ambitions, especially during the 1960s and 1970s: for example, Brasil para Cristo, and the Iglesia
ni Kristo in the Philippines. In Korea, new developments go further, suggesting that religious structures and beliefs can be made over by religious entrepreneurs and reintroduced to the world market in forms that are even more

effective than the original American exports.

In Korea, as in many parts of the world, Protestantism has fragmented more rapidly than has its American counterpart, although along the same lines: the older denominational system is stagnant; new independent church entities have emerged. Fragmentation can occur within existing old denominations as well as through the development of new sects; Presbyterians in Korea had splintered into forty-one groups and churches by 1981.[40] (They were not of equal size, however, and the two largest sub-denominations still claimed the loyalty of most Presbyterians.)

Now that a Pentecostal revival seems to be sweeping many parts of the Earth, the fresh appeal of Christianity is often linked to the tiny "templos," chapels, and tents that seem to pop up overnight for every would-be pastor who has heard the call. The egalitarian impact and the individual spiritual empowerment of such an accessible faith, unimpeded by hierarchy, is not to be denied; those who have documented the Pentecostal trend[41] find much of its strength in its very fragmentation and atomization. On the other hand the very newest Pentecostal and charismatic churches are involved in something different, a reaggregation and reorganization of Christian believers into new, large-scale forms. This is even occurring in the poorest countries, as well as in the more developed nations. In the United States, where traditional denominations remain large and institutionally influential, the entrepreneurship of the evangelical broadcasters reflects the larger reality of evangelical success: conservative, fundamentalist, and Pentecostal church members now outnumber the so-called "mainline" stalwarts of the National Council of Churches.

We should not be surprised by the reaggregation within this fundamentalist/Pentecostal mix, especially as the lives of believers become more settled and they find a big organization appealing for its identification with success and spiritual power. If this is the modernizing trend, then within Korea we find the most modern developments in the form of highly organized megachurches and parachurches that are led by strong entrepreneurial pastors with entourages of subpastors and elders. David Martin has identified the Korean Protestant scene as "a spiritual enterprise culture" that requires "in the top echelon, a kind of international manager 'of the spirit.'"[42]

The concentrated ownership and hierarchical control of the Korean chaebol, so effective for an export-oriented, state-controlled manufacturing economy, is mirrored in church and parachurch structures, particularly the Yoido Full Gospel Church of Paul Yonggi Cho and the Unification Church of Sun Myung Moon. Cho and Moon are impressive entrepreneurs; in addition to their spiritual leadership qualifications, they have strong technical backgrounds: Cho with degrees in technology and law, Moon in electrical engineering. One is the church builder par excellence; the other the creator of the most impressive worldwide parachurch, a quasicorporate entity that can raise and dispose of billions of dollars in many parts of the globe.

These men have their parallels in the United States, most notably in the field of evangelical broadcasting. Jeffrey K. Hadden and Anson Shupe, in documenting the ascendency of Robertson, Falwell, Swaggart (and many lesser figures) stress their businesslike approach to the task: "Many broadcastors pastor churches, but they have independently incorporated their broadcast ministries as autonomous *parachurch* structures, answerable only to boards they have hand selected."[43] Moreover, the televangelists have successfully identified their market "[the] niche within the broader context of the free-enterprise system. Evangelicals have a product to sell. The product is Jesus Christ and his gift of salvation to those who will accept." Hadden thinks the new evangelical and charismatic forces have simply outmaneuvered the more out-moded church structures:

> Denominational bureaucracies are cumbersome structures for the creation of new initiatives....The mainline Protestant and Catholic traditions simply don't have the organizational structure or fiscal resources to successfully compete with evangelical broadcasters. The entrepreneurial model, free from the constraints of church bureaucracy, is simply a more efficient means for developing a television ministry."[44]

Protestant behavior in the late twentieth century seems to turn Weber on his head: rather than religious asceticism allowing for the development of capitalist behaviors (presumably inculcated in a society over a century or two), we now have capitalist behaviors adopted in order to accelerate the efficacy of religious faith (with results expected within a decade or less). There is no better place to see this phenomenon at work than in South Korea.

Paul Yonggi Cho

In 1952, the Pentecostal churches in South Korea barely existed; eight congregations with five hundred members between them met to form the Assemblies of God.[45] Six years later, Yong Gi Cho, a twenty-two-year-old pastor trained by the Assemblies, launched a tent church outside Seoul with a membership of five people.[46] In 1961, Cho acted as interpreter for Samuel J. Todd, an American Assembly of God healer who was staging a revival tour in Korea; Todd's example inspired Cho to use revivalist techniques and display divine healing powers in order to enlarge his own church.[47] The revival center established for Todd's tour became Cho's Yoido Full Gospel Central Church in 1962. Because Pentecostalism established itself rather late in Korea, Cho's presence has been instrumental in promoting the "third wave" association between the church growth movement and the Pentecostal boom.

Furthermore, because the late start of Pentecostalism was more or less simultaneous with postwar Korean economic success, the "spirit-filled" faith was not a church of the poor, as Pentecostal churches often were in their early years in the United States and Latin America. Cho's church was not associated with material deprivation or the denial of worldly goods. Therefore, it was possible for Cho to build a gigantic Assembly of God Church on his own terms, having a heterogeneous membership that had a strong middle-class component: by 1974, only twelve years after founding the Yoido Church, a new ten thousand-seat auditorium was built, the church hosted the Tenth World Pentecostal Conference, and the Full Gospel Prayer Mountain retreat was established. By 1994 Cho was admired worldwide for his success because he had built the largest church in the world, with eight hundred thousand members. For those who doubt the possibility of "real" church membership accommodating hundreds of thousands, a description of how worship services were held in August 1986, when the Yoido Church recorded an exact membership of 513,601, indicates that three hundred fifty thousand could be seated each Sunday:

> The main sanctuary of YFGC seats 25,000 members and is surrounded by 15 auxiliary chapels connected by closed-circuit television. A total of 50,000 members and participants can worship simultaneously together in one of the seven services on Sunday.[48]

The "economic miracle" achieved by the growth of the Korean chaebols has its parallel in the organizational and demographic miracle achieved in the religious "chaebol" of Paul Yonggi Cho; obviously such achievement is revered by all Protestant pastors who aspire to multiplying their flocks. Less obvious is the way in which Cho had a vision of the "cell principle" in 1976 and began to systematize the growth theories of Fuller Theology missiologist Donald McGavran and other Western evangelists. Cho writes that he followed McGavran's advice: "Men and women do like to become Christians without crossing barriers."[49] His strategy was to divide up his church into homogeneous cells made up of five to ten families. By homogeneous, he usually means common orientations or occupations (racial homogeneity being almost complete in Korea)—businessmen, schoolteachers, housewives—and gives this example:

> Mr. Chun the banker is in charge of the cell meeting, his cell will be comprised mainly of financial people. Their one hour cell meeting might take place in a local restaurant and look very much like a business lunch....They might spend some time praying for their specific needs....They will discuss one potential convert. Perhaps it is another financial person who has a problem.[50]

However, says Cho, he used the "homogenous principle" for developing
the cell system, not for the entire church: "We do not differentiate between
rich and poor, high and low, or well-educated and uneducated."[51] The cell
system allows Cho's Yoido Full Gospel Church to evangelize *Our Kind of
People* (the title of a church growth book by McGavran's successor at Fuller
Theological Seminary, Peter Wagner), and then strictly organize these cells
into a giant structure of more heterogeneous elements. As of 1990, when the
church had six hundred fifty thousand members, there was the following
hierarchy: 48,009 gome cell leaders, 48,009 assistant home cell leaders, 6,740
section leaders, 402 subdistrict leaders, 24 district leaders, 11 regional chapel
leaders, a director of pastoral care department, and Dr. Paul Yonggi Cho
himself.[52]

Of the above, about seven hundred people were salaried pastors whose
activities were planned on elaborate maps and charts in the main church:

> In fact, it looks like a military strategy room. This is a war we are fighting. The
> enemy is the Devil. The battlefield is the hearts of lost humanity. The objective
> is to get as many souls saved as possible before Jesus comes.[53]

As the quote indicates, Cho holds to a dispensationalist interpretation of history and awaits the return of the Savior. Like present-day American fundamentalists and their predecessors, the conservative missionaries who founded the Presbyterian Church in Korea, he believes in Biblical inerrancy. Cho
also celebrates the power of the Holy Spirit to heal disease and drive out evil
demons, and he encourages his followers to use the same Spirit to derive success and prosperity in this world. The emphasis on the Holy Spirit not only is
at the heart of Pentecostal faith, but it also echoes strong tendencies within
the new Korean religions mentioned earlier and the shamanistic tradition that
orients Koreans toward this-worldly application of their devotions.

Cho sees his organization Church Growth International as being part of
the work of the Holy Spirit, "who opened my eyes to see the reality of the cell
system as God's plan to cause growth of a new era of superchurches."[54] Jae
Bum Lee, a Korean pastor who attended Cho's Full Gospel Bible School and
then completed a doctoral program at the Fuller Theology School, has written
about the effect of Yoido Full Gospel Church on other Korean churches. He
points out that superchurches are a Korean phenomenon. This holds true in
the historic Protestant denominations: the largest Presbyterian, Methodist,
Holiness, and Baptist churches in the world are all in Korea, with sixty thousand, thirty thousand, six thousand, and forty thousand members respectively.[55] Of these four, only the Young Nak Presbyterian Church is not Pentecostal, although it does rely heavily on a cell system and intensive prayer
meetings similar to the Yoido Church. The other three churches have those

two characteristics and share distinct Pentecostal features including baptism in the Holy Spirit, healing miracles, and the exorcism of demons. The pastor of the world's largest Methodist church, Ho Moon Lee of the Soong Eui Church in Inchon, is a disciple of Cho who closely studied the workings of the Yoido Church.

The Sung Rak Baptist Church led by Ki Dong Kim began with only seven members in 1969 and was associated with the Southern Baptist Mission in Korea. Its growth to forty thousand members in eighteen years made it the fastest growing super church in the world[56] but also marked its departure from the Southern Baptist denomination in 1987.[57] The Southern Baptists, based in the United States, could not tolerate the strong emphasis on Pentecostal practice; the speaking in tongues and healings performed in prayer meetings, and the overwhelming emphasis on exorcism, were contrary to acceptable "old-style" Baptist fundamentalistism. Kim "believes that everyone who is a Christian can cast out demons and perform signs and wonders," and has written three books based on Biblical methods of eradicating evil spirits (aptly named *Demonology I, II, and III*.)[58]

If Kim's preoccupation with evil and sin may seem quite compatible with North American Baptist theology (his favorite piece of scripture is "The reason the Son of God appeared was to destroy the devil's work"[59]), his methods of dealing with them are not: his rites of direct attack through "power evangelism," as advocated by Cho and many other neo-Pentecostals and charismatics, indicate that independent Baptists in Korea and many other lands may be taking a different route than the comparatively staid approach of independent Baptists in the United States (the theology and decidedly non-Pentecostal practice of Jerry Falwell's giant, independent Thomas Road Baptist Church, for instance, are more or less identical to the Southern Baptist norm.)[60]

Paul Yonggi Cho has helped generate the movement of charismatic practice into the non-Pentecostal churches because he believes there is new intervention of the Holy Spirit on Earth. His goal is to make the Korean church and other Protestant churches around the globe "dynamically equivalent to the New Testament Church,"[61] so that Christians may reasonably expect the Second Coming of Christ and the Kingdom of God. On behalf of racially and ethnically diverse Christians around the globe, Cho hopes to accomplish what the apostle Paul did for the Gentiles in the first century A.D.; that is, to demonstrate that Christian power, through its use of Pentecostal and charismatic powers, is superior to all the lesser demons, diseases, false gods, and shamanistic exercises that people have heretofore feared and worshiped. It would not be inappropriate if he were to describe himself, not in self-praise but rather in the sense of his mission, with the words Paul used in Romans 15:18-19:

> I will not venture to speak of anything except what Christ has accomplished
> through me in leading the Gentiles to obey God by what I've said and done—
> by the power of signs and miracles, through the power of the Spirit.[62]

This conception of the purpose of "power evangelism" is not unique to Cho,
for much of it was developed and popularized at Fuller Theological Seminary
in California by John Wimber—"The explanation of the gospel" is accompanied by "a demonstration of God's power."[63] Many Koreans and many of
Cho's protegés study at Fuller's School of World Mission, where there are two
professors of Korean studies and one of East Asian studies. Fuller has facilitated the inclusion of charismatic and Pentecostal theological perspectives
into mainstream American evangelical training and is credited by Protestant
scholar George Marsden as being both the least doctinaire and the most
accomplished in scholarship of all theology schools that follow in the conservative tradition.[64]

Yoido Full Gospel Church has a highly developed program of world mission itself; it may seem ironic that Cho's evangelism is being aimed back at its
source and concentrates on the United States, where over half of its five hundred missionaries were sent as of 1992. Next in numbers are missions to two
other rich, but much less successfully evangelized countries, Japan and Germany. To facilitate its missions, the church has founded its own Full Gospel
Seminaries in Kobe (Japan), Los Angeles, Berlin, and New York. The church is
also expanding its broadcasting activities thoughout the world; the highest
concentration of its foreign television programming is in Japan, where it has
special plans for converting ten million Japanese souls.[65]

Skeptics might suggest that a church that gives primacy to a gospel of success and prosperity is simply following its instincts and heading, like Willie
Sutton the bank robber, "where the money is." This may be true in the same
measure that U.S. charismatic churches, catering to the middle classes, are
found disproportionately in prosperous suburban areas and shopping malls.
On the other hand, Cho and his followers in Korea and elsewhere are consciously targeting cities because this is "where the people are" in a rapidly
urbanizing world. South Korea's urbanization has been as rapid as any in the
world—75 percent of the people lived in rural areas in the 1940s, and an estimated 80 percent will be urban by the year 2000.[66] In addition there are
almost one million Korean-Americans in the United States—most of them
Christian, urbanized, and middle class—who can serve as a potential base
for building megachurches and launching evangelization efforts in other
countries.

Cho's Full Gospel Church is not so different from many megachurch and
parachurch efforts launched by American televangelists and neo-Pentecostal

revivalists. The entrepreneurial experiments of a charismatic authority figure take form in a businesslike and profitable sort of evangelism that finds many customers, people in need of that particular type of religion. There is a vertically integrated church bureaucracy with clear lines of authority to the top and the possibility of horizontal expansion into other lucrative or challenging fields: publishing, Bible colleges, old-age homes, overseas evangelizing.

In Korea, however, the modernization of Protestantism is more recent and less encumbered by past structures and the rubble of past doctrinal battles; and thus the possibility for unimpeded, innovative growth has presented itself to Pastor Cho, much as a few industrial families in Korea have been free to create giant chaebols that dominate manufacturing and distribution at home and abroad. Cho's religious chaebol features the clear-cut pyramidal structure of neighborhood leaders, subpastors, and pastors under his authority, but with sufficient lateral openness through the "cell system" that they do not necessarily threaten bureaucratic stagnation at a certain size; in fact, expansion in the religious market seems to promise an almost unlimited growth of adherents. Certainly as this chaebol gets larger and increases its revenues and its core of skilled and dedicated practitioners, it is all the more capable of funding and staffing new efforts at home and abroad. At this point no one knows if a church like Yoido Full Gospel can be institutionalized to the point of surviving Cho's demise (or can survive in the patriarchal, family-owned form common to both chaebol corporations and some American evangelical parachurch operations), but it certainly is inspiring many young evangelists around the world to mimic Cho's mixture of Pentecostalism, prosperity theology, and "church growth" structure.

In terms of pastoral business authority, Cho's accomplishments look very striking indeed, for he has taken a Pentecostal church of the kind that are forever splitting into more and more egalitarian little "sect" temples, and transfromed it into a centralized church that is as large as many established religious denominations. His Yoido Church deals in mass production, formulating and marketing a neat, standardized product, thoroughly American and Korean and internationally acceptable. Its beliefs, practices, and much of its structure can be immediately transplanted and replicated in one hundred cities on five continents.

In this sense, Cho is an able religious engineer/industrialist who has gathered together straightforward fundamentalist components, eliminated the quirkier elements that cause too much denominational friction, and thrown out extraneous old production habits and standardized the new ones. He has come up with a more appealing and more effective way to be religious—a better way, to quote Hadden, "to sell Jesus."

The Reverend Moon

The Holy Spirit Association for the Unification of World Christianity was founded by a young man whose family converted to Presbyterianism when he was ten years old. Six years later, on Easter Sunday 1936, he met Christ as he walked through the hills near his village in Northern Korea. "You are the son I have been seeking, the one who can begin my eternal history," said Jesus.[67]

In the years that followed, Sun Myung Moon had other direct communications with Jesus and God, as well as with Buddha and Moses, which led him to found the Unification Church in South Korea on May 1, 1954. Like other Korean leaders of new religions, he claimed that God had chosen him to play a semi-messianic role in the restoration of earthly paradise, "to restore the Kingdom of Heaven on earth," which he sees emanating from Korea: "All aspects of culture and civilization must bear fruit in this nation."[68]

American evangelical writer Richard Quebedeaux has called the Unification Church "a Korean form of Christianity."[69] However, the point here is not to establish the legitimacy of the Unification Church, which is tiny in membership, either as a world religion in its own right or as an accepted adjunct of conservative evangelicalism. Instead, let it be noted that an organization that calls itself "The Holy Spirit Association for the Unification of World Christianity" considers itself to be Christian. What is significant in relationship to Korea, and to the ways in which "modernization" and "modern" religious influence are intertwined in a larger global framework, is how the Unification Church has used its anti-communist supranationalism to exert worldwide influence. If Cho has modernized Pentecostalism and given energy and organizational direction to the "supershamanistic" aspect of Christianity (a first century "miracle religion" revitalized for the millennium 2000), then Reverend Moon has been very clever and businesslike in building a transnational religious and business web in which "supranationalism" is the most important element. Something larger than pure nationalism (or even simple empire-building) is at work, as Moon uses religion to conflate the goals of U.S. and South Korean anti-communism (attaching Korean destiny to U.S. manifest destiny rather than simply imitating it):

> America's existence was according to God's providence. God needed to build one powerful Christian nation on earth for his future work. Korea has replaced Israel as the land of the Messiah.[70]

Moon's peculiar genius has been to recognize that he could graft his Unification theology onto the universalizing trends exemplified by the growing hegemony (and possibly, global agenda) of the United States: anti-communism, free enterprise, and Christianity. He, perhaps more than any other religious leader, has demonstrated how effectively a religious organization can operate as an entrepreneurial business enterprise with political objectives; and how, in spite of small membership, the Unification Church can accumulate vast amounts of wealth and power in strategic areas of the globe.

Moon's operations are in a different league than the reasonably large-scale broadcasting/evangelizing business of American Christian entrepreneur Pat Robertson, which generated over $200 million in sales in 1987. In Moon's more varied, much larger and murkier portfolio, the profits alone, not sales, were likely to exceed that amount, if ever one could find a way to account for them. One scholar who has often written sympathetically about the church alludes to this mystery:

> One might, indeed, view Unification-related businesses, were they to be regarded as a single entity, as comprising a not inconsiderable multinational corporation. No one outside the movement has been able to work out precisely where all the money in the so-called "Moon Empire" comes from or goes to.[71]

Just to get an idea of the size and reach of this empire, consider just a few figures related to money raised in the 1980s: $20 million per year income within the United States; about $122 million annually from Japan, 90 percent of which was exported to other countries (including $800 million to the U.S. over a nine-year period); nearly $10 million in direct yearly profits from Korean industries, including Tong'il Industries, the armaments producer. By 1990, the church was credited with owning ten banks in Uruguay; other fresh funds were flowing to China, where the People's Republic had approved a $250 million investment in a new automobile factory.[72] Recent U.S. investments have included shared ownership of the Nostalgia Network on nationwide cable television and an interest-free $50.5 million loan that gained the church financial control of the bankrupt University of Bridgeport in Connecticut.[73] As of 1993, one investigator estimated "that the movement controls over $10 billion worth of business assets worldwide."[74]

The Unification Church's justification for its preoccupation with building up its wealth sounds remarkably similar to prosperity theology; an excerpt from a training manual tries to correct misinformed Christians:

> Christians think the Messiah must be poor and miserable. He did not come for this. Messiah must be the richest. Only he is qualified to have dominion over things. Otherwise, neither God nor Messiah can be happy.[75]

But unlike the charismatic "faith" churches, the Unification Church is not preoccupied with channeling prosperity back to individual members; quite the contrary. Individualism is discouraged and unselfish service to the

"Family," to the church under "Father" Moon, is paramount. Profits are plowed back into the "family" businesses.

In addition to investing in profit-making enterprises, the Unification Church spends large sums on political and journalistic activities. Since 1982 the church has continuously sustained multimillion-dollar annual losses at its influential right-wing newspaper, *The Washington Times*.[76] The paper was Ronald Reagan's main source of journalistic information during his presidency; it also served as the front organization for the Nicaraguan Freedom Fund, a nonprofit charity that raised $14 million for the Contra War when Congress denied the Reagan administration that amount of money in 1985. The Church has also produced other ultra-conservative newspapers that steadily lose money, including the *New York Tribune, Noticias del Mundo* (New York), *Ultimas Noticias* (Uruguay), *Middle East Times* (Crete), and *World Daily News* (Japan).[77]

Such activities, in which religious motivation is combined with the political will to counter leftist influences around the globe, are certainly not limited to the Unification Church. The fight against satanic communism has long been fertile soil for American evangelists who want to raise money, prove their patriotic mettle, or simply perform their Christian/American duties on the world stage. For example, Jimmy Swaggart's and Pat Robertson's efforts on behalf of the Nicaraguan Contras and the right-wing governments in Guatemala and El Salvador were substantial in the 1980s. And Robertson's Christian Broadcasting Network gives him the ability to interpret the news as he sees fit. However, his activities, and those of other American preachers, pale alongside Moon's ambitious range of networking apparatuses, which begin with very explicit, confrontational political organizations and end with seemingly non-ideological intellectual/scholarly associations.

On the political side, the Unification Church has spawned dozens of organizations.[78] The most prominent, CAUSA, has chapters and affiliates in many countires. CAUSA has mustered considerable right-wing cohesion within Central America, backed the legislative ambitions of a whole slate of conservative politicians in Brazil (fifty seven candidates in the 1986 elections), supported rebel activities against the leftist government of Angola, enlisted the vice president of the Philippines and his wife as spokespeople, actively assisted Low Intensity Conflict indoctrination in a number of countries, and otherwise been a very influential component of the World Anti-Communist League.[79] Concentrating mostly on geopolitical struggle, CAUSA only occasionally touches theological matters, referring to "Godism" as an antidote to Marxism.

CAUSA spends little time on evangelizing, being content to fight communism and socialism and other revolutionary movements in concert with whatever religious beliefs are held by its right-wing associates in any particular country. Within the church, however, leaders and theologians have emphasized that Godism is part and parcel of Unificationism, and it necessitates a global authoritarian theocracy ruled by the True Father, Reverend Moon. Godism is by nature undemocratic, wrote Chun Hwan Kwak in a church missionary magazine:

> Godism, however, has not been the majority idea. God's teaching has not been the majority teaching. Therefore through democratic elections, people have not selected God's will, goodness, True Parents, or the messiah. Our goal and purpose is to follow Godism.[80]

For more amplification of Church doctrine and its ultimate societal implications, one can look to church theoreticians who are removed from direct political activities; one leading thinker, San Hun Lee, laid out the ultimate social and theological goals of the movement in his 1985 book, *The End of Communism:*

> [the goal is] the eradication of Communism and the final synthesis of all sciences and philosophies under Unification Thought as the basis of a new world order.[81]

Within the United States, the Unification Church pursued an interesting course of influence building among the new Christian right, where it convinced a number of important political and religious operatives that its theology is substantially Christian (or at least not threatening) and that its money is acceptable (or, at least, that one can accept the money without endorsing the theology). Until the late 1980s, when their funding from U.S. sources began to wane, many new right leaders had stayed clear of Moon's organizations (not all did; Terry Dolan's National Conservative Action coalition collected $750,000 in 1984[82]).

By 1987, however, "conservative strategist and fund-raising genius" Richard Viguerie faced impending bankruptcy and was bailed out by Moon's top U.S. aide, Bo Hi Pak, in order to start the American Freedom Coalition, which promoted the direct alliance of the conservative Christian lobby, Christian Voice, with Moon organizations. Even evangelicals who had previously taken offence at Unification theology were won over: Ron Godwin, a former vice president of Jerry Falwell's Moral Majority, had attacked another American fundamentalist leader in 1984 for taking "Moon money," condemning him for accepting "support from a church whose founder believes he's divine." In 1986, Godwin joined *The Washington Times* as senior vice president and began acting as an "emissary to conservative Christian leaders."[83]

In the case of influencing the Christian Right, Moon and his deputies have great amounts of money to spend, but they do not usually demand public recognition or support for their theology, nor do they necessarily demand control over the message or the messenger, especially in the religious/cultural realm. For the Unification Church it can be a victory simply that their money is accepted. Howard Ruff, founder of influential conservative PAC "Free the Eagle," commented on the phenomena in 1987: "It's a brilliant plan to gain influence, prestige, and power, because Moon doesn't have to convert you to succeed."[84]

The Unification Church and its organizations have sought influence in the realm of journalistic, cultural, and academic circles that deal with politics and economics by sponsoring meetings and junkets. Journalists have been treated to group excursions to global hotspots or gathered for large, broadly based World Media Conferences. The church also supports academic conferences and scholarship; when the subject is economics or politics the personnel are generally conservative, free-market anti-communists who favor American geopolitical aims. The papers are often presented by retired American senior military and diplomatic officers, or by stalwart Asian members of the Professors for World Peace Academy. (PWPA is the organization through which the Unification Church purchased the University of Bridgeport in Connecticut in 1993; the organization represents several thousand scholars.) These contributions are published in a "PWPA Book" series through the church-owned Paragon House Publishers in New York City. Recent titles from the late 1980s, for instance, were: *Taiwan in a Time of Transition* (which, among other things, tries to explain and justify the transition form "hard" authoritarianism to "soft" authoritarianism); *Chinese Economic Policy*; *Political Change in South Korea*; and *The Strategic Triangle: China, The U.S., and The Soviet Union*.

Also working in the political realm is The Washington Institute for Values in Public Policy, funded with about $1.5 million per year for conferences and publications. The orientation of the institute is also toward conservative, anti-communist scholarship but offers more sophisticated treatment and allows for some dissenting viewpoints. For example, the institute's own press published *The Politics of Latin American Liberation Theology* in 1988; though most contributors were vigorous opponents of this left-leaning religious tendency, some offered more measured critiques emphasizing that the strength of liberation theology had been exaggerated, and one scholar who supported liberation theology was allowed.[85]

As Moon's search for legitimacy reaches into the cultural and theological realm, the sponsored discourse gets decidedly more liberal. Among the myriad church-funded organizations that are explicitly religious—such as the International Religious Foundation, the Religious Youth Service, Youth Seminar on World Religions, the Parliament for World Religions—the New ERA, or New Ecumenical Research Association, stands out. New ERA is dedicated to open scholarship and academic commentary on new religions, religious globalization, and the interpenetration of theological ideas that might "unify" world religions.

"New ERA Books" report the contributions that have been presented at various academic conferences sponsored by the church. Many volumes have been edited by very well-known scholars in the world of sociology and religion: *Religion and the Global Order*, edited by Roland Robertson and William R. Garrett, appeared in 1991; other volumes edited by Rodney Stark, Anton Shupe, Jeffrey Hadden, Bryan Wilson, and Joseph Fichter have appeared over the past ten years. Most of these books deal briefly with the Unification Church's point of view (one or two papers), but not always: a New ERA title called *World Religions and Global Ethics* (1989), seemingly a natural place to hear from a syncretist Christian viewpoint originating in the East, had no commentary on Unificationism.[86]

These scholarly activities proceed even though a millenarian Biblical worldview is certainly present in Unification teaching; the church has partaken heavily of the anti-communist Manicheanism that has featured post-World War II American fundamentalism:

> At the consummation of human history, both the heavenly side and the satanic side have come to operate on the world-wide level. Thus, the two worlds of democracy and Communism co-exist. But after the third world struggle the two worlds will be united. Seen from God's dispensation, the Third World War will inevitably take place. However, there are two ways for that war to be fought. First, the satanic world could be subjugated by a wholly internal fight through ideology. God does not desire judgment or destruction (Ezekial 33:14-16) but salvation. Thus he desires Satan to submit ideologically, and with the least amount of external sacrifice. If this fails, the satanic side will inevitably attack the heavenly side. The heavenly side must then defeat the satanic side by force.[87]

It is interesting to note how some conservative U.S. scholars, like Richard Rubenstein of the Washington Policy Institute, have translated the unification millenarian belief into a much more subtle explanation of benign "globalization" in religion and and societal relationships:

> As the growth of the Roman Empire rendered obsolete many of the earlier small communities based upon tribal and kinship bonds, so too the rise of Asia and the world marketplace calls for a new and more broadly based moral community than has previously existed. The rise of the Holy Spirit Association for the Unification of World Christianity and the teachings of Sun Myung Moon can be seen as an important response to that need.[88]

Such evalutions seldom deal with some important questions, such as how the structure of the Unification Church transcends common expectations of the religious "marketplace," even as practiced by televangelists and the religious right in the United States. The Unification Church has constructed a "chaebol" apparatus that is more business than religion, that merges authoritarian political objectives so completely with authoritarian business practices that no one can ultimately disentangle the spiritual, financial, and anti-communist connections that date back to the founding of the church in the 1950s.

Almost from the very beginning of the Unification Church, Reverend Moon recruited powerful lieutenants and formed invaluable liaisons in the world of politics and covert operations. In 1957, Bo Hi Pak—a Korean Army colonel, Korean CIA agent and assistant military attaché in Washington— joined the church and started directing many of its activities in the United States. This initiated a long and fruitful interaction between the church, militant ultraright groups around the world, and various government intelligence agents within Korea.[89] In the same year Moon founded a branch of the church in Japan, called Genri Undo, which ever since has performed three important support functions: it was the conduit for huge amounts of cash coming from Japan to Korea; it supported the Japanese branch of the World Anti-Communist League; and it provided close contact with ultraright Japanese business leaders.[90] Critics of the Unification Church in Korea are able to document a long history of direct involvement in harassment and intimidation, including violent attacks against its political opponents as well as against the wage laborers employed in its businesses.[91]

When the Tongil Industry Co., Ltd. (the largest manufacturing company owned by the Unification Church in South Korea) was beset by labor difficulties in 1987, it unleashed its own force: more than five hundred Kusadae attacked laborers as they staged a sit-in and inflicted many injuries on the workers. (Tongil is a weapons manufacturer and is named after T'ong-il-gyo, the short name for the Unification Church in Korean.)[92]

A different kind of gathering was met by similar violence on October 18, 1987, when "250 Moonie thugs" attacked speakers and beat priests at the Sekwong Church because they were holding a seminar on the Unification Church that was expected to be critical.[93] The Unification Church's use of violence is not only understandable within the Korean context, but also within the context of the Reverend Moon's view of the shortcomings of contemporary political societies. In 1983, he said:

> The more democratic a society is, the more serious the collapse of its traditional value system appears to be. This shows that democracy is failing to provide solutions to the problems facing our societies and the world.[94]

Korean Derivatives and the New Fundamentalism

On one level the Unification Church is tiny and does not appear very threatening to anyone: there probably were never more than two hundred thousand members worldwide, and the U.S. membership never came close to its goal of reaching thirty thousand faithful. In fact, many observers believe the number of adherents within the United States has declined substantially. When Reverend Moon was imprisoned for tax evasion in the United States, he won considerable support from both conservative and liberal Church groups who were concerned about threats to religious freedom (and possibly to the freedom of other "nonprofit" religious entrepreneurs, no matter what their persuasion, to raise money); however, this should not be construed as proof of his power.[95]

However, the remarkable wealth, influence, and breadth of activities of the Unification Church demand attention. As Eileen V. Barker has put it:

> Reverend Moon's most telling achievement lies not in the changes he has wrought in the lives of Unificationists…it lies, rather, in the networks that he and his followers have organized throughout those structures and cultures that lie beyond the boundaries of the Unification Church.[96]

The possibilities open to this new derivative of Christianity suggest that church structure, church businesses and concerns, and church belief systems may be greatly altered by the effect of new American fundamentalism taking root in other parts of the world. The new fundamentalism not only is free to grow or metamorphasize outside of U.S. borders, but it can also return to the United States in its new form.

In the case of Reverend Moon's religion, the Biblical inerrancy that we usually associate with Christian fundamentalists is somewhat lacking (although dispensational interpretations are still important), and there is more interest in intellectual exchange with other Christian traditions and other world religions than is shown by most of the religious right in the U.S. Within this church that operates like a giant chaebol, closely controlled by its "family" owners, it is difficult to ascertain which of the many tentacles and interests, spiritual and material, are most important. What is most striking in terms of fundamentalist Americanism is the degree to which American civil religion, in particular twentieth-century anti-communism as a central belief and driving force, has been grasped by Moon and embodied in the beliefs and activities of the Church. By the nature of Korea's special place on the battle line of the Cold War, the Church has been able to develop the eschatological confrontation between God and Satan into a global struggle between U.S./Korean Christian righteousness (and Manifest Destiny) and global communism. This is a special version of the fundamentalist connection to civil religion noted by Robertson and Chirico in respect to globalization and religious resurgence:

> the rise of the new fundamentalist Right can be seen as an attempt on the part of adherents to a particular world-view to establish their position as the civil religion of America (and American civil religion as the civil religion of the world).[97]

Not only has Moon seized upon this aspect of civil religion and made it global, or "unificationist," instead of merely American, but he has also managed to directly insert himself in the middle of the right-wing American theologization of politics and then provide some real "unification," at least through his substantial organizational and funding apparatus. Perhaps the instrumental services that he renders through his parachurch apparatus are more important than his church itself. By coming from the outside, from Korea, Moon entered the American scene with an agenda that was so acceptable to those of the Christian right that they overcame their theological doubts and disregarded the foreign elements of unification thought. The acceptance of Moon not only proves the strength of his funding largesse but, more importantly, indicates the primacy of anti-communism as a central binding value of the new fundamentalism.

In terms of Moon's elaborate and secretive relationships with authoritarian governments and political influences, it is not particularly clear who was using whom most effectively. The extremely powerful head of the Korean CIA, Kim Jong Pil, probably saw the Reverend Moon as his pawn; he thought that "the Unification Church should be organized satisfactorily to be utilized as a political tool whenever he and KCIA needed it." On the other hand, Moon's calculation was that if he was "serving the government, the government would be serving him."[98]

It is clear that Moon's authoritarian religion fits in rather nicely with the authoritarian goals of the state, and vice versa. The Unification Church features a psychological authority structure based on a father figure, dictatorial control exercised through the closely held ownership of assets, and precisely designated roles of good and evil. Such a structure seems ideally suited to helping merge fundamentalist belief and repressive political action in the late twentieth century.

SEVEN

Christianity in Liberia

*L*iberia is a small West African state with a lengthy evangelical Christian tradition.[1] The Protestant religion arrived with the first American slaves who were repatriated to Liberia in 1822 as part of a scheme of the American Colonization Society. Over the next forty years twelve thousand colonists settled there, until the American Civil War effectively stopped colonization. Also settled were fifty-seven hundred Africans who had been freed from their transport ships before they could be delivered into slavery. Today the descendants of ex-slaves, Americo-Liberians, form a small but dominant group in a nation of 2.5 million; the majority of the population (the Afro-Liberians) belong to sixteen principal tribes that never left Africa. In 1870 the Americo-Liberians created a political party, the True Whig Party, that ruled the country for over one hundred years. Liberia was a one-party, Christian state. When the party was dissolved in 1980, the president of the country was the chairman of the Liberian Baptist convention, the vice president was bishop of the United Methodist Church, and the chairman of the True Whig Party was the moderator of the Presbyterian Church.

Liberia was notoriously corrupt. In the 1927 election the victor was credited with two hundred forty-three votes and his opponent nine thousand, when the total electorate comprised no more than fifteen thousand. In other words, the winner's tally was more than sixteen times greater than the number of possible voters. This election has the title in the *Guinness Book of Records* of the "most bent" election of all time.[2] The rule of the True Whigs over the indigenous (Afro-Liberian) peoples was oppressive. Government forced labor was common and so open that in 1930 the League of Nations sent a commission to investigate reports of slave trading on the part of Liberian government officials. Officials used to round up youth in the interior and ship them to the plantations on the Spanish island of Fernando Po (now part of Equatorial Guinea) in a practice hardly distinguishable from slavery. A damning report publicized these abuses to the world in 1931 and recommended that Liberia be stripped of its independence and placed under a League of Nations mandate. The president and vice-president were forced to resign, as was the postmaster general, who was a ringleader in recruitment. There is some validity in the claim that it was very selective to single out Liberia for this crime; the U.S. State Department, which instigated the report, deliberately avoided annoying Spain in the inquiry. Nonetheless, the episode highlights the attitude of the ruling Americo-Liberians toward the local tribes.

The arrival of the Firestone corporation in 1926 began a new era for Liberia. Firestone, as part of a U.S. attempt to break the British monopoly on rubber in Malaya, was granted a lease of a million acres for ninety-nine years at six cents an acre, and at Harbel it established the world's largest rubber plantation. After Firestone came several multinational companies, tempted by what Liberia called its "Open-door" policy, led by iron-ore mining companies from America, Germany, and Sweden. Throughout the 1950s Liberia's growth rate was higher than that of any other country except Japan; between 1952 and 1957 it was about 15 percent a year. But the growth benefited a small number of foreign companies whose profits were largely repatriated. Nearly three out of every four dollars that Firestone made in Liberia were transferred to the United States. Between 1962 and 1973 the American-controlled National Iron Ore Company shipped nearly $300 million worth of ore out of the country; the Liberian share over a 16-year period around this time was $2.5 million. This very little benefit came to Liberia from this theoretical boom. As late as the 1960s the country had only ten miles of paved road.

The open-door policy is associated with the presidency (1944-71) of William V. S. Tubman, under whom the patronage state reached its limit. Under him the cult of the presidency attained its peak; he subverted every institution of society to enhancing it. He had a presidential yacht whose budget was greater than that for the country's justice system, and at one state inaugeration the appropriation for ceremonial bands surpassed the expenditure on public health.[3]

Tubman was succeeded by his vice-president, William Tolbert, who responded to pressure for change, political liberalization, and a curb on corruption. But members of his own family were among the prime offenders in the area of corruption. In 1979, as chairman for the year, Tolbert was to host the annual conference of the Organization of African Unity. He spent $100 million in constructing a conference center, and not long afterward announced that the price of rice would have to be raised. (It was not lost on the population that the Tolbert family, as the country's biggest rice producers, would derive most benefit from such an increase.) This was the final straw, and on April 14, 1979 rioting broke out with widespread looting. Order was restored, but the political scene steadily deteriorated till on April 12, 1980, a group of seventeen enlisted men overthrew the government, killing Tolbert and twenty-five others.

Staff Sergeant Samuel Doe, as the highest ranking among the seventeen, was declared chairman of the People's Redemption Council, which took over the government. Initially, this coup was immensely popular. However, by 1983 Doe had lost all popular support. The general feeling was that the system was unchanged (as Liberians said, "Same taxi, different driver") and, if anything, controlled by someone even more corrupt and inept than previous rulers. Doe set in motion the return to civilian rule, but totally manipulated the process (utilizing state funds, buying off opposition figures, making it a felony of the first degree to criticize him in the election campaign). Even so, on election day of October 15, 1985, after an enormous turnout for the elections, preliminary counting showed that he was losing, so in the early hours of October 16 counting was halted, and (against all the procedures laid down) all ballot boxes were ordered to be brought to Monrovia for counting. Doe set up a "non-partisan and broadly representative" committee to count the votes—a committee stacked with tribesmen and supporters. Doe issued orders that soldiers should arrest and flog anyone predicting that the opposition had won the elections. When the "official" results were announced on October 29, Doe was credited with 50.9 percent in the four-way race for the presidency, a result, claimed the head of the Elections Commission, "directed by the hand of God." The gloom that descended on Liberia that day has been compared to the national gloom and stupefaction that came over the United States the day President Kennedy was assassinated.[4]

The elections were barely over, the opposition parties were still protesting, when on November 12, 1985 a coup was attempted by Thomas Quiwonkpa, one of Doe's associates in the 1980 coup. Quiwonkpa had been a popular figure, continuing to live with fellow soldiers rather than adopt the luxury of power, and, through his constant harangues against corruption and insistence on speedy return to civilian rule, he had made himself popular with civilians as well. He was commanding general of the Armed Forces when, in November 1983, his popularity led to his dismissal by Doe and he fled to the U.S. In the early morning of November 12, 1985, he announced over Liberia's national radio that Doe had been toppled. There was unrestrained jubilation and dancing in the streets, and almost a carnival atmosphere. But the coup leaders did not go for the jugular and attack the executive mansion itself, nor did they take control over the total communication system. Later in the day

Doe came on the radio to announce that he was still in charge. The coup lost its momentum then, and army reinforcements arrived to stamp out the last traces of revolt. Unfortunately for many, the dancing in the streets earlier in the day had been recorded on video. Now reprisals began against those who had rejoiced. For days killings occurred at the executive mansion, and truckloads of bodies were buried at night. Reprisals took place in Nimba County, where support for the opposition and for Quiwonkpa was strongest. Also, because Quiwonkpa had indicated that he was not interested in power for himself but in turning over the government to the political opposition, Doe rounded up all the leadership of the opposition parties; some were still in detention months later. The unfortunate result of this failed coup was that it dissipated the protest over the stolen election and thus entrenched Doe more firmly.

This was the situation in Liberia when the Second Republic was launched on January 6, 1986, with the inauguration of President Samuel K. Doe. However, the return to civilian rule was a fiction. The Second Republic was simply the perpetuation of the old military government in a new guise; the president was the former master sergeant, in a three-piece suit rather than battle fatigues. More importantly, the Second Republic was just the First Republic renamed. Doe claimed that his regime constituted a new social order, and that his only opponents were those with vested interests in the old order who wanted to turn the clock back. But nothing had changed since the Tubman/Tolbert days, except that in many respects the regime was more blatant in its abuses and more inept. Under Doe's oppressive and incompetent rule, health and education deteriorated, and the infrastructure collapsed. Corruption reigned supreme. This was the situation when on Christians Eve 1989 Charles Taylor launched the rebellion that led to the assassination of Doe on September 10, 1990, and to the total destruction of Liberia. The war was still unresolved as of this writing. Even were peace to be swiftly achieved, it would take generations to repair the destruction of the civil war.

A U.S. Colony

In geopolitical terms, Liberia was a client state—one might say a colony—of the U.S. There is some irony in this because the United States was very late in recognizing its offspring; in the first decades it offered little but neglect to its repatriate slaves. In this century, however, the U.S. forged such close links with Liberia that their relationship was almost symbiotic. Firestone and other U.S. firms made great investments in Liberia. The U.S. built up strategic interests. Robertsfield International Airport outside Monrovia was built by the U.S. as a military airfield, and the U.S. had landing and refueling rights for military planes on 24 hours' notice. Monrovia's port, too, was a U.S. military project. The U.S. had in Liberia its Voice of America transmitters for Africa and the Middle East, the CIA intelligence relay system for the whole continent, and the Omega tracking station, one of only a handful around the world that monitor the movement of all ships and airplanes.[5] Besides these commercial and strategic interests to protect, as Africa's colonies moved to independence, many of them committed to socialism, the U.S. needed a proxy among these black nations that could promote the American viewpoint ("a voice of moderation"). For all these reasons, the U.S. wanted a stable government of unwavering loyalty and support.[6]

In return for this support, the U.S. was prepared to ignore the rampant corruption, mismanagement, and injustice, and the neglect, if not oppression, of the majority of the population. So U.S. Vice President Humphrey could describe Tubman, in a tribute after his death, as "a man who devoted a good part of his life to the development and welfare of his country.... Liberia stands today as a living monument to his labors. He died a statesman, a great President, and a beloved human being. The world mourns his absence and praises his achievements which stand stalwart against the tide of time."[7] Likewise President Carter, on his stopover in Liberia in 1978, spoke fulsomely of Liberia as a place where "individual human freedom" and "the liberty of the human soul" flourished. He said how impressed he was by "how much (Tolbert) knew intimately and personally about the needs of the average citizen in Liberia."[8] Of course, such tributes disguised the true reality, but were judged necessary if the U.S. was to keep its strategic interests, repatriate its profits, and keep its loyal proxy in international gatherings.

Interestingly, it was during the later Tolbert years that Liberia seemed to be gaining some degree of independence. Whereas Tubman had always offered diplomatic excuses to Soviet invitations—in 1950 he was simply told by the U.S. State Department not to go[9] —Tolbert had by mid-1972 established full diplomatic relations with Romania and the Soviet Union. Then in rapid succession, links were established with Czechoslovakia, Hungary, Poland, East Germany, North Korea, and Cuba. In February 1977 Tolbert established diplomatic relations with the People's Republic of China, and consequently lost any link with Taiwan.[10] In June 1978 he visited Peking. Tolbert justified this major shift in Liberia's foreign relations, saying that his policy involved "genuine non-alignment" and "forging new friendships" while "strengthening existing ties."[11] Along with these new links, Tolbert was prepared to sever relations with Israel in 1973 in keeping with an Organization of African Unity decision. He also donated money to African liberation movements. All these were indications of a growing independence from the U.S.

After the coup, it seemed that Liberia was moving toward full independence and genuine non-alignment. But because of Liberia's isolation (out of distaste for the excesses of Doe's coup) and because of a collapsing economy, Liberia was pressured more and more to return to its "special relationship" with the U.S. This reversed the trend of the Tolbert years, and made Liberia a U.S. puppet as never before. Those with independent views began to be weeded out of the military government. Libyan diplomats were expelled in May 1981. In August 1983 Liberia became the second Black African state (after Zaire) to resume diplomatic ties with Israel. Doe made a state visit to Jerusalem in September 1983 (the first by an African leader since 1971). Doe called on the rest of Africa to "adopt a new and constructive attitude to Israel."[12] In October 1983 the Soviet ambassador was expelled for alleged collusion in an anti-government conspiracy, and in July 1985 the Doe regime severed relations with Moscow altogether for alleged links with student activists. Liberia rejected Polisario's claim to recognition as the sole representative of the people of Western Sahara, supporting Morocco's claim instead. Doe became a defender of U.S. policy in international meetings—for example at the 1986 meeting of the Non-Aligned Movement in Harare, after which he was commended by Reagan.

In return for returning so faithfully to the U.S. fold, Doe was amply rewarded. First, he was awarded a full state visit to Washington in 1982 (where Reagan welcomed him as "Chairman Moe"). And when he returned to address the United Nations General Assembly in 1983, Reagan met him again in New York, and described him as "a dependable ally—a friend in need."[13] More important, though, Doe received aid, both military and civil. From a level of $20 million in 1979, by 1985–86 the level of U.S. aid had grown to over $90 million. In his first five years Doe received roughly half a billion dollars; Liberia was receiving more U.S. aid per capita than any other African nation, such aid constituting over one-third of the nation's budget. Between 1980 and 1985 Washington gave Doe $52 million in military aid.[14] Military aid to Liberia decreased afterwards, but that indicated no dissatisfaction with Doe. For U.S. military policy, Africa was the very lowest priority, and military aid to Africa was slashed from $147.6 million in fiscal year 1985 to $25.25 million in 1988—a decrease of 83 percent. Liberia was simply affected by this general policy.[15]

In return for coming back to the fold, the U.S. was very accommodating to Doe's shortcomings. Initially Washington hoped that elections would take place as scheduled and that a civilian government would duly come to power in January 1986. But the U.S. made little effort to use its influence to push for human rights and freedoms. Quite the contrary. All observers recognized that Doe had stolen the 1985 election.[16] But Reagan sent Doe a congratulatory telegram, hailing the election of October 15, 1985: "On that date, the people of Liberia expressed their strong commitment to civilian democratic rule."

That is true, but that expression had immediately been trampled on by the very man Reagan was congratulating.[17]

Two months later, Assistant Secretary of State Chester Crocker, while admitting to some "shortcomings," praised what he said were "noteworthy accomplishments" in the elections.[18] Similarly, in his remarks about the November coup attempt, Crocker obscured both the scale of the abuses and who was responsible.[19] Crocker went on to describe the outlook for Liberia's Second Republic in a manner that can only be described as cynical: "There is in Liberia today a civilian government based on elections, a multi-party legislature, a journalist community of government and non-government newspapers and radio stations, an on-going tradition among the citizenry of speaking out, a new Constitution that protects those freedoms, and a judicial system that can help enforce those provisions. The government is committed publicly to that system."[20] Similarly, Reagan's secretary of state, George Shultz, visited Liberia in 1987 and complimented the Doe regime: "There is freedom of the press here, there is an opposition, there are no political prisoners. So there is genuine progress."[21]

So it continued. U.S. aid was reduced from its peak, a greater percentage of the aid was channeled to NonGovernmental Organizations, and there were frequent appeals to improve the human rights record or face losing U.S. aid. The appeals came from Congress, but were ignored by the Reagan administration. The symbolic and ritualistic nature of these appeals became evident in mid-1989, when U.S. Representative Mervyn Dymally visited Liberia for a public affairs forum on "The Rule of Law in a Democratic Society." Dymally insisted that Liberia would have to give "clear signals" to Washington that it was serious about improving its record if it wanted to continue receiving aid. Such signals included: "the existence of a free press, free speech, free association, the observance of the rule of law, not only by the people but also by the government."[22] Two weeks later, Doe closed down indefinitely the Catholic radio station ELCM. The pretext was an ELCM news bulletin that announced that deaths had occurred at an accident at a soccer match; the real reason was obviously the independent character of its reporting. All the following week the Catholic Church, opposition parties, and local journalists protested at this abuse on the part of the government. On June 21 the *Daily Observer* carried on its front page more protests against the closure, and alongside the protests the news that the previous day Liberia had received a $9.5 million grant from the U.S.; at the signing ceremony, Doe had been praised for his "stalwart leadership and foresight."[23]

As Liberia under Doe received massive U.S. aid, many Liberians began to ask what the aid was for: was it to buy a compliant leader, or to further the development of the Liberian people? Clearly it was the former; Americans

chose dealing with a dictator over pressing for democatic rule. This was particularly evident when military aid was considered. In July 1987 the Liberian
army numbered fifty-three hundred, with a coast guard of four hundred fifty
and a paramilitary of two thousand. In 1987 it was announced that a separate
navy and air force were to be formed. Defense expenditure was estimated at
$37.7 million in 1986/87, or about 10 percent of total budget spending.[25] What
was this army for? Liberia had no external aggressors. Doe's only enemies
were his own people, and all this manpower, U.S. equipment and Israeli training were required solely to keep himself in power and his people in subjection.[26] More and more Liberians came to see the U.S. as the greatest single
support for the repressive regime under which they suffered. As an American
missionary, deported by Doe, explained to the U.S. Congress: Liberians "have
become entirely disillusioned with regard to America's much vaunted commitment to justice, truth, democracy and principled action (because) the support—both political and economic—forthcoming from the U.S.A is recognized universally as the single most potent influence perpetuating this dictatorial, corrupt, inept government in Liberia."[27]

The Role of Religion

The role of Christianity in Liberia is linked to Liberia's special history. When
the modern nation was founded by American slaves, large numbers of these
repatriates were Christians. The Christianity that had helped them endure
their bondage in the United States became a key component of the self-under-
standing of the Americo-Liberians who were to control Liberia. There was,
however, one significant change in this slave Christianity when it moved
from America to Liberia. Whereas in America the faith had given the slaves
identity and courage to survive under oppression, in the Liberian context
Christianity gave the small settlements of repatriates an identity distinct from
that of the tribal people inland. It contributed to the feelings of superiority
that led to Americo-Liberian oppression of the inland tribes.

Christianity became part of the structure of dominance. The Americo-
Liberian oligarchy presided over a monstrously unjust social system; and
Christianity was one of the key pillars on which the whole oppressive structure was built. One observer expresses it: "Belief in the Christian faith, membership of the Masonic Lodge, and Americo-Liberian background were the
prerequisites for admission into the oligarchy."[28] Another makes the point
slightly differently, although agreeing about the crucial role of Christianity:
"The professing of Christianity, the wearing of Western style dress, and the
use of the English language were the main cultural features differentiating the
Americo-Liberian community from the surrounding tribespeople, and became
the three chief characteristics of the Americo-Liberian way of life."[29]

This identification of Christianity with the structures of oppression was clear at the time of Doe's 1980 coup. As already mentioned, the three pillars of the establishment were the president, the vice-president, and the party chairman, who in turn were the heads of the three oldest churches, the Baptist, Methodist, and Presbyterian. They were also among the hardliners, determined not to give an inch, resolved to maintain their position whatever the cost.

But there was more. Christianity was not only structurally identified with the system; it also provided an ideology to explain events, to legitimize power, to justify True Whig dominance, and to mask the often sordid reality in high-flown Biblical rhetoric. In the nineteenth century, according to historian Amos J. Beyan, Christianity "enabled (Liberian leaders) to easily veil their political and other mistakes. No wonder Christian thoughts and values were encouraged, or, in some cases, made compulsory in Liberia."[30]

In the latter years of Tolbert's presidency, some of the mainline churches tried to distance themselves from the establishment and to be more vocal in denouncing the regimes's graft, corruption, and abuse of human rights. Some churchmen cooperated with opposition campaigns; some sat on government committees trying to introduce changes; some in their sermons denounced abuses. Some used their position to protect people from torture. The Baptists, Methodists, and Presbyterians joined the other historical denominations—the Lutherans and Catholics, neither of which had been quite part of the establishment, and the Episcopal Church, which in the twentieth century became even more identified with the ruling elite than the earlier churches—to form the Liberian Council of Churches. In the first years of Doe's regime the council made some courageous pronouncements, denouncing the government for intimidation, urging it to return to the rule of law, calling on Doe to stop arbitrary arrests, mysterious disappearances, and extrajudicial trials. They denounced abuses in the long runup to the 1985 elections. But by the mid-1980s the council was becoming less outspoken. Its effectiveness was diminished by scandals in the ranks of church leaders, and intimidation on the part of the government. Two churchmen, however, refused to be silenced: a leading Baptist, and the Catholic Archbishop of Monrovia, who continued to issue pastoral letters on abuses in Liberia.[31]

Besides the mainline churches, a sizeable group of Christians belonged to the Evangelical Fellowship of Liberia. This organization was dominated by such bodies as the Sudan Interior Mission (and its main Liberian subsidiary, the radio station ELWA), the Assemblies of God, the Worldwide Evangelization Crusade, the Carver Mission, the Christian Reformed Church, The Great Commission Movement of Liberia (Campus Crusade), Child Evangelism Crusade, Scripture Union, and the Bible Society. For the most part, the evangelical churches reacted against the close identification of the mainline churches with the establishment; they thus turned their back on "political involvement" of any sort, distinguishing their "Biblical Christianity" from the "political Christianity" of the mainline churches. This did not, however, make their Christianity non-political. Theirs was a solid vote for the status quo, an unfailing support for the beneficiaries of the system.[32]

The conscious decision to leave the social system unchallenged was completely political, and this was the stance Doe wanted the churches to adopt. Doe wanted all the churches to preach personal piety, resignation, obedience, peace, and avoidance of politics. A Ministry of Information press release of September 15, 1987 claimed: "In Africa today Liberia has an enviable record of stability, civil liberties as well as freedom of press, speech and religion. Indeed Liberians are proud that Dr. Samuel K. Doe emerged as President after a vigorous nationwide campaign, a national election based on universal suffrage, the adoption of a constitution based on a multi-party system, and a democratic government with three separate branches." The release went on to appeal "to religious bodies and others to continue to promote unity and peace in Liberia for the development and prosperity of the nation and its people."[33] The picture of Liberia painted by the Ministry of Information was, of course, a travesty; but Doe wanted Liberians to eschew political pronouncements,[34] and wanted to coopt the churches in bringing this situation about.

One of Doe's contentions was that the mainline churches, in their occasional and tentative political statements, were forsaking their properly religious role and creating confusion in the country.[35] Often the evangelical churches would echo Doe in this, in coded attacks on the mainline churches. Under the headline, "Leave Politics with Politicians—Church Leaders Urged," the *Daily Observer* reported on a sermon that urged "church leaders to perform their spiritual duties and leave politics with politicians." The preacher reminded "spiritual leaders who are out to politicize religious affairs that the passages in the Bible are mainly intended to win souls, saying that the passages are not intended to create confusion, disorder and destabilization."[36] Under a headline: "Religious Leaders Advised to Shun Politics," the *Herald* reported a church spokesman telling church leaders "to stop using the pulpit to express their political views and instead strive to win more souls to Christ."[37] Another *Daily Observer* story headlined "Preach the Gospel, not Politics" reported another pastor preaching the same message: "The Gospel preacher, like Jesus, tells the poor about hope and treasures that are beyond earthly riches. The poor with this hope remain calmly content within any tumultuous society. The preacher urges the literally poor to trust God and work industriously while on earth. The true preacher does not tell the poor to support chaos in the nation. The true solution for literal poverty is the peace that Christ gives.

This is the Gospel."[38]

An influential bishop of another church, at an ordination ceremony, was reported to have "urged Christian leaders to do away with discriminating acts and politicking. He admonished them to get on their feet for the total evangelization of Liberia."[39] The founder of the African Christian Fellowship in Liberia "called on Christians in the country to put aside their differences (politics) and embrace the Lord as their personal saviour." The Rev. Ernie Brown of the Baptist Fellowship Mission Agency in the U.S., the invited speaker at this African Christian Fellowship week-long convention, spread the same message. "The time has come for Liberians to put aside everything and seek God's blessings for peace and unity in the nation," a news account of Brown's talk said. "The American preacher stated that the responsibility of Christians was to go out and spread the Gospel of Jesus Christ."[40]

The attitude that Christians must withdraw from all political involvement was thus fairly widespread in Doe's Liberia. Obviously this quietism has many parallels in evangelical history; it was probably given a certain intensity from a conscious repudiation of the political manipulation of Christianity so common in Liberia's history. However, Liberia's evangelical Christianity was itself undergoing considerable modification throughout the 1980s as a result of huge growth in the number of charismatics. This transformation occurred in several ways, two of which can be illustrated here in some detail. The first was the process of affiliating with American charismatic churches.

Consider the following case. In 1984 Bishop Dixon was head of the Christ Pentecostal Church, with thirty-one churches and thirty-five preaching posts. This was the time of a particularly fierce recession in which many of his church members lost jobs. His revenue dried up; his building plans had to be abandoned. He took the route of writing to American churches, seeking a link. He received six replies, but (he claims) upon checking their doctrinal statements he found that five were not orthodox. He therefore did not pursue them, but chose the only orthodox candidate, Don Stewart Ministries of Phoenix, Arizona. Dixon travelled to the U.S. in 1986, and negotiations were completed by March 1987, when Dixon's church became the Don Stewart Christ Pentecostal Church. Don Stewart had taken over the ministry of A. A. Allen of Miracle Valley, Arizona, when Allen died in 1970. By 1989 Don Stewart had about fifteen hundred churches worldwide, known as Miracle Life Fellowship International.

This link certainly was a great boon to Dixon. Don Stewart's agencies began operating in Liberia on February 17, 1988. In September 1988 the newspapers published photos of a truck unloading powdered milk worth $17,250, and stated that the church was catering for eight thousand children at four centers in Monrovia. In August 1989 the church reconditioned a road in a

Monrovia suburb at a cost of $3,000. The newspaper account said that the church would soon tackle the suburb's problem of erosion along the beach, and stated that it had 2,700 pupils in its schools around the country. The 16-member Liberian delegation that returned from Don Stewart's international convention in Phoenix in October 1989 announced that it had received a $470,000 gift of textbooks. All this aid benefited the local church, and brought Bishop Dixon such prestige that other churches sought to join him.

But Don Stewart benefited too. When Don Stewart first visited his newly adopted Liberian church in 1989, there were three others in his party. One was the editor of his fund-raising magazine, the two others (not members of his church) were professional filmmakers. Dixon had acquired government permits for them to photograph in the most squalid areas of Monrovia, which they did. Don Stewart's fund-raising *Feed My People* magazine is noted for its photos of distended stomachs and emaciated limbs. Thus the link has the result that Don Stewart can more effectively raise funds back in the U.S., some of which find their way to Liberia.

Dixon's church, which had begun life as an offshoot of the Pentecostal Assemblies of the World, was originally a "Jesus only" or non-Trinitarian church. The merger with Don Stewart, a classic example of America's new charismatic "faith-Gospel" movement, has theoretically changed the theology of Dixon's church. In this case, though, the conscious rethinking required was minimal.

A second method through which charismatic Christianity spread was the Bible school. Consider the Monrovia Bible Training Center, run by a group of missionaries, all graduates of Kenneth Hagin's Rhema Bible Center of Tulsa, and linked to Jim Zirkle's Living Waters International in Guatemala. This ministry opened its doors in September 1987. The influence of this school rapidly became incalculable.

This training center functioned each Saturday, from 9 a.m. to 4 p.m., in a rented public secondary school. In the morning there were two hour-long lectures and an hour's worship; lunch was then provided; two more hour lectures followed in the afternoon. The year consisted of four terms of eight weeks, and the cycle of courses changed each term. For each course, set books and course outlines were distributed. Each course had an exam (twenty-six true/false questions). Students successfully completing one year received a certificate, and students who successfully completed the two-year course were given a diploma. Graduation ceremonies, held at Monrovia's Centennial Pavillion, in many ways eclipsed the graduation ceremonies of the University of Liberia. The total cost for a student was U.S. $56 a year in 1989. The school was operated very efficiently—procedures were spelled out and insisted on. Its first fully operational year was 1988–89; when it opened for the 1989–90 year, the number of students enrolled had reached 828.

The other schools in the Monrovia area are tiny in comparison. The Church of God Bible College had twenty-two students; the Seventh Day Adventists had four Liberian students; the Mid-Baptists had forty; the Carver Institute and College together had sixty-five; the Episcopal and Methodist evening schools had about twenty each; the Association of Independent Churches of Africa's School of Personal Evangelism had about twenty; the Baptist seminary had eighty-two; the United Pentecostal Church's Maranatha Bible College had about forty. Thus within the space of about three years, the Monrovia Bible Training Center had increased to train more than twice the number attending all the other schools put together.

Even more significant is a denominational breakdown of the training center's 828 students. They came from 183 denominations. These included all the historical denominations, Anglican, Catholic, Lutheran, Baptist, Presbyterian, Methodists, African Methodist Episcopalians, and Wesleyans. More importantly, they included scores of African Independent Churches, older ones like the Church of the Lord (Aladura) and newer ones like Bethel, Philadelphia, the Refuge Temple, the Four Square Gospel Church, the Salvation Church, Baffu Bay Pentecostal Church, the Trump of God International Church, Transcea, and countless others.

The 828 students included seventy-five pastors, most of them from small African Independent Churches. Such pastors were keenly aware of their lack of theological education, and this Saturday school that provided books was very attractive. Some churches used the center as training for at least some of their pastors; besides numerous independent churches, the AME Church followed this policy.

Nor was the influence of the training center limited to Monrovia. In September 1988 similar schools opened in Kakata and Gbarnga, with eighteen and thirty-one students respectively. Staff and students of the Monrovia Center conducted these schools one day each week, traveling by van. Then in September 1989 nine more schools were opened around the country, and operated in the same way. So by 1989, every major center in the country except for those in the two southeastern counties had a Bible school of this type. This is where the Monrovia training center probably exerted its greatest influence, molding the evangelists and pastors of the churches of the interior. Altogether about thirty pastors attended these eleven extension Bible training centers. Total enrollment of students in all twelve schools for 1989–90 was 1,153.

The theology of the Monrovia center and its subsidiaries was the pure "faith theology" of Hagin and Copeland. The set books distributed in the fourth term of 1988–89 were Copeland's *Sensitivity of Heart, The Force of*

Righteousness, The Decision Is Yours, You Are Healed; Kenneth Hagin's *The Believer's Authority*; and *Courage,* by Ed Louis Cole, another prosperity proponent. The books distributed for the first term of 1989 were Copeland's *Our Covenant Making God,* and *A Ceremony of Marriage*; Hagin's *Understanding How to Fight the Good Fight of Faith, New Thresholds of Faith,* and *Don't Blame God*; Ed Louis Cole's *The Potential Principle: Living Life to Its Maximum*; and Billy Joe Daugherty's *The New Life*.[41] In the first year at all twelve schools the following courses were offered: Faith, Obedience, Blood Covenant, Healing, Authority, Demonology, and Christian Stewardship.

Thus the theology of Tulsa's Rhema Bible Center found its way into 183 different denominations. The seventy-five pastors took it back to their congregations, and this message spread even more widely. Liberian law made provision for the Bible to be taught in public schools. Often this was not done, because there was no one to teach it. (The mainline and historical evangelical churches gave this little priority.) The Monrovia Bible Training Center proposed to the Ministry of Education that their students and graduates do this teaching; the Ministry agreed, on the grounds that the center was non-denominational. So 110 of its students and graduates taught the Bible every week to twenty-one thousand pupils.[42] In 1988 the director brought one hundred fifteen thousand copies of various publications from the U.S. as support literature. In two years, he claimed Living Water Teaching had distributed sixty thousand tracts, two thousand Gospel portions, twenty thousand elementary level children's magazines and booklets, twenty-five thousand junior and senior high books, and more than seven thousand teaching books.[43] These publications for schools all expounded the faith gospel, and included Billy Joe Daugherty's *This New Life,* and *Honeycomb, the Family Magazine* from Willie George Ministries, of which one issue concerned banishing sickness, which comes from Satan.[44] At the Monrovia center's graduation ceremony on May 31, 1989, the director of religious instruction in the public school system spoke and thanked the center for its contribution; in the course of his remarks he urged the Liberian Council of Churches to "forget about politics and raise money for the center to spread the Gospel through Liberia."

Moreover, the center's staff were invited to speak at various churches around the country. The series of talks given to launch the Lutheran Good Samaritan organization in May 1989 were all given by the center's staff, and they preached on Sundays at various churches. The MBTC team exerted their influence not just individually the center was institutionally linked with Bethel World Outreach Center, which was one of the fastest-growing churches in the country.[45] The Bethel pastor had his office with the Monrovia center's office, and he taught the stewardship course at the center. This pastor was Liberian, but had spent ten years studying at Oral Roberts University in

Tulsa, Oklahoma. He too preached the faith gospel of health, wealth, and miracles.

The center had institutional links, too, with the Liberia Fellowship of Full Gospel Ministers; the director of the center was the driving force behind setting up the fellowship. This fellowship had as its aims: "1. To provide an opportunity for denominational Full Gospel ministers to meet and interact with independent Full Gospel Ministers. 2. To sponsor an annual Camp meeting/Convention that will bring together Full Gospel Churches and Christians for several days of spiritual retreat and revival. 3. To promote unity and strength for the purpose of winning Liberia, deterring the spread of false religions and cults in this nation."[46] In establishing the fellowship, great effort was made to include as many influential churchmen as possible. At the ceremony marking the formation of the Liberia Fellowship of Full Gospel Ministers, the American AME bishop preached, and the superintendent of the Assemblies of God inducted the office bearers. Among the five office bearers were the director of the Monrovia Bible Training Center and the pastor of Bethel (as well as an assistant at a UMC church who has attended Copeland's seminars in Britain).

Christian Zionism and the Muslim Threat

One aspect of Liberia's charismatic Christianity that deserves special mention is Christian Zionism. It stems from the dispensationalist understanding that many Biblical prophecies refer to the modern state of Israel. This generally leads its exponents to give uncritical support to Israel at all times. Lester Sumrall, for example, who visited Liberia to be a major speaker at Monrovia's "Jesus Festival '89", argues that America's refusal to support Britain, France, and Israel in their 1956 attack on Suez caused the decline of America: "What has become of the United States since 1956? Note carefully, we have lost the last two wars we have fought, in Korea and Vietnam. Our society has begun to fall apart rapidly. Violent rebellion broke out on our college campuses. The drug problem, sexual sin, and divorce have exploded. Our economy has become far less stable and far more vulnerable to foreign competition. All these things may seem unrelated on the surface, but that is not the case. It is not a coincidence that these problems erupted after our desertion of Israel in 1956."[47]

Zionism has come to occupy a crucial place in American Christianity. It spans all sectors—Fundamentalists like Falwell, neoPentecostals like Robertson, Southern Baptists like Criswell, and has even permeated the mainline churches through the charismatic movement. The Christian media networks all disseminate it. And, despite the Biblical references adduced in its support, the spread of this Zionism is a product of contingencies in America's recent history. Geopolitically, Israel has functioned as a proxy for furthering American interests in the Middle East; Christian Zionism provides a religious justification for pursuing these interests.

The obverse side of this fervent Zionism is a marked hostility to the Arab cause and Islam. When this Christianity comes to Africa, the anti-Islamic element becomes tremendously important.[48] In Liberia, relations between Christians and Muslims were traditionally fairly amicable. Partly this is explicable because, whatever their numbers, the Muslims were woefully underrepresented in positions of influence or power.[49] This is attributable mainly to their comparative lack of education. But in the 1980s, with an influx of money from Kuwait and Saudi Arabia, the Muslim community began to assume a higher profile. Another complicating factor had nothing to do with religion at all; this was a shift in economic strength. In Doe's Liberia, an estimated 70–80 percent of the retail and wholesale trade was controlled by the Lebanese, many of whom were Muslims. But more significantly, two tribes were emerging into economic prominence. The Mandingos enjoyed almost a monopoly in the transport business, and also in rural retail shops. The Fulahs, French-speaking and not Liberians at all, began to dominate the nation's taxis—seemingly Liberia's one lucrative business. Their economic ascendancy was resented, and because both were Muslim tribes, the resentment on commercial grounds took on religious overtones. There were signs, too, that Doe's government was not loath to stir up these religious tensions for political gain. Dr. Caine, chairman of Doe's National Democratic Party, in September 1989 alleged that the Unity Party had promised to make Liberia an Islamic state. The Unity Party quickly rejected the allegation as "infantile propaganda."[50]

In opposing Islam, a clear divide exists between the mainline and non-mainline churches. The mainline churches, in theory if not always in practice, accept Islam as a valid monotheistic religion. This does not commit them to the view that all religions are equal, but it does enable them to respect Islamic doctrines as valuable insights into the nature of ultimate reality, and to respect Islamic practices as significant responses to that reality. As Liberia's Catholic Archbishop Michael Francis, half of whose family are Muslims, publicly stated, "We worship the same God." The Catholic weekly *Herald* published several official documents on the nature of Christian-Muslim dialogue.[51] The Liberian Council of Churches actually initiated such dialogues.

However, the non-mainline churches regard this attitude as a denial of basic Christianity. In September 1985 Archbishop Francis's statement drew a lengthy series of rebuttal. The American expatriate missionaries were most vocal about the Muslim threat; the directors of the Monrovia Bible Training Center seemed incapable of speaking without insisting that Liberia is a Christian country and must be preserved against the Muslim threat. At their commencement ceremonies on May 31, 1989 the two people who gave personal testimonies as part of the ceremony had both been Muslims. To great applause they explained how they had come to be saved.[52] The previous year's graduation had also featured testimony from a Muslim convert.[53] The Liberian Fellowship of Full Gospel Ministers had as its third objective: "To promote unity and strength for the purpose of winning Liberia, deterring the spread of false religions and cults in this nation"—code for combating Islam.[54]

Among Liberian pastors (even mainline church leaders) a curious double standard was evident. The fact that Kuwait and Saudi Arabia were sending money and missionaries into Liberia was taken as evidence of something sinister; the fact that Christian money and missionaries kept Liberia operating seemed quite natural. Similarly with media programs—the fact that even one Muslim program was introduced on TV (there were at least seven Christian programs) was taken to indicate that the Muslim director of ELTV was trying to eliminate all Christian TV.

This is not a purely theological issue, but is linked with the American origins of much missionary Christianity. That this attitude stems from America's preoccupation with the Middle East is confirmed by the fact that Islam has been accorded a special status among "other religions." A "world prayer missionaries' map" produced by a California ministry and found in some Liberian churches illustrates this.[55] The world is divided into countries that are "mostly free" (51 percent), Communist (33 percent), Marxist-socialist ("leaning towards communism") (2 percent) and Muslim (14 percent). Logically, there is no basis for distinguishing Muslim countries from Buddhist, Shinto, or Hindu countries. According to evangelical theology, all are on the same footing; all are equally lost without Jesus. But Muslim countries are given a special category, the others are not. The grounds of this division are obviously not religious but political. The distinction being made in the map is between U.S. allies (the "mostly free" countries, at the time the map was made, included Haiti, then under military rule, and the dictatorship of Zaire) and various categories of its supposed enemies (communist, Marxist-Socialist, and Islamic). Islam's special status among non-Christian religions has come about because the development of this evangelical Christianity coincided with the rise of Islam as a perceived threat to the U.S. These were the years of OPEC and the oil price increases; these were the years in which Gaddafi and then the Ayatollah came to be demonized as America's great enemies. The time of the forging of this new evangelical coalition was the very time of the Iranian hostage crisis and America's humiliation at the hands of the Ayatollah, an event more traumatic for Americans than the disaster of the Vietnam War.[56] The anti-Islam component is another indication of just how conditioned by recent U.S. history much missionary Christianity is. Lester Sumrall's *Jihad, the*

Holy War: The Destiny of Iran and the Moslem World, can be used to illustrate this. The first part is a "Biblical history" of Iran. Then he moves to the 1979 attack on the U.S. Embassy in Teheran, "a day of infamy and shame."[57] Iranian Moslems "are the ultimate fanatics."[58] The Western world had not yet recognized "the titanic struggle in the breast of the Moslem to destroy Christianity and Judaism off the face of the earth."[59] Moslem hatred is "satanic in origin."[60] Sumrall deals with the abortive rescue mission that ended in disaster in the desert two hundred fifty miles from Teheran: "I personally asked God why such a nation as America with the finest equipment on the face of the earth and the best fighting men on the face of this earth should fail in a mission such as this. It was not only for me—it was for the whole Western world."[61] God gave Sumrall an answer that mitigated the humiliation, because the mission failed through no fault of the Americans but in accordance with the divine plan:

> God said, 'I stopped the Americans in the desert before reaching the city, because had they done so, there would have been more bloodshed than has ever been imagined.'
>
> I tremble to think of this. I thought of how it might have triggered the confrontation with Russia—and how it could have been a world war which would have aroused the whole of the Arab world with a JIHAD such as history has no record of. God gave the Russian world further opportunity to seek His face, repent of their sins, and ask His blessings upon their lives.[62]

This answer permits Sumrall to answer his own anguished question—"Were we a first class nation or not?"—in the affirmative.[63]

After the collapse of communism, the anti-Islam component promises to assume ever greater prominence in this theology. Let Sumrall provide further illustration. Just before the Iraqi invasion of Kuwait on August 4, 1990, Sumrall in his ministry's magazine could write about the Soviet Union's "predicted" attack on Israel, but it was no longer the Soviet Union as communist (that word was never mentioned) but the Soviet Union as Islamic. "Currently living in the lands of Magog, Rosh, Meshech, and Tubal (southern Russia and modern Turkey) (Ezek 38:3) are the largest concentrations of Muslims in the Soviet Union. The Islamic growth rate in these regions is five times that of the rest of the Soviet Union. The Soviet armed forces are currently made up of about 35 to 40 percent Muslim troops." He concludes: "With Islamic motivation, revival and zeal sweeping the U.S.S.R and the Middle East, it is only a matter of time before Ezekiel 38:15–16 is fulfilled, partly by the Soviet Union's Muslim people." Also taking part in this invasion of Israel, he claimed, according to Ezekiel 38, will be "Persia (Iran), Ethiopia, Libya, Gomer (southern U.S.S.R.) and Togarmah (eastern Turkey)." Identifying Ezekiel's nations in this way not only enabled Sumrall to include a number of America's enemies in the Biblical list of God's enemies, but to draw the conclusion he wanted: "The one united feature of all these nations is Islam."[64]

It was hard to see how Liberia could avoid serious Muslim-Christian confrontation. Monrovia's street evangelists, led by the evangelist who insisted against Archbishop Francis that Muslims do not worship the same God that Christians do, commonly led their listeners in an action song with the words, "Satan power is powerless power, but Jesus power is super-super power." In subsequent verses, the phrase "Satan power" was replaced with synonyms like "Juju power." Sometimes the evangelists inserted, as another synonym of Satan, "Muslim power"—and this in the middle of the main street, with Muslims passing by. An instructor at a Muslim school was quoted in a news report as calling for the creation of a religious bureau within the government to control religious activities in the country, because "certain groups of Christians are in the habit of preaching in the streets only to criticize and sabotage other religions."[65] By 1989 Muslims were fighting back—in July anti-Christian notices were appearing at the university, posted by the University of Liberia Muslim Students Association.

Ali Mazrui has argued that Islam is not so much anti-Christian as anti-Western. He claims the two Third World movements expressing hostility towards the U.S., Marxism and Islam, are both of this character. Third World Marxists' hostility is directed not so much toward capitalism as a form of economic and social organization, but towards economic imperialism as a means of external domination. So, too, Islam's hostility is directed against American cultural imperialism. "Despite what many in the U.S. and elsewhere believe, the Iranian revolution was not anti-Christian but anti-Western. The chief focus of hostility was not the Vatican, but Washington; not the crucifix, but the star-spangled banner. Iranian motivations were no doubt religious, but the targets were secular."[66] In Liberia, the conflict sharpened because the Christianity that Muslims met was so obviously an American cultural product. If Christian leaders had been more concerned to make their Christianity genuinely African, the religious sting might have been taken out of the conflict.

In Liberia, all the Christians most opposed to Islam, both American missionaries and local pastors, gave the same reason for their opposition: "Liberia is a Christian country." In making this claim, they were merely reverting to the language of True Whig Party stalwarts. "Liberia is a Christian country" was nothing but a shibboleth used in the fight to preserve the status quo. Christianity was seen as an essential plank of the system, and it was the system that they were determined to preserve.

Conclusion

Liberia is far from unique. Sub-Saharan Africa has long been distinguished for its oppressive, inept, unaccountable dictatorships, propped up by East or West in pursuit of their Cold War interests. At the time the Cold War ended and Doe's Liberia imploded in a savage civil war, most of Africa began a move toward democratization in what has been termed Africa's "Second Liberation Struggle." The results of this movement have in its first few years been rather mixed.

The same movement is bringing about a re-examination of the role of Christianity in Africa. It is too simple to say, as is sometimes heard, that African Christianity is focused on liberation. South Africa was one area where a sector of Christianity consciously addressed political issues, in a "black theology" rather similar to Latin America's liberation theology. But the Christianity of sub-Saharan Africa was, like Liberia's, generally not characterized by such political awareness. On the contrary, most African Christianity was, like Liberia's, of an avowedly "non-political" kind, and increasingly marked by charismatic influences which, if anything, made them even less of a challenge to Africa's dictators. Some Africans, however, are consciously involved in a reappraisal of Christianity's role in Africa's changing circumstances. The call for re-evaluation is eloquently expressed in these words of one of the most articulate of Africa's theologians, Jean Marc Ela of Cameroon: "The human condition in today's Africa is characterized, on the one hand, by the imperialism of the developed countries and the cultural and technological domination of the West, and on the other hand, by injustice and oppression, in all of its various forms...ultimately, the denial to millions, individually and collectively, of their basic human freedoms, at the hands of bureaucracies that are rotten to the core....The cry of the African—of the African human being— ought to move the churches to question themselves as to what they are, what they are saying, and what they are doing in Africa."[67]

EIGHT

The "New" Christianity in Africa: The Charismatic Explosion

> Take the continent for Jesus. From Cairo to Capetown.
> —Reinhard Bonnke

*B*onnke is the world's most successful tent evangelist, and he frames his religious objectives in the same terms that Cecil Rhodes once used on behalf of the British Empire. The Trinity Broadcast Network (TBN), based in Orange County, California, used similar language of Christian conquest, calling its first African television station "a strategic beachhead...on the dark continent."[1] Both Bonnke and TBN are contributors to a Protestant wave of conversion in Africa, a process that combines generous quantities of local enthusiasm with significant charismatic (or neo-Pentecostal)[2] influence from abroad. Yet some observers talk rather glibly of Africa's flourishing new "non-denominational" or "interdenominational" or "Biblical" churches as if this were a spontaneous African revival that is leading to something quite African, or at least some kind of "Third World Christianity"—in short, something quite new. This view is sometimes taken further by those who speak of the Third World missionary movement as "the great new fact of our times."[3]

True, a great Christian revival is spreading throughout Africa. The oft-quoted figure is sixteen thousand and four hundred new Christians every day, but in fact it could be nearer to twenty thousand.[4] Given Africa's phenomenal economic and social collapse, and the state of dependency this has created, Africans are vulnerable to resourceful outside interests that radiate success, professionalism, and enthusiasm. Thus the continent has become receptive to a new form of Christianity that derives primarily from the United States.

In reviewing this phenomenon, there is a danger of giving the impression that the countries of sub-Saharan Africa are quite homogeneous. This is not the case. Considerable differences exist among these nations, which are inhabited by different peoples (for example, Bantu, Nilotes) who have organized their societies according to different traditions, from centralized kingdoms (Buganda in Uganda, Ashanti in Ghana) to acephalous tribes. The modern countries date from the nineteenth-century partition of Africa into colonial states by Britain, France, Germany, Portugal, Spain, and Italy, as well as (in his personal capacity), King Leopold of the Belgians. Minor redistributions were made at the end of the First and Second World Wars, when Germany and Italy lost their colonies. Only Liberia and Ethiopia were left out of this partition.

This partition explains the division of modern Africa into language blocks: anglophone, francophone, and lusophone. Some of these countries (notably Kenya, Rhodesia, Angola, Mozambique) were settled by colonists; others (most of West Africa) were never settled, merely administered, by the colonial power. Ghana was the first of these to become independent (1957). Most received independence in the 1960s, a few much later (Mozambique and Angola 1975, Rhodesia [Zimbabwe] 1980, Namibia 1990). Most came to independence peacefully; others (particularly the Portuguese colonies) after bitter wars of liberation. Some opted for capitalist modes of development (notably Kenya and Cote d'Ivoire), others for socialist (notably Tanzania). The former established alliances with the West, the latter tended to form links with the Eastern bloc, the Soviet Union, China, and North Korea. Some have been characterized by instability or military coups (Togo, Ghana), others have been remarkably stable (Malawi was ruled by Hastings Banda 1964–94; Zambia by Kenneth Kaunda 1964–92; Cote d'Ivoire by Felix Houphouet-Boigny 1960–93). The totally arbitrary borders of these colonial states have given rise in some to considerable ethnic tension (Uganda, Nigeria); other countries have not seen open warfare, but the ethnic factor has been crucial in subsequent development (Kenya); a few are lucky enough to comprise essentially only one tribe (Lesotho, Botswana). In some, Christian-Muslim tension has added another element of friction (Nigeria, Sudan, Tanzania). Some are naturally rich in resources (Zaire in minerals); others are relatively poor. All these factors, and more, give rise to major differences between countries. We should also note that the situation in Africa is not static; major sociopolitical changes are afoot, particularly since a general move towards democratic practices began about 1989. For our purposes here, however, we can leave all these considerations to one side, without, it is hoped, oversimplifying the picture.

In the 1980s, black Africa experienced increasing social, political, and economic collapse. In Nigeria—and one out of every six Africans is a Nigerian—when Babangida left office in mid-1993 the real income per head was one-tenth of what it was when he came to power eight years earlier.[5] In Cameroon income per head fell by half between 1985 and 1993.[6] According to the head of the United Nations Economic Commission for Africa, commenting on the failure of the U.N. Programme of Action for Africa's Economic Recovery and Development (1986–90), the average African received 40 percent less real income in 1991 than in 1980.[7] A general collapse has occurred in the areas of education and health and economic infrastructure. By any standards of reckoning—statistics for life expectancy, child mortality, health, education, gross domestic product—Africa has fallen well behind other developing areas of the world. The continent is slipping out of the Third World and into its own bleak category of the "nth" world.[8] Moreover, Africa is being increasingly marginalized, and few people outside the continent notice or care. This was evident at the height of the crisis in the former Yugoslavia. At that time, the carnage in Angola, where after losing an election the rebel movement UNITA took up arms again, was even more complete; but the Western media gave great coverage to Bosnia and almost ignored Angola. In this context of precipitous decline and international indifference, governments collapsed and retreated from all kinds of areas. Non-governmental Organizations (NGOs) flooded in to take their place, and in extreme cases such as Mozambique, they exerted more power than governments.[9] Over the same period, in a similar way, missionaries have flooded into Africa, often with an effect on the Christian landscape just as substantial as that of the NGOs on the sociopolitical terrain. Many of these new missionaries are linked to Africa's Pentecostal movement. Already by the mid-1960s the mainline Protestant missionaries had been surpassed in numbers by those from non-ecumenical evangelical and "unaffiliated" agencies. This trend has proceeded apace. For example, Guinea (Conakry) under Sekou Toure (1968–84) took a very harsh line towards Christian missions; at the time of Sekou Toure's death in 1984, only Catholic and Anglican churches were permitted. By 1991, however, the country had only eight Catholic missionaries and one Anglican, but over 100 evangelical Protestants, mainly American.[10] These new missionaries to Africa are normally not working in development or schools or clinics; the vast majority are concerned with evangelization pure and simple. Indeed, many of them are influenced by the "church growth" school of California, and target their people groups, with their charts and graphs and projectiles and quarterly returns.[11]

Although the missionaries often claim they are working for the local churches or networks, or are "partners" with them, one must make full allowance for the disparity of resources and education. The missionaries and the pastors they link with do not meet as equals; and the effect of this on the Africanness of the African churches needs to be researched. The claim that churches are "independent" or "autonomous" may sometimes disguise foreign influences that are increasing rather than diminishing.

The fact that these missionaries are predominantly North American is important. It is not easy to plot trends in this matter. For one thing, statistics are not always collected on exactly the same basis.[12] This American influence appears to be growing even though the percentage of American missionaries is not increasing.[13] However, against this must be set other considerations. First, mission agencies have consciously adopted a new strategy: to support locals, rather than send North Americans. Locals are both "less expensive and less culturally intrusive." In 1992 U.S. agencies fully supported 24,213 locals and partially supported 17,737.[14] Also, a new factor has entered the field of missions today, made possible by leisure and easy and cheap travel. Many evangelical Christian colleges in the U.S. now provide opportunities for students to spend at least some of their summer vacation in mission fields; one estimate put the number of Americans in such short-term missions in 1989 at one hundred twenty thousand.[15] It must be said that much of this short term work, even when it involves non-Americans, is on behalf of American multinational agencies like Youth With A Mission. Also, an important and novel feature of the contemporary scene is that many missionaries are genuine "independents," sent from independent, charismatic churches in North America; they are often not counted in statistics compiled according to mission agencies.

Comparing a representative number of African countries between 1989 and 1993, one finds that in general, full-time American Protestant missionaries have increased: Ghana, for instance, had 158 American Protestant missionaries in 1989, and 184 in 1993; Kenya increased from 1,225 to 1,337; Malawi, 155 to 199; Nigeria, 486 to 487; Zimbabwe, 23 to 309; however, over the same four-year period the U.S. missionaries decreased in Cameroon (247 to 213) and in Zaire (899 to 715, although the decline in Zaire can easily be explained by the general flight of Western missionaries from the chaos engulfing Zaire since 1989). An additional 359 Protestant missionaries were accredited to "Africa" generally in 1993.[16]

These missionaries have established countless ministries, fellowships, and churches of their own kind, and (through their workshops, literature, and media involvement) have profoundly influenced already existing churches. So Africa now has a rapidly growing sector of Christianity that is closely related to and heavily dependent on the United States, and it is this sector that we will focus on here.

However, it must be stressed that Africa has a context considerably different from that in the U.S. In the U.S. fundamentalists focus their energy on particular issues—abortion, homosexuality, the equal rights amendment, "welfare," the teaching of evolution in schools, New Age movements, the alleged humanism of the Supreme Court, and the media and the educational system. But in Africa, whatever the policy of religion enshrined in a particular constitution, few of these issues are significant. In almost all African states, governments are very opposed to abortion, "gay rights" are not an issue, women are subservient, welfare systems almost nonexistent, and the courts usually very subservient to the executive. Also, the electronic technology (cable TV, free phone networks, computerized mailing) that has been an inseparable part of the emergence of the U.S. fundamentalist coalition simply does not exist in Africa. Just as significant, the freedom of speech that enables U.S. fundamentalists to denounce their government for all sorts of alleged inadequacies is not widely honored in Africa, and so strong public denunciations are out of the question in most of Africa.

Thus a completely different dynamic obtains in Africa. The terms "fundamentalist" and "evangelical" cannot be used in Africa to suggest any distinction from "Pentecostal." Even though in the West, in the U.S. particularly, this distinction is often important, in Africa today these three terms seem virtually interchangeable. In Africa today most fundamentalist evangelicals are Pentecostal as well. In what follows, the term "fundamentalist" will always be used to include Pentecostal Christians. But, more importantly, in its classical Christian sense of denoting some belief in the Bible as inerrant, almost all African Christianity is fundamentalist, for nearly all African Christians approach the Bible rather uncritically. They love to quote it, refer to it, support any position by alluding to it. This is true of Christians of the mainline churches and is doubly true of what are called the African Independent (or Instituted) Churches. This was well expressed in a report on the history and theology of a group of Independent Churches, written by the Independent Churches themselves. After writing of how seriously they take the Bible, they continue: "Some people will say that we are therefore 'fundamentalists.' We do not know whether that word applies to us or not....We do not have the same problems about the Bible as White people have with their Western scientific mentality."[17] The different contexts must continually be borne in mind in what follows.

Mergers

Africa's economic collapse is crucial to understand, for it explains the most significant phenomenon among traditional African Independent Churches, namely their increasing dependence on U.S. churches. As Africa's economies have collapsed, many African churches have been reduced to a state of penury. All independent churches know that Lutherans and Methodists have "overseas boards" that fund them and enable them to run the schools and clinics that give them and their pastors such status. In their poverty, pastors and churches have been reduced to writing to U.S. churches in an effort to establish links with them—which most often means offering to become the

African branch of the American church. African pastors look for addresses of churches and ministries on the backs of magazines and tracts. The more literate borrow from missionaries, or consult at the nearest United States Information Service, reference books like Melton's *Encyclopedia of American Religions,* which lists all North American denominations and their addresses. One bishop of a recently formed breakaway church in Liberia wrote fifty-two letters and received thirty-seven replies, of which eighteen were positive. He thus had his choice of eighteen American churches. In this case he chose the Church of God of the Mountain Assembly. There is nothing secret about this general scramble for U.S. affiliation; it is simply regarded as a necessity.

This same tendency toward dependency on the U.S. even applies to whole organizations or fellowships. For example, the United Evangelical Churches of Kenya is an umbrella body of about two hundred fifty pastors representing about sixty different churches. Most of these are of the newer American-influenced fundamentalist wave, although about sixty of the pastors would be classified as of the traditional African Independent Churches. In 1992 the organization came into existence by effectively placing itself under a parent body in the U.S., the United Evangelical Churches of America, a group of one thousand pastors under Rev. Charles Hardin of Georgia. In this body, in theory, Kenyans and Americans join as equals, but Hardin was elected the overall head. This American link has brought trips for the Kenyan pastors, and a team of Americans led by Hardin came for the Fellowship's Kenyan convention in November 1992. By 1993 the organization was moving to include pastors from South Africa, and the United Reformed Ministers Council of Uganda, a body of over two hundred pastors of different denominations, was pressing to join.

In all these mergers (more correctly, given the economic reality, buyouts) the overriding motive seems financial. In fact, this phenomenon of seeking U.S. patronage is so widespread that many U.S. ministries now deal explicitly with this matter in the material they send to Africa. Thus Melody Green's Last Days Ministries of Lindale, Texas, includes a letter in communications to Africa stating, "We are sorry, but Last Days Ministries is not equipped to provide Bibles, clothes or anything not listed in our catalogue, including financial assistance, airplane tickets and finding you a job in the USA." The most important feature of this amalgamating phenomenon is the theological impact on African churches. We can note in passing that the drive for amalgamation is not only on the side of the Africans. With "church growth" the vogue in the U.S., and "expanding one's share of the market" the goal, U.S. churches are often desperate to establish branches overseas. Taking over an already existing church is often the easiest way of achieving this.

But this general tendency to form links between churches is only one of the instruments by which U.S. fundamentalism is propagated. We will discuss others under the headings of crusades, conferences, pastors' workshops, Bible schools, and media.

Crusades

Crusades or revivals are now an important feature of life in any African city. In many cities, almost every week a new crusade team arrives. Since they are held in the evenings, and since in many African cities not much is provided in the way of free entertainment, they usually draw sizeable crowds.

Crusades take place normally in late afternoon, although on weekends they begin somewhat earlier. Saturday is sometimes Holy Spirit day; that evening all are taught to speak in tongues or "baptized in the Spirit." The crusade ground normally has the main platform near the center; on this platform the preacher has his wife and other key members of the crusade team. Often another platform is erected nearby for important civic and church leaders. Around the edges of the ground are numerous stalls selling Christian literature, tapes, T-shirts and hats. These wares are often touted (sometimes at bargain rates) from the platform.

The crusade itself is divided into three sections. The first can be called a "warm-up" session, lasting between one and two hours. In this section, professional artists and the best soloists, instrumental groups, and choirs from the participating churches take their turn in performing. Many of them are superb. This period of time serves to make everyone totally responsive and involved; as the emcee at one Kenyan crusade told the crowd: "Before we were saved we used to dance in night clubs; now we dance for Jesus. This is a sanctified rumba, so don't feel inhibited." This section ends with an offertory, taken up by hundreds of trained ushers.

The second section is the sermon. This lasts an hour or ninety minutes. Normally the preacher preaches in English, with an interpreter translating into the (main) local language after every two or three phrases. This is always a virtuoso performance, and contributes immensely to the effect of drama, as both men interact, move around the platform, and act out little scenes. The preaching is normally direct and simple, full of illustrations and anecdotes— many of which feature the preacher and his (always victorious) encounters with "witchdoctors," faithless mainline Christians, and atheists on television. The preaching is highly personalized. The appeals and questions achieve the total involvement of the crowd. Regular appeals are: "If you are listening, wave", "Wave if you are saved", "Are you happy?", and "How many of you are free?" At times the preacher breaks into tongues, whereupon the crowd joins in.

After preaching comes the healing. Because of the size of the crowd it is not possible to call people to the front, or to cure them individually. Normally the preacher tells those desiring healing to place a hand over the affected organ or area. Then, after rebuking the spirits responsible for countless ills and invoking God's power in all these areas, he calls for the healing of everyone together. Thereupon those who claim to be healed are asked to make their way to the platform to testify. There they demonstrate their healing by performing actions previously impossible for them; for example, by running around the platform if they had been lame, by talking if they had been dumb. This section, which could last an hour and involve twenty or thirty testimonies, invariably arouses the greatest excitement.

We can illustrate this by referring to the most high-profile of all these Western crusaders in Africa, Reinhard Bonnke. Bonnke, a German, trained at the (non-Pentecostal) Bible College of Wales. But his theology is of the "faith gospel" movement; he has an office in the U.S., regularly stages revivals in the U.S., and has on his platforms such prominent U.S. revivalists as Ralph Mahoney and Kenneth Copeland, or U.S.-trained revivalists such as South Africa's Ray McCauley.

Bonnke's headquarters since 1986 have been in Frankfurt, but he began his ministry in Southern Africa. His mission is to evangelize throughout Africa, reaching to the Islamic countries of the north. He tells often of his vision of a "blood-drenched Africa." He conducts about twelve crusades a year in sub-Saharan Africa, and by 1993 only Liberia and Equatorial Guinea had not had at least one of his crusades.

More impressive than the number of his crusades are the numbers he attracts. In the last few years he has claimed audiences at single meetings of two hundred fifty thousand in Ougadougou, Burkina Faso; two hundred thousand in Ilorin, Nigeria; two hundred thousand in Lome, Togo; three hundred thousand in Kinshasa, Zaire; three hundred sixty thousand in Mbuji-Mayi, Zaire; and biggest of all, five hundred thousand at the closing session of his 1990 crusade in Kaduna, northern Nigeria. These figures become even more impressive when fitted in their context; his crowd of one hundred forty thousand in Warri, Nigeria, was said to be half the total population of the area; his seventy thousand in Goma, Zaire, was out of a total population of one hundred twenty thousand; in Butembo, Zaire, his fifty-five thousand was of a total population of ninety-four thousand; the one hundred seventy-five thousand who attended the Saturday afternoon session of his 1993 crusade in Kumasi, Ghana, was 40 percent of Kumasi's entire population; the crowd of three hundred sixty thousand in Mbuji-Mayi was of a possible population of four hundred thousand. In the year from October 1990 to September 1991 he preached face to face to over eight million people. Equally impressive is the number said to have committed themselves to Jesus: in Ougadougou, forty thousand in two days; in Ibadan, Nigeria, over one hundred thousand in total; in Kaduna, two hundred thousand throughout the course of the crusade; in Kinshasa, two hundred thousand. Of the millions he preached to between October 1990 and September 1991, he claims two million responded to his call.

A large part of Bonnke's success is attributable to the local churches he involves in preparing for the crusades. Preparation can take up to a year. For a month prior to his ill-fated 1991 Kano, Nigeria, crusade, Bonnke had a team of twenty in the city. (The largely Muslim population of the area felt so threatened by the prospect that they rioted, leading to disturbances resulting in untold destruction and hundreds of deaths, which caused the crusade to be abandoned.) In Nigeria, two hundred fifty local churches were involved in the Jos crusade, two hundred seventy in Warri, four hundred (of one hundred different denominations) in Ibadan, one hundred twenty in Ilorin. Sixty-five were involved in Bamenda, in Cameroon, two hundred in Nairobi in Kenya. In Kaduna, Nigeria, in 1990, it was claimed that every church in the city was involved in some way or other. Bonnke is able to ensure the participation of all sorts of churches that one would not normally expect to be involved. Of the churches involved in the 1991 Nairobi crusade, at least fourteen were Anglican. An Anglican clergyman was on the Ilorin committee; the chairman of the Kano crusade was an Anglican; the Anglican bishop opened the meetings in Kaduna. The Kaduna and Kano crusades were both sponsored by the Christian Association of Nigeria, the umbrella body for all Nigerian Christians, including Catholics. The Lutherans in Tanzania have been prominent in supporting him. (In Kuala Lumpur, Malaysia, the local Anglican, Methodist, and Lutheran bishops all appeared on Bonnke's platform.) Bonnke's theology is that of the modern U.S. charismatic variety, and the networks that he creates through staging his crusades are one of the chief conduits of this Christianity, and are an important influence in modifying existing churches toward this brand of charismatic Christianity.

Many other prominent overseas "men of God" also visit Africa. In March 1993, Paul Yonggi Cho of South Korea came to Kenya. (Again, although not an American, his message is the faith gospel.) A committee prepared for this crusade months in advance; the crusade committee was in large measure the same as prepared for Bonnke two years previously. Countless local churches were involved, and publicity in press and on TV was plentiful. President Moi attended, too.

Even Billy Graham contributes to this process. In mid-1989 Billy Graham held a crusade in London, and three evenings of this crusade (29 June–1 July) were broadcast to Africa. Some African countries received the transmission live via satellite and relayed it directly over the national TV channel. In these countries TV sets were placed in churches, and a normal revival took place in each church, led by trained local preachers. Then, at the appropriate time, the TV sets were switched on, and the revival sermon was delivered by Billy Graham by satellite. After his altar call, the TV sets were turned off and the local counselors in each church took over. Many other African countries which for various reasons could not take over the national TV on those particular nights, received videos from London, and these videos were later relayed over national TV, and the same procedure was followed. Billy Graham's Mission World prepared thoroughly for this; they held training sessions in Zimbabwe for those who would run the operation in each country. (They later also took several Africans to Hollywood to translate the three sermons into their own languages so that later these videos could be shown to rural people.)

This Billy Graham TV crusade is noteworthy because it reveals an important shift in African evangelical Christianity. Bonnke, Cho, and the countless others who come to Africa are almost invariably charismatic; a long healing service is an integral part of the crusade. Billy Graham is not charismatic. But, as in so many African settings, a Billy Graham crusade sermon was forced into the local charismatic framework. It was preceded by the exuberant preparatory singing and dancing, and followed by the equally exuberant healing miracles. The majority of African Christians would not have realized that some of Billy Graham's followers in the United States would have a problem with this.

Bonnke, Cho, and Billy Graham are just the best known evangelists. In Africa's major cities—Lagos, Nairobi, Accra, Kinshasa—crusades preached by visiting revivalists are becoming almost continual. Some teams do this regularly; in other cases, individual churches save for one trip as part of their mission outreach. For example, in August 1989, the Voice of Pentecost Church from San Francisco flew a team of fifty-eight people, including two different choirs, to Monrovia, Liberia, for a four-day crusade. This church is part of the United Pentecostal Church in the U.S. and the crusade was theoretically under the auspices of Liberia's United Pentecostal Church. But in fact, the crusade was totally the initiative of the American church, and the local church just had to fit in with that. Some of the local people expressed resentment at the purely passive role allotted to them.

The crusade phenomenon is on the increase all over Africa, and by the 1990s had become part of the local scene. The vast majority of the preachers are American teams, and when they are local they replicate as much as possible what they have heard and observed from their foreign models. We noted above that visiting preachers usually preach in English, with a translator interpreting after every few phrases. Sometimes a local preacher who knows the local language perfectly will still choose to speak in English so that he can make use of the services of an interpreter. Thus the English sermon with interpretation is considered part of the ritual.

Conferences

If crusades are generally evening revivals, conferences, camp meetings, and conventions are usually daytime events. These may take place over a period of three days or more, with lectures by a variety of speakers of sufficient distinction to attract people from far afield. This too, is becoming increasingly more common in Africa's bigger centers.

Bonnke, in coordination with his crusades, often conducts "Fire Conferences" or special teaching seminars. The first was held in Harare, Zimbabwe, April 21–27 1986, and drew four thousand delegates from sixty countries, most from the forty-one African countries represented. Of these delegates, Bonnke paid for about one thousand. The key speakers at this conference give a good indication of the kind of Christianity being spread: Loren Cunningham, the founder of Youth With A Mission; Gloria and Kenneth Copeland of Fort Worth; Wayne Myers of Mexico; Ralph Mahoney of California; Ray McCauley of South Africa (but educated at Rhema in Tulsa); Benson Idahosa, the founder of the Church of God Mission International, one of Nigeria's megachurches, and a regular on North American platforms. Bonnke has conducted similar conferences in Europe—Euro-Fire '87 in Frankfurt, Euro-Fire '88 in Birmingham, and Euro-Fire '90 in Lisbon—and regional ones in Africa. The Fire Conference held in conjunction with his 1991 Kinshasa crusade drew four thousand Zairian delegates. He was to hold another regional Fire Conference during his aborted Kano crusade in October 1991; his Fire Conference in Dar es Salaam, Tanzania, in February 1993 drew four thousand pastors and evangelists from all over the country, including the Kilimanjaro region and Zanzibar.

The United Evangelical Churches of Kenya, organized by Maurice Mutimba of World Intercessory Ministries, held a conference in Nairobi in October 1991 with speakers from Israel, U.S., South Africa, and Sweden. In November 1993 his speakers were Paul Tan of Singapore; Bob and Esther Fort of Salinas, California; Alex Scoble of South Africa; Amos York of Houston, Texas; and effectively his director, Charles Hardin of Georgia, the head of the United Evangelical Churches of America.

The Zimbabwe Assemblies of God Africa (ZAOGA Forward in Faith), which was founded in 1968 by Ezekiel Guti, in February 1993 held a much publicized International Christian Leadership Summit for Africa at Harare's International Conference Center, certainly the most impressive conference center in black Africa. The theme was "Restoring purpose of life for this generation. What will Africa be by the year 2000?" This convention was hailed as the first genuinely African conference ever held on the continent, an event led by one of the African Indepent Churches. The major speakers, with the exception of Mensa Otabil of Ghana, were all from the U.S. or the Caribbean.

The whole conference was a replica of Summit '92, held in 1991 at Nassau in the Bahamas. The speakers were almost entirely those at Nassau. At one stage in Harare the dynamics were revealed most forcefully when the wife of the pastor of Harare's Rhema Bible church (an American trained at Gordon Lindsay's Christ for the Nations in Dallas) said that the convention's main speaker, Myles Munro of the Bahamas, had been in her class at Oral Roberts University, where another key speaker at the convention, Dr. Jerry Horner (now the dean of Pat Robertson's Regent University), had been their teacher. She said that she little suspected then that all three of them would be on the same platform in faraway Africa years later. For all that was made of the fact that this was the first conference run totally by Africans, this vignette provided a more telling insight into the central dynamics of the conference.

Morris Cerullo has evolved a variation on the institution of the conference. He has offices in several places in Africa, and runs video conferences (they are misleadingly billed as the Morris Cerullo Global Satellite Network School of Ministry) in many key cities. In Nairobi, for example, on the first Saturday of each month, Maurice Cerullo Ministries hires the Kenyatta International Conference Center, and on giant video screens from 8.30 a.m. to 5 p.m. they play videos of Cerullo himself preaching at crusades elsewhere, or of other Americans preaching at Cerullo crusades. On sale are cassettes, audio and visual, and books by Cerullo and others. Each video conference attracts up to four thousand people.

Pastors' Workshops

Increasingly, the crusades are accompanied by pastors' workshops. An open invitation is extended to office holders in local churches to attend day meetings given by the revivalist or members of his team. All Bonnke's crusades are coupled with pastors' workshops.[18] In his April 1993 Kumasi, Ghana, crusade, two thousand pastors attended the functions put on for them.[19] Paul Yonggi Cho's crusade in Kenya was advertised everywhere as Holy Spirit Expo Crusade and Pastors' Conference.

All these churches and ministries give these pastors great priority. Consider the Potter's House, a church (whose branches also go under the name "The Door") founded by Wayman Mitchell in Prescott, Arizona. In the space of a few years this church has made considerable inroads into Africa. Its Liberian branch began on Sunday, August 14, 1988. Its first outdoor crusade, with five visiting Americans, took place in November 1988. During the day, the visiting Americans conducted a workshop for pastors; "200 delegates attended our first Pastors' Conference," reported the denomination's magazine. A few months later, concurrent with another crusade conducted by four other Americans, they ran another pastors' seminar, attended by one hundred ten church leaders. At the same time others from the denomination's U.S. churches were conducting crusades in Kenya. The church's magazine reports that in Kenya during one single crusade, "Up to 400 native pastors attended our seminars."[20]

Youth With A Mission (YWAM) also operates with this philosophy. YWAM has three ships, the Anastasis, the Good Samaritan, and the Pacific Ruby, which travel the world, calling at Third World ports with teams of volunteers who perform dental and facial surgeries, involve themselves in agriculture and construction of buildings. From November 1992 to the end of January 1993 the Anastasis was docked in Freetown, Sierra Leone, at the invitation of the Sierra Leone Ministry of Health. From February to April 16, 1993, it was berthed in Dakar in Senegal. One of the volunteers' central ministries in these Third World countries is to conduct workshops for pastors. By mid-1993 they claim to have reached thousands of pastors through their workshop teams on these "mercy ships."

Also, fellowships or associations set up in particular countries set out to do the same thing on a more permanent basis. The Liberian Association of Full Gospel Ministers, effectively the creation of four American missionaries of Jim Zirkle's Living Waters International (and all graduates of Kenneth Hagin's Rhema Bible Training Center), was set up in 1989; one of its aims is to "sponsor an annual camp meeting/convention" that brings pastors together, and to "promote unity and strength" among them. Their first convention, held in mid-1989, consisted of four days of preaching/lecture sessions, at which the speakers were four Liberians, two visiting Ghanaians, and four visiting Americans, among them that epitome of the American charismatic revivalist, Lester Sumrall of South Bend, Indiana. Another example is the Africa Fellowship of Christian Ministers in Zimbabwe, which meets for two days every two months, and sometimes draws over one hundred twenty pastors to its seminars. The fellowship is the creation of the American pastor of the Rhema Bible Church, and meetings are held to coincide with the visit of such people as Ed Louis Cole, Casey Treat, and Ray McCauley.

There are even American ministries in Africa that exist solely to help provide education through seminars and workshops for pastors. Such a ministry is Clarence Matheny Ministries, in Nairobi, Kenya, which conducts week long seminars for local pastors (and for pastors from Uganda and Tanzania, too), often over two hundred at a time, at heavily subsidized rates. The ministry boasts of the "international speakers" it is able to provide.

Here we find in sharp relief the genuine novelty in African Christianity. For this is totally new. In the past, Africa's African Independent Churches (AICs)—churches that have either split off from mission churches, usually because of perceived racism, or have been established to incorporate local elements that the mission churches would not countenance—were largely ignored, even despised by mainline or mission churches. In the 1980s, the AICs saw their lot change because the newer, generally American charismatic churches or ministries have none of this attitude. Although they are very negative when confronted with what they consider "deficient" Christianity, U.S. missionaries are very accepting and accommodating of churches or pastors that are open to receive "true Biblical Christianity." These missionaries have a totally new ecclesiology, according to which the true church is made up of all born-again believers, and has nothing to do with those organized bodies traditionally called churches. Many of these missionaries are not primarily aiming to plant or spread their own churches, which has traditionally been the agenda of mainline missionaries. These new missions are more than ready to influence existing churches, so they positively court these AICs. This is the first time these pastors have been taken seriously by Western missionaries, the first time these churches have been taken into the ambit of Western Christianity. Most of the AIC pastors are well aware of their lack of theological training, and are hungry for it. They flock to the opportunities these new ministries provide for them.

Bible Schools

Probably the greatest single instrument for spreading U.S. Christianity is the rash of Bible schools appearing all over the continent. Many of them, besides enjoying access to American funds, books, and media equipment, also grant degrees from various American institutions. Africans generally have an enormous hunger for education; often it is seen as the only way out of the enveloping chaos. As education facilities have deteriorated all over the continent, these Bible schools stand out as very desirable centers of education. Often the best way to obtain education is to go to one of these schools; the best way to get overseas is to be given a scholarship from one of these schools. In the previous chapter, we have already provided a lengthy description of such a Bible school.

Media

The three giants of Christian broadcasting (ELWA, TWR, and FEBC) have been active in Africa, and (until ELWA's destruction in 1990 in Liberia's civil war) covered the whole continent. All are thoroughly American and thoroughly fundamentalist, even when broadcasting in local languages through local people. ELWA rigidly excluded and TWR fairly strictly excludes what they consider liberal (i.e. mainline) Protestants, although FEBA broadcasts for the Lutherans. At the other end of the theological spectrum, however, the broadcasters were and are just as exclusivist. ELWA rigidly excluded Pentecostals (and such African Independent Churches as the Church of the Lord [Aladura]); TWR theoretically excludes Pentecostals, although in practice this is not an issue in Africa. Only FEBA welcomes Pentecostals. But there is a wide range of Pentecostals, and a good many of the most prominent in the U.S. today are frowned on by all three radio ministries, all of which predated the current charismatic revival. Some of the U.S.-produced material that cannot be aired on the big three finds an outlet on other stations in Africa. The most interesting case of this is in Swaziland, where programs that could never be accepted by TWR are often found on Swazi Commercial Radio, a private station owned by the South African company Kirch Investments. Thus Herbert Armstrong of the World Wide Church of God and such faith preachers as Kenneth Hagin can be found here.

Another station that has operated in a similar, purely commercial way is "Radio Africa," from Bata in Equatorial Guinea. This is the shortwave service of Equatorial Guinea's state radio system, and can be heard as far west as Sierra Leone. R. G. Hardy of Baltimore and Marty Drake of Walled Lake, Michigan, are among the American preachers who have broadcast from here. In 1989 the rates were U.S. $50 for fifteen minutes, much cheaper than most American stations.

In Africa, many state radio systems will broadcast Christian programs—indeed will broadcast almost anything—provided U.S. dollars are paid. In Kenya, traditional religious broadcasting times are offered to the local churches free, and other religious programs are aired. Paul Yonggi Cho's *Invitation to Happiness* is broadcast on both Kenyan state radio and state TV, with a local contact address. (The Kenyan subsidiary ministry that handles the program locally is called the Success Club World Mission.) Zimbabwe's ZBC, too, offers James Dobson's *Focus on the Family*, paid for by the local branch of the Church of the Nazarene, in addition to programs produced by local churches.

Christian television is something new on the continent. Two religious networks in the U.S., Christian Broadcasting Network (CBN) and Trinity Broadcasting Network (TBN), have major international operations that feature charismatic programming. TBN began broadcasting in 1973 and is known for featuring prophecy. (Popular apocalyptic writer Hal Lindsay has his own show.) TBN has over one hundred TV stations in the U.S., and more than twenty stations in other countries. TBN plans to build a $16 million nationwide South African network. TBN established its first station, the first independent religious station in Africa, in the South African "homeland" of Ciskei in 1987. Its second station was built in the "homeland" of Transkei in December 1989. TBN has also been allowed by the South African government and the governments of Bophuthatswana and the Transkei, to use state networks until the entire South African TBN network is completed. TBN also provides the national Swazi TV network with programming on Sunday afternoons.

Most of the TBN programming in the Ciskei (about 90 percent of its transmission time) comes from the U.S. The station broadcasts its own programs made in Southern California, as well as programs from other U.S. televangelists, including Robert Schuller, James Kennedy, Kenneth Copeland, and (in happier times) Jimmy Swaggart. But TBN has also begun to produce local South African programming.

The homeland government of the Ciskei and the South African government work in close partnership with TBN. In 1988 TBN sponsored a series of three evangelistic rallies, sometimes with crowds of more than 10,000. The entire Cabinet, except for the president of the Ciskei who was out of the country, attended the TBN rally in the homeland capital. Ciskei government departments and schools closed for the event. The homeland government also provided transportation for some eighty-five busloads of people to attend the rally. TBN recorded 6,000 "decisions for Christ."

CBN is the largest and most ambitious international religious TV network but, unlike TBN, owns only one TV station outside the U.S., Middle East Television in Israeli-occupied Lebanon. In Africa it sells its programs to the state systems. In this way CBN's international *700 Club* has been shown in South Africa, Kenya, Uganda, Zambia, Zimbabwe, Nigeria, Bophuthatswana, and Liberia. In these countries CBN has an aggressive follow-up program, through "ministry centers" where viewers can telephone or write. This is the normal way in which U.S. televangelists screen their programs in Africa; state systems readily provide time for prior payment in U.S. dollars.

Whereas Africa's Christian TV tends to be charismatic, its radio has been more traditionally evangelical. But in line with so much else, the movement even on the airwaves is markedly toward the charismatic.

The situation in Africa is changing very rapidly as political and economic upheavals affect the continent. (For one thing, the South African homelands were abolished in that country's move to democracy.) Whereas most African governments for the first twenty or thirty years of independence kept tight control of all forms of media, and total control (and ownership) of broadcasting and television, they have now been forced by economic collapse to consider deregulating radio and television. They are therefore prepared to consider granting licenses to any who make an attractive offer.[21]

But quite apart from the specific content of radio or TV broadcasts, what the newer churches take from U.S. Christianity is a media consciousness. This serves to differentiate them sharply from mainline churches. These charismatic churches, even the poorest and newest of them, move in a media culture. A public-address system is the first thing they save for. As soon as they are established they record pastors' sermons. Soon they move to videotaping pastors' sermons. It is standard procedure to advertise tapes and books of the pastor at services.

This emphasis on media has been learned from the West. At Bonnke's Harare Fire conference some of the visiting American speakers donated a cassette of their talks to every participant. Africans quickly recognize the importance of cassettes.

Easily assimilable literature is extremely important to the new churches. In many African countries throughout the 1980s, crises in foreign currency meant that books were very difficult to obtain. Universities and schools were hard pressed for printed matter of any kind.

In this context, a ministry importing and distributing books can have an enormous impact. The impact stems not just from the number of books, but from the nature of the product—usually beautifully produced glossy magazines, or cheap booklets of thirty-odd pages, the format Hagin and Swaggart made their own. This literature is available all over Africa.

In Sierra Leone in 1991 the Anglican bookshop contained only 18 books, of which three were Baha'i, and three Seventh-Day Adventist. The Catholic bookshop sold rosaries and a few devotional tracts. By contrast, the evangelical bookshop, the only bookshop of good quality in the country, contained numerous books, including a wide array of Kenneth Hagin's booklets. Similarly, in Zambia's evangelical headquarters, the greatest single number of publications was Hagin's booklets. (Significantly, both these evangelical fellowships would have been considered non-charismatic just a few years ago.) In the shop/lending library of World Intercessory Ministries in Kenya, the same pamphlets and booklets are for sale and distribution.

In Ghana, in the Methodist headquarters, there is a Rhema bookshop owned by a local architect. It is a good example of a bookstore that disseminates North American charismatic Christianity. In mid-1993, the shop had one book by C. H. Spurgeon, and another by John Stott (an English evangelical in the classical sense); apart from those, the authors were Ralph Mahoney, Paul Yonggi Cho, Roberts Liarden, Watchman Nee, John Osteen, Colin Urquart, Smith Wrigglesworth, E. W. Kenyon, Fred Price, Maurice Cerullo, Josh McDowell, Ed Roebert, James Dobson, Bill Subritsky, and whole sets of the writings of Robert Schuller, John Avancini, Reinhard Bonnke, Lester Sumrall, Kenneth and Gloria Copeland, T. L. Osborn, Oral Roberts, and

Gordon Lindsay. The only African authors on sale were Emmanuel Eni (a Nigerian demonologist) and Abraham Bediako (who is of a piece with the Americans listed here). Besides books, there was a free audio tape stand consisting of tapes by Kenneth Hagin, and a free videotape stand, on which the majority of tapes were of Benny Hinn. Also in Ghana, Action Faith Ministries, one of the most high-profile churches in the country, has its own bookshop. In February 1994, its stock consisted of only thirty titles. Five were by John Avancini, six were by Lester Sumrall, and of the nineteen others, three were by Reinhard Bonnke and one each by Paul Yonggi Cho, Maurice Cerullo, Watchman Nee, and Robert Schuller. An assistant pastor explained that the Avancini and Sumrall books were there because both had preached at that church in the fairly recent past; they had brought their books with them.[22]

This phenomenon is also having an impact on the mainline churches. Methodists visiting their headquarters in Ghana buy these books. And in central Ghana, this influence appears to be seeping into the Catholic Church. Just outside Kumasi is the headquarters of Christian Hope Ministry, which was founded by Catholics in November 1984. By 1994 it drew about three hundred people (mainly women) daily, and for its general deliverance services on Thursdays it drew between two thousand and three thousand people. At the beginning of 1994 the mainly Catholic leadership was insisting that it was not a church, just a ministry. No services were held on Sundays and all adherents attended their own churches. The leadership had even wanted to be formally included in the Catholic diocese, and the bishop had begun discussions with them, but found too many anomalies (not least of which was the resort to exorcism for everything) to follow this up. However, in 1994, the three-quarters of the leadership that was Catholic dutifully attended Mass every Sunday. When questioned as to their theology, though, they openly admitted that the influences on them as (in the order they gave them) Billy Graham, Morris Cerullo, T. L. Osborn, Benny Hinn, Derek Prince, Bill Subritsky, A. A. Allen, Don Basham, Kenneth Hagin, and Kenneth Copeland.

Christian bookshops and roadside vendors sell translations of U.S. material even in such French-speaking countries as Gabon and Ivory Coast. In Mozambique, where literacy is very low and the country has been destroyed by civil war, the literature brought in by ministries for mass consumption consists mainly of Portuguese translations of Gordon Lindsay's pamphlets.

It is thanks to the saturation of airwaves and the quantity of material in bookstores that in many places in Africa this charismatic Christianity is called simply "Christianity."

Elements of Africa's New Charismatic Christianity

American sources and missionaries are systematically flooding the continent and forming a crucial, dynamic part of the African revival. It is not claimed here that all these new churches in Africa are identical, or that Africans are totally passive in merely absorbing this aggressive U.S. Christianity. But America's global theological emphases are increasingly characteristic of these churches, even in areas where strong African traditions and preoccupations might seem to be sufficient.

Demonology

In African cultures, belief in spirits, witchcraft, and spiritual agency of many kinds is widespread. Likewise, a highly developed demonology has evolved in Africa's modern charismatic Christianity. The best known of these is Emmanuel Eni's *Delivered from the Powers of Darkness*, which recounts his story as a servant of "the Queen of the Coast," at whose orders he killed several people.[23] However, in 1985 Jesus appeared to Eni and saved him, since when he has worked for Jesus. Eni's account is from Nigeria, but a similar and almost equally famous account is *Snatched from Satan's Claws: An Amazing Deliverance by Christ*, by evangelist Mukendi of Zaire.[24] Mukendi claims to have been born through magic and breastfed by a mermaid. His father initiated him into advanced degrees of sorcery. In the early 1980s Mukendi was introduced to Satan himself, who invited him to the international satanic school, where he began on January 1, 1981. In this school he saw a video of Lucifer's fall, learned the various categories of his servants, the ranks of his government, the times and seasons of satanic or divine authority. The one hundred forty students in Mukendi's class also learned how to misuse the Bible to mislead people. Satan gave Mukendi only eight years in this role, since those receiving power directly from Satan are not permitted to live beyond the age of twenty five. He was due to die in 1987; in fact, most of Mukendi's classmates were killed in the various aircrashes of that year. But just before his appointed death, Mukendi was saved by the power of Jesus. Through the help of a pastor, over a period of seven years, Mukendi was completely delivered from the power of Satan.

There are other similar testimonies, including some from East Africa, among them Symons Onyango's *Set Free From Demons*.[25] Those from Nigeria tend to have more local flavor. There are even booklets exclusively about local spirits, such as Victoria Eto's *Exposition on Water Spirits*.[26] This contains a full exposition of the important modern cult of "Mammy Water" spirits. "Mammy water refers to the type of water spirits that are half fish, half human, mainly females.… After Adam lost control of the earth to satan and satan divided the earth among his followers, the demon of Marine was given the seas, lakes and clear water rivers to possess and rule." The book includes descriptions according to habitat, which lists amphibious, stone, tree, river ("the commonest marine in Southern parts of West Africa"), lake, lagoon, and sea marines. It distinguishes various kinds of marine: crown marine, marine vampire, bridal marine, celebate marine, sensual marine, marine withcraft, marine Lucifer, marine Dada, and ubiquitous marine. It describes local marines, or spirits attached to landmarks in her part of Nigeria. It describes manifestations of marine, marine deposits (the things that the marine puts in the body of her victims, like beads or snakes or cowries), and gives techniques for exorcising marine possession. Numerous case studies show the overriding importance of the sexual in this scheme of things. Almost everything is subjected to a sexual interpretation.

A whole popular literature (usually pamphlets rather than books) is emerging on evil spirits or demons.[27] Obviously, much of it is particularly African, for example, the West African Mammy Water Spirits. But U.S. charismatic Christianity also gives enormous prominence to demonic beings. This is evident in Peretti's best-selling novels and in Rebecca Brown's books.[28] Like its African counterpart, the U.S. demonology gives much play to the sexual, and to child murders and cannibalism.

In some circles, the U.S. demonology may be more influential than the African belief in spirits. A pastor of Broken Yoke Foundation, of Bolgatanga in the far north of Ghana, said he felt the need to begin a new church. Each church and minister ought to have their own specialty, he explained, and his was demonology. Asked whether his demonology was similar to that of Emmanuel Eni of Nigeria, he responded quickly: "No, I don't have that attitude so much," and volunteered that the books he finds most helpful in this matter are books by Lester Sumrall, Kenneth Hagin, or Gordon Lindsay. Another minister at Tamale in central Ghana reported a similar orientation. The resident pastor of the World Miracle Bible Church said the specialty of his church was demons. Asked if the congregation's understanding of demons was that of Emmanuel Eni, his reaction was again swift: "Some of those Nigerian books are not well based, but frightening. Some are weird and exaggerated. We don't take them as true, especially Nigerian books. We just concentrate on Frank Hammond's [*Pigs in the Parlor*] book."

These two strands—the African and the Western—reinforce one another, feed off one another, and in certain circles tend to coalesce. Thus a Kenyan Christian magazine, in advertising a forthcoming conference, could categorize Rebecca Brown and Eni as the same thing. It states simply: "The evangelist Emanual Eni and Rebecca Brown *who were Satanists before converting to Christ*, are scheduled to attend."[29] Undoubtedly the U.S. charismatic demonology has considerable harmony with traditional African beliefs; but the demonology of Africa's contemporary charismatic churches may well be getting its special character through the power of American literature.[30]

The Faith Gospel

The faith gospel has seemingly taken over Africa's charismatic revival. According to this, Jesus has met all our needs on the cross, and every believer should now share the victory of Christ over sin, sickness, and poverty. A believer has a right to health and wealth—in fact, a believer should be distinguished for his or her health and wealth. This teaching is characteristic of almost all Africa's charismatic megachurches. This is not, however, to say that all these churches are identical in their teaching, that they advocate prosperity in the same way or employ the same hard-sell techniques. Some are just as crass as many in the U.S. For example, Benson Idahosa of Nigeria, probably the best-known church leader the Pentecostals have produced in Africa (and who is frequently to be found on American platforms), preached a crusade in Douala, Cameroon, in May 1993. In the course of one sermon, Idahosa claimed that his faith had brought him so many clothes he did not know he had them; a car that even Nigeria's President Babangida could not match ("When my car passes in Nigeria, people gape"); so much food that he simply collapses.

In the final session, one of Idahosa's associates (who later admitted that his only theological training was in Kenneth Copeland seminars) invited the crowd to come forward to receive an anointing, which would change their lives as it had his. He explained that before his anointing he traveled economy class; afterward he always traveled first class; before the anointing, his wife and he had always had to go without food if they had guests; since then, whenever a guest came, he could afford to kill a cow; after the anointing he got a better car, one with air conditioning and a chauffeur, and he expected to have a Mercedes 500 Concorde before November. Before the anointing he had a three-bedroom house; afterward he had a seven-bedroom house, but he expected to have 12 bedrooms by the end of the year. He ended, "Greatness is on the way; my home is in heaven, but let me see the one here first. Are you ready for your anointing?"

For Idahosa and his team, the agenda clearly was fund raising. Idahosa said, "God has told me to start the first Christian university in Africa. Wouldn't you like in the future through Nigerians to have a Christian university in Cameroon?" Then he gave his hearers the chance "to sow" 10,000, 5,000 or 1,000 CFA (at that time, U.S. $1 was worth about 270 CFA). For 30 minutes he lined up those who wanted to sow, first 10,000 then 5,000, then 2,500, then 1,000 CFA, insisting "God will bless every seed sown," and "I wish I were you, so that I could sow and expect a miracle." Immediately after that, he invited everyone to come forward to buy a book he had written and a magazine "for only 1,000 CFA." Nearly everyone took part in both parts of this exercise.

But, by contrast, consider Mensa Otabil of Ghana. His International Central Gospel Church in Accra is a faith movement church; the one who believes will receive. He insists "God did not create you with failure in mind, but with success." But there is a different way to success. For Idahosa, success was achieved instantly (and magically) through faith, anointing, and giving to God (or Idahosa). For Otabil, success is reached through confidence, pride, determination, motivation, discipline, application, courage—and by skills and techniques that Otabil sets out to teach his congregation.

There is an obvious reason why the prosperity gospel should be so readily received in Africa: African traditional religion was primarily concerned with health, fertility, and abundance. But one might ask how this faith gospel can be received so readily where poverty is so widespread. Otabil's church is primarily for the upwardly mobile—young, educated, urbanized people who are determined to profit from the chances that Ghana's structural adjustment offers them. Otabil's preaching is a high-powered incentive to set goals, to aim high, to discipline oneself, to improve oneself, after the manner of the power of positive thinking made famous by the Rev. Norman Vincent Peale. Otabil actually quotes Robert Schuller, another prominent exponent of this power of positive thinking.

But an important qualification should be made here. Positive thinking played such a large role in U.S. Christianity in the '50s and '60s because there was an expanding economy, near full employment, a climate of business confidence, low inflation to encourage savings; there was peace and stability, a judicial system increasingly enforcing equal opportunity, even for blacks; and there were good elementary schools and expansion in higher education. This context is crucial. Ghana, although brought very low, has been struggling since the mid-1980s to introduce order into a situation of considerable social disintegration. Some opportunities still exist: there is some scope for advance, and is a framework of some predictability, a structured, rational environment where those with confidence, discipline, and ability can get ahead. The faith gospel can have great appeal where the chance of progress remains.

However, in Africa generally throughout the 1980s, the movement was backward. In Liberia, Sierra Leone, Zaire, Mozambique, where the economy was in precipitous decline, obviously this Christianity could not serve such a function. All the discipline, determination, and effort in the world could not raise you out of the enveloping chaos. All it could do is enable you to suffer with more dignity than most. Even in Ghana, for the vast majority, life became increasingly precarious. Why these Africans should persevere in the faith gospel is hard to say. Perhaps it is still too early to predict whether they will persevere in it. But we must not assume that increasing penury automatically discredits the faith gospel.

In 1990 Liberia was totally devastated by a civil war; one third of the population were turned into refugees, economic activity ground to a halt, and almost every family lost someone in the savage fighting. The Monrovia Bible Training Center managed to finish its academic year in May 1990, but because of the civil war was unable to reopen in September 1990. The American missionary directors therefore immediately moved to Freetown where they opened their Freetown Bible Training Center, with four hundred students, in January 1991. In mid-1991 the directors of this Bible school were asked whether, in the light of Liberia's destruction, they had reason to rethink their faith message, particularly that part of their profession of faith that explicitly states that "God intends for his body to walk in total prosperity, spiritual, mental, physical, financial, social." They gave assurance that they did not. God had indeed been good: to their ministry, which had moved to Sierra Leone and was flourishing; to Christians in general, for in the Liberian war very few Christians had been killed—countless individuals could testify that God had miraculously delivered them.

Pressed to explain how any true Christian could have been killed—one training center teacher died in the war—they had numerous answers. Some initially implied—arguing from Romans 7:25, which suggests that one can receive Jesus in the mind but not in the spirit—that this teacher had not been the true believer he appeared. (However, when pressed, all denied that those who had died must have lacked faith.) Some said he was a martyr. Some (citing Heb 11:25) argued that one could *choose* to die; and still others said that he had prospered after all, because he had gone to be with God. In no case, however, did anyone admit to any rethinking being necessary.

Christocentric Exclusivism and Islam

In this starkly dualist world of fundamentalist Christianity, anything "outside Christ" is automatically "in the domain of Satan." This has profound significance in two areas. First, African traditional religion and culture. Many preachers can find nothing good in African culture and categorize all of it as "witchcraft." They have no understanding of, say, the varieties among Africa's traditional healers. All institutions through which Africans have been humanized over the centuries are despised and rejected. Thus Bonnke could describe the results of a crusade in the interior of Zaire: "Satanic structures as old as the hills were smashed."[33]

But equally important is the profound significance this Christocentric exclusivism has for coexistence with Islam. In this regard, consider Nigeria. The dynamics of interreligious tension in Nigeria are enormously complex, but one contributory factor is the kind of Christianity becoming so prevalent there. This Christianity sees Muslims as part of Satan's empire, or as agents of Satan. This view is graphically presented in a Christian book titled *Who is this Allah?* in which G. Moshay argues, with breathtaking lack of subtlety, that Allah is actually Satan. "The devil" is holding all Islamic countries "in bondage of false religion and demonic influence," he declares, and goes so far as to suggest that the evil spirit inspiring Mohammed was the same spirit that inspired Hitler.[34] Published in July 1990, the book needed a second edition within four months.

If Muslims are part of Satan's empire, there is no question of dialogue. All a Christian can do for Muslims is convert them. As we mentioned in the discussion of Liberia, the Christian Zionist component of U.S. millennialism leads these Christians to mount agressive campaigns among the Muslims. Officials of Benson Idahosa's Church of God Mission International claim they are establishing five churches a day in the north. ("The north" is code for "among the Muslims.") Similarly, according to an American lecturer at its Jos seminary, the Evangelical Church of West Africa, the church of the Sudan Interior Mission, founds three churches a week among Muslims.

Muslims hear these figures trumpeted incessantly. Sometimes the justification for the claims is more theological than historical; that is, they are based less on what is actually happening on the ground than on the theological conviction that in these last days God is bringing his divine plan to completion. *Who is this Allah?* exemplifies this thinking. "This decade is very crucial in God's programme," it states. "In these last few years God has decided to save fast and *en masse* and there is nothing Muslims can do to stop him....The wall of the Islamic world is also going to crumble very soon."[35]

Emphasis is placed not only on the quantity of converts, but also on their quality. An American lecturer at the Jos seminary stated that 56 *mallams* (Islamic teachers) were converted in the late 1980s in the Jos area alone.[36] (Each brought all his pupils with him as well.) And *Who is this Allah?* concludes with the testimonies of two converted Muslims, one "son of the heir to the Sokoto caliphate," and the other "from the Sultan of Sokoto's royal family." Thus, Moshay asserts, the best and brightest of Islam are being won to Christianity.

In October 1990, Sword of the Spirit Ministries of Ibadan, with preachers from London's Kensington Temple and Elim Pentecostal Churches of Scotland, launched their Operation GAIN with a five-day crusade in Sokoto, the historic seat of Nigeria's caliphate. The ministry's magazine referred to "this formerly renowned Islamic stronghold" as "this land of inheritance," and spoke of the "wretched state of the multitudes of the state's indigenous, held in bondage to deceit, oppression and sin." The operation was "directed at destroying the enemy's strongholds and deceits in Sokoto"; the preaching "unveiled the enemy's oppressive weapon of deceit in the lives of the people";

and by the end "well over 4,500 adults had been delivered from the devil's clutch."[37]

The theology outlined here is not that of mainline Protestant churches nor that of the official Catholic Church. Their teaching is that Muslims worship the true God, that the Holy Spirit moves among them, that they are included in God's plan of salvation—indeed, that they possess spiritual values from which Christians can learn. But this mainline theology is not heard much in Nigeria. Nigerian Christians have formed the Christian Association of Nigeria, an almost unique body for Africa in that it combines all strands of Christianity: Catholics, the Christian Council of Nigeria, the Pentecostal Fellowship, the independents, and the fellowship of the Evangelical Church of West Africa and the more mainline churches based in the north. And although the top officials of the Christian Association of Nigeria are mainline (the national president is the Catholic Archbishop of Lagos, and the general secretary is the Methodist head of the Christian Council), and its constitution weights voting rights in favor of Catholics and the council, the attitude toward Muslims seems to be that of the new fundamentalists. All branches of Christianity seem to have adopted the one view, in another example of charismatic influence over other churches.

Evangelization and Political Support

A fourth element of the American mix, at least in some formulations, has considerable political significance. This Christianity can give an almost exclusive emphasis to evangelization, which can be expressed with truly apocalyptic fervor. The speaker closing Nigeria's Fifth National Congress on Evangelization in September 1988 stated: "If you are born again, the only reason the Lord is keeping you behind is to evangelize.... Everything else you are doing is just to get enough food to eat and clothe yourself, so that you can evangelize. If you don't see your life in that perspective, then you have missed the mark."[38] This belief in evangelization as the only concern of a Christian usually carries with it a criterion for assessing governments that is rather simplistic. Since evangelization is all that is required, a government that allows this is a good government and one that does not is a bad government. One that positively encourages the work of missionaries is regarded as an *excellent* government, whatever its record might be sociopolitically. This attitude has been used by several African dictators.

President Moi in Kenya continually plays on this. Let us consider some examples. Kenya's state-controlled media continually portray Moi as a God-fearing leader, guided by Christian principles of "peace, love and unity," the motto of his party KANU. Every Sunday evening the first item of KBC TV news is Moi's attendance at church that morning. Often this takes half the time devoted to national news. One Sunday in February 1992, when he was under considerable internal and external pressure to lift his ban on opposition political parties, Moi attended the Gospel Redeemed Church, and that evening the television news carried lengthy coverage of the church leader's sermon. The leader was shown preaching: "In heaven it is just like Kenya has been for many years. There is only one party—and God never makes a mistake." He continued: "President Moi has been appointed by God to lead the country and Kenyans should be grateful for the peace prevailing....We have freedom of worship; we can pray and sing in any way we want. What else do we need? That's all we need."[39]

A few weeks later, Moi attended a harambee (communal fund raising) of this Gospel Redeemed Church. An enormous flag of KANU flew over the platform, dwarfing the Kenyan flags elsewhere around the ground. The church leader (echoing the rhetoric of KANU politicians) delivered a ringing denunciation of Kenya's socially involved clergy: "People should shut up, accept the present leadership, and prepare to go to heaven." Moi then spoke for 15 minutes, stressing the freedom of worship he allowed in Kenya and noting that some of the emerging opposition parties would not allow this because they believed in witchcraft. "Others visit witch doctors, while we in KANU believe in the God of Abraham, Isaac, and Jacob. Other gods do not appeal to KANU."[40]

After the service came the fund raising. Moi contributed 400,000 shillings ($13,000), and—from the entourage that he brought with him—the Vice President and Minister of Finance George Saitoti gave 20,000s, four Cabinet ministers, the Nairobi KANU chairman and the Nairobi police chief each gave 10,000s, and three assistant ministers and the attorney general gave 5,000s each. Nearer the December 1992 elections Christian charismatic support for Moi grew. In November 1992 Charles Hardin and a group of Americans came to Kenya for a major convention of the United Evangelical Churches of Kenya. Just before the convention Hardin, his colleagues and Kenyan leaders paid a visit to President Moi "to confer and to pray with him." Moi took the opportunity to denounce the World Council of Churches for betraying the full Gospel message by accommodating to the world, and warned his visitors to avoid ungodly behavior, to defend the faith without compromise, to have no antagonism to the state, and to stay out of politics. Then he promised to loan six buses from his Nyayo Bus Company to ferry participants to the United Evangelical convention. In the Kenyan context Moi's message was quite clear, for by this time the mainline Protestant National Council of Churches of Kenya (the local equivalent of the World Council) and more lately the Catholic Church had come out with statements on the political scene that were harshly critical of Moi. Moi's message was not lost on the United

Evangelical Groups. The United Evangelical Groups convention became something of a promotion of Moi, and led to a statement signed by the group's leaders challenging the negative pronouncements of the National Council of Churches. And again, two days after the elections, which Moi won (but through such irregularities that the opposition and the National Council of Churches were still debating whether to challenge the results) the United Evangelical leaders went on TV rebuking the National Council and urging the opposition to accept the results.

Similarly, Paul Yonggi Cho came to Nairobi for a crusade March 25–31, 1993. He had a well-publicized reception with President Moi at State House, where Moi referred to his preaching as a "blessing" for Kenya. The media printed pictures of Moi and his entourage attending the closing day of the crusade. A report noted that Cho "called on Kenyans to have faith in God in order to be delivered from the economic crisis facing the country. He said that Kenya was a blessed country because it had a God-fearing leader. The South Korean preacher urged Kenyans to trust in Jesus in order to prosper…(and) that God gave the President wisdom to lead the country."[41]

To appreciate just how political this preaching was, it is necessary to understand that exactly that week, on March 22, Moi had reversed Kenya's economic liberalization program, showing, according to London's *Financial Times*, "the stranglehold corruption has over" the Kenyan economy, and "the power wielded by a handful of politicians who have stolen millions of dollars by manipulating economic controls in their personal favor."[42] At a time when foreign and even the Kenyan press were pointing out that the root cause of Kenya's parlous economic situation was the unbridled corruption of the ruling clique, a visiting "man of God" was preaching to thousands, amid great publicity, that Moi was ruling with wisdom given by God himself, and that it was only the deficient faith of Kenyans themselves that was preventing a glorious and prosperous future for Kenya. Cho's preaching may or may not have been a blessing for Kenya, but it certainly was for Moi personally.

Even some formulations of demonology can have political implications. In March 1991 there was a weeklong crusade in Mathari Valley, one of Nairobi's biggest slums. The crusade drew a large crowd; on the final afternoon it was estimated at one hundred forty thousand people. At various times during the crusade, spirits were referred to as the cause of cancers, heart diseases, ulcers, skin diseases, fevers, tuberculosis, lung complaints, paralysis, and countless other ills. The fact that this slum lacks drains and latrines, that its people are mostly unemployed and undernourished, that they lack resources and education, was never mentioned. One of the books on sale at this crusade (written by a Kenyan, but one who acknowledged his profound debt to Derek Prince of Florida throughout), after explaining at great length that everything evil is to be explained by demonic agency, concluded that those who "do not know this cause, including a majority of Christian believers, blame the government and their leaders." In other words, no Christian who properly understood spiritual causality could blame Kenya's ills on the government. It is not irrelevant to note that the preface to this book was written by Daniel Tarap Moi, President of the Republic of Kenya.[43]

Conclusion

The head of the Evangelical Association of Ghana has remarked: "I work for two evangelical groups; I exercise charismatic gifts both privately and publicly; I worship in a Methodist church where I am a lay preacher. I am a typical Ghanaian evangelical."[44] Behind this statement was the belief that in some way Africa is transcending the historical theological differences that have split Christianity in the West. There is no doubt that Africa does not feel the sharp divisions that are still felt in the West. For example, in Accra, there is a central ecumenical church, shared jointly by Anglicans, Methodists, and Presbyterians. In February 1994, notices displayed in the foyer advertised a Catholic function, the Campus Crusade training center, the Sudan Interior Mission's Bible College, and an Anglican crusade billed in the following terms: "Let Jesus take over your problems; let your business be revived; let your joy be restored; let your marriage be healed, as you become a brand new person in Christ Jesus." The Bible study that morning, led by the Anglican pastor, was quite fundamentalist: "If you are a wife, you know your level, that you are to succumb to your husband." The sermon, also by an Anglican, was on the importance of the Bible: "Anglicans are lazy about the Word; we hate to hear about it.... Let's forget this tradition business. Only Jesus, only Jesus, only Jesus." (In the course of his sermon the Anglican preacher brought in the totally dispensationalist notion of "the rapture.")

Of course, there is no reason why the issues that once separated Zwingli and Calvin and Luther should be of great importance to modern Africans. But even though those differences have little meaning in modern Africa, we should not conclude that the Christianity that is evolving is a genuinely African construct, arising from African experience and meeting African needs. Of course African experience and needs are a huge force in forging the Christianity emerging on the continent. It could not be otherwise. But an overriding influence is present, too: a particular kind of Christianity is presented under the label "biblical," and this claim, by and large, is accepted at face value. This form of Christianity is new and fundamentalist and American. Through its resources, personnel and technology, it may be exerting an influence every bit as great as the colonial Christianity of the last century.

NINE

Spreading the Word:

Organizational Techniques, Theological Emphases, and Pastoral Power

*F*undamentalist churches have become central to the lives of many millions of people because they successfully combine various parts of the evangelical/Pentecostal/charismatic Christian heritage. They offer community and a sense of order, psychically for the individual and socially on the grass-roots level of the congregation. Because their appeal is highly personalized, yet collectively powerful, their influence cannot be reduced to economic developments or political orientations favored by North American businessmen or missionaries. This religious tradition helps people exercise control in a seemingly uncontrollable world through strict standards of "right living." Incomprehensible cycles of poverty and violence are made comprehensible through an all-encompassing theology and by the personal authority of the pastor. And, access to an everyday miracle religion empowers people; it gives them hope of negotiating the insurmountable obstacles of an unknown future.

Although primarily developed in the United States, Christian fundamentalism appears acultural or transcultural in the sense that it can be exported almost anywhere. Differences in emphasis, receptivity, and form exist. But what is striking is not so much the subtle variations among the new Christian groups both intra- and interculturally, but rather the degree of similarity in terms of form, content, and style that are strongly influenced by North American models. One can immediately recognize a "Christian" service no matter whether the tongue is English, Tagolog, Spanish, Korean, or Swahili.

It is undeniable that one of the greatest appeals of the new Pentecostal groups is the manner of worship. Services appear spontaneous, experiential, and exuberant.[1] They are "muy allegre," filled with singing, dancing, and clapping.[2] The comparison with early Methodism and other forms of "enthu-siastic" religion in England, which David Martin has documented, is fitting. For those whose everyday existence is difficult and drab, the air of celebration can be both stimulating and cathartic. People are enraptured. The service is driven by music, often quite professionally orchestrated with drums and gui-tars, so that the rhythm of expression evokes the appropriate expression of grief or joy. Emotion sways the crowds until the speaker holds forth and deliv-ers his message of religious salvation. The general effect, according to a Guatemalan widow who attends the Church of God, is that "Se calma mi corazon"—"It calms my heart."[3]

Whether lower class or middle class, rural or urban, the worship is partic-ipatory. The relatively egalitarian structure "negates the principle of hierarchy, as well as clerical privilege, and the rigors of social stratification of the larger society."[4] Some churches have choirs, which at times perform for the fellow-ship, but most of the service consists of songs sung by the entire congregation. The words are usually simple and frequently repeated, or the words are pro-jected onto the wall for all to see. The function of the lively instrumentation is essentially to carry people along in the lively singing, not to give the musi-cians a forum to perform in their own right.

The individual coming into this spiritual realm receives a kind of attention which should not be underestimated—*you* as a person are important, and *you* can have a sense of belonging here as a child of God. Individual and group identities are set up to nurture and complement rather than compete with one another. People are involved in small, intimate groups that create a sense of belonging. The individual matters—to God, to Jesus, to the pastor and fellow parishioners. This is powerful stuff, and it gives people a share in the super-natural locus of control that is attributed to God, Christ, and the Holy Spirit who "lives within." There is the immensely comforting offer of Jesus as both Savior and Friend—the one who understands your problems and is here to support you.

While individuals may be relatively powerless to change large-scale social and political structures, within the sphere of their private lives they can bring control, order, and dignity. Within the church and family, individuals can suc-ceed, be faithful and prosper by concentrating on individual solutions: no drinking, smoking, gambling, or committing adultery. It is not that this is always easy, but it is in the realm of the possible. Moreover, the individual is recognized as weak, as a sinner who may repent and ask forgiveness, and then try again to "live cleanly."

The question of how this kind of individualism is promoted within a tight-ly ordered fundamentalist framework is an interesting, complex, and para-doxical one. While individual salvation and nurturing are stressed, one of the strongest appeals is the sense of belonging that fundamentalist groups offer. The church provides a community of people who care about individuals, but only as long as they conform to the dictates and principles of the collective. Frank Lechner argues that fundamentalists tend to go against the modernist grain of offering greater autonomy to the individual:

> Ego interests are typically given up for a Higher Cause....."Selflessness" becomes a value. On the other hand, dominating collective sentiment translates into superego, keeping the lid tightly shut on the id...."Self-discipline" becomes the rule.[5]

Group cohesion has a particular appeal because so many people have been displaced from their communities of origin. Intensive rural-to-urban migration creates a vacuum into which fundamentalists can effectively interject their values, taking advantage of the massive upheaval in family kinship networks and traditional patterns of life. Since the individual is already torn away from his traditional home, there is not so much to sacrifice in this bargain—and if it works, much to gain. Furthermore, in most parts of the world, and especially some of the countries dealt with here, the act of demanding social reforms through political channels may be a dangerous undertaking. Attributing unemployment, landlessness, poverty, and military abuses to demonic spirits and individual sin may be the safest explanation in a world turned upside down. Pointing out social inequalities and violence might invite reprisal.

Yet, by self-definition, evangelicals are neither cowardly nor weak—they are prayer warriors, soldiers in God's army. They are encouraged to rail against the evil forces, to name them and to demand that they "get out." Thus women and men can express strong emotions without fear, for they are not challenging or accusing officials or institutions per se. The psychological consequences may be substantial. People may feel more empowered and act in more confident ways, especially when buttressed with community support.

These voluntary associations offer adherents a "free social space" where they can find some sense of belonging, solidarity, and psychological security unencumbered by past alliances. The new community allows them to forge new notions of the self—"for in Christ, the old man is made new." Their churches "create a kind of spiritual cocoon, a congregation of like-minded people who are bound together by a common and particular corpus of rules, moral codes, and theological beliefs."[6] Self-discipline and limited self-government are stressed; within the context of the congregation, people may shed their passivity and entertain goals and ambitions of strength, courage, leadership, and responsibility. One does not need years of training in a seminary to take on a leadership position; instead, one can rise to authority and be accepted and respected on the basis of one's talents, abilities, charisma, and achievements. The importance of this, especially in places where such opportunities are limited, cannot be overestimated.

When the layer of Pentecostal/charismatic experience is superimposed upon old-style Protestant fundamentalism, religious practice within the church service is characterized not just by speaking in tongues, but by testimonies, miracle stories, and prophecies. People who may, in the larger world, count for little have the chance here to demonstrate to others how the Holy Spirit triumphs in their lives. According to South African Pentecostal David du Plessis there is a "restored emphasis on our oral tradition, spoken spiritual autobiographies."[7]

Oral testimony and expression of faith is especially appealing in Third World countries where literacy rates are low, and disproportionately so among women. It offers access to the consumption and production of knowledge among those who may not have the skills or resources to read much printed material. Orality shapes the nature and meaning of the expressions of worship that distinguish Pentecostalism; the outpourings of the gifts of the Spirit, such as speaking in tongues and prophecy, are directly accessible regardless of education, erudition, or social class.[8] Anthropologist Emilio Willems, one of the first to study the growth of Pentecostal churches in Latin America, argues that part of the appeal of Pentecostalism is that the Holy Spirit "as a personal experience, available to all, is mystical identification with the deity and a form of messianism that redeems here and now, rather than in the future."[9]

Organizational Techniques: The Parachurch

If spreading the Word of God requires this special kind of human enthusiasm, it is also dependent upon material resources and effective techniques. American Protestants have generated an abundance of all three as they have fielded missionaries at a steady and impressive rate for the last two hundred years. For most of the nineteenth century, their main objective was the evangelization of the frontiers and cities of the United States as the population expanded into new rural and urban territories:

> American Christianity could keep up with the population movement only by being entrepreneurial.... [They developed] new modes of Christian thinking—adventism, apocalypticism, the holiness movement, Pentecostalism.[10]

After 1900 the idea of winning the whole world for Christ gained paramount importance. As the twentieth century progressed, the changing focus of missions was accompanied by a great shift in the origins of Protestant missionary fervor. A century ago most missionaries, whether they were conservative and biblically literalist or more liberal in their outlook, were sent abroad by the old mainline denominations. By 1953, the two new strains of twentieth-century Protestantism, fundamentalism, and Pentecostalism, had helped to even the score: the National Council of Churches sent out 9,844 full-time personnel to other countries, while 9,296 people were dispatched from more conservative evangelical sending agencies, which included both old-style fundamentalists and Pentecostals. By 1985, the National Council of Churches' number had fallen dramatically, to 4,349, while conservative evangelical, Pentecostal, and independent agencies built up an impressive eightfold advantage, supporting 35,386 missionaries.[11]

In part, the mission statistics reflect some changes in denominational strength within the U.S. For instance, the Southern Baptist Convention, with its majority now firmly committed to fundamentalist doctrine, outnumbers the largest National Council church, the United Methodists, almost 2 to 1. The Southern Baptists nearly equaled the foreign missionary efforts of all National Council members in 1993, with 3,950 long-term representatives in 131 countries.[12]

This denominational competition, however, has become a secondary matter as the parachurch and megachurch have surpassed the denominations in the effectiveness of their proselytizing efforts. The parachurch functions as a transnational coordinator of religious activities operating separately from church memberships themselves. The megachurch is a mushrooming church/business apparatus based within a single, large independent congregation under the control of a powerful minister.

Influencing the worldwide course of Christianity through foreign missions is no small task. In 1900 only 17 percent of all Christians resided outside of Europe and North America, today 56 percent do.[13] Of the 1.7 billion to 2 billion Christians in the world, roughly half, nine hundred million to one billion, are Catholic, perhaps as many as one hundred seventy-five million are Orthodox, and six hundred million to seven hundred million are Protestant. Of the last group, over three hundred million might fit into our broad description of the new fundamentalists, which encompasses the Bible believing, millennialist evangelicals and most of the Pentecostals and independent charismatics.[14]

Building up a following of three hundred million, mostly outside of North America, has required new structures of outreach. Parachurch organizations have proved themselves indispensible for rapid evangelization, and represent a major share of the evangelizing effort in terms of dollars spent and personnel supported, both in the U.S. and abroad. They are generally nonprofit, non-denominational religious institutions that operate very much like multinational corporate businesses. They serve a wide variety of fundamentalist,

Pentecostal, and conservative evangelical churches rather than the old-line moderate and liberal denominations. The range and scope of their activities around the world can be demonstrated by describing a few of the largest parachurches.

The Campus Crusade for Christ dates back forty years, and was established and is still controlled by the strong hand of evangelist Bill Bright. Originating in close connection to Youth for Christ and Billy Graham, Campus Crusade has promoted revivals and the conversion of students throughout the world, always putting a strong emphasis on anti-communism. Within the last ten years it has allowed full Gospel and charismatic missionaries to join its ranks. It has offices on over seven hundred college campuses in more than one hundred fifty countries and operates high school ministries as well. The total staff, full- and part-time, numbers some sixteen thousand people, most of whom raise their own salaries by finding church or individual sponsors. Campus Crusade has been controversial in such countries as the Philippines where tensions between Catholics and zealous evangelicals run high. (For example, the University of LaSalle in Negros Occidental forbade them to organize on campus.)

Youth With A Mission is the openly charismatic organization of Loren Cunningham, which also aims at young people, supports medical missions, and concentrates resources on fielding teams of students for mission/vacation trips in the summer. Thousands of American youth go abroad for evangelistic and church building activities that last from two weeks to two months. According to *The Dictionary of Pentecostal and Charismatic Movements*, "YWAM sends 50,000 short-term volunteers...has 6,000 full-time workers; has more than 100 Discipleship training Schools with a five month curriculum; offers a two-year degree at the School of Urban Missions in Amsterdam; operates the Pacific and Asia Christian University in Hawaii."[15]

World Vision International is an evangelical relief organization that concentrates on supplying medical care and food to the poor, often in conjunction with foreign-aid programs operating through the U.S. government. It is more dedicated to long-term social amelioration than many evangelizing agencies, but still emphasizes the primacy of aggressively Christianizing the world with its charismatic theology. A subdivision, the Mission Advanced Research and Communications Center, publishes the *Mission Handbook* and dedicates itself to "Great Commission" research and defining "the unreached peoples." World Vision has in recent years had the largest budget of any Protestant missions agency in the world (nearly $300 million from the U.S. and Canada in 1992).[16]

The Summer Institute of Linguistics (also known as the Wycliffe Bible Translators) is an organization that dates back to the earliest twentieth-century fundamentalist missionaries. It was founded by Cameron Townsend, who worked in Guatemala for the Central American Mission. The Summer Institute puts particular emphasis on translating the Gospel into tribal languages and reaching the most primitive and isolated peoples. It has frequently employed anthropologists and helped to generate a version of Christian anthropology that is dominant in many religiously oriented colleges and universities in the United States. Its ranks now include both traditional evangelicals and charismatic believers, both dedicated to Biblical inerrancy and dispensationalist thought. It has produced Bible translations in over two thousand languages and dialects.[17]

The Full Gospel Business Men's Fellowship International started in 1952 in Los Angeles, and now claims more than one million members in ninety-one countries. Believing in faith healing, "baptism in the spirit," and speaking in tongues, it draws a very broad membership ranging from Pentecostals to Catholics. Although it is an exclusively male organization, members' wives established a parallel organization known as Women's AGLOW. Wealthy fellowship members helped support the launching of Pat Robertson's Christian Broadcasting Network, Phil Crouch's Trinity Broadcasting Network, and Jim Bakker's PTL Club. Military terminology pervades the group's discussions, for it periodically sponsors "Military Prayer Breakfasts"; men's "advances" (not retreats); and "airlifts," such as the one to the Philippines in 1986 that included tours to schools, plants, factories, and military bases.[18]

Serving more as a charismatic/Pentecostal Rotary Club than a hierarchical missionary agency, the Full Gospel Business Men's Fellowship's middle-class and upper-class constituency provides important contacts for other parachurch and megachurch groups coming from the United States. It encourages a very broad, inclusive definition of "born-again" and "full-gospel" experience; Catholic charismatics are often welcomed into local chapters and even, as in the case of the Guatemala City branch, have filled leadership positions.[19]

While the Full Gospel Fellowship is organized more or less like a fraternal order or religious Rotary Club, other entities such as Pat Robertson's Christian Broadcasting Network represent expanding parachurch organizations that are true multinational businesses dedicated to profit-making activities. In 1993, CBN was expanding business; this included purchasing a European animation firm in order to create new programming aimed at Eastern Europe and Russia, and gaining free access to Mongolian state television so that it might provide children's Bible history programming.[20]

Interestingly enough, the organizations listed above, with the exception of the Christian Broadcasting Network, all originated in Southern California; perhaps this suggests something about their modernity and their affinity with the political conservatism epitomized by late twentieth-century suburban life in the United States. Some scholars[21] have noted the proximity of this evangelization machinery to some of the largest U.S. military installations and defense contractors in Southern California. This would find a parallel in Pat Robertson's location near the huge naval facilities at Newport News, Virginia. Also there is the burgeoning growth of national and international parachurch groups in Colorado Springs, Colorado, the home of the U.S. Air Force Academy and other military installations. Of the more than seventy groups now in residence there, James Dobson's Focus on the Family organization is one of the largest, with a budget of $100 million per year and 1,100 employees.[22]

This is not to suggest that military conspirators are running the parachurch organizations, but rather that certain compatibilities may exist between the subculture that has been charged with the task of imposing American order upon certain parts of the world and those who would like to extend God's covenant with America to the rest of the world. Also, many U.S. military men certainly share the civic inspiration we have called "fundamentalist Americanism," and would appreciate the zeal of the fundamentalist Christians even if they are not prepared to join their churches. There is frequent coordination of activities between former U.S. military personnel in evangelical missions and the aid and training functions of the U.S. Armed Forces and various foreign armed forces. Usually these contacts are open and informal (rather than secretive and illicitly organized, as with the Unification Church or Oliver North); their connection is based on a shared understanding of what is "good" for America and the world.[23]

The Megachurch and the International Faith Missions

Some parachurch activities can also be carried out by the megachurches, which we have described in some detail, especially in regard to Korea and Paul Yonggi Cho. There is no determinant size for a megachurch, although the membership must have the financial resources to support a large church building and a variety of educational and support activities. This probably necessitates a congregation of at least a few thousand, even in well-to-do neighborhoods or suburbs of U.S. and foreign cities. Since fundamentalism was first spawned by the rapid urbanization of the U.S., Sandeen has noted that dispensational millenarianism was most effectively promoted by the big-city pastors who could motivate and mobilize large congregations:

> Never rural or in any sense a grass-roots sentiment arising from the congregations, millenarianism had taken hold first among urban pastors, particularly in New York, Boston, Philadelphia, and Chicago.[24]

Today's megachurches typically are under the command of charismatic, male authority figures who generate more and more activities with which to encompass the lives of their congregations. Their situation resembles that of the big-time pastors at the beginning of the twentieth century, who have been described as "male fundamentalists invested heavily in protecting and expanding the minister's role, an occupation with declining prestige in American society."[25] For instance, the addition of such educational activities as elementary and secondary schools, and Bible colleges enhances the minister's influence and control and will serve as a form of outreach to like-minded Christians in smaller churches that cannot provide these services.

The hierarchical lines of control and authority usually resemble the family-held corporate model, even if ownership is not formally in the hands of the pastor. Like a closely held capitalist business, the decision-making process is controlled by a paternalistic figure, and the division of labor is organized along rather clear patriarchal lines. Most of the laborers in both spiritual and practical matters are female, but most of the higher positions are held by males. Often male authority is transferred down to the next generation of males in the pastor's family. Although the pastor's wife can be an important church representative, as an evangelist or preacher in her own right, she is also an important decorative item. In the megachurch she is on display and full of charm, well-coiffed and well-dressed in the latest American fashions, the epitomy of Western business success.

In the parachurch and megachurch, the legitimacy of the organization is tied to its businesslike aura. Americanizing elements of business clothing and imagery follow the precedent set in the Moody era, and later expanded internationally through such groups as the Full Gospel Business Men's Fellowship International. The missionary and pastor are conducting important business and should wear suits and ties. They should look Western. Currently such faithfulness to the standards of business is being stressed in the various foreign Bible schools, just as it once was in missions training programs within the United States at the turn of the twentieth century:

> In the period in which the new American missions were coming to life it is plain that a whole aspect of American culture—the association of business methods, efficient organization, and financial reward—was unquestioningly accepted not only as a fact of life but as something that could be consecrated to God and employed in Christian activity.[26]

An obvious corollary to the admiration and reproduction of American business culture is the study of English by pastors in many lands. This has obvious educational advantages, as in any field of study, for it allows the advancing preacher to read books published in English, to win a scholarship to the U.S., and to converse with visiting missionaries. But it is also the language of dispensational fundamentalism, the "world language" of divination as well as commerce. We have aleady described how the greatest global evangelists, such as Bonnke and Swaggart, use the international tongue, English, while their very skillful interpreters give an equally moving performance in the local language, complete with facial expressions, hand gestures, and choreography.[27]

The charismatic explosion has led the parachurch and megachurch to promote new developments in the use of old techniques. We have already described, for example, the primacy in Africa of the crusade, which may be America's greatest single contribution to world Christianity. The crusade is really a twentieth-century form of the large, open-air camp meeting that revolutionized the spread of enthusiastic religion on the American frontier. Even then, in the early 1800s, camp revivals were taken abroad from America by U.S. evangelists. Lorenzo Dow's camp-style evangelization so excited lower class English Wesleyans that they were expelled from the Methodist Church and founded their own denomination in 1811, the Primitive Methodist Church, which in many ways was a forerunner of the twentieth-century Pentecostal movement. Historians remind us, however, that the camp meeting was not an American invention, but rather an outgrowth of the "field meetings" of Presbyterians and their breakaway sects, especially the Covenant churches and other reform groups in Scotland, the Northern English border counties, and Ulster. The Six Mile Water Revival in Ulster in the seventeenth century is often cited as the original source of this mass participatory effusion of faith. The Scots-Irish immigrants to America (that is, Scottish and English Protestants who often arrived in North America after a generation or two as tenants on the plantations of Ulster and other Irish counties) brought their revivalist traditions with them, especially to the broad stretch of Appalachia where they were most likely to settle.

Pastors' conferences and Bible schools are two more tools which have been refashioned to promote late twentieth-century fundamentalism. They are just as key now as they were to Dwight Moody in his efforts to change the foundations of American Protestantism at the end of the nineteenth century.[28] The connection between large independent churches under charismatic, patriarchal leaders and ambitious Bible schools is not new either. One hundred years ago the churches of America's greatest revivalist preachers set up "Premillennial Faith Missions." The most prominent independent premillennialists, Scofield, A. J. Gordon, A. T. Pierson, and A. B. Simpson, used their powerful urban churches, among the largest in the United States, to generate the zeal and resources required to create their own missions programs, such as the Central American Mission and Christian Missionary Alliance. Such missions work required substantial revenues, as A. F. Walls points out:

Missionary societies could not have emerged where substantial cash surpluses were not available or where application of such surpluses was subject to outside control.[29]

By the beginning of the twentieth century, these large independent churches demonstrated that they were efficient competitors with the denominational missions: "For the voluntary society to be a principal organ of Christian activity requires, in fact, an atomized church, decentralized and dispersed."[30] "Decentralized" in this case does not mean a small church, but rather a strong, localized entity detached from the national networks of the denominations, which might be seen as a drain on resources.

Generally the megachurches are not dependent upon upper-class largesse, but rather on a cross section of urban residents with strong representation of working-class, middle-class, and upper-class members.[31] This, too, follows the pattern set by the great churches of early twentieth-century fundamentalist leaders. Studies of the William Riley's First Baptist Church of Minneapolis and T. T. Shields's Jarvis Street Church of Toronto show that they exemplified "a type of *cathedral*, a central, urban church with a membership scattered throughout the city."[32]

Both of these preachers had taken over predominantly upper-middle-class churches that soon divided because of controversy over the institutionalization of fundamentalist doctrine. While some prosperous members split off to form smaller, more liberal churches, the pastors succeeded in attracting a much larger congregation of believers from across the class spectrum, all of whom identified strongly with "traditionalist middle class values." According to Martin Riesebrodt, "Fundamentalism's appeal was by no means directed toward the lower socioeconomic classes....The upper and middle classes remained overrepresented."[33]

In addition to the broad economic base of the megachurch, which can support rapid proselytizing within a nation, it is important to consider the relative prosperity of all classes of fundamentalist believers in the industrialized countries when compared to the vast majority of world citizens. Church members who see themselves as lower-middle-class (and this would include many from the skilled working class), can be mobilized to support missionary efforts abroad. Pentecostals in the U.S., such as those in the Assemblies of God in the 1950s and 1960s, were generally not members of the economic elite, but they could no longer be fairly characterized as the disinherited, marginalized urban and rural poor. Prosperous postwar America gave them the means to muster impressive material support for missionary ventures in poor countries.[34] When this potential support is combined with the zeal of the congregation and an evangelical calling to perform Christian service in unfamiliar foreign settings, it translates into a substantial export of cultural and religious influence.

This combination of economic wherewithal and power of the Spirit was harnessed and expanded in the 1950s because the independent faith missions were reborn in conjunction with the Pentecostal healing revivals in America (for example, Gordon Lindsay's Christ for the Nations, Lester Sumrall's church building and evangelizing activity in the Philippines). These missions' efforts, often built on the entrepreneurial efforts of a single pastor, have grown steadily until the present day. One of the most interesting networks of Faith Missions and contemporary evangelization revolves around Kenneth Hagin's Rhema Bible Center in Tulsa, Oklahoma. Rhema claims over fifteen thousand seven hundred graduates in its twenty years of operation, 757 of them completing the two-year full-time training program in 1994, including fifty-three international graduates from twenty-seven different countries.[35]

Many churches throughout the world call themselves Rhema and openly admit their dependence on Hagin. Of these, Ray McCauley's Rhema in Randburg, a suburb of Johannesburg in South Africa, is one of the most influential.[36] Zimbabwe also has a Rhema church that is almost as significant in its own local scene. Numerous churches that are not called Rhema are also strongly influenced because their pastors trained at the Tulsa Center, or because all their literature originated there. In our chapters on Liberia and Guatemala, we noted that the Living Water (Agua Viva) Churches and their Bible schools, both prominent players on the Christian scene, have personnel who were educated by Rhema in Tulsa.[37]

Hagin himself does not control or necessarily sanction most Rhema offshoots, even if founded by graduates of Rhema Bible School in Tulsa. He grants official Rhema Bible association to only three schools: McCauley's in South Africa, one in Ontario, Canada, and another in Australia. The Rhema church and Bible school in Zimbabwe, its counterparts such as Livets Ord in Sweden, and the Living Waters in Guatemala and Liberia are all independent (from Hagin and each other).[38] In fact, this particular "faith" tradition is particularly effective at creating pastors who can pursue their own independent ventures.

Livets Ord (Word of Life) is a charismatic megachurch in the Swedish university city of Uppsala, founded and pastored by a Rhema graduate. This church boasts the largest charismatic church (seating over four thousand) in Europe and the continent's biggest Bible school, with courses taught in Swedish and English. Coming to the English sessions on scholarship are large numbers of Africans, who return to Africa to spread the influence of Hagin. Livets Ord has begun a concerted drive to evangelize the former Soviet Union and Eastern Europe. By the end of 1993 it had trained one hundred fifty pastors from CIS, a Russian denomination, in its Bible school in Uppsala. It worked with nine Bible schools and five hundred churches, and founded two of its own new Bible schools in Sofia (Bulgaria) with three hundred fifty students and in Tirana (Albania) with two hundred students. Livets Ord was planning to open another Bible school in Moscow shortly thereafter.[39]

Kenneth Hagin's influence through Rhema is not unique, for other prominent American preachers have similar independent faith missions throughout the world. Lester Sumrall (already mentioned in regard to Guatemala, Liberia, and the Philippines), founded a church in the Philippines in the 1950s that he claims was the biggest church in Asia at the time. Since then Sumrall has toured the world from his megachurch base in South Bend, Indiana. He is a featured speaker at global charismatic conventions and has written one hundred twenty books, which are distributed widely, often at heavily subsidized prices. He has TV and radio stations; his World Harvest Radio International transmits shortwave to Latin America, Canada, Europe, Russia, and North Africa.[40]

Sumrall's books teach the prosperity gospel associated with Hagin, but display a slightly different tendency. Whereas Hagin's are generally "Biblical" and inspirational, and could be termed unintellectual, Sumrall, in his wide-ranging forays into politics, history, and sociology, is jingoistic, more aggressive, and positively anti-intellectual. Like Hagin's, his ministry is something of a family business: Kenneth Hagin Sr. is assisted by Kenneth Hagin Jr. and his grandson; Sumrall's three sons are all involved in his ministry.

Another evangelizing presence in Liberia and the Philippines is the ministry of Don Stewart. Stewart, like Sumrall, is a direct extension of the 1950s Pentecostal revival that has kept prospering into the 1990s; he took over the ministry of A. A. Allen after Allen's death in 1970, and is now based in Phoenix, Arizona. Allen was the first to develop prosperity preaching into a successful fund-raising ploy. Unlike Hagin and Sumrall, Don Stewart runs his own denomination of churches (see the Liberia chapter). By 1990 he had about fifteen hundred churches worldwide, known as Miracle Life Fellowship International. Three hundred or four hundred of these are in the Philippines, where they are known as Miracle Revival Inc.[41]

An American with a different pattern of international ministry is Jimmy Swaggart. His message, solidly rooted in the American South and its expressive Gospel tradition, was often strongest in its fervent anti-communist support of repressive host governments (Chile, Guatemala, South Africa), but he was not, in contrast to the others, an exponent of the prosperity gospel. Nor did he attempt to establish his own churches, for he was an integral part of the Assemblies of God outreach. His special field was crusades and televangelism, and in many countries he could outdraw all others. In November

1987, under the aegis of the Assemblies of God, he conducted the biggest crusade in Liberia's history; in Guatemala he was the clear television favorite.
Since his sexual scandals in the late 1980s and disassociation with the Assemblies of God (at its insistence), Swaggart has been much less visible in the
international arena. Still he operates an office in Zimbabwe for Jimmy
Swaggart's Relief Ministries and Jimmy Swaggart Child Care International,
both of which concern themselves with refugees in Mozambique; he also continues his TV broadcasts within the U.S. and his Bible school in Baton Rouge.

Theological Perspectives and Religious Practice

Although we have referred to the common theological perspectives of the
new Christian fundamentalism throughout this book, it may be useful to
briefly discuss these elements here. Protestant beliefs range widely, so it is not
our intent to catalogue them or specify exactly which combination might
qualify a particular conservative evangelical to be part of a global fundamentalist movement. Some of these beliefs are wedded to old Protestant traditions
of empowering the individual to lead an exemplary life. Others are related to
twentieth-century excitement over miraculous interventions that are sum-
moned, awaited, perceived, and acted out in the everyday life of charismatic
and Pentecostal Christians.

The conjunction of many of these beliefs, some grounded in "book-cen-
tered 'rational' fundamentalism," others in "experience-centered charismatic
and Pentecostal fundamentalism," is relatively new. The Pentecostal worshipers of the early twentieth century, no matter how much they labored to
"put themselves right with God," were generally excluded from the narrower
Christian fundamentalism of the 1920s. Because of their poverty and emphasis on the gifts of the Spirit, they were not invited to, nor did they particularly desire to join Baptist and Presbyterian inerrantists in trying to preserve (or
transform) American society. This religious movement endeavored to transform the Puritan heritage of the "rationalization of the daily conduct of life"
into the "rational fundamentalism of world mastery."[42]

Martin Riesebrodt, in his comparison of 1920s U.S. Christian fundamentalism and recent Iranian Shi'ite fundamentalism, makes an important distinction between the separation of the rational and the charismatic that once
prevailed in the United States and the opposite case in in contemporary Iran:

> In Shi'ite Islam, rational, ritualistic, charismatic, ecstatic, and magical elements
> are woven together in religious practice...[and] "heterodox" popular religion is
> integrated into "orthodoxy."[43]

Today it is precisely this mixture of theology and practice—the combination
of rationalistic and charismatic elements in the new Christian fundamental-

ism— that is generating such power in the current global revival of Christianity. Its inclusiveness is more apparent abroad than in the United States, but even at home the exclusive elements of particularistic evangelical traditions are giving way to tolerance, if only so that disparate fundamentalist groups can participate in a movement toward "world mastery." The charismatic orientation of many fundamentalists today does not disqualify them from worldly action; in fact, they feel it arms them more fully for the battle to Christianize the world.

From the common fundamentalist basis, Pentecostal and charismatic beliefs have expanded the realm of the active supernatural influence of God. Speaking in tongues and the acceptance of the healing powers of the revivalist are common to most Pentecostals. Added to this, especially in the charismatic or neo-Pentecostal churches, is the notion that divine power may be transmitted to more and more people—so that members of the congregation and the local pastor may heal (laying on of hands) and drive out demons. The final accretion of all these supernatural powers, including the path to material prosperity, is most characteristic of the charismatic megachurches.

This kind of theological underpinning is regarded by many evangelical theologians as heretical, a kind of Godism wherein the believer acquires the attributes of the Divine. The various forms of "Word ministry," "faith-formula" theology, and "positive confession" promise the believer that divine words taken selectively from the Bible can be used efficaciously, and to miraculous effect, in everyday life. Such doctrines, particularly as they relate to wealth and health, have been derived by Hagin, the Copelands, and other "faith" practitioners from the writings of E. W. Kenyon. The right to assert heavenly dominion over material goods, the person's body, or a wider territorial sphere, is invested in the charismatic believer. Hagin claims that, "Within our right of dominion is the privilege of speaking into existence the purpose of God.… In this way we create with God new things and destroy the works of darkness." He derives this from 1 Corinthians 15:32: "Because we are his legal stewards of this planet, it is important for a human being to speak out an authorization for action on the part of the angels."

He finds many other Biblical justifications as well, including:

Mark 11:23–24: "Whatever you ask in prayer, believe that you receive it, and you will."

Deuteronomy 28:2: "All these blessings shall come upon you…if you obey the voice of the Lord your God."

Hagin's Rhema doctrine teaches that God gives men and women the use of Godlike powers and direct access to the blessings of the Kingdom through speaking the Word; hence, the "faith" movement is also called the "Word Ministries." Yonggi Cho's theology is very close to Rhema's. He teaches that through the spoken word the Spirit-led believer can "create and release the presence of Jesus Christ." One need only visualize and specify exactly what is needed in order to secure success, prosperity, or good health.[44] Hagin, Cho, and a legion of others have been criticized for such theological perspectives by other evangelicals, but this has not deterred their growing influence.

The Healing Impulse

Probably the most common exercise of divine power through human agency is the act of healing. Certainly this is the means by which many of the most famous evangelists, both American and international, began their revivalist careers. It is the emphasis on miracle faith that most distinguishes the great revivals now being staged in Africa, Latin America, and Asia from the North American revivals of Billy Graham in the 1950s and Dwight Moody one hundred years ago. Normally, the miracles of healing are performed in front of the crowd, though many evangelists, among them Idahosa of Nigeria, also like to recount previous instances in which they have raised the dead to life.

A touch or a word from the pastoral figure may suffice to drive the sickness out of the afflicted, following the model of Jesus's many feats of healing in the Gospels.

> Acts 5:12–16: "All of them were cured."
> Acts 10:38: "Jesus cured all who had fallen under the power of the devil."
> Acts 9:32–35: "Aeneas, Jesus Christ cures you: arise, and take up your bed."

Normally healings are of the blind, deaf, or dumb; sometimes they are more spectacular, of cripples who throw away their crutches or who leap out of their wheelchairs. Barren women are restored to fertile status. When claims are made of reviving the dead, they are usually newborns or infants. Demonstrations of the power of the Christian healer over omnipresent demonic elements (which are often accepted as normal presences in daily life in many traditional societies) may be more common in Third World countries. Then again, many of the American faith healers of the 1950s revivals explored the field of demonology, and fascination with demonic (and angelic) influences is increasing in the U.S. and other Western countries. This suggests that the differences are not so great as might be imagined, and that more research is needed to understand local pre-Christian elements (in Africa, Asia, or South America) as opposed to standard Western charismatic elements in this mix. In both the West and the rest of the world, demonic spirits are always deemed responsible for the ills that need to be cured; thus healings are inevitably seen as exorcisms.

Apart from barrenness, a major concern at every African crusade (a cure for which is by the nature of things not immediately verifiable), the majority of cases are obvious physical disabilities that are in theory verifiable. There is little evidence of any outright fraud; quite the opposite, for there are always people claiming a cure from an affliction that all too obviously they still possess, a temporary embarrassment that even a little manipulation on the part of the organizers could have avoided. This healing part now looms so large in crusades that a non-Pentecostal crusade will simply no longer work. Visiting revivalists are increasingly billed for their miracle-working capacity.

The Full Gospel and the Great Commission

Although Christians in older, established denominations may be skeptical of the seemingly magical elements in the new fundamentalism, those who practice "full Gospel" Christianity feel that there is substantial theological precedence for their faith. They trust in the Biblical certainty that their methods of worship represent a return to the "true," full-powered Christianity of the New Testament and the first century A.D. The believer expects the presence of the Holy Spirit to be present in everyday life. Supernatural "blessings" serve both as benefits derived from Christian faith and the necessary elements for continuous evangelization of the faith.

Biblical quotations such as the one attributed to the apostle Paul are used to explain the necessity of having a "miracle religion" if Christians are to reach all the unconverted peoples of the earth:

> I will not venture to speak of anything except what Christ has accomplished through me in leading Gentiles to obey God by what I have said and done—by the power of signs and miracles, through the power of the Spirit. (Romans 15:18–19)

This longing for a fresh, reinvigorated Christianity that can empower believers today as it did the apostles has ample precedence in American history. Andrew Walls suggests that American Protestant evangelism of the nineteenth century, even without all the miraculous components of the twentieth, followed an "absolute" New Testament pattern and depended on a special feeling of affinity with the original apostles:

> The success of frontier evangelism…must constantly have brought the sense of bringing the church to birth or rebirth, of starting Christian history again.[45]

A similar feeling seemed to empower the early Pentecostals. T. B. Barratt, the apostle of European Pentecostalism in the early part of the twentieth century, insisted that the movement was distinct from all the evangelical awakenings that preceded it:

It is seen therefore that much of what is taught are *fundamental* truths, accepted in all evangelical denominations. Yet *there is a difference,* as the Pentecostal
revival seeks to return as much as possible to the *doctrine, faith, and practice of
original Christianity in all manners.*[46]

The key element of this original Christianity, the faith in the "full Gospel"
and the practice of miracles in the present day, is what leads Pentecostals to
believe that they can fulfill the Great Commission. The Holy Spirit will help
them bring the Word to all the world's people, thus setting the stage for the
Second Coming.

Speaking in Tongues

The presence of the Holy Spirit is often indicated by the ability of many
Pentecostals and charismatics to speak in tongues; this gift of glossolalia is
connected to the Biblical injunction to evangelize in all languages of the Earth.
In fact, the first Pentecostal missionary efforts generated by the Azusa Street
Revival were generally considered failures because the evangelizers had
departed ill-prepared, believing that they really were speaking the tongues of
India and China. Their newspaper, *Apostolic Faith,* which operated from 1906
to 1908, told its readers: "God is solving the missionary problem, sending out
new-tongued missionaries."[47]

Yet the real significance of this "gift" may have little to do with the mastery of tongues, for the initiates give up control over their words and sounds
in a rite of submission to God's authority. The direct line to divine inspiration
allows the believer to bypass more worldly authorities and gain direct sanction for the new religious practices; in this new scheme of things, established
figures in the old religious and social hierarchy lose a great deal of power. For
many new Pentecostals and charismatics, speaking in tongues is a sign of ini-
tiation and group acceptance into the new faith; for those who have come
from a conservative evangelical or Catholic tradition, the surrender to glossolalia may mark a decisive break with rigid interpretations of religiosity that
rely only on the written word or ecclesiastical authority. Hollenweger feels
this has the significance of joining a new "tribe":

> This function of a "tribal mark" is largely supplied by the baptism of the Spirit,
> with the objectively ascertainable sign of speaking in tongues.[48]

Anthropologist Richard Van Dijk offers an interpretation of the charismatic one-upmanship practiced in the African country of Malawi, where youthful street preachers have used speaking in tongues as a way to defy the elders
who control the one-party government and business community:

> The born-again identity is constructed in such a way that it fosters a sense of

assertiveness among the young by suggesting that religious and moral authority is exclusively reserved and restricted to the "true" Christian [i.e., those who practice speaking in tongues and other Pentecostal behavior].[49]

The "infilling" by the Holy Spirit gives the young a source of power over the old. By making their most spiritual discourse unintelligible to the elders, the younger generation distinguishes their activities from the "gerontocratic" relations that also characterize the older, non-Pentecostal Protestant churches.[50]

In Malawi, as in many other societies around the world, magical rites and contact with ancestors have traditionally been under the control of the oldest members. In this context the speaking in tongues by the new Christian represents something distinct from magical incantation, and, according to Van Dijk, should not be interpreted as a handy form for mimicking folk magic. The orientation of the young preachers is "global," if only in the rudimentary form in which they identify with Christian evangelists whom they hear on tapes and radio from around the world. They identify with city, not rural, life; they want to form nuclear, not extended, families that can function in the modern labor market; they do not want to become new local head men, but rather aspire to be preachers of an international charismatic religion. When young people use their Pentecostal powers they are not making a "bridge" to traditional magic practices. They are being modern, actively repudiating customs that they feel are corrupt and have great negative sway over the elderly who run their faltering society.

Prosperity and Meeting Material Needs

The individualized miracle power of faith theology, directed toward others or oneself, can be utilized for any positive purpose whatsoever, so that it might overcome any and all material obstacles that the Christian encounters. There is nothing wrong in calling upon God's power through prayer in order to meet material needs: not only health, but wealth, are the just deserts of each Christian. This is not interpreted so much as a reward for faith, but rather a duty of God to follow through on His side of the bargain: You believe and He will reward you a hundredfold. Again there is no lack of Scriptural justification:

> Philippians 4:19: "My God will supply every need of yours according to his riches in glory in Christ Jesus."
> Mark 10:29–30: "There is no one…who will not receive a hundredfold here in this life."

Evangelist Gloria Copeland, a "faith" practitioner like Hagin and others, contends that such verses can be interpreted literally: "You give $1 for the

Gospel's sake and $100 belongs to you.... Give $1,000 and receive $100,000."

Prosperity theology has spread rapidly from the United States to other relatively prosperous middle-class groups of Christians who have access to the
global consumer culture (and might be seen as having an unlimited number of
"needs" to be met) in such places as Sweden and South Africa, in up-and-coming economies such as South Korea, and within the better-off classes in many
Third World urban areas (Guatemala City and Sao Paulo, for example).
However, prosperity theology is also embraced by Christians among the
poorer classes. A great many individuals live in rapidly collapsing societies,
yet are exposed to the same advertising and media images of wealth and plenty that tempt more affluent believers. Perhaps this encourages the poor to
think they have the right to arrive at "elect" status, and certainly they must be
enchanted by the prospect of a miracle cure for their own and their societies'
economic maladies.

Power Evangelism and Spiritual Warfare

In a sense, the new fundamentalism is steadily evolving in its powers, cir-
cumscribing an ever greater range of individual and social situations that can
be dealt with through the application of spiritual influence. The notion of
"power evangelism" denotes the ability to convert people to Christianity by
demonstrating the superior "power" of the Holy Spirit in confronting demonic forces. Thus in the battle of Christianity against sinfulness the faithful
engage in "spiritual warfare" on many levels. First, demons can be exorcised
from the body or the soul of an individual who is possessed. Secondly, God's
power can be invoked to destroy evil forces that inhabit neighborhoods and
cities, as well as the territorial demons who might cause drug abuse, prostitu-
tion, poverty, and other social afflictions. Third, perhaps the ultimate level of
spiritual warfare, is to confront Satan's greatest powers, the global false religions of communism, Islam, and secular humanism.

Peter Wagner notes that one function of the "Third Wave" (a term he
coined in 1983) is to avail pastors and evangelists of the "power encounters"
that demonstrate the faith; this allows them to participate in "charismatic-
type manifestations without disturbing the current philosophy of ministry
governing their congregations." "Avoidance of divisiveness at any cost" is the
watchword in Third Wave and church growth circles; the gift of speaking in
tongues is de-emphasized in contrast to classical Pentecostalism. In fact, in
referring to individuals, "terms such as 'charismatic' and 'Spirit-filled' [are]
rejected because of their alleged implication that those who are so labeled
form a sort of spiritual elite of first-class as over against second-class
Christians."[51]

Possibly the Third Wave expansion of the spiritual powers of full Gospel believers is significant in attracting non-Pentecostal fundamentalists toward the new faith. The identification of sinfulness and the full-scale engagement in the battle with demonic forces has resonance with the old-style (non-Pentecostal) fundamentalist preoccupations with evil. The added element is that now Christians are empowered to destroy evil rather than simply avoid it. The military imagery so common to evangelistic campaigns and missionary societies of the past ("Onward Christian Soldiers") has been assumed by new contingents of "prayer warriors," who actually dispatch themselves to various parts of the globe to intervene on the side of Good. Cindy Jacobs, author of *Possessing the Gates of the Enemy*, says that she and other evangelical women are "invading countries, covering them with prayer and engaging in spiritual warfare." This activity is particularly attractive to women, who form the majority of members on these "assault" or S.W.A.T. teams ("Spiritual Warfare and Tactics"). They have mounted incursions around the world such as striking down Macumba witches in Argentina and removing the curse of Satan that was fixed on Red Square in Moscow (the latter accomplished by the Strategic Prayer Council of Aglow International in July 1990). It seems significant (and representative) that one of the high-powered groups that gives itself military rank, "The Generals of Intercession," has fifty members who are divided in terms of their fundamentalist outlook; although half are charismatics and half are evangelicals who do not otherwise worship through gifts of the Spirit, all are able to devote themselves to the concept of international prayer warfare.[52]

Dominion and the Covenant of the Chosen People

The idea that Christians must engage in the struggle with evil at the social and political levels as well as the personal, involving institutional or government corruption as well as private wrongdoing, merges nicely with a longstanding American notion: that when true believers have entered into a covenant with God, they are granted dominion over the territories they already inhabit or intend to inhabit. Although the most extreme promoters of American theocracy, reconstructionists such as Rushdoony, are a very small minority unassociated with Pentecostalism, the attraction of dominionist belief is considerable for many neo-Pentecostal believers. The power of the Holy Spirit may be invoked by those who enter directly into the largest arenas of political confrontation and purification (like Pat Robertson and Reverend Moon).

Such empowerment may have encouraged Pentecostals, once on the margins of political engagement, to join other Christians in maintaining the "election of America" as God's chosen country. In fact, the ability of Pentecostal practice to transcend geographic and cultural boundaries may offer a kind of conduit to covenant religion, which used to favor rationalistic, reformed nationalism. Such churches—be they American, Dutch, Scottish, Northern Irish, South African—once had difficulty overcoming their nationalist pretensions to sanctity and superiority, and often were more successful at conquest than conversion. The neo-Pentecostal churches often see themselves as covenant communities whose mission can expand into the political and economic realms of the whole nation. The influential Verbo Church in Guatemala City, for instance, can envision "stewardship" over the country by a theocratic leader (like Rios Montt) as compatible with Christian "stewardship" over the nation's resources on the part of responsible capitalist owners.[53] Perhaps such an open-ended interpretation of worldly dominion suggests that American culture, through charismatic power, can be expanded or tailored into a mass, one-style-fits-all covenant.

Miracle History (or Salvation History)

Dispensationalism, millennialism (pre- and post-, or a mixture of the two), and apocalypticism are staples of both old and new fundamentalism. They are a constant attraction to a great many Christians along the fundamentalist/ Pentecostal spectrum; perhaps they are indispensable in light of a return to "first-century Christianity" and the urgency of the Great Commission.

In this scheme the passing of history (2,000 years is little more than the steady accumulation of sinfulness and the examples of humanity's failure to fulfill Christ's message), the Great Commission will put an end to the dispensations and, of course, to the liberal (or secular humanist, or Marxist, etc.) preoccupation with temporal history. Dispensationalist belief has merged with Pentecostal miracle religion and dominionist ideas to "empower" new fundamentalists in other parts of the world to identify their destiny with that of the United States. The points of history reconstructed by American fundamentalists consist of a linear connection from the Israelites to the apostle Paul to the Pilgrims, to George Washington and the Founding Fathers, to the year 2000. Korean believers have connected themselves to the original covenant by postulating that their ancestors were a tribe of Israelites lost on the East Asian peninsula.

In many places, however, the conditions of social disintegration, plague, famine, and endless violence may simply add up to the real experience of apocalypse for both believers and non-believers. For new Christians in these locales, an explanation of the "end times" (the literal end of history and its attendant suffering) can be found via studies of prophetic scriptures (Daniel, and Revelation, and sometimes Ezekiel). Alternately, in what might be seen as the more practical short term solution, there is identification with the United States as its "chosen" status becomes globally recognized through the interpretations of the various fundamentalist Bible schools. The distinction between premillennial pessimism and postmillennial optimism, blurred throughout the evolution of U.S. Protestantism, ultimately becomes unimportant, like two sides of the same coin being flipped by the Creator.

Endowed with the power to negate notions of secular history, to graft miracle history onto the expanding covenant of U.S. values, fundamentalist/ charismatic interpretations can cover all bases. If the new global culture can replace the unworkable old local cultures, ending the familiar apocalypses without a final Apocalypse, this is acceptable. The new Christians want to demonstrate that terrible events and political confrontations in the present are part of the imminent final conflict between God and Satan. However, they would settle for an outcome in which the painful tribulation is canceled because the millennium has already been decreed.

Biblical Inerrancy

Although Biblical exegesis has always been common to Protestant interpretation of the world, belief in the literal inerrancy of each word of the holy text was not common until the nineteenth century. For early Protestants the association of Bible reading, literacy, and the individual's ability to engage himself in the activities of the world did not require such rigidity. Biblical interpretation of everyday life and the exciting discoveries generated by other forms of written knowledge were not mutually exclusive, rather they both promised the believer more mastery over the world.

A belief in the all-encompassing, literal truth of the words of the Bible has taken on a magical, incantatory power for fundamentalists of all stripes, and it is intimately connected with the nineteenth-century development of various schemes of dispensationalism. The task of Biblical interpreters is not to show the reasonableness of the Biblical text or explain away apparent contradictions, for in their view the Word of God requires no such justification by mortal beings. Fundamentalists use Biblical passages as markers to which they can attach isolated historical incidents, sacrificing the sequence and movement of historical events to the certainty of God's plan. The object is to delegitimize secular explanations, or any historical or scientific interpretations that lie outside the realm of the preacher or the reference Bible. At times, the notion of inerrancy adds immense authority to the pastor, for it is precisely his ability to focus on and emphasize certain words and passages (and ignore others) that limits the movement and intellectual range of his flock.

Locus of Order and Pastoral Control

The foregoing list of theological features ought to suggest some of the range of the new Christian fundamentalism as it affects the believers' comprehension of order and disorder in daily life, their trust in divine power, and their spiritual engagement with their church and the larger world. Beyond the personal relationship that each believer can have with Jesus, as offered by evangelicalism in general, there is a fundamentalist belief system and interpretive matrix that allows an immense opportunity for the minister to orient and even steer the church member. When combined with the paternalistic, personalistic control of the actual church organization by the pastor/businessman, especially the megachurch and the parachurch apparatuses as described above, this particular all-encompassing theology can motivate intense evangelizing outreach and strong charismatic identification (in the Weberian sense) with the father figure who heads the church. The faith and the business apparatus enhance each other; this in turn results, potentially, in the immense enhancement of pastoral power.

It is not our purpose here to analyze the dynamic of psychological submission to the pastor and to the boundary system of fundamentalist theology, except to venture that some rather rigid establishment of psychic, spiritual order seems to be acceptable, even necessary for the individual church member. It does not matter especially how one interprets this submission to order. In the negative sense such faith could relate to such things as a profound state of fear among the believers, the real or perceived conditions of anomie in society, and an irrational hunger for miracles. On the positive side, such a belief system legitimates a longing for a spiritual community offering safe and orderly patterns for the expression of love and caring, an approved medium for expressing positive thoughts and feelings, and an actual means of empowering people to accomplish remarkable deeds in the real world. In either case, the pastor wields a great deal of control, and this is legitimate in the eyes of the church member.

There is a fortunate conjunction of forces: the pastor's own evangelization goals and business objectives fit nicely with the personalistic-patriarchal principles that mark the fundamentalist tradition. The large-scale independent mission churches and the related evangelization ministries are essentially entrepreneurial outgrowths of the most "charismatic" of the charismatic and Pentecostal preachers. In the days of Dwight Moody and big city preaching impresarios like A. J. Gordon, this type of impetus and organization corresponded to the personal empires established by many U.S. capitalists, both large and small. Thus it was not surprising that the "pro-business" pronouncements of Moody stirred up considerable support among the leading businessmen of whatever large city welcomed his revivals. Such a direct connection, although to some extent important in regard to such organizations as the Full Gospel Business Men's International, no longer links the efforts of the evangelists to the American business elite. The most powerful segment of the business class today is dominated by impersonal, rationalized giant corporations that are run by CEOs who are generally not sympathetic with the full Gospel evangelistic concerns.

The megachurches have more in common with the traditional, paternalistic, middle-class business forms that were marginalized by corporate growth in the early twentieth century; but at the same time they are innovative and up-to-date in terms of the product mix they manage to instill in their congregations. Their pastors address the individual needs and wants of the congregation and they manage to lead fundamentalist believers toward engagement in social and political matters that old-style Pentecostals and fundamentalalists used to avoid. There is a correspondence between such newfound powers and church structure.

Jim Williams, pastor of the largest Assembly of God church in New Zealand and a member of Yonggi Cho's crew of church growth specialists,[54] recommends that pastors use a Presbyterian model of government by elders, common to many Pentecostal churches as well as Reform/Presbyterian churches, because it concentrates pastoral power. This is preferable to centralized control over pastors by bishops and congregational control by the membership because, as he explains, "it is almost impossible to inspire and revive a church from the ground up. It must come from the top."

This desire for pastoral authority over the church membership, as well as over the interpretation of the Bible, suggests that the megachurch and parachurch models are leading the new faith toward new kinds of hierarchy. When one looks at areas outside the focus of our direct investigations, the most convincing research indicates a tendency toward increasing pastoral control and congregational respect for authority, and even tolerance of authoritarianism. This is happening among older Pentecostal traditions as well as neo-Pentecostal upstarts.

The world's most established Pentecostal church is probably the Methodist Pentecostal Church in Chile, founded in 1911 by "born-in-the-spirit" renegades from the Methodist Church. It has been relatively free from direct foreign influence ever since. This denomination of about one million people, one tenth of all Chileans, is controlled by a hierarchy composed of bishops and very powerful pastors. In the 1970s the Methodist Pentecostals and most other Pentecostal churches in Chile became the enthusiastic supporters of General Pinochet's military coup and right-wing dictatorship. When other Christian groups, both Catholic and Protestant, were petitioning the government to respect human rights, thirty-two Pentecostal groups took out a full-page newspaper ad in the capital in order to declare their unreserved support for the "maximum authority" of the junta. Since then, the Methodist Pentecostal "cathedral" in Jotabeche has grown into the world's second largest church with over three hundred thousand members.[55] The pastor/bishop of the church, Javier Vasquez, was even invited to be Pinochet's minister of religion (Pinochet being a Catholic in a country that was over 80 percent Catholic at the time); Vasquez declined but continued to provide other valuable services to the regime.[56]

Lalive d'Epinay's studies of Chilean Pentecostalism in the 1960s suggested that pastors served as surrogates for the "patrones," the landowners who had previously set all the rules in the rural hacienda culture.[57] His model of analysis, in which pastors of little churches of the poor were helping to herd their flocks into the modern age, took on a different aspect in light of the evolution of Methodist Pentecostalism and the changes in Chilean society. As Pentecostalism developed significant large hierarchies of its own, the relationship and deference to authority became more structured and included strong themes of nationalistic obedience; this was entirely compatible with the kind of free-market militarism that ruled the country.

If the structure and historical circumstances of the Methodist Pentecostal Church are peculiar to Chile, they bear comparison with the circumstances of another, large body of Pentecostals, the Assemblies of God in Brazil. Worldwide, the Assemblies have probably grown faster than any other large Protestant denomination: from 1,632,531 adherents in 1965, to 4,594,780 in 1975, to 13,175,751 in 1985, to 25,448,373 as of December 31, 1993. Assemblies in the United States, though still very influential, make up less than 10 percent of the total, 2,271,718 members. Brazil has become the overwhelming leader in adherents, claiming over 14,400,000 members in 1990, or more than 50 percent of the worldwide total.[58]

The spirit-filled influences and open structures of the Assemblies have, in the past, allowed strong-minded individuals to experiment with independent endeavors. Out of the Assemblies have come many great evangelical innovators. There are those who stayed associated with the denomination, like Cho and Swaggart (until he was dismissed), but there are a great many who left to become independent charismatic leaders, healing revivalists, and faith practitioners (Kenneth Hagin, Lester Sumrall, Morris Cerullo, A. A. Allen, Loren Cunningham).

One of the best known, and most unusual of the Assemblies' breakaway talents in the 1960s was the Brazilian revivalist Manoel de Melo, who left the denomination to found his own very large, socially progressive church, Brasil para Cristo. When de Melo pushed his Pentecostal church into affiliation with the World Council of Churches in order to battle for social justice, he explained:

> While we convert a million, the devil de-converts ten millions through hunger, misery, militarism, and dictatorship.[59]

De Melo's success led many observers of the Pentecostal scene, including Hollenweger, to be optimistic about the future of Pentecostal engagement on behalf of the rights of the poor and grass-roots democracy. But Brasil para Cristo proved to be an anomaly, as did the appearance of an inspired Pentecostal defender of the disenfranchised, the congresswoman Benedita da Silva.[60] Instead the major Protestant movement into worldly affairs consisted of the rather sudden, conservative politicization of the Assemblies in Brazil in the mid-1980s, as they formalized new kinds of organizational hierarchies. "Pastores/presidentes," the leaders of state and regional church organizations, began to direct their constituents toward right-wing political conformity. Abandoning their previous apolitical stance of "believers don't mess with politics," the pastors campaigned openly on a "brother votes for brother" theme. Slates of twelve Pentecostal candidates were elected in the 1986 and 1990 congressional elections.[61] Once having chosen political activity, the Pentecostals had an advantage over other religious traditions; sociologist Paul Freston indicates that this was because of their churches' "capacity to control large areas of members' lives, including the ability of pastors to tell their flock how to vote, and a sufficiently strong church/world cleavage to prevail over competing political influences from outside."[62]

Rowan Ireland, in his in-depth local study of religion and politics, suggests that pastors have led congregations in the Brazilian Assemblies to "enter into social formations that link the poor and powerless to agents and actors of the ruling classes in an authoritarian and non-negotiable mode."[63] Ireland draws on the analysis of the foremost Brazilian observer of Pentecostalism, Francisco Cartaxo Rolim, and concludes that many Pentecostals have limited options:

> They are not freed from dependency, rather they are doubly dependent: their religious consciousness is formed in submission to the established social order, and they are then tied to the interior authority of their sect and congregation.[64]

In this fashion the interests of the increasingly bureaucratized Assemblies ended up corresponding more closely to the right-wing political agenda of the newest neo-Pentecostal churches, which explicitly serve a middle-class, urban clientele. The older Pentecostal breakaway Brasil para Cristo abandoned its activist social role under pressure from increasingly conservative church elders in the 1980s. In its place arose such organizations as the Universal Church of the Kingdom of God, representative of a Rio-based "third wave" of Pentecostalism in Brazil, said to be "founded by home-grown products of a slightly higher cultural level and whiter skin."

That church, which owns Brazil's fifth largest TV network, managed to elect three national congressmen from its ranks in 1990. "The Universal Church shows a frankly pragmatic relation to politics, characteristic of a

business empire expanding on many fronts." The whole religious apparatus is
rigorously controlled by the founder, Bishop Edir Macedo, who keeps lower
pastors in line by moving them frequently from church to church. The church,
nearly one million strong, uses prayer warfare in full-scale battle against
Umbanda, the popular form of spiritualism which attracts millions of middle-
class and poor Brazilians. It also embraces prosperity theology and teaches its
members how to pray for economic success. One researcher in Brazil remarks
that this church "may be peripheral consumer capitalism's most definitive
answer yet to the Methodism of the industrial revolution....The very name of
Universal Church reflects the trend to worldwide economic integration, so
distant from the nationalism of Brazil for Christ."[65]

Furthermore, the rapid movement of people—from rural to urban areas,
downward or upward in status—helps change the priorities of the congregants. The Universal Church in Rio is aggressive in many ways, and tena-
ciously controlled from the top down, but not regarding the individual habits
of its consumers. Much of its appeal is based on its lack of the stringent dress
requirements and behavioral norms that would be expected in traditional
Pentecostal churches. This trend is found wherever globalizing consumer
norms gain hold; in Guatemala City, for instance, where some Assemblies'
congregations grow larger and more solidly middle-class, the pastors find they
must downplay the old legalistic restrictions banning makeup, pants for
women, dancing, and music. Otherwise they would lose the loyalty of their
more prosperous families, particularly the younger generation who are enam-
ored of imported American video culture.[66]

It is important to note that increased latitude for superficial lifestyle pref-
erences among the more prosperous churches does not signify a liberalization
of theology and pastoral direction. The tendency toward more hierarchical
megachurch structures means that different segments of different social classes must be afforded a comfortable place in the congregation without being
censured for matters of taste. The pastor, in turn, is freer to pursue more
potent issues, and can mobilize his congregation toward larger fundamentalistic goals: control over schooling, influence on politics and the media. By no
means are most of the new fundamentalists middle-class people, but a
substantial number are, and this lends a middle-class aura to the whole
movement.

The "middle class" label has been used in derogatory ways by some critics
who denigrate or underestimate the power of the neo-Pentecostal faith on the
grounds that it is linked to desires for prosperity and anxiety about being
financially secure. That link is valid, but should not be used to dismiss the religiosity of churches that are generally serious about all the theological points
we have listed, and often have a varied membership in terms of social class

(and there is no denying the idea that wealth, or even slightly better prospects, can be quite appealing to the poor and working classes). Keep in mind too that the assumptions of middle-class adherents in regard to access to the political process, to education, to various kinds of social involvement are infectious, and have inspired other believers to support an activist course that invigorates Christian fundamentalism as a conservative social movement. The middle-class members often have the time to assume leadership positions in local and regional Christian organizations, and their class connections provide access to resources that are unavailable to Pentecostal churches of the poor. This explains, in part, why older Pentecostal traditions are being drawn toward the neo-Pentecostal, charismatic theological positions, which are simply more available in print, on tape, and in broadcast forms. The globalizing tendencies of the megachurches and parachurches and their quick identification with American trends are not at all liberalizing, but they are adding to pastoral power. In urban and suburban areas of Brazil, Chile, and a number of other countries, the most modern and dynamic trends may be the most fundamentalistic, just as they are in the United States.[67]

tradition still palpable in American Protestantism, which tends to identify misfortune with sin. Moreover, the lower classes in the United States often belonged to non-Protestant confessions, but in Iran they were, as a rule, adherents of the same creed.[2]

Many Muslim cultures are intensely resisting both Westernization and Christianization. They believe social disintegration is caused by economic and cultural imperialism and that globalization on the grandest scale, the modernization of production, is a force dictated outside the boundaries of Islam. The Islamic renewal is allowing nations to modernize and urbanize, helping individuals withstand the pain of relocation and readjustment. However, it also contains the rate of change, so that believers do not fear absolute social destruction and the apocalyptic conditions that have undermined other religions and aided the spread of the fundamentalist rival of Islam.

In contrast, the Christian fundamentalists celebrate capitalism, offer their own solution to the Apocalypse, and demonize the Muslim faith. The aggressiveness with which they implement the Great Commission is illustrated by an advertisement for the evangelizing group "Frontiers" that appeared in *World Christian* magazine.[3] A few words were set in white letters against a full-page purple background:

> In the time it takes
> you to read this ad
> a dozen Muslims will
> have died and gone to
> Hell.
>
> But then,
> who really cares?
>
> FRONTIERS
> Declaring Christ's glory among Muslims!

Frontiers is a smallish charismatic group that fields about 200 full-time missionaries in Muslim countries; it is said to have made a "stirring presentation about reaching Muslims" at the InterVarsity conference for college evangelical Christians at Urbana, Illinois, in 1993. "Urbana…devoted much time to the Muslim world." Of more than seventeen thousand young people attending, over nine thousand pledged to do missionary work after completing college.[4]

The mainstream evangelical weekly *Christianity Today* featured a cover story called "Muslim Mission Breakthrough" at the time of this conference, and gave very favorable coverage to the Christian offensive in Islamic nations. In its analysis it referred to experts at Fuller Theology's School of World Missions, including Dean Gilliland, an African specialist. He acclaimed the effects of the "power encounters" mounted by the charismatic evangelists, in which good spirits overcome the bad: "Folk Muslims are seeing more power in Christianity than in Islam and much more evidence of God."[5]

The growing intensity of rhetoric points to the meaningfulness of global religious competition for many North Americans, even though the real conflict is taking place in far-removed places (as in our African examples, the Filipino confrontations on Mindanao, and the potential antagonism between a re-Christianizing Russia and the Islamic ex-Soviet states that lie on its southern borders). The consciousness of American Christians has plenty of preparation for such interreligious conflict. Since the nineteenth century the dispensationalist tradition has identified the destiny of the U.S. with Israel, two chosen peoples with common infidel enemies. This concoction has been reheated by recent geopolitical pressures (see the version popularized by evangelist Lester Sumrall, described in the chapter on Liberia). In the Gulf War of 1991, there were evangelical chaplains in the U.S. Army who inspired their troops by invoking God's wrath against the demonic rival faith and the satanic Saddam Hussein.[6]

Clearly, the new Christian fundamentalist movement has redefined globalization for its own purposes, which are to conquer and homogenize the world through prayer and evangelization. Muslims may be the largest enemy faith, but others can qualify in their absence. For example, the January 1994 newsletter from MARC (the missionary affiliate of World Vision) reported on a prayer walk into the obscure Himalayan kingdom of Bhutan. Christian activists (including MARC's director of "unreached peoples") were making a "spiritual assault" on the "darkest place on earth," which happened to be the capital's main Buddhist shrine. The same issue also recommended a book to its readers: *Operation World: The Day-to-Day Guide to Praying for the World*, by Patrick Johnstone, calling it "a handy reference for the more experienced globalist."[7]

Anti-Communism

> Christians are the best foes of communism. Therefore, evangelism helps to create a bulwark against communism.
>   —Campus Crusade for Christ's Christian Embassy[8]

Only lately have the fundamentalist Christians been concentrating on the Muslim infidels, because their principal enemy for the past fifty years has been global communism. During the Cold War era, the civil religious impulses of American Protestantism led American citizens to accept an ever broader definition of their Manifest Destiny. Anti-communism became central to the faith because it alerted Americans to the satanic competing world power, the Soviet Union, which was said to have imperialist plans that would turn back the onward march of the "American free enterprise system." By association, the anti-communist beliefs also demonized the scores of little nations that adopted Marxist revolutionary rhetoric and waged anti-colonialist wars to escape direct European/American domination.

As we know, the identification with this dual U.S. "mission" against big and little communism helped rally public support for intervention in Latin America, the Caribbean, the Philippines, Korea, and Vietnam. Although the Evil Empire rhetoric reached its culmination in the Reagan era, the anti-communist phobia had pervaded North American life for some time and had considerable influence on all the churches, Catholic, mainline Protestant, and evangelical. In other countries, too, "communism" became an umbrella term for evil in general. In South Africa, for example, The Suppression of Communism Act effectively defined a communist as anyone who "aims at bringing about any political, industrial, social or economic change" of which the Pretoria regime disapproved.[9] For many years, the traditional evangelical churches of South Africa supported anti-communism as well as the institutionalized racism of apartheid. When this ideological alliance crumbled, in particular as the Afrikaner Reformed Church became more liberalized, so the hard-line commitment to white rule began to break down.

In our discussion of South Korea, the Philippines, and Guatemala, we noted that the new Christian fundamentalism has spread in part because of its affinity for expressions of American political hegemony. The connections between anti-communism, the establishment of localized national security states, and the ideological preparedness of the good Christian are unmistakable.

One need not see this relationship as generally conspiratorial (although occasionally it is, as with Oliver North and his compatriots), but rather as an extension of compatible religious and political ideologies that often overlap. Sociologist Sara Diamond flatly asserts the political connection: "The Protestantization of vast portions of the Third World in recent decades is intimately tied to the Cold War orientation of U.S. foreign policy."[10]

This particular intimacy between religion and politics, as we have mentioned before, had its origins after World War II in the calls for revival by such elite luminaries as John Foster Dulles. He and many others saw communism and socialism as religious competitors, systematic "faiths" upon which many people around the world staked their hopes for changing the world. Not only that, but many socialist adherents held atheistic viewpoints that were openly anti-supernatural and anti-Christian (and anti-Muslim, for that matter). They believed that most religious traditions had assisted or condoned the control of elite classes that owned the productive forces and the cultural machinery of various societies throughout history.

To conservative and especially to fundamentalist Christians, such thoughts represented the ultra-rationalistic webs of Satan, woven to confuse the mind and soul. Communism was a rival that offered to "cure" humanity of its afflictions; it worshiped the false goal (or idol) of building an earthly rather than heavenly paradise. When linked to popular movements in underdeveloped countries, especially where leaders also championed a new kind of nationalism, communism seemed to inspire its own messianic loyalty among its followers. How could those who truly believed in both Christ and America accept this?

Americans' conception of Manifest Destiny had long since transcended North American boundaries; they assumed that the orchestrated spread of American ideals and free enterprise was natural and good. American nationalism had a messianic, universalistic quality of its own. As had been the case at earlier times in U.S. history, the postmillennial trust in America as God's promised land mingled with all manner of premillennial expectations of the end of history. One way or another, whatever their particular mix of dispensational and Arminian interpretations, the fundamentalists would agree that only Christ's Second Coming could cure humanity.

For many years a great deal of popular literature in the United States, much of it not religious except in the "civil" sense, expressed a steady demonization of communism and any remotely related leftist ideologies. The widely distributed writings of government ideologues like J. Edgar Hoover of the FBI and innumerable articles in such places as *The Reader's Digest* gave most citizens their only information and perspective. This is still true today for fundamentalist Christians. Contemporary charismatics, for example, go to such sources for historical confirmation of how Christians have used the Holy Spirit to fend off the Anti-Christ.

For instance, Cindy Jacobs, writing in 1991 on the power of prayer intercessors to effect global political events, used a 1964 *Reader's Digest* article, "The Country that Saved Itself," as evidence of women who are "modern enforcers" of God's will. In her words, the middle-class women of Brazil "rose up" and fought off the impending "communist takeover" with their prayers; "spurred on by these brave women and other resistance groups, the Brazilian army and navy rose up and routed a Communist attack with the leader slipping away in the night." What she was actually describing was the Brazilian military coup against a social democratic, elected government, an event followed by twenty years of military dictatorship. Such simplistic and misleading justifications of major political events was typical fare for *Reader's Digest* and other mainstream media in the early 1960s. The fact that this account can be invested with authority and reworked into the new fundamentalist jargon, with little regard to the real consequences for Brazil, is indicative of the pervasiveness and staying power of the anti-communist message.[11]

Spiritualism confronts communism not just over historical interpretation, but also regarding the "faith" that many modern intellectuals have in the social and natural sciences. The scientific rationalism that so many fundamentalists distrust is not the sole province of atheistic communists, for it survives within more liberal Protestant churches and the humanistic traditions of the Catholic Church. For the fundamentalists, these lukewarm, cerebral Christians (as opposed to those who practice true "religion of the heart") are too tolerant of humanistic influences and other intellectual exercises that explain the human predicament. This not only weakens their application of the true faith, it makes them vulnerable to direct satanic influence in the intellectual sphere, where rationalist thought has proved its susceptibility to the egalitarian ideals of the communists and has tried to give them spiritual relevance.

In the fundamentalist view, the respect that liberal Christians show for the social sciences has resulted in such heresies as liberation theology. A Christian doctrine of social liberation is not just a theological error (or the result of inappropriate emphasis, as some of the more polite critics at the Vatican would say); it provides an opening for satanic communist influence to completely corrupt the Christian faith and turn it into its opposite: an anti-American, anti-free enterprise, anti-spiritual exercise by secular humanists attempting to change the world. Those practicing liberation theology may be characterized on the one hand as dangerous revolutionaries, on the other as silly dupes of communist agents who will lead them astray. To many conservative evangelists in the U.S. in the 1980s, there was no distinction at all. Campus Crusade, for example, characterized liberation theology Christians as nothing more than "masked communists."[12] This same dynamic obtained in the Philippines, in Korea, and particularly in South Africa.[13]

The popular movement to incorporate liberation theology into Christians' daily religious practice has been largely a Catholic phenomenon in such places as Latin America and the Philippines (although some Protestant churches, theologians, and pastors have also embraced its tenets in various parts of the world). This made it possible for Protestant fundamentalists to link their pro-American anti-communism to their rivalry with Catholicism.

Anti-Catholicism and Christian Conflict

Fundamentalists sometimes go so far as to suggest that Catholics are idolaters and not Christians at all. This goes beyond the issue of saints and statuary and sacred relics. In part this stems from the traditional evangelical distrust of a hierarchical institution and its leader, the pope, that are not firmly based in U.S. culture and can never be totally American. But the question of political trustworthiness is only one factor contributing to the antagonism.

The major cause of conflict is undoubtedly the attempt by evangelicals to convert Catholics to "real" Christianity. In parts of the world where Catholic missionaries had secured the allegiance of the masses for hundreds of years, a serious competitor arrived. Heretofore, Protestant presence had been a minor intrusion that appealed generally to a limited number of rural townspeople or an isolated portion of middle-class, educated city dwellers. Even when Protestants wielded substantial influence because of political change, as when the liberal government disestablished the Catholic Church in Guatemala at the end of the nineteenth century, no great conversions of the population were realized.

The new fundamentalist crusaders are much more successful. They have more tools, such as computers and the electronic media, and more money and more missionaries. In certain countries they may be tolerated by an elite class that no longer trusts in the reliability of Catholic support for their system of oligarchical rule. The success of the newcomers relies mostly on their ability to appeal to people who are already religious. No wonder the tremendous success of new religious groups has caused alarm in many countries. In Africa, Gabon actually passed laws in the 1980s banning new groups; other countries such as Ghana, tried to regulate them. Zimbabwe restricted the movement of religious groups in such places as camps for refugees from Mozambique, fearing the right-wing political agenda they espoused. But in none of these cases did the banning of new movements have any effect.

In Africa, the Catholic Church is not the sole player, as it has been for so long in Latin America or the Philippines, but it is a formidable presence. Many of its senior churchmen are important public figures, so important that in the national conferences in Benin, Gabon, Togo, Congo, and Zaire, set up after 1989 to oversee some opening to democracy, Catholic bishops presided over the whole process. Catholic institutional involvement in health and education is unparalleled, especially as civil authority continues to disintegrate in the 1990s.

The defection of Catholics to new churches has become so serious that in 1991 a Catholic project was set up to respond to the challenge. The project produced a booklet, circulated in English and French, titled "New Religious Movements in Africa and Madagascar," which set out the reasons for their success, and suggested some strategies Catholics could adopt in response. These suggestions (which echoed those put forth by the Catholic bishops in the Philippines) included: increase participation in worship; give the Bible greater place in sermons and pastoral letters; attend to the particularities of the local scene; and give the laity a greater role in running their churches.[14]

Still, it must be said that the Catholic understanding of the nature of the new Protestants is limited. The Church's African synod (April–May 1994) focused on the rise of new religious movements; but in the submissions of one of the Catholic dioceses of Ghana, "sects" were indiscriminately defined as anything that was not Catholic, including Buddhists, Hindus, Mormons, and the Full Gospel Business Men's Fellowship. The Catholic Church in Latin America, likewise obsessed with the problem of the "sects," has usually failed to recognize that, despite the plethora of identities and superficial differences, most groups making up the Protestant onslaught are not separate little religions, but rather distinct parts of the dominant Protestant tradition.

If Catholics often fail to recognize that the new fundamentalists are legitimate Christian groups, there is certainly a corresponding disparagement from the other side. The newly arrived Christians feel that Catholicism is weak because it is not infused with the full Gospel that allows for the complete range of religious expression on the part of the believer (with the possible exception of charismatic Catholics). Worse in the eyes of the Protestants is that Catholicism has permitted syncretist religious elements to be practiced side by side with Christianity in many Third World countries and does not mount a full-scale attack against the "satanic" influence of old indigenous ceremonies.[15] Even practices that belong to the Catholic Church, such as the veneration of Mary, seem pagan to these Protestants.

According to the newcomers, Catholicism's failure is evidenced by the fact that it has been the prominent religious presence for hundreds of years. It must, they think, be partially responsible for economic underdevelopment, as well as the lingering sinfulness and immorality that are rampant in these countries. In this sense Catholicism is associated with the corrupt culture of the Spanish conquest in Latin America and the Philippines, as compared to the commendable Anglo-Saxon culture emanating from North America. Catholicism is not seen as American, at least not outside the United States. It is Latin, permissive, decadent; it is African, pagan, overwhelmed by the "Dark Continent."

The leadership of the Catholic Church is choosing to fall back upon patterns of rigid structure and doctrine just as the new Protestants are proving that the absence of hierarchical control energizes their evangelistic campaigns. One of the extraordinary advantages of the Pentecostal and charismatic groups, once they become a sizable presence, is their ability to replicate themselves at will. They would say it is the will of God, who continually calls upon new preachers to arise from the existing congregations and start brand-new churches. Hierarchical direction through the Catholic seminary or the mainline Protestant divinity school is terribly cumbersome by comparison with the constant dynamism of the new churches.

The new Protestants may seem to disregard large-scale bureaucratic structure and organizational stability, but they certainly have their own reverence for a chain of command mandated by heaven. The fundamentalists believe in the "natural" hierarchy whereby God confers direct authority on the pastor. This minister is not just an individual, but the exemplary leader of his own nuclear family. Most cultures that are open to evangelization are well along in the transition from traditional cultures of the extended family to new formations made up of smaller, husband-headed families who rely primarily on their own efforts for survival. In this environment the pastor and his wife represent the perfect couple who have taken it upon themselves to be the foundation of a new church community.

This religious enterprise is not an egalitarian affair, however, for the wife is subservient to the husband. The fundamentalist Christian worldview, which has no need to impose the logistical, bureaucratic framework of a universal Church, does choose to maintain psychic and doctrinal order through the re-subordination of women. If women do not constitute an "enemy" faith, as communism does, the question is why and how the freedom of women in the modern world somehow threatens the fabric of the faith (in fact, of all three faiths: fundamentalist Protestantism, Catholicism, and Islam).

Re-enforcing Patriarchy

People turn to religion in their search for coherence, and this is no less true for fundamentalists who long for order and certainty, especially in their primary relationships lived out in the context of family, church, and school. Here they are unabashedly supportive of patriarchal beliefs and structures. Authority is clearly patriarchal, invested in male superiority and the designated female role of avoiding conflict.

This reinforcement of patriarchy is the trait that Christian fundamentalism most clearly shares with the other forms of religious belief that have also been called "fundamentalist." In his comparative studies, Bruce Lawrence has concluded that: "Fundamentalists are secondary-level male elites. They claim to derive authority from a direct, unmediated appeal to scripture, yet because interpretive principles are often vague, they must be clarified by charismatic leaders who are invariably male."[16] Patriarchy is particularly evident across the Abrahamic tradition of the three monotheistic religions: among fundamentalist Israeli Jews, within both Sunni and Shi'ite Moslem communities in various countries, and within the current revival of evangelical Protestantism emanating from the United States. All three seek to control women and the expression of sexuality, and simultaneously celebrate the status of mother and wife. As Goodwin points out in relation to contemporary Islamic fundamentalism and Bendroth in relation to North American Protestant fundamentalism, changes in the status of women pose a fundamental threat to the traditional cultural order and societal structures.[17]

Martin Riesebrodt, in his comparison of Islamic and Christian fundamentalism, found that the restoration of male power was the most powerful underlying motivation in both religions: "fundamentalism is primarily a radical patriarchalism."[18] In his view fundamentalism represents a protest movement against a universalistic trend in the globalizing world market, where women as consumers and wage earners are becoming more and more equal to men. This feminization of the market may or may not represent a deepening of the democratic process in any particular country (in some advanced countries it allows for women to enter influential professions, but in many places it is connected to the exploitation of young female workers), but it surely is linked to the bureaucratic depersonalization that accompanies the expanding influence of large corporate and state apparatuses. Middle-class men want to maintain dominance of the middling areas of society where jobs are increasingly contested by women, but in many areas of managerial and professional work they no longer have the ability to do so; control was long ago ceded to the "first-tier" male elite who actually run the corporate world.[19] Thus the reference to fundamentalism as the realm of "second-tier male elites" relates to fundamentalist insistence on controlling the means of social reproduction, in particular in the major socializing institutions of family, church, and school. Within the vast majority of fundamentalist, Pentecostal, and charismatic Protestant churches spreading inside and outside the United States, the downward lines of authority are being firmly reinforced: God—> pastor—>husband—>wife—>children. At least rhetorically, this model is particularly well-suited to promoting patriarchal patterns of obedience within the nuclear family; it may represent the most clear-cut way of asserting dominion when other social constraints over female roles are disintegrating and gender roles and relationships are being challenged and transformed by economic and cultural changes in the society at large.[20]

In the early twentieth century, the original U.S. fundamentalist movement explicitly stated that reining in women was essential to maintaining social cohesion; one periodical, *The King's Business*, stated: "There is a full-fledged rebellion under way, not only against the headship of man in government and church but in the home."[21] Evangelists noted with alarm the declining appeal of religion among men and sought to pump some manly appeal into the faith. Bendroth explains: "Feminine piety was something revivalists could take for granted," while "masculine indifference to religion clearly threatened Protestant hegemony in a rapidly secularlizing, increasingly non-Protestant,

American culture."[22] The shift from an agrarian to an industrial society had made it more difficult for men to live out "traditional" notions of masculinity:

> Urban middle-class culture seemed to allow fewer and fewer opportunities for masculine self-determination and patriarchal control. The closing of the frontier, the rise of pacifism, and declining opportunities for the self-made man to succeed in the urban, business world made the quest for authentic manhood elusive and difficult.[23]

While the Boy Scouts of America were trying to devise new ways to create "real men" out of boys,[24] the revivalists were echoing the challenge from the pulpit. Addressing the Winona Bible Conference in 1909, John Balcom Shaw "observed that 'virile preaching' aimed at the 'sturdy and thoughtful' had replaced the 'effusive, mushy, story-crammed, platitudinous' preaching of a past generation."[25] The Victorious Life Movement emphasized filling the young man with the Holy Spirit so he "can of course do what a thousand cannot do.... He is the strong man, the wise man, the effective man." W. B. Anderson went even further:

> Jesus Christ has never asked that man should make this living gift an emasculated human being, or that any of man's normal, vital members be cut off. [Christ came] not to destroy but to fulfill. He came not to curtail life but to release it. ("Victory in Christ," Princeton Conference, 1916)[26]

A kind of militant, virile masculinity became the hallmark of the Christian warrior: "Masculine language and comradery became a rallying point for those who chose to do battle with the devil in modern Babylon."[27] This is no less true today.[28]

The patriarchal elements of early fundamentalism are unabashedly proclaimed in contemporary circles. The director of counseling for Jerry Falwell's Thomas Road Baptist Ministries issued the simple directive: "The Bible clearly states that the wife is to submit to her husband's leadership."[29] And evangelist James Robison's comment on working women speaks directly to the male fear of lost prestige: "The man's attraction is to a woman, not to a 'professional person,' and certainly not to a competitor whose success makes him feel inadequate in his God-given role as a provider."[30]

As women are entering the paid labor force in so many parts of the world, we can find evidence of the anti-feminist bias in the kinds of religious "fundamentalism" that otherwise do not resemble Judaism, Islam, or Christianity very closely. Fundamentalist Hindus in India resemble their American counterparts, according to John S. Hawley, precisely because, "Both groups are loathe to see a woman claim an identity outside the matrix of husband and family."[31] Young men and ascetics upset by the intrusions of women are the most active in trying to "restore Rama" and the most likely to excuse the re-emergence of such customs as bride-burning. They have taken Rama out of the pantheon of Hindu gods and goddesses and elevated him to the status of a male monotheistic God; Rama is a symbol of both male supremacy and right-wing Hindu nationalism.[32]

In Japan, where Christianity has been very slow to take hold, new religions have emerged that have little in common with U.S. fundamentalism other than their extensive practice of faith healing and their opposition to changes in female lifestyle. Historian Helen Hardacre reports that "the branch of American religious life identified as fundamentalist has registered sustained horror at these changes and seeks to return to an idealized past when men were men and women knew their place. This reaction of horror is what most unites American fundamentalism with the new religions of Japan."[33] The new religions want to restore the Japanese model of the patriarchal family idolized during the Meiji era. Male leaders can make the most misogynous proclamations without alienating their predominantly female memberships. "It's the men who are superior, and the women who are behind all the trouble in the world," announced one man to an all-female audience at a Risshokoseikai gathering (a religion founded by a woman in 1938 that now has as many as five million members).[34] The women who follow such leaders are looking for confirmation of traditional hierarchies they learned as children, while still engaging in the new modern roles that have expanded their freedoms.[35]

The dominance of women by men, common to the cultural patterns of most all civilizations in the last few millenia, appears to be the longest lasting and most basic level of authoritarianism. The persistence of male authority, perhaps, has more resonance for the average citizen (female as well as male) than any other arbitrary assumption of power conferred by tradition.

As various cultures are eroded by the force of the global market, by the cash nexus, by the commodification and homogenization of information flow and entertainment, many people cling to the notion that man rules the family because this has always seemed "natural" in their society. When the world seems incomprehensible or spinning out of control, people will seize upon the oldest traditions of keeping order. According to Karen McCarthy Brown:

> When the mind and the spirit are cut off from the body, women become the magnets for the fear raised by everything else that seems out of control. The degree to which control is exercised over women is therefore a key to the profundity of stresses felt by most persons and groups. Fundamentalism is a product of extreme social stress.[36]

Hawley's description of the fundamentalist Hindu movement, where the traditional status of middle class men is threatened on many fronts, correlates nicely with the assessment of both early twentieth-century fundamentalism in the U.S. and Shi'ite fundamentalism in Iran. Religious activism is often generated by the traditional business, landowning, and shopkeeper classes (and their children) because they are the ones being left behind by social change. In Riesebrodt's assessment: "the basic experiences of the traditional middle class are thus economic insecurity and an enormous loss in cultural prestige."[37]

Christian fundamentalists want to reassert a secure male image of a man who can exercise personal, patriarchal control now that parameters of social class and the family are being redefined by larger social forces. In many cases extended families are not only less helpful than in prior economic configurations, they are a hindrance to economic success and mobility. Traditional systems of religious obligation outside the family, once required for promoting community solidarity within the town or village, often cannot cement together social relationships as fast as they are collapsing. The independence of particular Protestant churches (especially the new megachurches) makes them very adaptable to meeting the needs of newly established nuclear families.

To women, who may be able to assume new job roles in the modernizing economy but are not necessarily "ready" to compete at all levels with career-minded males, the megachurch can offer countless outlets for spiritual work and devotion. Part of Yonggi Cho's success at Yoido Full Gospel in South Korea relates to his systemized appeal to women, who make up the majority of church members just as they do almost everywhere in the Christian world. Women are deemed suitable for evangelizing at the neighborhood level and performing certain ministerial services, but are restricted from holding the highest posts in the Church. Their labor is usually free, and they are suitably deferential and devoted to the male leaders.

This may seem incongruous with the historical pattern of Pentecostal revivals, since their churches have allowed females more prominent opportunities as preachers and evangelists than any other Christian tradition. However, examples of female leadership and equality with male preachers have usually been characteristic only in the start-up phase of the Pentecostal traditions. Margaret Paloma's study of the Assemblies of God in the United States indicates that female leaders, preachers, and evangelists became much less common as the church, both as a congregation and as a denomination, grew larger and more institutionalized.[38]

Yonggi Cho began his tiny revival church at Yoido in 1956 by sharing the pulpit with a woman faith healer, his future mother-in-law, but as the church grew he assumed complete control over the pastorship. By the 1980s, when writing about the importance of women in his church, he referred to his reservations about trusting women with the Word, which derived from the apostle

Paul's directive: "Let the women keep silence in the churches." Yonggi Cho found justification elsewhere in the Bible for permitting a woman to assume ministerial roles, "as long as she was under the authority of the church." He explained that to create an expanded role for women in an Asian society that is accustomed to male leadership "was more revolutionary than to establish the cell system itself."[39] His willingness to accommodate, even as he and other men held onto the highest status as defined by male pastorship, is instructive about the negotiation of gender and familial power relationships, and the redefinition of patriarchy. The new fundamentalist megachurch is a site where male and female roles can be redefined while male prestige is reasserted.

This indicates one of the difficulties in discussing the gender politics of fundamentalist Christianity in regard to a range of different cultures. What appears to be an evangelical liberalization of sex roles and a softening of patriarchal power compared to the dominant tradition within many Asian and Latin American societies is still the conservative definition of rightful male authority according to U.S. standards. A number of studies, among them Elizabeth Brusco's assessment of evangelical church culture in Colombia, suggest that the Protestant models of nuclear family life and protective church community diminish the display of machismo while offering safe space for women to assume new responsibilities.[40] It is not a contradiction to point to the importance of male authority within the new fundamentalist framework, while allowing that this authority may be wielded in a more humane and respectful manner than in the predominant familial and religious traditions of a particular culture. In this way the church can provide a modernizing influence, by offering a revised family structure that is more congenial to social reorganization without betraying the legacy and expectations of patriarchal control.

Even in the United States the primacy of the male-dominated nuclear family is still at the heart of Protestantism, whether liberal or conservative (witness the current antagonism to women clergy among many mainline church members), and is glorified by the religious right in their "family values" representation of patriarchy. Submission to the father, celebration of the mother, and the containment of sexuality are nearly always linked together.

Nowhere has this tendency been more exaggerated than at the periphery of the movement. For instance, in the Unification Church the Reverend Moon has always sought ways to control the sex lives and sexual energy of his followers. Moon, as "True Father," decides which members should mate with each other, and he and Mrs. Moon are designated as the "True Parents" of bride and bridegroom.[41] The Holy Wine Ceremony, the church's official ritual of engagement, is said to purify the blood of the partners and begins the long period (often three years) of imposed chastity before the couple can be married.[42] Moon, in his book *Divine Principle*, explained that "the traditional sacraments of Baptism, Eucharist, and Holy Matrimony happen all at once."[43] The marriage, with all its symbolism of the ultimate communion, also becomes a purification rite. The partners are freed from sinfulness, including the sin of "fornication," which Moon identifies as the key to satanic rule on earth.[44] The Unification Church's pronouncements on family, like its endorsements of anti-communism, may be extreme, but they suffice to put Moon on the side of "good" versus "evil." They certainly insert family values into dispensationalism in a novel way:

> The restoration of marriage is understood to be the beginning of the restoration of mankind in the last days.[45]
>
> DIVINE PRINCIPLE shows the family-centered foundation for the coming divine kingdom. An ideal society can be erected once a truly God-centered family comes into being.[46]

Unification Church theology is an exaggeration of fundamentalist evangelical principles (ridiculously stringent rules about marriage have probably limited church membership). Nonetheless it indicates one of the primary tasks of the new churches: to offer idealized versions of the proper nuclear family in modern society. The pastor and his wife are the perfect couple, he leads and she follows (if he is strong and she is beautiful, and both are well-dressed, all the better). They stand in contrast to their Christian rivals: family values under the supervision of Catholics may seem suspect because there is no family unit at the head of each church. What does the priest (or the nun, for that matter) have to offer in terms of exemplary behavior? What experience does he have in marriage, or in disciplining and raising children? No wonder, say the new Protestants, that family life under Catholicism is falling apart.

This is not to deny the role of patriarchy in the Catholic tradition, and certainly it would be hard to argue that any feminist agenda is coming to the forefront of a church that keeps insisting on the importance of an all-male clergy and hierarchy (the pope insists that the matter is not even open to discussion). However, "feminine" aspects of Catholicism contrast with the masculinity of Protestantism, particularly the "muscular" Christianity that evolved out of the late nineteenth-century evangelization campaigns in the U.S. and still characterizes fundamentalist evangelicalism. In the 1920s evangelist Billy Sunday used to tell his male converts that Christianity was "a man's religion," not a "pale, effeminate proposition.... Jesus was no ascetic, but a robust, red-blooded man who lived to the full."[47] In the 1980s, Ray McCauley, a body builder and former Mr. Universe (and now the pastor of the Rhema Church outside of Johannesburg), would flex his muscles as he gave his testimony at crusades throughout South Africa. Among the latest versions of constructing a notion of virile Christian masculinity are the giant rallies staged exclusively for male believers in U.S. football stadiums under the auspices of a group called the "Promise Keepers."[48]

In contrast, the Marian theology within Catholicism—the worship of Mary for her womanly Christian strength, love, and devotion—may be interpreted as undermining the predominant male role (and, in the view of some Protestants, a secret way of incorporating a female deity into the faith). The celibate priesthood and other ambiguities of gender may make the Catholic application of patriarchal values shaky by comparison with the fundamentalist brand. Are priests and male religious leaders supposed to be examples of sexually neutral care givers? Can they transcend sexual roles and offer both masculine and feminine support to parishioners without favoring particular familial connections? Is this any way to promote Christian discipline?

The power of Mary within the Catholic frame of reference has no Protestant equivalent. Her importance is evidenced by the frequency with which her intervention, rather than that of the Father, Son, or Holy Spirit, is sought by prayerful believers and those who await miracles. Her image in statuary and painting, physical and earthly, often takes on the features of local populations. Theologically, too, the influence of Mary carries great weight within the most controversial questions confronting Catholicism. The Vatican's discussion of liberation theology, in which it tries to incorporate much of the liberationist message as a legitimate concern of the Catholic Church, has relied heavily on the Marian tradition. Thus, *Redemptoris Mater,* issued by John Paul II in 1987, clearly designates Mary's words in the Magnificat as defining the Catholic Church's preference for the poor and oppressed: "the truth about God who saves cannot be separated from the manifestation of his love and preference for the poor...celebrated in the Magnificat...later expressed in the words and works of Jesus." The true Christian is implored to trust Mary, who in anticipation of Jesus's birth directed the Christian message toward the world's disinherited when she emphasized: "the importance of the 'poor' and of 'the option in favor of the poor' in the word of the living God. These are matters and questions intimately connected with the Christian meaning of freedom and liberation."[49]

The question here is not to evaluate whether the Vatican really wants to incorporate liberation theology into the Catholic faith, nor to speculate about whether the enormously rich (and often conservative) sectors of the Church in Europe and North America are actually willing to put their resources and faith behind the majority of Catholics, who now reside in the Third World. Rather, we note that the Catholic Church, as a universal body, faces difficulty in condoning the social consequences of worldwide capitalist expansion even as it struggles with the issue of maintaining its own sense of male authority. Some liberal American Catholics, among them sociologist Andrew Greeley, sense that the Vatican is retreating rather glumly into a state of obstinate male withdrawal, a process that, if it lasts for long, may have the effect of reducing the size of the church in order to purify it. Or, according to Greeley, this may simply represent a last gasp of exasperation on the part of males who will one day have to share power within the Church.[50]

In any case, the Catholic dilemmas concerning wealth and sexuality, and the kinds of authority that should control them, have no counterpart among fundamentalist Christians. Their evangelization will keep proceeding apace, perhaps more quickly in the midst of Catholic consternation. Their new faith is simply more adaptable to the present cultural and economic patterns of globalization.

ELEVEN

The New Spirit of Protestantism and the Global Consumer

According to some observers, the new evangelical movement, because it is accompanying the global dissemination of American products and Western values, substantiates the idea that Protestantism can propel economic development. That is, it can help usher in modern industrial capitalism. According to one scenario, Protestantism and capitalism might now combine to create a bright era of material prosperity and democratic institutions,[1] thus following the pattern that was played out successfully in England, Northern Europe, and the United States.

The ethics of emergent capitalism, especially where they embody frugality, self-discipline, and social discipline, are not peculiar to Protestantism. Historian Fernand Braudel found these qualities amply available to Catholic merchant and banking families in the Italian city states; their capitalist values percolated upward and influenced Northern Europe well before the Reformation.[2] Moreover, twentieth-century social scientists have found similar ethics in Eastern, as well as Western, civilization. Some have speculated that various Confucianist traditions are more Protestant than Protestantism, at least as far as preparing people to apply their ethical traditions in the achievement of worldly endeavors.[3]

While we can imagine some kinds of capitalism without Protestant religion, it is nearly impossible to imagine Protestant activity without the background of a culture of emerging capitalism and crumbling precapitalist society. This is not because of economic determinism, nor for that matter religious determinism, but because of the particular historical conjunction of capitalism and Protestantism. The new Christianity of the sixteenth and seventeenth centuries helped break the bonds of feudalism. The spirit of Protestantism, a "religion of the heart" and intense faith in the individual's direct connection to God, was key to freeing people from their traditional patterns of subservience. Historian Christopher Hill describes the process as it took place in Puritan England:

> But men did not become capitalists because they were protestants nor protestants because they were capitalists. In a society already becoming capitalist, protestantism facilitated the triumph of the new values. There was no inherent theological reason for the protestant emphasis on frugality, hard work, accumulation; but that emphasis was a natural consequence of the religion of the heart in a society where capitalist production was developing.[4]

This faith did not represent a retreat from the world, nor timid piety in a world turned upside down. Rather it braced individuals for an exciting engagement with the world and freed them from the constraints of past social barriers and practices. This core value of Protestant theology, common to the seventeenth century as well as the twentieth, loosens the psychological shackles that keep people from attempting what heretofore seemed impossible. American missionaries, and the enthusiastic members of new churches in various countries, go about their tasks with such a high degree of energy, dedication, and reliability that they often overcome deficiencies in technical skills, language, or cultural understanding. A belief in the self, inextricably linked to God, allows them to persevere. As one observes this in developing nations throughout the world today, it is no less remarkable than what Hill described in Puritan England:

> What is so astonishing was that so many people had at the same time the same miraculous experience of conversion: thanks to God's direct intervention, grace made them free...there was no salvation in the old priestly magic, because that no longer gave them control over the world of economic fluctuations in which they now had to live. Only assertive self-confidence could do this.[5]

The individual feels compelled to take action—"We teach that only Doers shall be saved," announced the Puritan preacher Thomas Taylor.[6] This kind of spiritual power seems virtually unstoppable when old social structures are falling apart, especially when combined with the adaptability of the new faith—that is, with its ability to change organizational forms, theological emphases, and cultural loyalties in accordance with what is operational and emotionally satisfying.

As Protestantism has reinvented itself in various forms that correlate with significant changes in the nature of modernizing societies, it has deemphasized some of the qualities that were so potent in the seventeenth century. Then, for instance, the newfound independence of merchants, small farmers, and artisans who thrived in the cities was closely related to their intellectual curiosity; their equality before God helped prompt their willingness to experiment with social forms that would lead to democracy. Many Puritans and nonconformists, in particular, felt free to open up their minds to scientific experimentation, and the literacy learned from the Bible gave them an appetite to devour knowledge and stretch their intellectual engagement with the world. In contrast, today's new fundamentalists have often been proud of their anti-intellectualism, a factor we shall discuss later.[7]

While we would agree with part of the Weberian hypothesis, that Protestantism is connected to the spread of capitalism, we would suggest that both the requirements of the faith and the parameters of the economic system have changed. This is particularly true when we consider the realms of freedom and equality today. As we have pointed out in our case studies, the new fundamentalism is compatible with authoritarian environments and often displays authoritarian dimensions of its own. The repressive element of the faith, as R. D. Tawney liked to emphasize, has been present from the beginning. Martin Luther warned:

> Therefore stern hard civil rule is necessary in the world, lest the world become wild, peace vanish, and commerce and common interests be destroyed.... No one need think that the world can be ruled without blood. The civil sword shall and must be red and bloody.[8]

When more egalitarian forms of governance were developed by early Protestants, they too used terror to instill civic discipline. The rule of the middle-class Calvinists in Geneva "involved the systematic use of torture, the beheading of a child for striking its parents, and the burning of a hundred and fifty heretics in sixty years."[9]

The kind of zeal that was energizing to the individual artisan, merchant, and entrepreneur became something else—more stern and frightening—when wedded to the civil religious task of imposing order on other people. When Cromwell's Army landed in Ireland and eagerly dispatched the souls of the local infidels,[10] Scottish Calvinists were inserted among the lowly Catholics in order to legitimize British domination.[11] The Scots (or Scots Irish) were no more than a low to middling class of tenants in Ulster, themselves exploited by rich English landlords. Nevertheless they were convinced of their elect status and displayed unwavering enthusiasm in maintaining discipline over the unlucky Irish natives. This kind of militant righteousness had a persistent lineage, extending to the annihilation of the Native Americans by the settlers of Appalachia and subsequent projections of American Manifest Destiny;[12] today it is still found in the devotion to Americanism shown by contemporary evangelists and their followers.

In spite of such episodes, the last three hundred and fifty years of Northern European and North American history have also demonstrated that democracy, capitalism, and Protestantism are compatible. The benign side of the faith encouraged individuals to control their own destinies and contributed to liberty and middle-class equality in the Protestant nations—Holland, England, and the United States—which successively dominated an expanding world system of commerce and trade. These countries in turn attributed their successes to their moral superiority and their righteous ways of living.

At the beginning of the twentieth century, liberal elites welcomed Weber's confirmation of a special connection between capitalist endeavor and Protestant habits. Capitalism was under intellectual attack, not only from social democrats and revolutionary Marxists, but from Christian socialists as well. No sooner had Weber delineated the connections between capitalist asceticism and Protestant morality than other historians countered with myriad examples of capitalist greed and exclusivity cloaked in the selective use of Protestant truisms. Tawney enjoyed pointing out that as Puritan vigor had waned, social inequality had increased in Restoration England, and so did theological contempt for the poor:

> A society which reverences the attainment of riches as the supreme felicity will naturally be disposed to regard the poor as damned in the next world, if only to justify making their life a hell in this. Advanced by men of religion as a tonic for the soul, the doctrine of the danger of pampering poverty was hailed by the rising school of Political Arithmeticians as a sovereign cure for the ills of society.[13]

Analyses of the capitalist/Protestant connection still abound; one popular viewpoint contends that the American brand is the most advanced product of "Judeo-Christian Western Civilization." There has been a strong current within American sociology, economics, and political science—whether dealing with development, modernization, or democratization—that assumes that American patterns and institutions and even cultural sensibilities are the necessary carriers of progress (and the culmination of Western civilization to this point.) We find this even today, in different measures, in two recent studies that provide a wealth of useful information and interpretation concerning the new wave of Protestantism. David Martin anticipates that the new brand of "enthusiastic" religion, Pentecostalism, will perform a service akin to Methodism in preparing working- and lower-middle-class people for the frugal enjoyment of prosperity, polite public discourse, and democratic citizenship. David Stoll, who was once pessimistic about the ability of evangelical Christians to free themselves from the conservative agendas of their U.S. sponsors, now wonders if Latin American evangelicalism/Pentecostalism might yield positive results as a moral-reform movement.[14]

This tendency, understandable enough in researchers who witness first-hand the high level of religious commitment among the new fundamentalists, takes a different turn among other scholars. To some who have been battling anti-capitalist interpretations of recent history, the new Protestant growth represents a vindication of Western ideals. Neo-Weberian Peter L. Berger feels that a reliance on Protestant belief is necessary to counter opposing radical belief structures because "the political culture of capitalism cannot inspire, and thus cannot *by itself* counter the mythopoetic inspiration of the egalitarian and socialist visions."[15] Moreover, Berger expects glowing results from the current wave of evangelization: "What one may expect is that the new Protestant internationale will produce results similar to those of the preceding one—to wit, the emergence of a solid bourgeoisie, with virtues conducive to the development of a democratic capitalism."[16]

Is Protestantism really conducive to the development of local capitalism and the expansion of democracy? Is a Calvinist/English/American religious ethic spawning a propensity to individualism, freedom, and grass-roots economic enterprise in various parts of the world? In the parts of the world that we have examined, and in other regions of the world investigated by others, we are inclined to answer: no.

We agree that an important Protestant movement is afoot, maybe even some sort of "revolution." But it should be noted that other political/social upheavals—the Puritan Revolution, the Industrial Revolution, and the American Revolution—were all imbued with different kinds of Protestantism that fit the needs of the day. Even if Protestant Christianity is capable of significant and rapid adaptation to new social requirements, there is no reason to assume that this change should always be progressive or that its alliance with free markets will guarantee freedom of expression and democracy.

Western notions of individualism, a central tenet of Weberian analysis, are lacking in the most successful examples of capitalist development in recent years. In regard to the East Asian "tigers" or "dragons"—South Korea, Taiwan, Singapore, and Hong Kong—the political freedoms that are supposed to accompany individualism have been, for the most part, sadly lacking.[17] Instead the values of "collective solidarity and discipline," not to mention "respect for authority," that are learned in Confucian societies of the East have proved very conducive to their adaptation to capitalism, far outweighing influences imported from the West.[18] Scholars have hypothesized about the ways in which Confucianism could be the Eastern functional equivalent of Protestantism, that is, especially conducive to the work ethic.[19] This implies an altogether different kind of Westernization: the integration of new peoples into a smoothly running international system requires an expansion of the realm of order and the doctrine of orderliness.

In the previous two chapters we touched upon how the new Christian fundamentalists give order to their world. Their theological framework connects them with the power of Good in its multiple confrontations with Evil, and it also connects the individual believer to the exercise of pastoral authority, particularly as regards re-establishing patriarchal norms within realms that can be affected by personalistic dominion over the family. These conclusions are clearer and easier to arrive at than the next level of questioning: how does this new version of Protestantism relate to the much broader question of "order" on the level of political economy? Does the new fundamentalist Christian worldview lead to the legitimation of a new "global order?"

Political and business authoritarianism is one of the characteristics of modern capitalist society that fundamentalist Protestantism adapts to quite handily. From both Calvinist and dispensationalist roots, the faith expresses an extreme desire to impose order on human relations and world events. This does not always represent approval of violent suppression of disorder, but it certainly recommends that people subject themselves to those in power. An admonition found in *Christianity Today* in the 1950s still rings true in the 1990s: "The principle of subjection is with us on every hand: wife to husband, children to parents, citizens to state, congregations to elders and bishops. This is not our arrangement but God's."[20] As our evidence from Guatemala and South Korea (and to some extent, the Philippines and Kenya) suggests, such fundamentalist tendencies are not limited to the religious right in the United States. Research in such places as Chile, Brazil, and Peru tends to confirm that the compatibility of Christian fundamentalism and authoritarianism is not limited to places where the presence of the United States—economic, military, or otherwise—is most pervasive.[21]

As we took pains to point out in our chapter on Korea, modernization and democracy are not necessarily produced in conjunction with one another, even when dynamic Protestantism is present. Steve Chan, analyzing *East Asian Dynamism*, notes that "one of the hallmarks of the capitalist East Asian economies has been political subjugation of their industrial workers"; the developmental state is characterized by strong centralized control and "the stewardship of authoritarian and developmentally oriented bureaucrats."[22]

This demonstrates how misleading it is to confuse the East Asian "work ethic" with the classic "Protestant ethic," the latter presupposing the internalized willingness and desire to work energetically, especially in some unsupervised and independent vocation, which in turn prepares individuals for democracy. The work ethic can be imposed by force and maybe even internalized by populations who endure many years of long and dreary industrial labor. When the "work ethic" is thrown around rather recklessly these days as the *sine qua non* of successful capitalist development, it may connote the very opposite of democratization.

Il Sa Kong, former chief government economist in South Korea, wrote with regret (in 1993) about the period of democratization in his country in 1987–89: "Korea's favorable work ethic and worker-management relationship began to erode rapidly."[23] Of course, in reality Korean workers had not suddenly become lazy; they simply pushed vigorously to form independent labor unions (withstanding massive repression as indicated in Chapter Six) and succeeded in winning long-withheld wage gains; their increases averaged 20.5 percent per year from 1988 to 1990. For Il Sa Kong, the "work ethic and worker-management relationship" are clearly euphemisms for subservience to capital, and were acceptable to the sponsors of his book, a mainstream economic institute in Washington that is attuned to the international viewpoint of American multinational corporations and banks.[24] American think tanks also have sponsored positive sociological and political evaluations of the phenomenal growth in South Korea, Taiwan, and Singapore; their assessments of the dictatorships that underpinned the economic development have been kind: "their regimes, while not democratic, are authoritarian in a generally benign way."[25]

As a result, a body of literature exists that celebrates or tolerates the supposed necessity of authoritarian rule in developing states.[26] Some writers hope that the middle class prosperity resulting from growth under harsh political regimes will lead to democratic openings, such as that which occurred in South Korea in 1992. However, the democratization process in that country has just barely begun; its successes are due more to massive working-class rebellion in the 1980s than to middle-class enlightenment, and could easily be reversed. Democratization in Singapore is almost non-existent, and in Taiwan so recent as to be untested by political confrontation. Given their high levels of prosperity, these countries have very weak records of democratic practice.

This confusion of the work ethic with respect for (or involuntary submission to) authority was hardly what Max Weber had in mind with the Protestant ethic. He lamented the fact that Germany lacked the individualistic Puritan history of England; instead he saw a stagnant Lutheran bureaucratic state with institutions that were "peculiar to feudalism and conservatism, the officers' corps and feudalized civil service." Weber felt the German state had rendered the middle class impotent, quite unlike the seventeenth-century religion that had liberated the middle-class English for self-confident action.[27]

The parallel that was missing in late nineteenth-century German capitalism, almost as much as in late twentieth-century global capitalism, was the conjunction of the habits of daily living and religious values that typified Puritanism. Certain trends emerged simultaneously among the Puritans:

egalitarian striving among the lower and middling ranges of society; small-scale experimentation by independent traders, farmers, and craftsmen; and new religious invention by inspired individuals. Thus, in seventeenth-century England (and Massachusetts, for that matter), an optimistic fusion of self-discipline and freedom energized the common people:

> What mattered was that protestantism appealed, as medieval heresy had done, to artisans and small merchants, whom it helped to trust the dictates of their own hearts as their standard of conduct. The elect were those who felt them-selves to be elect.[28]

Perhaps it was an awareness of historical limitations, the futility of trying to fit a maturing, modern capitalism into an older Puritan framework, that led to Weber's pessimism about how much freedom "the iron cage" of modernity would permit. He feared that the narrow rationalism of bureaucratic capitalism left little room for the individualism he admired in Calvinism.[29] The authoritarianism we find imposed in modernizing countries today, and the space created for certain kinds of new Christian practice, are more indicative of a different kind of human agency also emphasized by Weber, the power of personal charisma to shape human consciousness. In his introduction to *Economic Ethics of the World Religions*, Weber wrote:

> The legitimacy of charismatic rule thus rests upon the belief in magical powers, revelations, and hero worship...Charismatic rule is not managed according to general norms, either traditional or rational, and in this sense is "irrational." It is "revolutionary" in the sense of not being bound to the existing order.[30]

Weber was certainly not thinking of charismatic or Pentecostal Christianity when he wrote this, and although he sometimes entertained longings for charismatic rulers who might transform modern Germany, he probably would not have given up the ascetic rationality he admired in Puritanism in favor of charismatic transformation. We might speculate, however, that something resembling such a tradeoff has been made in the emerging new fundamentalism. The present age, dominated by transnational corporate capitalism, does not require much ascetic rationality from most people who produce things (or only in very limited doses and in areas confined to the performance of a certain function). Thus Protestantism can concentrate instead on developing the charismatically expressive, irrational side of its nature, particularly if it seems to be satisfying widespread emotional needs that legitimize newly evolving social and economic structures.

To many people the power of charismatic and Pentecostal fundamentalism offers substantial promise. The Holy Spirit not only grants psychic certainty in very uncertain times, it also holds out the possibility of miracles that will enable material and physical survival. Although such beliefs have relevance to middle-class existence within a global consumer culture, they also relate to the practical strategies of those who are not now and probably never will be middle class.

In the poorer nations, rigorous Protestant practice in daily life can help orient newly displaced people toward modern patterns of work and urban living. But does this bring economic betterment, as it seemed to do in nineteenth-century Britain and North America among Methodists, Baptists and other denominations? In the late twentieth century Pentecostals and other fundamentalist church members are often recognized as particularly honest and hardworking individuals by their fellow citizens in various parts of the world. On the other hand, no one has demonstrated that these qualities are bringing economic success to the new Protestants (either in absolute terms or in relative terms in comparison with their non-Protestant neighbors).

In studies of Protestantism in Latin America in the 1960s, Emilio Willems pointed to the rising expectations and economic successes of the believers; they appeared to be an upwardly mobile group of the disinherited, with some similarities to Weberian models. Willems emphasized the psychological significance of insular Pentecostal communities in breaking the pattern of control exercised by the economic and Catholic hierarchies: "Pentecostalism thus turns out to be a symbolic subversion of the traditional social order."[31] Such egalitarian commitments still can be found in thousands of small congregations in many countries, yet their spiritual defiance of unfairness and evil in the world has not yet led the Pentecostals to transform the social order. In fact, as Pentecostalism has become more widespread and more identified with the established order, evidence of particular economic achievement has diminished. In East Asia no definitive picture emerges of Protestants performing better than others; many have done well as societies have achieved significant overall advances in standard of living, but the Confucianist, Buddhist, and animist ethics seem to be at least as rewarding as the Protestant one. In the rest of the developing world the situation is worse. In the most recent twenty years, 1975–1994, and especially in the "lost decade" of the 1980s, most people, including Protestants, suffered deep cuts in their standards of living.

Francisco Cartaxo Rolim, who has studied Brazilian Pentecostalism extensively, carefully designates the class positions of those who join the new religion. He identifies 80 percent of believers in greater Rio as members of "the lower levels of the petite bourgeoisie."[32] Many are street vendors and owners of tiny, marginal shops; they are a "dependent" class outside of "direct production," neither working-class nor real owners of production; they are generally thwarted, rather than rewarded, in their attempts to move upward. Rolim's pessimistic appraisal of upward mobility is consistent with evidence from elsewhere in the world: the new fundamentalist Protestantism does not necessarily correlate positively with improved economic performance. For example, a survey of Salvadoran Protestants found: "Contrary to Weberian visions of a Protestant ethic lifting poor converts into higher social strata, our data give little sign that Protestantism has led to upward mobility in El Salvador."[33]

And in Guatemala, a recent anthropological study of Mayan widows concludes that survival is much more important than advancement: fundamentalism is not a "religion of repression," although it was at first for many widows, "nor the religion of advancement," but a "religion of survival," "a space in which the women are able to reclaim some authority over their lives."[34] Earlier research by Bryan R. Roberts in Guatemala City in the 1960s suggested a similar state of affairs: "Under the unstable conditions of Guatemala, Protestant families are not notably more successful than others."[34] Roberts also pointed out that Protestants spend considerable amounts directly on their religious activities: "contributions to church building, visits to other churches, and maintaining the pastor consume as much as 15–20 percent of family income."[36]

The Religious Method of Methodism

Those who have linked Protestantism to the development of capitalism have identified both the individualistic qualities that make potential capitalists and the orderly habits that create good workers. For instance, in the eighteenth and nineteenth centuries, Methodists and Baptists were known for keeping their noses to the grindstone without complaint; they were welcomed by the property-owning elite because they made dependable employees and tended toward political quietism. In England, the early Methodist ministers openly opposed political and trade union organization for their members to ensure that the Anglican authorities would not interfere with the rapid growth of their church. An early Methodist leader, Richard Wilberforce, put the message in clearly subservient class terms:

> Practical Christianity [that is, Methodism] makes the inequalities of the social state less galling to the lower orders...reminding them that their more lowly path has been allotted to them by the hand of God.[37]

This fit with the spiritual mission of John Wesley, who felt his task was to build up the fortitude of individuals, so that they would earn the respect of the higher classes and prove the efficacy of the Methodist "method." In the judgment of social historian E. P. Thompson, common people could have achieved even more progress in terms of democratic and economic rights if only the religious non-conformists had stayed out of the way; in his view the religious enthusiasm of the new sects undermined class solidarity and appropriated the energy needed to sustain such groups as the Chartists and the Workingmen's Party.

If Thompson was harsh in his judgment, others saw Methodism more favorably, as an indirect route toward an egalitarian society. Robert Wearmouth claimed that the religious practices of the Methodists promoted social reform because it was one viable form of active expression and practical organization left open to people. Since the Anglican Church in eighteenth-century England had a strong similarity to the Catholic Church in twentieth-century Latin America—that is, a very small priesthood celebrated mass for a small percentage of the population, which was over-represented by communicants from the upper classes—there was space for religious and social experimentation among the lower classes as long as they could avoid suppression by the state.

In the United States, the presence of the evangelical churches was also tied to industrialization. In the "Rockdale" era of small-town textile mills, the elite and the working class often lived within sight of each other; they could take note of how each other lived out the ethical and social requirements of their common religion.[38] Evangelicalism helped develop the cultural hegemony that taught "respect for authority" among all classes, while it also justified God's rewards for those at the top of the local social structure.[39] The local development of industry required a harsh labor system and the obsession with disciplining workers, adults and children alike, that had been part of "practical Christianity" since the beginning of the industrial revolution in England:

> The proverbial Non-Conformist mill owners, with their Methodist overlookers, and their invidious reputation as weekday child drivers, work[ed] their mills till five minutes before midnight on the Saturday and enforc[ed] the attendance of their children at Sunday school on the Sabbath.[40]

How much is the method of Methodism replicated in the Pentecostal churches of today? Peter Fry—in comparing the industrial development of Sao Paulo, Brazil, and Manchester, England—concludes that Pentecostalism in one sense follows the path of Methodism in Manchester, for it produces extremely devout and conscientious workers for the new industrial enterprises, people who can survive the brutal regimen. He notes one major difference, however, compared to Thompson's view of England and Wallace's picture of the United States: bourgeois Brazilians, whether factory owners or otherwise, are not found in the ranks of the Pentecostals.[41] The Brazilian industrialization process, though an imposing undertaking, does not seem to require the same

Protestant orderliness and rigor on the part of manufacturers that was required for the economic development of England and North America.

Obviously the historical and cultural circumstances of Britain and Brazil, the one epitomizing the earliest capitalist inventions and the other the latest in capitalist expansion, cannot converge in the long run. Above all, the social reordering of the present world is a rapid and gargantuan task. Both industrial development and demographic change are compressed into a much briefer period of modernization, with the major instigator being the movement of multinational capital and the requirements of a globalizing corporate culture. This late modernization does not necessarily need the spirit of democratization that characterized the Puritan revolution; nor does present-day socialization necessarily require the egalitarian rigor of nineteenth-century Methodists and Baptists, whose ambiguous stance, halfway between independence and docility, was fitting to their historical position, midway in the development of a Protestant/capitalist culture.

The Irrational Order of Global Consumerism

Why do models of earlier centuries, of Puritan application and Methodist enthusiasm, fit rather poorly with the modern world? Part of the answer lies with the fact that the developing nations are neither inventing their own models of capitalism nor fashioning particularly indigenous kinds of Christianity. They must conform to the rules of a global network of business and finance, and to the enticements of the expanded marketplace. The superficial overlay of culture that accompanies this network, in language, images, and popular trends, is increasingly American. People have no choice but to accommodate themselves to this culture, just as they generally have no choice about whether to go to work for companies, subcontractors, and plantations that ultimately are connected to the operations of transnational corporations.

Fundamentalist Protestantism from North America is drawing people from various classes into a belief system that encourages submission to authority. Paradoxically, a limited kind of individualism, rather than any reverence for capitalist values, is contributing to this process. The "free-market" version of neo-Pentecostalism offers individual Christians an exciting, but narrow range of religious experiences tailored to U.S. specifications. Believers are encouraged to select personally efficacious items from the racks of religious commodities and then bear witness to the astounding change in their personas. In Latin America, for example, many middle-class Christians are jettisoning the wornout fabric of aristocratic Latin Catholicism in favor of attractive charismatic and neo-Pentecostal lines. They usually avoid another available choice, a new kind of grass-roots Catholicism. This other new faith might offer them more significant opportunities to reconfigure their lives, but at a cost: it would challenge their significant social privileges and demand spiritual sacrifice, rather than fulfill their desires for spiritual consumption.

The Catholic experiment in non-hierarchical religion may be more "Protestant" than the new fundamentalism. The base communities of poor Catholics, inspired by liberation theology, are expanding their world of competency and creating their own patterns of self-direction. Daniel H. Levine has studied these grass-roots communities as they have spread throughout many parts of Latin America[42] and he emphasizes that their importance lies neither in their revolutionary potential nor in their destabilizing tendencies (as has been hypothesized by outsiders who either applaud or condemn the movement). Instead their successes are due to "elective affinities" that peasants and urban migrants are finding between their attempts to create a rational social order and their efforts to practice an ethical religion.

Although the original Protestant ethic was generated by artisan and petit bourgeois groups at a particular time in history, Weber noted that the existence of such groups did not guarantee a movement toward "ethical religiosity." In fact, he thought a slight possibility existed that "the peasantry will become a carrier of religion," but "only when it is threatened by enslavement or proletarianization."[43] The immense peasant population of the globe has been proletarianized at an incredible and increasing rate throughout the twentieth century. But what evidence exists that they can embrace a religion that is both ethical and rational?

The ways in which the popular Catholic groups read their Bibles and relate the message to practical problems in their daily lives is new to them. Their insistence on arriving at knowledge independently of hierarchical instruction, their attempts to understand the social worlds that control their destiny, and their willingness to confront inegalitarian political and economic forces are indicative of a transforming force that is similar to early Protestant faith. These Christians are "particularly open to opportunities for the construction of reason, sociability, and community that are, at least for them, fundamentally new."[44] Their ability to organize themselves and give order to their activities, whether related to instituting public health measures, cooperative marketing, or political networking, depends on a very "Puritan" faith in the efficacy of their own reasoning powers.

Furthermore, Levine suggests that this grass-roots religious movement has much in common with Protestantism:

> The base communities stress the Bible and the value of literacy, they make informed participation a marker of faith, and they look to the personal within congregational structures. As was the case for the Puritans who occupied Weber's attention, the spirituality...is decidedly of this world.[45]

Because much attention has been given to the connection of base communities to the propagation of the more political aspects of liberation theology, it
is sometimes neglected that these communities represent the major Catholic
response to massive social and cultural change and the delegitimation of old
kinds of authority. These popular groups are religiously innovative, for they
give infinitely more opportunity for the lay religious person to create, broad-
en, and take charge of day-to-day church responsibilities. For lay people,
especially women, other benefits are "education, companionship outside the
home," and experiences that build up self-image.[46] Bible study groups are very
popular and utilize Bible stories in the interpretation of personal dilemmas
and community interactions. Because base communities also represent the
self-conscious decentralization of a very hierarchical organization, they have
great success in offering the very qualities of worship that the evangelical
churches emphasize: "intensity, personal warmth, and equality of believers."[47]

Assessing how powerful this religious trend is in comparison with the new
Protestant fundamentalism is difficult, because the internal reformation of the
Catholic Church has been hotly contested. The Vatican has been mounting a
determined campaign to control and thereby minimize the independence of
the base communities since the early 1980s. In its counterreaction, the
Catholic Church wants to make use of base communities, but under tight
supervision as befits the lowest parts of the already existing hierarchy. In
Colombia the conservative Catholic bishops have taken over control of base
communities and are attempting to orient them toward activities dictated
from above, which is manifested through the program for "One Hundred
Pastoral Agents," and financed through the largesse of the West German
Church.[48]

Reasserting control over the base communities is just one of the Vatican's
attempts to reaffirm the wisdom and power of hierarchical guidance; the tendency is manifest "in a host of conservative ecclesiastical appointments,
purges of seminaries, training programs and publishing outlets, and a consistent effort to control autonomous groups."[49] Consistent pressure is applied on
women's religious orders because an essential component of restoring the traditional order is the need to control the activities of women and reinforce
their subordinate position.

Whether or not such life experience and faith make the base communities
the twentieth-century equivalents of seventeenth-century Protestant movements, it is safe to say that the popular Catholic groups have found increasing congruence between their religious ethics and the freedom to rationally
structure their social world. This does not mean that the political and social
goals supersede the religious ones, but that the religious commitment can
make the social mobilization possible.[50] The popular church of the Catholic

poor may not succeed. After all, there is ample opposition to many of its goals, both in the kinds of structural economic readjustments demanded of poor nations by world financial bodies and in the hierarchy of the Church. Nonetheless, within this religious and social movement of impoverished people, the search for ethical rationality and egalitarian social forms is generally compatible with their spirituality and immersion in Bible study.[51]

The example of the base communities should be contrasted with the more ambiguous case of neo-Pentecostal fundamentalism, which appeals to a broad mixture of social classes. These new Protestant groups are often open to poor congregants, but they are usually led by a core of middle-class pastors, elders, and members who have more economic and educational opportunities. The members' experience in various church activities and Bible study groups might seem to prepare them for the practical tasks of reordering their disintegrating societies. Their broadening identification of sinfulness in the social arena, and the powers they call forth to eradicate evil, show that part of the Calvinist heritage is present—they want to prove their mastery over the wicked world. But the undeniably spiritual nature of their faith does not necessarily imbue it with the old Protestant ethic, which emphasized rational appraisals of earthly phenomena and the postponement of material gratification. This religion tends toward instant gratification and anti-rational thought; it is characterized by anti-scientific enthusiasm for creationism and anti-historical leanings toward Biblical dispensationalism.

Within the United States, a sizable minority of the population believes in millenarian dispensationalism, a tendency supported by the inclination of the majority: Gallup polls have shown that "62% of adults in the U.S. affirm that Jesus will literally return to earth."[52] Paul Boyer points out, in *When Time Shall Be No More: Prophecy Belief in American Culture,* that no longer can those who believe in dispensationalism be written off as deprived (in the sense of the classical sociological deprivation theory about compensatory beliefs for the very poor and alienated members of society).[53] The majority of those in the U.S. who adhere to fundamentalist expectations have experienced some form of middle-class or stable working-class existence, and there is a sizable representation of upper-class adherents, too.

The new theology is devoted to a form of hyperindividualism, a transformation of one's personal relationship with Jesus into regular concentration on one's own piety, one's own feelings, one's own health, and one's own financial security. As Ray McCauley, pastor of the Rhema church in South Africa, advises: "Be concerned about yourself rather than everyone else around you. If you have Jesus he will take care of others as he sees fit."[54] On one level, too much attention to troubling external events could be interpreted as disturbing "the power of positive thinking" that was incorporated into fundamentalism via the charismatic revival. In the personal psyche of the "new Christian," the "rational" and the "positive" could very well be at odds: "Rational thinking, doubt, and uncertainty are regarded either as demonic, or as avenues for Satan to penetrate human defenses."[55]

The negative power of rationalism to disrupt the individual's aura of certainty goes beyond questions of personal efficacy. Anti-rationalism is particularly obvious in the new Christian right's response to ideas that challenge Biblical authority. Gary North, whose dominionist tracts are especially influential in their advocacy of Christian commitment to both the free market system and theocratic government (the reconstructionist position), would be considered an intellectual spokesperson of the movement. Yet his instructions for fighting such dangerous ideas as evolution rely on the sentiment of positive thinking rather than on reasoned refutation: "Scientific creationists have not yet successfully attacked the soft underbelly of Darwinism: historical despair."[56] The weakness of Darwinism, for North, ultimately lies in the fact that it does not make people feel good; it challenges their status as the beings chosen by God for eternal pre-eminence on the earth and in heaven.

In the view of some evangelical intellectuals who embrace religious conservatism but resist fundamentalism, the current anti-intellectual emphasis relates to the nature of mass popular culture. George Marsden, for instance, has observed:

> The fundamentalist message is also peculiarly suited for large segments of society in the technological age....The larger the audience the simpler the message must be....The ancient simplicities have been given a contemporary shape by the same forces that produce the efficient production and sales of, let's say, McDonald's hamburgers.[57]

This idea—a simple, one-thought-feeds-all approach of a contemporary theology for the masses—has some attraction, for it does relate to the ease with which the theology is reproduced, particularly in the Bible school businesses, which can set up shop successfully in almost any urban center in the world. On the other hand, the McDonaldization of culture can be seen as an elitist attribution: intellectuals, be they conservative evangelical scholars or skeptical liberals, may infer that the mass acceptance of such theology is due to the simple-minded nature of the American audience or the inability of foreign believers—be they Korean, Nigerian, or Guatemalan—to get it quite right. To counter such bias, it must be remembered that this "feel good" theology has often originated among the upper strata of society. Norman Vincent Peale, when he addressed his educated, upper-middle-class audience in Manhattan, sounded just like Yonggi Cho:

> Learn to pray correctly, scientifically....There is enough power in *you* to blow the city of New York to rubble.[58]

How could one claim that Peale meant this metaphorically, but that Cho is speaking more naively if he makes a similar pronouncement in his "power encounters" with members of his congregation, be they Korean factory workers or bankers?

The super-charged religious scientism and the empowerment of the individual through the use of the Word are potently combined in the charismatic developments of the "faith" ministries. The spiritual powers offered to each believer (or marketed to each religious consumer) by these new fundamentalists are not unusual in one sense; they represent the typical enhancement of individualism found in late modern societies, the kind described by sociologist Anthony Giddens in *Modernity and Self-Identity*.[59] The constant experience of consumption, as everything is commodified under fully developed capitalism, means that it is difficult for almost anyone to distinguish between the "personalized" and the "commodified" experience. In these circumstances such concepts as individual free will are tied to "standardized consumption patterns promoted through advertising and other methods," which in turn "are central to economic growth." In this kind of world, where mature capitalism cannot only meet, but define the needs and feelings of any person, "individualism becomes extended to the sphere of consumption" and "market-governed freedom of choice becomes an enveloping framework of individual self-expression."[60] For many, the meaning of the "freedom to choose" has been reduced to the democratic interaction between the shopper and the supermarket shelf.

In fact, neo-Pentecostal preachers would be the first to admit the connection between their "sales pitch" and the methods of the most successful marketing companies. One Norwegian evangelist, Aril Edvardsen, compares "multi-level evangelism," with its pyramidal cell structure for church growth, to the "multi-level marketing" of the fast-growing American Fortune 500 companies Mary Kay and Amway, which produce neither goods nor services but manage to sell a broad range of cosmetics and other personal effects. As companies operating with an explicitly evangelical Christian corporate ethos, their coordination of group and individual enthusiasm for their various commodities is a model for all Christians: "Amway, Mary Kay...have done tremendous business and have grown tremendously because they have used the same system which is really a biblical system."[61] The aura of salesmanship surrounding Christ was first sketched in by advertising tycoon Bruce Barton in his 1920s bestseller, *The Man Nobody Knows* (Jesus is characterized by Barton as having "picked up twelve men from the bottom ranks of business and forged them into an organization that conquered the world").[62] The image of the Christian salesperson has been much more fully delineated today in intentional networks of proselytization and consumption, highlighted by the televangelism beamed out of the United States. It is the one television product in which there is absolutely no distinction between the program and the advertiser, the actor and the pitchman. (Although increasingly, some cartoon programming for children approaches this level of ambiguity in order to sell more toys and accessories.)

If one is looking for religious consumers who are more circumspect in their buying habits, one can find them on the outermost edges of the global system, where the consumption of advertised life experience is not yet second nature. Anthropologist Leslie Gill, in her studies of Bolivia, indicates that the arrival of Pentecostalism on the world periphery may be no more than an epiphenomenon in the local marketplace, its staying power still in question. Her description of poor, predominantly Indian women—who are mixing religious associations, moving in and out of sects, and frequently being dissatisfied with the efficacy of the religion—makes one suspect think they are "shopping" for a spiritual solution but still are capable of walking out of the market.

> As the ties that bind the poor Bolivians to each other are fractured by economic chaos and the growing commodification of social life, they face the world as individuals, which forces them to create personal solutions to their problems.... Changing religious allegiance...is part of the ongoing drama.[63]

Such women will not be interested in the distinctions that are said to divide modern life from post-modern life. They stand on the brink of rough assimilation into capitalist consumer culture, and they see no signs of rational modernization of the kind projected by U.S. theorists in the middle of the twentieth century. Their world has been enveloped by a chaotic modern/post-modern mix, where any sense of order is ephemeral: "From the point of view of premodernity in which stasis is the norm, modernity can only appear as the maelstrom in which 'all that is solid melts into air.'"[64]

The immersion of the poorest Third World citizens in advertising images and pseudo-information is only partial in comparison with the situation of middle-class citizens in the First World, who already have been submerged by the commodity machine that has, according to Stuart Ewen, "the ability to stylize anything: toothpaste, roach spray, food, violence, other cultures around the world, ideas, etc. and provokes a comprehension of the world that focuses on easily manipulated surfaces. Most notably, as the evanescent becomes increasingly 'real', reality becomes increasingly evanescent."[65]

Confronted with this "reality" of shifting surfaces, the individual fundamentalist believer in developed countries is seldom denied in his search for personal psychic order. He or she may choose the most current personalized means to deal with anxieties about money, romantic love, sickness, and loneliness. Outside of individualistic preoccupations with the path to salvation and access to earthly "blessings," however, the individual may eschew freedom in favor of overt social control, opting for discipline imposed from above. The next layer of order and discipline above the self, pertaining to family and the church, falls back on the paternalistic control of the authorized male: the father, the husband, and the pastor.

As we emphasized in the previous chapter, this kind of patriarchal order seems to characterize almost all current religious movements that have fundamentalist tendencies. This restoration of an older middle-class model has a desperate quality about it, in part because the existence of independent middle-class life has been under attack by large-scale enterprise for a long time (since the early part of the century in the United States). Today the boss or manager is not necessarily an available father figure, and vice versa, the father is not very likely to be a boss. The loss in personal prestige also means a loss of moral agency. The religious emphasis on male, fatherly dominion, whatever its mixture of traditionalist and modern elements, becomes fundamentalist in nature because it tries to impose religious thought as a strict social program. Behind the fundamentalist desire to control life lies a fear of chaos.

In this regard, according to Frank J. Lechner, "fundamentalism is very modern indeed" and "can be seen as one kind of functionally appropriate response to globalization."[66] The attempt to structure thought and behavior, to maintain regular and predictable patterns based on absolutist values, to stabilize a world that has become far too "differentiated" for many people, seems to demand a "decomplexification" (or dedifferentiation) that can be achieved through religion.

Fundamentalist fears of social disintegration, of course, are not imaginary, for anomie and chaos are symptomatic of drastic reordering within globalizing cultures. People of developing countries are faced with cultural changes and adaptations that are extremely rapid and jarring; a world economic system is imposing an industrialization process much more quickly than that experienced by many advanced capitalist countries in the past. No wonder, Lechner writes, people are seizing upon a certain kind of religion in order to maintain functional patterns in their lives:

> An externally induced, sudden, late and deep modernization experience is likely to present a more favorable environment for fundamentalist tendencies."[67]

As various peoples must incorporate themselves into a global system, they pass through a common regimen of modernization, which includes (among other things) urbanization, industrialization, and what we might call nuclearization of the family. Of these, only nuclearization, the reformulation of micro or family structures, is really addressed through restorationist fundamentalism. At the macro levels of reordering complex social structures, fundamentalism—whether Christian, Muslim, or Hindu—may acquiesce to change, but hardly comprehends the nature of the globalizing imperatives. It is sufficient for the new Christian fundamentalism to counsel deference to hierarchical structure and subjection to modern forms of social discipline—the state, the military, and the transnational corporate system—so that believers can function in the changing world. On the other hand, the faith has a special proclivity for powers that are compatible with individualistic consumption. The "freedom to choose" as applied to the believer's personal needs, both spiritual and material, has been introduced in such a way that it can co-exist with the lack of options in other areas of modern life. The fundamentalist movement, particularly in its charismatic form, can grow because it does not chastise its adherents for individualistic worship, nor does it exclude them from participation in the infinitely expanding universe of commodities.

For the new Christians, the "world mastery" of the Puritans is severely restricted; the rational imposition of the ethical life is bound so closely to the personal context that it becomes possible to escape or rise above the forces that are dismantling old national and cultural systems. Historian Stanley Johannesen sees the fundamentalist religious experience, especially Pentecostalism, as a way of translating the literal disembodiment of culture (including the loss of one's national language) into comprehensible terms.[68] There is in Pentecostalism the possibility of a global religion that can transcend boundaries and origins; perhaps, writes Johannesen, it "is only the final mass-movement phase of a Calvinist 'moment' that has been Christianizing mobile, commercial, and frontier populations since the sixteenth century."[69]

The detachment of the Calvinist faith from responsibility for the larger structural elements in society, especially a nebulous coming-into-being global society, has interesting spiritual possibilities. Perhaps it is the world, not the self, that is detached from reality, separated from the concrete:

> Where the Holy Ghost is invoked we may expect to find...a dissolving of the territorial character of the world. The world becomes a "medium," flowing in and through the self, and extending the will of the self by unmediated stages or progressive territorial conquest to its heart's desire anywhere in the world. When the medium is held, in Fundamentalist fashion, to be literally and truly the habitat of the Holy Ghost, we can see clearly the ground of the evangelical energy and success of the Pentecostal movement. The corresponding sense of political virtue, conceiving of the world as continuous from the desires of the

self to all the imaginable needs of the world, is a fair description of the piety of that other institutional legacy of Calvin's war on medieval Christianity, the American Republic.[70]

But hold on. This ought to remind us that in Pentecostalism and neo-Pentecostalism the power of evangelism and Americanism have been mixed anew. It is rather difficult to have a disembodied world when Calvinistic piety and a sense of political virtue are wedded to the faith. Because the American sense of Manifest Destiny converges with the overwhelming sense that the Great Commission must be fulfilled at once, the new Christian fundamentalism cannot simply lose its identity with the United States and become a diffuse, floating, world phenomenon. But what does this portend? Actual conquest, the literal extension of U.S. frontiers and direct political control? Or something different, something new in the annals of cultural conquest?

TWELVE

The Mystery of the Capitalist Ethic

Once again the spirit of Protestantism is accompanying the expansion of capitalism in many parts of the world. Alongside the globalizing economy, where the needs of nation-states are being rapidly subordinated to those of an expanding world system, a particularly American kind of fundamentalist Christianity is able to reproduce itself. Although the world is said to have entered a "postmodern" age, where old liberal certainties of rational cause and effect are suspect, it certainly is not "postindustrial," for there is more industry and production than ever. Industrial production is merely being transferred and reorganized in other parts of the world. The process requires that hundreds of millions, perhaps billions of people must adhere to new systems of discipline, often under very harsh conditions. Their traditional beliefs and cultures can no longer sustain them, and the chaos of the city makes them long for new order and connections to others. No one can yet know what the cultural requirements of the completely restructured world system will be, but our research suggests that new forms of fundamentalist Christianity are particularly well suited to exist alongside the nascent social, economic, and political networks.

Most of the countries we have discussed stand out as extreme cases, in terms of the rate of religious change, the severity of social and political conditions, the speed of economic restructuring or collapse, and the degree of direct U.S. involvement. Our assessment of this trend has been more negative than some other very informative studies, but this should not be construed as reflecting hostility to religion or an attempt to reduce religious enthusiasm to a category of religious opportunism subordinated to political and economic factors. Despite the fact that an American religion has accompanied the diffusion of American culture, often in congruence with American military presence, we do not suggest that the proliferation of fundamentalist Christianity is conspiratorial, or functions because of cleverly thought-out political calculations.

We have emphasized grim social and political factors because they seem especially pertinent to this period of global restructuring, or as the World Bank and the International Monetary Fund call it, "structural adjustment." Destructive mechanisms have been present in other eras of capitalist development, indeed have been part of the very definition of the social upheaval accompanying the capitalist creation of wealth. The current period of economic modernization (especially the last thirty years, 1965–1995) has been no exception, having imposed heavy demands on many regions of the globe. Is the payoff of development—a higher standard of living and democratic participation in society for most people—in sight? This is clearly not the case. The economic picture in most places where fundamentalist Christianity is spreading is rather bleak. While economic growth has stagnated even in the highly industrialized countries, it has been much worse for many developing nations. In most parts of Latin America and Africa, and some areas of Asia, conditions of depression have existed, destroying the already meager living standards of most people. Although a second round of industrialization is now encompassing the whole world, it has not yet proved itself to be beneficent to more than a handful of nations.

We have reflected upon the ways that the new Christian fundamentalism relates to this kind of globalization and have suggested how the new version of Protestantism fits the conditions of our era: it tailors the Protestant spirit to the specifications of modern corporate industrial society, and it helps the individual believer assume his or her place in the irrational order of global consumerism. In the course of the book, we have referred to the power and excitement generated by this religion, but describing that phenomenon is not our primary purpose. Authors Harvey Cox and David Martin have already ably demonstrated how the strong Pentecostal strains within the new Christian fundamentalism are uniquely suited to producing enthusiastic and genuine religious experience among the most diverse peoples. We accept that as a given.

The diverse populations who embrace the new Christianity are linked together by systems of production and consumption. Hundreds of millions of people are now plugged into industries as wage laborers; millions more are peddlers and small merchants, throwbacks to economic relations that long predated capitalism. Yet the plans, efforts, and aspirations of all these people are not the core of late twentieth-century economic dynamism, which rests upon the export production efforts of large national and multinational conglomerates. Common people, whether petit bourgeois shopkeepers or members of the working class, have to work and work and work, in an atmosphere that is shrouded in mystery. They might well ask themselves: Who gets the real economic rewards in the globalized business culture? And why?

The world economic system, as it turns more homogeneous, also is becoming more extremely unequal. Rising inequality is the norm, whether in regard to the income awarded to the rich industrialized countries versus the rest, or in relation to the compensation given to the upper classes within almost any country as compared to the middle and working classes and the marginalized poor. Figures from the United Nations Development Programme demonstrate how global wealth and income are becoming more and more skewed to the benefit of the developed countries: in 1960, the richest 20 percent of the world's citizens earned nine times as much as the other 80 percent per capita; in 1980 the ratio had increased to 12 to 1; and by 1989 the richest 20 percent, slightly more than a billion people, earned twenty-four times more than the remaining 80 percent, who numbered more than four billion.[1]

The facts of this situation run contrary to the classic post-World War II theories of developmentalism and developmental functionalism that were advanced by Parsons and refined by other scholars such as Hoselitz. They had promised that rather painless economic development, with growing wealth and equality among all social classes, would follow the transplantation of American institutions. Developmentalists still exist in American academia, but their outlook is considerably less optimistic; the most sophisticated analysis dispenses with the equalizing claims of older models (that growth benefits most citizens), and reveals that often 60 percent or more of the population in developing countries is absolutely, not just relatively, impoverished by the modernization process under capitalism.[2] This is now called "realism"; it reflects a post-Cold War sensibility in the highly industrialized countries that such an outcome is regrettable but necessary.

With this set of economic relations in mind, let us note some ways that late capitalism, in its final enclosure of global resources and labor power, has a different relationship to crusading Protestantism than did early capitalism. The world scene has some of the following roughly drawn characteristics:

1) The primacy of capitalist business organization has created a universalistic model of accumulation and control within the workplace, but there is no corresponding universalistic culture that legitimates the hierarchy and authority found in corporate life. Fundamentalism legitimates authority, but because the ultimate economic authority resides in places so remote from everyday life, and is exercised through a labyrinth of networks incomprehensible to the ordinary citizen, this authority is quite mysterious. The invocation of miracle religion for a whole variety of material needs indicates that even those people

who are moderately comfortable are afraid of instability and have little concept of their own individual agency within the political economy.

2) The political/economic elites, the investing classes, on the national level but especially the international level, are very remote from middle-class measures of rectitude and orderliness. While leading industrialists and merchant capitalists sponsored Moody's crusades and other revivals in the nineteenth century, working hand in hand with middle-class ministers and educators, this is seldom the case throughout the world today. Upper-class control of ownership and management is more secure than ever, but the elite are nearly invisible. The moral and intellectual energy of many middle-class fundamentalists, found within the "second-tier male elite," is concentrated (or overconcentrated) on producing "puritanical" social behavior within the narrow realms that are left open to them.

3) The intellectual processes used in scientific and educational enclaves are separated from the thinking and experience of the middle and working classes; this has the effect of disconnecting scientific theory from the practical implementation of science in production and work processes. Many people in the eighteenth and nineteenth centuries enjoyed the hands-on experience of experimenting with practical science and the dispersion of new ideas in both industry and social organization. Today there is no comparable application of scientific rationality. Instead many intelligent people are exposed to a plethora of rather complicated rationalizations of natural processes from "age old" and "new age" sources ranging from astrology to the power of body auras. Dispensationalism, if separated from its Christian context, would hardly be more than another "new age" systemization of fact and fancy, offering compartmentalization and order to the agitated individual mind. When joined with the evangelical rigor and the charismatic community of Christian worship, it serves as the mental ballast that stablilizes a system of personal, communal, and divine ethical authority. This religious substantiation only encourages the Biblical dispensationalist element to develop creationism and other pseudo-scientific theories on a grander scale.

4) Increasing inequality within almost every nation, and among nations, hampers the growth of universalistic faiths, ideologies, or even programs of practical cooperation and reform. The pressure on states, regions, and nations to compete in supplying low-wage labor to the multinational giants of production undercuts their ability or inclination to agree on universal social programs, human rights, or labor laws. For the poor, economic immiseration is the rule. Austerity programs for the working and middle classes have become the world norm, whether in regard to public services or privately promised benefits. The middle class is generally not growing proportionately to population growth, even in advanced countries (perhaps an exception could be

granted to the NICs, the newly industrializing countries of Asia), and as a result is not inclusive. Changes in access to middle-level jobs (now open to women and ethnic minorities) are threatening to the type of males who once understood that these jobs were meant for them. A return to patriarchal values enhances middle-class male prestige, at least superficially; however, the shrinkage in middle-class jobs that offer prestige means that many people, both young and middle-aged, are putting more energy into religious fundamentalism. The rapid rates of modernization, urbanization, and social dislocation may deepen this fundamentalist commitment.

5) Apocalypticism rings true, at least metaphorically. Even if the whole world is not being destroyed, certainly the social worlds and cultures of many people are being destroyed as they are being required to join a new "global" culture and adapt to its rules. It may seem that the old cultures have degenerated and have become debilitated by satanic forces, either by old evil spirits that have become emboldened or by new temptations and dangers brought from the outside. Perhaps the old habits that once seemed benign now seem fraught with demonic influence; extended families and rules laid down by elders may not be functioning as they once did, thus are blamed for inviting destructive influences. Fundamentalists have been said to be otherworldly in their anticipation of the Second Coming; they also may be very future oriented in a practical way. As they find a new "family" in the church, they may repudiate the past, severing ties to cumbersome extended families and losing contact with old community networks.

In a world with these five characteristics, many people, not just conservative Christians, may want to see some kind of order and control imposed. A general longing for authoritarian discipline can be found in many places where semi-apocalyptic conditions exist. Economic immiseration and total descent into chaotic violence (as in parts of West Africa and Guatemala) are accompanied by all kinds of physical suffering: hunger, disease, and constant vulnerability to crime. Elsewhere, even in nations as highly developed as the United States, where there is no immediate threat of social chaos, real material conditions are deteriorating. In the U.S., the perception of social collapse is fed by the immense differences between urban and suburban standards of living. At a certain point, the maintenance of order becomes the major social/ political goal of the upper middle-class and a large part of the lower-middle and working classes. If poverty, lowered standards of public morality, and clashing expressions of cultural values all seem destined to get worse—and if the society seems incapable of mounting programs of social amelioration (because government or private agencies are too disorganized or have committed themselves to fiscal austerity)—many frightened people will settle for "law and order" as the paramount requirement of government.

Christian fundamentalists do not create the authoritarian atmosphere at the highest levels of business and the state, although they may be better prepared to accept it than other citizens because of their own emphases on patriarchal control and order. Likewise they may be less ready to dispute the calls for austerity by governments and private industry; after all, pastors and congregations are eager to extend the realm of their private services—in education, counseling, and charitable endeavors—and would rather not compete with a government taxing apparatus that seeks money for the same purposes.

The hierarchical command structure of modern business, as we have mentioned, is so removed and bureaucratic that it borders on the incomprehensible. Amoral corporate standards and behavior are thus outside the purview of the paternalistic family model of conduct projected by fundamentalists. Large economic decisions that shut down factories, weaken labor unions, open up new plants, and increase or decrease disposable income seem like acts of God, either natural disasters or rationally inexplicable mega-blessings. The high-ranking international managers who make decisions on profitability and visit bad or good news upon various communities are less than morally neutral; in fact, they long to be invisible in moral terms. In the last two decades of the twentieth century, the generalized effect of their activity has been to drive down wages and impose social austerity on most parts of the globe (even in the United States, though certainly not to the same degree as in poorer countries). The elite managerial and stock-owning class, whose loyalties to each other through international connections are superseding sentiments of nationalism, can only claim that this is "necessity" at work, while hedging about the degree of suffering and dislocation that is caused. They crave national anonymity when their actions might be deemed harmful to their own particular nation's economy.

Small wonder, then, that there is a moral vacuum and a crisis of values. Elite Americans, corporations, and financial institutions (and much the same could be said for other national elites) can no longer correlate their self-interest with the national interest in the way that they could when they were rebuilding Europe and giving the United States a commanding presence in world affairs immediately after World War II. The Manifest Destiny tradition—the covenant of nationalist pride, militarist righteousness, and outright American superiority—still exists, but no longer serves as a direct adjunct to American policy objectives. "Faith in the nation," although it still resonates through socially conservative, military-connected networks inside and outside the United States, has been appropriated in a symbolic sense by the fundamentalists. It justifies their role in realizing global evangelization and revitalizing Americanism. Operating as "a second-tier elite," clearly not privy to transcorporate and international financial decisions, the fundamentalist leaders can project a spiritual sense of mission.

The appropriation of the American civil religion by the new Christian right in the United States is viewed by some as cause for alarm. Perhaps it is conceivable that somewhere, in times of utter turmoil, the new fundamentalist faith and the old sense of militarist Manifest Destiny could coalesce in some common purpose. As we have seen, evangelizing activity in the Philippines (as well as other countries aided by the United States) includes conservative, anti-communist indoctrination within the Army; and U.S. influence in South Korea helped foster notions of a messianic Korean nation allied with the U.S. global mission. On the other hand, the new Christian militancy does not necessarily further the military or economic objectives of the United States. Charismatic fundamentalism may promise the violent intervention of supernatural forces, but it is incapable of stopping the slow slippage of the United States from its dominance of geopolitics and the world economy. The establishment of a global empire through the directed dissemination of a new global faith—that is, the purposeful congruence between political domination and a system of heavenly dominion—does not seem likely.

Still, the spread of the new Christian fundamentalism as a global mystery religion can proceed unabated because it tacitly accepts the multinational hegemony of economic capital as a realm that cannot be understood or challenged. On what grounds would it oppose the operations of a corporate business, American or otherwise? To borrow an extreme example from our Korea chapter: how could the manager of a Radio Shack store in the U.S. be held responsible for the fact that Korean kusudae thugs are beating up the women wage earners who are producing the low-priced products for his corporation and his customers?

It is unlikely that this store manager (or, on a higher level, the district manager, or area cost accountant) would know anything about Korean factory conditions, nor could he find out through mainstream corporate media sources. If, by chance, any of these middle-management employees were informed about the abuse of human freedom incorporated into particular material goods merchandised by Radio Shack, and then attempted to discourage the sale of such items, he or she certainly would be fired. This inability to make moral choices, or even to locate causality and human responsibility, would be common to the middle-management personnel of almost any multinational corporation, no matter how "rational" and efficient their systems of production, marketing, and investment might be. In a similar vein, the global imperatives of production and distribution tend to paralyze policy makers and planners within government bureaucracies. The failure within one nation to impose environmental pollution standards on an international mining company would be seen as regrettable but unavoidable; the

willingness of another country to permit a multinational manufacturing con-
glomerate to employ child labor at less than subsistence wages would be
objectionable, but not reproachable or enforceable as a matter of human
rights. "Realism," the absence of moral contingency, is the order of the day on
the macroeconomic level.

Lest we become too moralistic about where the new Christians are likely
to ignore the absence of morality, let us consider their point of view. Although
we could interpret the two C's, commerce and civilization, as signs of corruption of the Christian missionary endeavor, the missionary might counter,
quite cogently, that we are lacking in reality perception. The cynical realism
of the transnational investor is outside of a church's control. Part of the job of
the missionary or pastor is to notice which way the wind is blowing. It is not
a question of whether the new economic order will be triumphant because
some missionaries are there greasing the wheels of industry; capitalism is
already established as a world system and will expand of its own accord.
Should not reasonable evangelicals be given credit for accepting the world as
it is?

From this vantage point, we should consider the charismatic/Pentecostal/
fundamentalist claim that their religious movement is now enabled and
empowered to accomplish in the twentieth- and twenty-first-century world
what the original Christians sought to do in the first and second centuries.
They compare their movement with the evangelization of the apostle Paul,
who was a Roman citizen who noticed that history was on the side of the
empire. Paul had taken note of the futility of worldly revolt on the part of the
Jews (a fact that would be emphasized most dramatically in 66-70 A.D.,
almost immediately after his death). Thus he and his followers in the early
church could accept the notion that Christians must work within the framework of Rome's political economy. The parallels with our era of global capitalism are not difficult to lay out: the entrenchment of the Roman system in
the first century A.D., all powerful and efficient, was hardly open to question
except on the most utopian terms; Christians, after initial persecution, made
peace with the empire and, while not approving of its worldly vices, developed the miracle faith that could live alongside the exercise of arbitrary power
by the Romans. Of course evil existed, but Christians could not overcome it
with rational plans and moral instruction in social programmatics, so they
faced evil by believing Christ would return to eliminate the world and replace
it with a new, perfect one.

Today's fundamentalists see themselves as a universal church of the spirit,
true to Paul's vision, and are either untroubled by or unaware of the fact that
they share many of the American cultural attributes that propel a universalizing political economy. Evangelists often trumpet the advantages of American

free enterprise, but do they have much understanding of where the ethics of capitalism are hidden? It does not seem that religious justification is sought by the American business elite, who are not dominated by Protestants any longer nor even by believers in Americanism. In a globalizing world, neither religion nor nationalism seems to exercise much influence over the decision-making web of managers, investors, owners, and diplomats. Is it possible that the reigning capitalist ethic is nothing more than an obligation to seek the highest return on investment?

The influence of the new Christian fundamentalism must operate on levels below the mysteries of the global marketplace, where the authority of the churches can fill the voids that have appeared in the old American covenant. Among the unmet obligations are the fading American dream of middle-class security, the lack of paternalistic commitment on the part of corporate business toward its employees, and the uncertainty of how to chart heroic, patriotic missions in world affairs. The emotionally charged religious communities have the potential to grow exponentially in these areas. The faith in individual prosperity as a divinely provided blessing not only replaces the increasingly shaky premise of the nation's connection to material providence, but it carries that prosperity message out to the rest of the world much more effectively than outmoded American, government-sponsored developmentalism.

The projection of "spiritual warfare" into the social and political sphere is an apt replacement for the periodic military pursuit of American Manifest Destiny. The rhetoric of Christian conquest may have little relation to imposing the rules of the World Bank or promoting the more or less peaceful intrusions of transnational corporations on foreign shores. Fundamentalist S.W.A.T. teams might be seen as a relatively harmless way to blow off steam (in a way that requires far fewer finite resources than actual armed forces) when they confront communist/Islamic/demonic hybrids and other shape-shifting enemies.

If economic globalization proceeds logically for transnational companies, spreading patterns of consumption and work discipline with less and less social disruption, the aggressive Americanist side of the new Christianity may begin to recede in importance. But the faith would still have properties that give it a global edge. The pseudo-sciences of creationism and dispensationalism, backed by Biblical inerrancy, form a kind of systematic theology/augury that can transcend barriers of class and race. They are much more effective than the nineteenth century pseudo-science of Social Darwinism, which was only adequate for soothing the anxieties of middle- and upper-class Anglo-Saxon Protestants (and their non-religious brethren, of course.) Moreover, these beliefs easily match the properties of a host of "new age" systems. The infusion of the Holy Spirit within each individual signifies a kind of

258   Steve Brouwer   Paul Gifford   Susan D. Rose

unrelenting progress, and supplants the faded Arminian optimism of past Protestant eras. The undaunted movement forward—which once was epitomized by the power to keep pushing the boundaries of the American frontier—can include each person in the world who chooses to join in the faith. Charismatic fundamentalism has transnational characteristics, with real abilities to overcome barriers of ethnic identity. The fact that it can be detached from territorial and cultural specificity, as the world becomes a spiritual medium for the transport of each "self," suggests that the Christian covenant can be transferred as never before. Perhaps there are now no limits to the expansion of the Calvinist "elect."

However, there is a caveat: the United States may remain the major military power in the world, the master trainer of armies, and the leading merchant of weapons for many decades to come. If this role becomes elevated as other U.S. economic interests are humbled, and global political disturbances keep erupting in places where the new Christians have some influence, then "spiritual warfare" may portend more frightening things. Currently, in the mid-1990s, the impressive influence of the highly motivated Christian Coalition in U.S. politics and the elevation of charismatic Christian leaders such as Oliver North and Pat Robertson demonstrate that there are growing legions of disgruntled middle-class citizens. Americanism is treasured by many millions of angry people, fundamentalists and social conservatives alike, and they clearly favor a deepening of authoritarian values at home while wanting the United States to keep dominating the world scene as a Christian superpower nation. This is not necessarily the most rational way of serving U.S. investment and macroeconomic interests; such conservative intellectuals as Samuel Huntington are already charting a more defensive course, preparing for a more limited global sphere of influence for the United States.[3] But to fundamentalist Christians, now the carriers of the torch for fundamentalist Americanism, such a course would be unacceptable, a retreat.

The American charisteristics of this religion do not disappear as they are internationalized; rather they proliferate at the same time that U.S. economic and military power retreats from its globalizing role. As the traditional kinds of U.S. presence recede, the new evangelists are eagerly intervening in their place. The incredibly fast infiltration of evangelical churches—conservative, fundamentalist, Pentecostal, and charismatic—into the former Soviet Union and Eastern Europe since 1989 indicates that the interventional energy of ordinary American Christians (and some of their missionary brethren in Western Europe and Asia) is very high.[4] We could even say that the investment of "religious capital" is outstripping the activity of financial capital.

Take the example of Soon Yan Lee, a Korean-American missionary from Los Angeles who went to Russia on behalf of a conservative Presbyterian church in Seoul. She and her minister husband founded a church of six hundred families in the southern Russian town of Mozdok. They are dedicated to simultaneously attacking sin, the remnants of communism, and Islam; a difficult task, Lee explained in the spring of 1995, because: "The Russian soul is rotten. Whatever is written in the Bible, they do the opposite." Mozdok had become a war town, the staging area for fierce Russian attacks that virtually destroyed the city of Grozny, which lies less than one hundred miles away in the secessionist state of Chechnya. The war effort, which has torn up the fabric of the predominantly Muslim culture in Chechnya, will ultimately provide a point of access to evangelizing groups, including Soon Yan Lee and her husband. They want to build a church there when the fighting ends. "I want Grozny to become a city of the blessed," said Soon Yan Lee. "Russia is vast and rich. Everything is here. If people would only turn to God."[5]

The origins and purposes of her mission are very American, but also complex. What kind of hegemony is being furthered? Christian, capitalist, American, Korean? Our predictive powers are necessarily quite limited. Our speculations about where the new fundamentalism fits into the social chaos that accompanies global restructuring are meant as stimulants to discussion rather than definitive indicators. Our concentration on the presence of U.S. religious models, faithfully implemented, may obscure contributions from local religious traditions, for it is very difficult to measure the degree of depth to which the new religious practice penetrates or displaces older cultural forms. Thus there is no way to know whether fundamentalist, Pentecostal, and neo-Pentecostal evangelicals are likely to maintain their spectacular growth rates, or even hold on to all the converts they have made so far.

It does seem likely that the influence of the older American Protestant denominations will keep fading, but we have no way of knowing whether the new fundamentalist churches will be successful in restoring their idea of Americanism at home or in extending a culture of American hegemony throughout the world. We know that Protestantism in Africa, Latin America, and Asia is swiftly taking on various fundamentalist features, but it is yet to be seen how this charismatic/Pentecostal enthusiasm might be further molded into a sort of transnational covenant. We can, however, hazard the guess that the new fundamentalists and the conservative evangelical base that supports them will soon represent the majority of Protestants in the world. Perhaps they already do.

We have suggested that the new fundamentalist Christianity has appeared at a time when there is no discernible ethic of capitalist behavior. No particular religious tradition has attached itself to multinational corporate activity; in fact, there is little effort to justify the morality or oppose the amorality of the economic superstructure. Capitalism is, rather suddenly, accepted as a given, almost a force of nature, an ocean or a glacier governed by its own natural laws. In such a spiritual environment we must ask: why is there no other equally dynamic, but socially independent and intellectually open Christian faith moving throughout the world? Why have the more liberal elements within Protestantism, and the liberalizing trends within Catholicism, failed to project a religion with strong universal appeal, one that combines its spirituality with an ethic of profound social engagement?

To some extent liberal Protestantism became too liberal to sustain its old ties to the American political and business elite. This conflict arose in the Cold War era, when many Protestants doubted the inherent goodness of U.S. nuclear weapons arsenals, and it deepened with their outright opposition to U.S. military presence in Asia. On a different plane, these expressions of doubt were troubling to many other citizens who did not want to relinquish their faith in American power and righteousness. The break with fundamentalist Americanism not only robbed liberals of trust at home, it diminished their will to evangelize, too. Although many mainstream Protestant theologians and ministers were genuinely sympathetic with the plight of poor and marginalized people in the U.S. and throughout the world, they no longer wanted to impose their cultural system upon other societies. Furthermore, they had no fresh conception of how to proselytize successfully among them.

The position of Catholics is more complex, since they equal or outnumber all other Christians in the world combined. We have noted that significant religious experimentation and rejuvenation within the Catholic Church have taken place within the loose parameters of the popular church and liberation theology, and in a way that suggests affinity with the creation of new social worlds where the poor and working classes can assert themselves as fully human persons. If we knew that fifty years from now this would be the dominant Catholic direction, and that it was wed to significant egalitarian and democratic gains in the lives of Christians worldwide, then we could imagine how Catholicism might maintain its position as a universalizing faith. This would constitute a reformation of Christian values to fit human needs of the twenty-first century (and put an end to Weberian and Marxist antagonisms over the social role of religion). An egalitarian, tolerant, truly catholic faith would provide the "elective affinities" between a religious social movement and the transcending need of common people to control their own lives and assert their universal interests over a world system of production.

The Catholic Church, however, has turned ever more surely against the liberationists, both by protecting its traditional certainties within the old patriarchal hierarchy and by comforting the conservative and economically comfortable factions of the laity. This may not be cynicism, but rather the guarded realism of religious custodians who have much more to lose than the erstwhile and scattered Pentecostals and neo-Pentecostals. Perhaps the internal transformation of the Catholic Church appears to be a process of self-reformation that is too risky.

Meanwhile, the aggressive new evangelicals, having knocked over their staid Protestant rivals in many parts of the world, are squaring off against the immense presence of the Roman Catholic Church. This struggle for influence and warm bodies in the congregations will be crucial to the future of Christianity over the next fifty years. The anxiety of the Catholic Church is probably warranted, but not in terms of how they can explain away the phenomenon of the swarming "sects" or how they can ward off vilification (for they are not demonized nearly as much as Moslems and socialists). If the present degree of social dislocation and economic crisis persists in Latin America, Africa, and Asia, the major challenge facing Catholics and older Protestant traditions will be how to create churches that offer as much spiritual dynamism as the new Christian groups. If local cultures do not return to the more stable patterns of the past, both Catholicism and liberal Protestantism are likely to keep losing ground because they cannot match the pastoral entrepreneurship or the congregational intensity of the fundamentalist Protestants.

In the 1990s there is no compelling doctrine of equality, democracy, and prosperity being proclaimed in the advanced industrial nations that were the founders of Protestantism. In place of liberalism and social democracy, which require some degree of optimism about human nature, the rational provision of civic services, and the growing prosperity of both working and middle classes, a profound pessimism has taken hold. A crude, harsh brand of capitalist relations is ascendent within almost all nations and is pushing out most notions of economic fairness and egalitarianism. Democratic reform movements, socialist experimentation, and organized labor resistance are declining precipitously in most nations. Even in the richest countries, various universal commitments to the citizenry in terms of health care, unemployment insurance, and retirement benefits are under attack.

In the United States some of this pessimistic worldview stems from the fact that liberalism never lost its roots in an elitist project that tried to foster American-style progress throughout the world and reproduce bourgeois social values; it never entirely rejected the Social Darwinist belief in the inevitable usefulness and superiority of a class-based society. Even in the 1950s and 1960s, at the height of American power and prosperity, U.S. liberalism needed anti-communism to energize the Christian revivalist element in the national civil religion, to mold a consensus about American Manifest Destiny.

Now, the middle classes and working classes are decidedly shrinking. The American dream, which was once credible and attractive as a universal dream, is slipping away quickly, and guarded ferociously and angrily by those who would struggle to maintain their share of it. Liberalism is gone because inclusiveness does not seem possible, either within the United States or in the world arena. Practical applications of socially progressive measures seem so pointless that they are hardly ever proposed. This opens up an immense terrain for a global church that can promise miraculous transcendence of material barriers to health and prosperity, that tolerates systems that impose order on unruly citizens, and that chooses enemies, such as Islam and socialism, that happen to be impediments to the full flowering of a global consumer society. The spirit of the new Protestantism can be supportive of capitalism because this association seems to accelerate the transmission of the faith, not because there is an ethical core hidden in the heart of the transnational business culture.

The Christian fundamentalists offer their kind of power at an auspicious time, in place of the diminished potency of a nation, the United States, that can no longer manage the affairs of the globe. The older Christian traditions are avoiding one path that could seriously challenge the new Christian fundamentalist dynamic: a countervailing Christian devotion, attracting Catholic and Protestant alike, to a renewed vision of social progress and cultural tolerance.

Definitions and Perspective

What Is a Fundamentalism?

In our far-ranging field studies of Christian evangelists and our review of literature concerning both Christian fundamentalism and the fundamentalistic aspects of other religious faiths, we have found that very few people want to be called "fundamentalists." For many religious people, it carries a derogatory tone that they would rather avoid. Among Muslims and Jews, for instance, it would be difficult to find any mullah or rabbi who feels that his religious doctrine and practice is "fundamentalist." Among American evangelical Protestants, only a few—found at places such as Bob Jones University—want to be known as fundamentalists; and abroad evangelical Christians are even less likely to identify themselves as fundamentalists.

On the other hand, nearly a century after it gained attention as a religious term describing a U.S. Protestant tendency, the word "fundamentalism" has taken on global significance because it is a convenient way of describing a wide range of religious revivals. There has been much academic discussion of the merit of studying "fundamentalism," and we were privy to a number of thoughtful exchanges about the subject through our connection to the Fundamentalism Project of the American Academy of Arts and Sciences. Many scholars, for a number of reasons, took exception to the blanket term "fundamentalism" because they thought it was not particularly helpful in understanding the workings of diverse cultures. Also, perhaps, it was seen as insulting or alarmist to label others with an American term of specific origin in conservative evangelical Christianity.

The organizers of the Fundamentalism Project and most of its participants came to refer to a broad range of "fundamentalisms" within different religions

and societies; the idea being that the term captures both the intensity of the
cultural changes taking place and the single-minded devotion of the believers.
Fundamentalism requires an intense belief in making one's own religion into
the central guiding principle of one's society and nation—this can be an
extremely large project, as for Hinduism in India. Such religiosity can be so
powerful that it pours over borders and emerges as transnational religious culture, a phenomenon which is currently evident in both Christianity and Islam.
Martin E. Marty and R. Scott Appleby, editors of the multi-volume series of
the Fundamentalism Project, devised a working definition of "family traits"
that applies to fundamentalisms across a range of religious traditions. This
definition, which helped guide our appraisal of the new Christian fundamentalism, is as follows:

> Religious fundamentalism has appeared in the twentieth century as a tenden-
> cy, a habit of mind, found within religious communities and paradigmatically
> embodied in certain representative individuals and movements, which mani-
> fests itself as a strategy, or set of strategies, by which beleaguered believers
> attempt to preserve their distinctive identity as a people or group. Feeling this
> identity to be at risk in the contemporary era, they fortify it by a selective
> retrieval of doctrines, beliefs, and practices from a sacred past. These retrieved
> "fundamentals" are refined, modified, and sanctioned in a spirit of shrewd prag-
> matism: they are to serve as a bulwark against encroachment of outsiders who
> threaten to draw the believers into a syncretistic, areligious, or irreligious cul-
> tural milieu. Moreover, these fundamentals are accompanied in the new reli-
> gious portfolio by unprecedented claims and doctrinal innovations. By the
> strength of these innovations and the new supporting doctrines, the retrieved
> and updated fundamentals are meant to regain the charismatic intensity today
> by which they originally forged communal identity from the formative revela-
> tory religious experiences long ago. ("Introduction" to *Fundamentalisms and the
> State,* Chicago: University of Chicago Press, 1993, p. 3.)

We feel the new Christian fundamentalism that is generated in the United
States fits this description of an all-encompassing social revival. The idea of
fundamentalism would not be useful if it merely described lesser phenomena:
a renewed interest in religion; individual absorption in various acts of piety; a
swing toward more "conservative" social practice: a correction in the interpretation of holy writings which are seen as too loose or imprecise; or a tendency to want to practice one's faith more openly and enthusiastically. These
practices may be present among fundamentalists, especially in an accelerated
or accentuated form, but they only really become fundamentalistic when they
are put in the service of social/political religious movements (which often
embrace very strong nationalistic beliefs). Fundamentalists feel they must

remake entire societies, and in order to do so they they must overpower a number of secular influences with their religious purity. Their rigidity of doctrine and their sense of sanctification is intensified as they go on the attack (and as their ideas are rejected by others): they generally target non-religious educational systems, secular versions of civic ethics, manifestations of greater equality between the sexes, and public figures and intellectuals who believe in other religions or philosophies.

This religious intensity (which is distinct from holding strong beliefs) is predicated upon the necessity of overwhelming others with the righteousness of one's religious worldview, and it is currently the driving force of Christian evangelization that we are calling fundamentalist. Some may be offended by our broad conception of the defining elements of the new American Protestant fundamentalism and its global offspring. We would only ask that those within the Protestant tradition attempt to perceive their religion as others might, from the outside (as if looking at fundamentalist Hinduism or fundamentalist Islam, which are also complex and broad-based). Because the new fundamentalism is an amalgam of several currents within American evangelicalism and not a derivative of one or two narrow sectarian influences, and because it is in the process of innovating and empowering itself all the more, some evangelical Christians may feel unfairly branded by our interpretations. The belief system we have outlined in Chapter One—including Biblical inerrancy, dispensationalism, and millenarianism, along with strong doses of Americanism—helps indicate which evangelical traditions contribute the most toward the fundamentalist movement. Groups that fit into our definition of fundamentalist belief include most Pentecostal and neo-Pentecostal churches, a good part of the Southern Baptist Convention (given their recent consolidation of doctrine), a great many other independent Baptist churches (such as Falwell's Liberty Baptist), most charismatic covenant churches, some holiness denominations, and particular conservative secessionist groups (such as Reformed Presbyterians.) There is reason to believe that there are many fundamentalist members in conservative evangelical churches that stop short of fundamentalism in their official doctrine (Reformed Church, Lutheran Missouri Synod, etc.).

Obviously, not all (or even most) evangelicals are fundamentalists, but evangelicalism does form the seedbed from which fundamentalist Christianity has sprouted. Our purpose, however, is not to affix a label to each church and each believer, but to provide guidelines by which to judge the American and world religious landscape in terms that are comparable to the way other religious traditions are judged as "fundamentalistic." A particular qualifying belief, such as accepting the idea of Biblical inerrancy, does not automatically make one a fundamentalist; but it may indicate a proclivity toward accepting the rest of the fundamentalist package. On the other other hand, the number of Americans who believe in inerrancy is striking: "a 1976 Gallup Poll found that 46 per cent of Protestants believe the Bible is 'to be taken literally, word for word'" (Nancy Taton Ammerman, *Bible Believers: Fundamentalists in the Modern World,* New Brunswick: Rutgers University Press, 1987, p. 217). If the belief in Biblical inerrancy could be measured among Protestants globally, we would expect the percentage to be much higher: Protestants outside North America and Europe tend to be more fundamentalistic in their thinking and much more Pentecostal in orientation. However, they are not very concerned about distinctions that different Protestant groups (or scholars) in the U.S. might use to distinguish between the purely fundamentalist and the not-so-fundamentalist heritage of particular denominations. They are not fighting merely to restore a vision of the American Gospel, but also to spread that Gospel everywhere; they have taken the strategies and beliefs once used to "preserve the identity of beleagured believers" in the United States and adapted them to converting the rest of the world.

What Are Pentecostal and Charismatic Churches?

We cannot be perfectly precise with definitions of Pentecostal, charismatic, and neo-Pentecostal churches partly because the labels vary worldwide. In many areas of Latin America, the word charismatic is reserved only for a segment of distinctly Catholic believers still practicing their religion in the Catholic Church, while the term neo-Pentecostal is used for the newest variations of Pentecostal and charismatic Protestantism. In Africa, however, the newest Protestant "full Gospel" churches spawned by American evangelistic campaigns are more often referred to as charismatic. We hope the reader is not confused by terms that might shift a little in different contexts, and we offer the following rough guidelines: the term Pentecostal refers generally to the one hundred year trend of "full Gospel" Protestantism, thus including both charismatic and neo-Pentecostal labels; or, at times, it is used more restrictively to describe the historic Pentecostal denominations, such as the Assemblies of God and the Church of God. Charismatic and neo-Pentecostal are considered interchangeable terms in this book, but to avoid confusion with charismatic believers within both the Catholic and mainline Protestant traditions, we often use the term neo-Pentecostal, meaning new expansionary variations on "old" Pentecostalism. This would include congregations, both independent and denominational, that are pursuing a more middle-class orientation and teaching a "health and wealth" message; the "church growth" and "third-wave" churches of the kind associated with Paul Yonggi Cho and the Fuller Theology School; the Bible schools associated with the "faith" doctrines of Hagin, Copeland, Sumrall, and others; and most of the international sources of televangelism, such as Robertson, Cerullo, and Bonnke. Note that the independent neo-Pentecostal churches generally call themselves charismatic (as does Pat Robertson); they belong to such associations as The International Communion of Charismatic Churches, the Charismatic Bible Ministries, and the International Convention of Faith Ministries.

The difficulty in nomenclature is evident in sub-Saharan Africa, especially in Nigeria. There the older Pentecostal churches (Assemblies of God, Apostolic Faith, etc.) have come to be called "holiness" churches in common usage, because of their emphasis on strict behaviors and the sanctified life. The newer charismatic churches, with easier dress standards and prosperity themes, are the ones now labeled "Pentecostal" by the religious customer. Ruth Marshall's investigations in the urban vicinities of Lagos revealed that:

> It is obvious that while in the "holiness" churches the categories of prestige center around attaining the personal qualities associated with leading a blameless, simple and Christlike life, in the 'Pentecostal' churches for the most part, the economy of prestige is based on the acquisition of both spiritual power, expressed in the ability to heal, exorcise, and prophesy, and material success as evidence of God's favor.

One Nigerian believer unfavorably described the congregation at a "holiness" church in Lagos called Deeper Life as "mostly people who were servants, who were clerks...they have this attitude about dressing, about sin, they have a condemnatory attitude." He compared it to the new "Pentecostal" church which he preferred to attend: "at Christ Chapel you could wear jeans; they allowed people not to cover their hair; people flocked down...people were seeing results, miracles, speaking in tongues, a lot of things happening" (Ruth Marshall, "Pentecostalism in Southern Nigeria," in *New Dimensions in African Christianity*, ed. Paul Gifford, Ibadan, Nigeria: Sefer, 1993, pp. 19–20).

What Is Being Left Out of Our Discussion of Evangelicalism?

Unfortunately we do not have room in this book to discuss all the kinds of evangelical churches that exist and prosper around the world. The situation is complex, for in every part of the world where there is great evangelical activity there is also room for a variety of influences; some of these work in contrast to the new fundamentalist/Pentecostal/charismatic model that we have emphasized, offering clear and modern alternatives to the social conservatism of the new fundamentalists, even from within the Pentecostal tradition. In Central America, for instance, the Church of God (Cleveland), while still holding to a full-Gospel message and an emphasis on strict individual comportment, has trained its ministers to be aware of social inequities and their consequences. When necessary it has kept a low profile in such educational efforts so as to avoid government repression and the opprobrium of more conservative Protestants. In the countries where more political discussion and activity is permitted (Nicaragua, Costa Rica), a number of Bible-believing Pentecostals and evangelicals have allied themselves with progressive political movements. In Guatemala, among poor Indian communities and urban dwellers, we have encountered individual Protestant churches from mainline traditions (Presbyterian, Episcopalian) that pursue a course of worship and action remarkably similar to the base communities that have grown out of popular Catholicism. They encourage a socially progressive reading of the Bible, an emphasis on the equality of men and women, and various kinds of cooperative economic arrangements compatible with Mayan community heritage. These phenomena are less isolated in such parts of the world as South Korea, the Philippines, and South Africa, where greater political openness has led some evangelicals and Pentecostals to join other Protestants and Catholics in battling dictatorial regimes and pushing for democratization. However, these groups are a minority. The dominant course of this globalizing religious culture is going in the other direction.

In regard to fundamentalistic influences, it should be noted that non-Pentecostal/non-charismatic churches continue to be important; large contingents of American missionaries are fielded by such groups as the Southern Baptist Convention and the Churches in Christ. We have underrepresented their activities in this book because their growth rates are modest, and they are not having the overwhelming impact of the Pentecostal/charismatic churches, parachurches, and Bible schools.

However, to every trend there is an exception, and one very interesting example of an atypical fundamentalist church is the New Apostolic Church. It is not a product of the United States but of Germany, and is growing very rapidly in Ghana and other parts of Africa. What makes this so interesting is that a church less Pentecostal, less flamboyant, could hardly be imagined. Its worship is sober, almost dour, with solemn hymns. It is hierarchical: in each governing district its grades are apostle, bishop, district elder, district evangelist, community elder, shepherd, community evangelist, priest, deacon, and subdeacon. It has no Bible colleges, though its ministers come together for occasional seminars.

In-depth studies of church growth in Ghana demonstrate that the traditional African Independent Churches are losing members rapidly, while mainstream Protestant and Catholic populations are stabilizing as the overall population rapidly increases. Really substantial growth in denominations over the five year period, 1987-1992, was, as might be expected from the experience in other countries, among the churches belonging to the Pentecostal Council (large, independent urban churches were not measured in the report, but were also doing very well). The New Apostolic Church also grew very fast, even though it does not fit this Pentecostal/charismatic model. There are no "gifts of the spirit," rather worship is characterized by a unified liturgy and sacramentalist devotions, combined with pietistic attention to personal sanctity. Also, it is a rural church, whereas the charismatic megachurch is an urban phenomenon. The New Apostolic Church is not a product of American enthusiasm, directly or indirectly. Still, the key may be that it is evangelism fueled very systematically from abroad. The German headquarters provides a set number of church buildings each year, all built according to plans drawn up in Germany and with money provided from Germany. In Ghana in 1994, there were 50 churches to be built in just one apostle-district of Ghana South. More research is needed on the New Apostolic Church, although it can be said that its figures are probably more solidly based than most, being rigorously calculated every year on computers (supplied from Germany). It has made rapid advance in several areas in Africa: in Sierra Leone (till the war devastated its area of activity), Uganda, and Kenya (where in 1992 it established over 1000 new congregations).

Why We Differ with More Optimistic Appraisals of the Global Revival

We have found the observations of David Martin (*Tongues of Fire*) and Harvey Cox (*Fire from Heaven*) to be very valuable as we try to make sense of the global Christian revival that we have witnessed first-hand over a number of years. However, we find their evaluations overly optimistic when they project the most favorable of historical American and British values into the current international scene. There is something attractive in this: Cox puts his emphasis on the African-American Pentecostal churches and the spiritual power of music, healing rituals, and other kinds of "experiential" religion; Martin's analysis resonates of such themes as the strong Arminianism of the Methodist tradition in frontier America, the role of non-conformist Protestantism in promoting social peace during the English industrial revolution, and the possibility that good Christian living habits will bring material well-being for all.

David Martin, however, does offer a point of departure from the rosy view of the new Protestantism, by discerning what is missing even in areas of high economic growth: "A technically sophisticated society, such as exists today in South Korea, does not require as by some inner necessity a humanist intellectual sphere equipped with appropriate moral, political and epistemological perspectives. It may advance, and advance spectacularly, by combining instrumental technical skills with conspicuous instrumentality in the sphere of religion" (*Tongues of Fire*, p. 142). And Harvey Cox, in his last chapter, admits that he is not so sure about the future of the Pentecostal movement, because "a sharp clash is under way between those who would like to capture it for the fundamentalist party and for the religious political right" on the one hand, and the experientialists who feel "that its authentic purpose is to cut through creeds and canons" (*Fire from Heaven,* p. 311).

When Martin and Cox draw historical parallels, whether to English Methodism or to early Pentecostalism among African Americans, we find them pertinent and interesting, but not convincing as a model for the current wave of global evangelism. The new fundamentalist Christianity does contain elements of "enthusiastic Methodism" and "experiential Pentecostalism," but we think a more balanced and critical appraisal must give equal weight to less optimistic comparisons. We would suggest that global Christian fundamentalism also contains other historical Protestant influences that have encouraged authoritarianism, an aggressive tendency to identify U.S. interests with God's interests, and an intolerance of people from different cultures. One of these influences, for instance, might be called "enthusiastic Calvinism," an amalgam of first century Christian Pentecostal miracle religion and the aggressive, sometimes violent covenant of seventeenth-century Scottish Calvinism. Important elements of religious and social experience among the Scots-Irish Presbyterians later came to influence the "American Gospel" of the "chosen land" and Manifest Destiny. The Scots-Irish were generally people of low-to-middling status inserted into stratified social/economic structures and asked to help subdue the natives, first the heathen Irish and then the heathen indigenous Americans. Later, conservative strands of Presbyterianism in the U.S. (no longer exclusively Scots-Irish) adopted dispensationalist belief systems and contributed to the original fundamentalist theology of the early twentieth century. Today the large independent neo-Pentecostal churches that are setting the global trends of worship and belief are essentially Pentecostal Calvinist covenant churches. In looking for historical roots, we note that the first Protestant revival was probably The Six Mile Water Revival, begun by Scots in Ulster in the seventeenth century, then transferred back across the Irish Sea to Scotland; that the "National Covenant," also a product of seventeenth-century Scotland, equated the divine sanction of citizenship with Presbyterianism; and that the "covenanting" churches of that time also provided a "strong endorsement of clerical authority" over everyday life (Ned Landsman, *Scotland and its First American Colony,* Princeton: Princeton University Press, 1985, pp. 54–55; also see Maldwyn A. Jones, "The Scots Irish in British America," in *Strangers in the Realm,* ed. Bernard Bailyn and Philip D. Morgan, Chapel Hill: University of North Carolina Press, 1991; Philip S. Robinson, *The Plantation of Ulster,* Dublin: Gill and MacMillan, 1984; S. J. Connolly, *Religion, Law, and Power,* Oxford: Oxford University Press, 1992).

We are not proposing the "correct" historical lineage of the current evangelical boom (the above sketch of the Scots covenant churches is but one interesting possibility); rather we are pointing out that alternative historical investigations might help us understand the hegemonic elements of the new Christian fundamentalism. Although they are contributing mightily to the Americanization of global culture, it is clear that the fundamentalistic evangelical organizations do not work under the direction of the elite classes or the transnational corporations. The efforts of sincerely religious people of lower and middle class origins (just like their Scots Presbyterian predecessors) are teaching the lessons of religious and social discipline to other cultures that are being overwhelmed, this time by the forces of worldwide industrialization and consumer capitalism (rather than the British Empire). Under the twin covenants of Americanism and their churches, the new fundamentalists are having a profound effect in promoting both an acceptance of American (U.S.) cultural norms and the kind of civic and psychic orderliness that does not question the rule of the powerful.

Notes

CHAPTER ONE
Introduction: Global Christian Fundamentalism

1. David B. Barrett and John W. Reapsome, "Seven Hundred Plans to Evangelize the World," Richmond: World Evangelization Research Center, 1988, listed 1.7 billion Christians, 1.1 billion regularly practicing; the *1993–95 Mission Handbook,* ed. John A. Siewert and John A. Kenyon, Pasadena: MARC, 1993, p. 3, estimates that by the year 2000 2.1 billion people in the world will identify themselves as Christians.

2. Benjamin R. Barber, "Jihad vs. McWorld," *The Atlantic,* March 1992, and the book of the same name, *Jihad vs. McWorld,* NY: Times Books, 1995.

3. John Davison Hunter, *American Evangelicalism,* New Brunswick: Rutgers, 1983, reported that 22 percent of Americans over age eighteen were evangelicals. Gallop Poll data has shown higher figures when asking Americans if they consider themselves evangelical/"born again" Christians: 33 percent said yes in 1986, increasing dramatically to 45 percent in 1993. Another Gallup poll in 1979 reported 19 percent of Americans considered themselves Pentecostals or charismatics, which presumably included some Catholic charismatics. Spokesmen at Liberty University claimed that 50 million Americans accepted the dispensational eschatology of the fundamentalists (quoted in Jeffrey K. Hadden and Anson Shupe, *Televangelism, Power and Politics on God's Frontier,* NY: Henry Holt, 1988).

Of Christians in the world, large groupings break down like this: Catholics, 925 million; Orthodox, 175 million; Protestants, 600 million. The Protestants are in overlapping classifications: for instance, Barrett and Reapsome list evangelicals at 220 million, and Pentecostals/charismatics at 333 million (which includes 63 million charismatic Catholics) but do not attempt to determine which churches were counted in both categories (Barrett and Reapsome, "Seven Hundred Plans..." 1988). By 1995, the number of born-again evangelicals worldwide, which should include Pentecostals, was probably higher than 300 million. Note that Harvey Cox in *Fire From Heaven,* Reading MA: Addison Wesley, 1995, p. xv, uses the figure of 410 million for the Pentecostal population alone. This may be a little high, but not unrealistically so.

4. William G. McLoughlin, *Revivals, Awakenings, and Reform,* Chicago: University of Chicago Press, 1978, p. 214.

5. Pat Robertson, *America's Dates With Destiny,* quoted in Hadden and Shupe, Televangelism, pp. 298–299.

6. Paul Yonggi Cho, "Mobilizing the Laity for World Evangelism," *Church Growth,* Spring 1992, p. 5.

7. David Stoll, "Introduction" to *Rethinking Protestantism in Latin America,* ed. David

Stoll and Virginia Gerrard-Burnett, Philadelphia: Temple University Press, 1993, p. 3.

8. Andrew F. Walls, director of the Centre for the Study of Christianity in the Non-Western World at the University of Edinburgh, "World Christianity, the Missionary Movement, and the Ugly American," in *World Order and Religion,* ed. Wade Clark Roof, Albany: State University of New York Press, 1991, p. 151. Walls says four-fifths of the 67,200 Protestant missionaries are North American. Other estimates are a bit lower, but none is under 50 percent.

9. Harvey Cox, *Fire from Heaven,* NY: Addison-Wesley, 1995, p. 16.

10. G. J. U. Moshey, *Who is this Allah?,* Ibadan: Fireliners International, 1990, p. 163.

11. Samuel P. Huntington, "The Clash of Civilizations," *Foreign Policy,* Summer 1993, p. 26.

12. Ariel Dorfman, *How to Read Donald Duck,* New York: International General, 1984, demonstrates that the cheerful missions of Donald Duck and Huey, Dewey, and Louie on behalf of Uncle Scrooge have made great primers on imperialistic benevolence for the youth of Latin America.

13. Jeffrey K. Hadden and Anson Shupe, *Televangelism,* pp. 192–193.

14. Marlise Simons, "Latin America's New Gospel," *New York Times Magazine,* 7 November, 1982, p. 117.

CHAPTER TWO
Fundamentalist Americanism and Christian Fundamentalism

1. Quoted in Hadden and Shupe, *Televangelism,* NY: Henry Holt, 1988, p. 96.

2. Anthony Wallace, *Rockdale,* NY: W. W. Norton & Co., 1978, p. 453.

3. Quoted in Hadden and Shupe, *Televangelism,* p. 272.

4. Jerry Falwell, *Listen America,* NY: Bantam Books, 1980, p. 18.

5. McLoughlin, *Revivals, Awakenings and Reform,* p. 190.

6. Ibid., p. 189.

7. Jeremy Rifkin (with Ted Howard), *The Emerging Order: God in an Age of Scarcity,* NY: Putnam, 1979, p. 167.

8. Mark Toulouse, *The Transformation of John Foster Dulles,* Macon: Mercer University Press, 1985, p. 177.

9. John Foster Dulles, *War, Peace, and Change,* NY: Harper, 1939.

10. Toulouse, p. 232.

11. Dulles quoted by George Black, *The Good Neighbor,* NY: Pantheon, 1984, title page.

12. David Stoll, *Fishers of Men or Founders of Empire?,* London: ZED, 1982, p. 23.

13. Quoted in Paul Gifford, *To Save or Enslave,* Harare, Zimbabwe: EDICESA, 1990, p. 5.

14. Ibid., p. 6.

15. Steve Bruce, "Fundamentalism, Ethnicity, and Enclave," in *Fundamentalism and the State,* ed. Martin Marty and Scott Appleby, Chicago: University of Chicago Press, 1993, p. 51.

16. Ibid., pp. 55–57.

17. We single out Moon because his church has made such a singular contribution to the new right within the U.S. Sun Myung Moon, *Divine Principle*, 1974, quoted in Irving Horowitz, "The Last Civil Religion: Reverend Moon and the Unification Church," in *In Gods We Trust*, ed. Robbins et al., New Brunswick: Transaction, 1981, p. 61.

18. Ibid., p. 64.

19. Lee Daniel Soonjung, *A Historical Study of the National Evangelization Movement of Korea*, dissertation, Fuller Theology School, 1988. Lee reviews various Christian nationalist influences, especially the founder of the National Evangelization movement, Rev. Shin Hyun Gyoon, who in 1964 wrote: "God chooses his people from the Semitic line. We Koreans are in the line of Shem, the first born son of Noah, a nation from the East, a single-race nation, and a small and weak nation. Korea is a nation divinely chosen for tomorrow." Pp. 208–209.

20. Interview by one of the authors with Church personnel, June 1992.

21. Interestingly, the spread of fundamentalist doctrine to Korea predated the post-war American military occupation, for it was carried throughout the Far East by the Bible Union of China and the Stewart Evangelistic Fund in the early 1900s. The latter was backed by Milton Stewart, who with his brother Lyman owned the Union Oil Company in Southern California and financed the publication of *The Fundamentals* from 1910 to 1915.

These origins have much to do with the fact that the majority of contemporary Protestants in Korea could be classified as fundamentalist: "It would be no exaggeration to say that main-line Protestant denominations are theologically fundamentalistic, even though they call themselves evangelical or conservative," writes David Kwang-sun Suh, "Forty Years of Korean Protestant Churches," in *Korean Church*, ed. Korean Council of Churches, Seoul: Christian Institute of Justice and Development, 1990. Suh provides a good explanation of how Korean Christianity is the "modernizing" faith of the nation at the same time that it is overwhelmingly conservative and leaning toward Pentecostalism, even within historical denominations such as Presbyterianism. Also see sociologist Kim Byong-Suh, "The Explosive Growth of the Korean Church Today: A Social Analysis," in the same volume.

22. Joseph Anfuso and David Sczepanski, *Efrain Rios Montt, Servant or Dictator?*, Ventura, California: Vision House, 1983, pp. ix–x. For good documentation of the vast array of fundamentalist Christian support supplied in Central America, see Sara Diamond, *Spiritual Warfare*, Boston: South End Press, 1989, and various reports from the Resource Center, Albuquerque, New Mexico.

23. Quoted in Steve Brouwer, *Conquest and Capitalism, 1492–1992*, Carlisle: Big Picture Books, 1992, p. 12.

24. Wallace, *Rockdale*, p. 373.

25. Ibid., p. 474. Wallace's book is extremely valuable for fleshing out the particulars, within one community, of one way in which evangelicalism provided for social control during an era of rapid industrialization. Not only were Rockdale's experiences common to many parts of the country, but its manufacturing families had influential connections to religious and political leaders at the national level and on the frontier. William Gilpin, governor of the territory of Colorado, whose earlier quotation on

Manifest Destiny probably represents the pinnacle of such belief, was the offspring of a capitalist family in nearby Brandywine; members of the Du Pont family were also close neighbors and friends of the Rockdale industrialists.

26. Appearing in 1886 and quoted in George Marsden, *Understanding Evangelicalism and Fundamentalism*, Grand Rapids: Eerdmans, 1991, p. 28.

27. Martin Marty, *Righteous Empire*, NY: Dial Press, 1970, p. 152.

28. Rifkin, *The Emerging Order*, p. 154.

29. Ibid.

30. Ibid., p. 155.

31. See Simon Smith Kuznets, *Growth, Population, Income Distribution*, NY: W. W. Norton, 1979, on the increasing equality of income across social classes after World War II. The opposite had been true from the Civil War until the Great Depression.

32. Steve Brouwer, *Sharing the Pie*, Carlisle: Big Picture Books, 1992; and Barry Bluestone and Bennett Harrison, *The Great U-Turn*, NY: Basic Books, 1988.

33. David Edwin Harrell, *All Things are Possible: The Healing and Charismatic Revivals in Modern America*, Bloomington: University of Indiana Press, 1975, pp. 200–201.

34. Ibid., p. 171.

35. Ibid., p. 172.

36. Quoted in Hadden and Shupe, *Televangelism*, p. 132.

37. Kenneth Copeland and his wife, Gloria Copeland, are a formidable evangelizing team, sharing a television show and publishing such titles as *The Laws of Prosperity*, Fort Worth, TX: Kenneth Copeland Publications, 1974, and *God's Will is Prosperity*, Fort Worth, TX: Kenneth Copeland Publications.

38. David Edwin Harrell, *Oral Roberts: An American Life,* Bloomington: University of Indiana Press, 1985, p. 158.

39. Ibid., p. 462.

40. Ibid., p. 424.

41. Capital letters are in the original from Kenneth Hagin's magazine, *The Word of Faith*, August 1993, p. 5.

42. Quoted in Gifford, *To Save or Enslave*, p. 11.

43. Robertson, *The Secret Kingdom*, San Francisco: Harper and Row, 1987, p. 117, quoted in David Edwin Harrell, *Pat Robertson*.

44. Marvin Harris, *America Now*, NY: Simon and Schuster, 1981, p. 151.

45. Ibid.

46. Ibid., p. 161.

47. Pat Robertson, *The Secret Kingdom*, quoted in Harrell, *Pat Robertson*, p. 117.

48. Harrell, *Pat Robertson*, p. 114.

49. Harrell, *Oral Roberts*.

50. Harrell, *Pat Robertson*, p. 41.

51. Tom Engelhardt, *The End of Victory Culture: Cold War America and the Disillusioning of a Generation,* NY: Basic Books, 1995, p. 301.

CHAPTER THREE
The Changing Theology and Practice of Fundamentalism in the Twentieth Century

1. Paul Gifford, *To Save or Enslave*, Harare: EDICESA (Ecumenical Documentation and Information Centre of Eastern and Southern Africa), 1990, p. 4.

2. Harrell, *All Things are Possible*, pp. 165–168.

3. Gifford, *To Save or Enslave*, p. 4.

4. Ernest R. Sandeen, *The Roots of Fundamentalism: British and American Millenarianism, 1800–1930*, Chicago: University of Chicago Press, 1970.

5. Ibid., p. 39.

6. Ibid., p. 61.

7. Ibid., p. 68.

8. Ibid., pp. 186–189.

9. See Rifkin reference, chapter 2, on sponsorship of Moody's big city revivals; in the case of producing *The Fundamentals*, Scofield and his colleagues were financed by the Stewart brothers, Lyman and Milton, owners of the Union Oil Company of Southern California; their religious intensity and largesse also pushed the fundamentalist line within the China Missions (the immediate cause of Henry Emerson Fosdick's attack on fundamentalism) and sponsored considerable evangelization in Korea. Cf. Sandeen, pp. 189–191.

10. Sandeen, p. 44.

11. W. McLoughlin, *Revivals, Awakenings and Reform*, Chicago: University of Chicago Press, 1978, p. 144.

12. Ibid.

13. James Weinstein, *The Corporate Ideal in the Liberal State: 1900–1918*, Boston: Beacon Press, 1968.

14. Gavin Wright, "The Origins of American Industrial Success, 1879–1940," *American Economic Review*, September 1990.

15. Richard Hofstadter, *Social Darwinism in American Thought*, NY: Braziller, 1965.

16. Stephen J. Gould, *Mismeasure of Man*, NY: W. W. Norton & Co., 1981.

17. Martin Marty, *Righteous Empire*, NY: Dial, 1970. See Chapter Fourteen, "A Decorous Worldliness."

18. Peter Berger, *The Sacred Canopy*, Garden City, NY: Doubleday, 1967, p. 159.

19. George Marsden, *Understanding Fundamentalism and Evangelicalism*, Garden City, NY: Doubleday, 1991, p. 175.

20. See Harrell, *All Things are Possible*; Walter Hollenweger, *The Pentecostals*, Minneapolis: Augsburg, 1972; Robert Mopes Anderson, *Vision of the Disinherited: The Making of Modern Pentecostalism*, NY: Oxford, 1979.

21. Marsden, p. 43.

22. Harrell, *All Things are Possible*, p. 16.

23. Ibid., p. 6.

24. Ibid., pp. 73–74.

25. "Many people mistakenly lump Pentecostalism together with fundamentalism," writes Harvey Cox, *Fire from Heaven*, p. 74. Cox's generally fine book stresses the

positive aspects of Pentecostal experience and devotion, areas that deserve attention and are given only brief mention in our more critical appraisal. However, he says in his last chapter that he is troubled by the many currents of Pentecostalism that are becoming or have become fundamentalistic. Our contention is that these represent the general trend, which is changing the very scope and definition of Christian fundamentalism. This in no way precludes the fact that many Pentecostals and, for that matter, conservative evangelicals are exploring more open, non-fundamentalistic approaches to religious tradition, the kind that Cox would prefer to see.

26. Donald McGavran, *Understanding Church Growth*, Grand Rapids: Eerdmans, 1970. For understanding the important role of the Fuller Theological Seminary, see George Marsden, *Reforming Fundamentalism*, Fuller Seminary, Grand Rapids: Eerdmans, 1987. Fuller has contributed immensely to softening fundamentalism, opening it up to full integration with Pentecostal influences; since 1947, Marsden says, the intention has been to make fundamentalism "more positive," to train real scholars. Dispensationalist training has been loosened up but not eliminated.

27. David Stoll, *Is Latin America Turning Protestant?*, Berkeley: University of California Press, 1990, p. 77.

28. Ibid.

29. *Church Growth Manual*, 1990. Seoul: Church Growth International, (3) December, p. 22.

30. Dick Bernal, "The Power of Faith," *Church Growth*, Spring 1992, p. 17, an excerpt from *Come Down Dark Prince*.

31. Kim Kyong Suh, "The Explosive Growth of the Korean Church Today," *International Review of Mission*, Vol. 74, January 1985.

CHAPTER FOUR
Guatemala: Protestant Modernization or Evangelical Apocalypse?

1. Bryan Roberts, "Protestant Groups and Coping with Urban Life in Guatemala City," *American Journal of Sociology*, 73(6), May 1968; Virginia Garrard-Burnett, "Jerusalem Under Siege: Protestantism in Rural Guatemala, 1960–1987," September 1989; Martin, *Tongues of Fire*.

2. The apparatus of the imperial Spanish Conquest, which first subdued most of America, has long since disappeared, and it has not been replaced by any systematized structure of dominance matching the orderly pattern imposed by occupying Spanish armies, settlers, priests, and friars. Nor do we find the nineteenth-century colonial patterns imposed by the industrial capitalist British empire, which effectively used the spirited evangelization of Anglican and religious nonconformist missionaries. Such a U.S. empire does not exist.

3. Susan D. Rose and Quentin Schultz, "An Awakening in Guatemala," in *Fundamentalisms and Society*, ed. by Martin E. Marty and R. Scott Appleby, Chicago: University of Chicago Press, 1993; David Stoll, *Is Latin America Turning Protestant? The Politics of Evangelical Growth*, Berkeley: University of California Press, 1990.

4. Bruce Calder, *Crecimiento y Cambio de la Iglesia Catolica Guatemalteca*, Guatemala

City and Austin: Seminario de Integracion Social de Guatemala and University of Texas, 1970, p. 51.

5. This secularization process refers mainly to the power of formal Catholic and Protestant institutions in urban areas and ladino towns; it is more difficult to assess whether there was any significant change in the depth or strength of the syncretist, Mayan/Catholic practices maintained by the indigenous peoples who continued to reside in highland villages.

6. Jim Handy, *Gift of the Devil*, Boston: South End Press, 1984; George Black, *Garrison Guatemala*, London: Zed Press, 1984; Richard Adams, *Crucifixion by Power: Essays on Guatemalan National Social Structure 1944–1966*, Austin: University of Texas 1970; Susanne Jonas, *The Battle for Guatemala*, Boulder: Westview, 1991.

7. Jose Miguez Bonino, *Doing Theology in a Revolutionary Situation*, Philadelphia: Fortress, 1975, p. 15.

8. Handy, *Gift of the Devil*, pp. 107–108.

9. Ibid., p. 128.

10. Ibid., p. 107.

11. Ibid., p. 129.

12. Noam Chomsky in Introduction to Jennifer Harbury, *Bridge of Courage*, Monroe, Maine: Common Courage Press, 1994, p. 25. The poverty rate in 1992 was 87 percent, up from 79 percent in 1980.

13. Black, *Garrison Guatemala,* p. 78.

14. Jonas, *The Battle for Guatemala*, p. 149.

15. Noam Chomsky, introduction to *Bridge of Courage*, p. 25.

16. "Assessment of Guatemalan Education" Guatemala City: Academy for Educational Development Report, 1985, No. 6; "Diagnostico de la Educacion Guatemalteca," Guatemala City: Ministerio de Educacion, Officina de Planeamiento Integral de Educacion, 1985.

17. Most revenues are raised through indirect, regressive levies rather than income taxes on the rich. *Guatemala 1986: The Year of Promises*, Infopress, 1987.

18. Calder, *Crecimiento y combio*, p. 54.

19. Daniel Levine, *Popular Voices in Latin America,* Princeton: Princeton University Press, 1992; Levine, ed., *Religion and Political Conflict in Latin America,* Chapel Hill, UNC Press, 1986; Philip Berryman, *Stubborn Hope: Religion, Politics, and Revolution in Central America,* Maryknoll, NY: Orbis Press, 1995; Penny Lernoux, *People of God,* NY: Viking, 1989.

20. Roberts, "Protestant Groups," pp. 764–765.

21. Ibid., p. 766.

22. Ibid., p. 761.

23. Ibid., p. 760.

24. Moreover, many Guatemalans who joined the Protestant *sectas* could more easily break away from the traditional *cofradía* system, which could be costly in terms of one's obligations to help support kin and community festivals associated with the Catholic Church.

25. Stoll, *Is Latin America Turning Protestant?* Berkeley: University of California Press, 1990.

26. Jose Miguez Bonino, "Protestantism's Contribution to Latin America," *Lutheran Quarterly*, 22 (1970), pp. 92–98.

27. Everett Wilson, "The Central American Evangelicals," *International Review of Missions* 77, Jan. 1988. pp. 99–106.

28. Garrard-Burnett, "Jerusalem Under Siege," p. 5.

29. Ibid.

30. Dennis Smith, "The Gospel According to the United States: Evangelical Broadcasting in Central America," in *American Evangelicals and the Mass Media*, ed. Quentin J. Schultze, Grand Rapids, MI: Zondervan/Academie, 1990, p. 281.

31. Garrard-Burnett, "Jerusalem under Siege," p. 5.

32. Steve Brouwer, *Conquest and Capitalism,* Carlisle: Big Picture Books, p. 34.

33. Black, *Garrison Guatemala*, p. 140.

34. Garrard-Burnett, "Jerusalem Under Siege," p. 7.

35. Joseph Anfuso and David Sczepanski, *Efrain Rios Montt: Servant or Dictator?*, Ventura, CA: Vision House, 1983, pp. ix–x.

36. In addition to his Guatemala connections, Pat Robertson was a preacher to the Contras as well as a major fund raiser. He has been a staunch ally of the Salvadoran army and the tiny economic oligarchy that stands behind it. Working closely with Senator Jesse Helms, Oliver North, and General Singlaub of the World Anti-Communist League, he wants to eradicate "communism" in Central America. For more detail see Diamond, *Spiritual Warfare.*

37. The documentation of violence during the Rios Montt era is extensive. See: "Politica Institucional Hacia el Desplazado Interno en Guatemala," Cuadernos de Investigación No. 6 Guatemala City: AVANSCO, January 1990; Chris Krueger and Kjell Enge, "Security and Development in the Guatemalan Highlands," Washington, D.C.: Washington Office on Latin America, August 1985; "Massive Extrajudicial Executions in Rural Areas Under the Government of General Efrain Rios Montt," *Amnesty International*, 1982.

38. Garrard-Burnett, "Jerusalem Under Siege," p. 7–8.

39. Ibid.

40. Bruce Larmer, "Guatemala: Evangelical Spurt Meets Spiritual Needs and Political Goals," *Christian Science Monitor*, 9–15 March 1989, p. 2.

41. Stoll, *Is Latin America Turning Protestant?* pp. 196–198.

42. Larmer, *Guatemala,"* p. 2.

43. See Garrard-Burnett, "Jerusalem Under Siege," p. 10–11.

44. Elizabeth Brusco, *The Reformation of Machismo,* Austin: University of Texas, 1994.

45. Julian Lloret, "The Gospel in the Mayan Culture of Guatemala," *Dialogo Hermanidad Maya 7(3),* 1978.

46. Quoted in Wilson, "The Central American Evangelicals," p. 99.

47. Ibid.

48. A 1989 SEPAL report indicates that Guatemalan Protestants are divided into

some three hundred denominations, one hundred of which have one thousand members or more, and two hundred of which have fewer than one thousand members.

49. Wilson, in "The Central American Evangelicals." Of the sixty-eight groups, of which eighteen report one hundred or more congregations, and thirty-eight report a membership of one thousand or more adults. The two largest denominations (Assemblies of God and Church of God) each account for 12 percent of the total active membership, leaving three-fourths of the evangelicals distributed among the remaining churches. The groups report an aggregate of five thousand organized local churches and two thousand other regular meeting places.

50. Dennis Smith, "The Impact of Religious Programming in the Electronic Media on the Active Christian Population in Central America," *Latin American Pastoral Issues* 15, July 1988, p. 76.

51. Maria C. Wert and Robert L. Stevenson, "Global Television Flow to Latin America," *Journalism Quarterly* 65, Spring 1988, pp. 182–185.

52. The one-half figure is from a survey conducted for one of the country's television stations. See Gustav Niebuhr, "Poor, Rich Alike Stay Tuned to TV Preachers," *Atlanta Constitution*, 2 March 1987, p. 6A. The "over one-half" figure is from a three-nation survey conducted by the Latin American Evangelical Center for Pastoral Studies (known by its Spanish acronym as "CELEP"). See Smith, "The Impact of Religious Programming," p. 77.

53. Smith, "The Impact of Religious Programming," p. 77.

54. About one-quarter of churchgoing ladinos regularly watched one of the four major radio or TV evangelists. Ibid., p. 78.

55. Ibid., p. 79.

56. See Rose and Schultze, "An Awakening in Guatemala."

57. Authors' interview with Rick Waldrop, July 1987.

58. Though according to Salazar, 80 percent of evangelical schools do not have a full evangelical staff.

59. Authors' interview with Christian school principal, March 1990.

60. According to Lernoux, *People of God*, p. 16, Swaggart alone spent $15 million dollars a year on overseas missions, including a private school system in El Salvador that educated over thirteen thousand children, and a similarly large one in Honduras.

61. Ibid., p. 16.

62. Fraternidad Cristiana, whose large church building resembles a fancy auto dealership in design, sits just outside of Guatemala City on the Pan American Highway near the glass-and-steel headquarters of several North American drug companies. The auditorium holds eight hundred people. Ushers are equal numbers of men and women, well dressed in understated light blue uniforms that resemble airline suits worn by pilots and flight attendants. Services at Fraternidad are lively and entertaining. Lopez is preceded by an imposing gentleman in a white jacket who is the lead singer, backed by a band and a well-dressed chorus of attractive young women. He alternates between leading the congregation in song and singing solos that have the sound of tasteful nightclub music. After about an hour, Lopez takes the stage and begins delivering a fast-paced sermon laced with humorous one-liners that evoke

laughter from his audience. Clearly the church is attracting many new members—the auditorium is packed for the three successive services held there every Sunday morning. In fact, extensive church and school construction is currently under way.

63. Rose and Schultze, "An Awakening in Guatemala." p. 440.

64. Interviews with the authors, June 1987.

65. Church service attended by the authors, June 1987.

66. David Stoll, "Jesus is Lord of Guatemala."

67. Ibid.

68. David Edwin Harrell, *Oral Roberts*, p. 158.

69. David Stoll, "Jesus is Lord of Guatemala: The Prospects of Evangelical Reform in a Death Squad State," in Emmanuel Sivan and Gabariel Almond, ed., *Accounting for Fundamentalism*, Chicago: University of Chicago Press, 1994.

70. Ibid. p. 95; speaking of spiritual warfare, an Army chaplain reported to Stoll that one-half of the four hundred cadets now in training at the Army service academy are evangelicals, p. 99.

71. Interestingly, Fujimora, a nominally Catholic agricultural engineer, was said to have his strongest support among Protestants in Peru, who generally backed his assumption of dictatorial powers in 1992.

72. Evidently ELIM's prophet/pastor asked Serrano to leave the church because he was not willing to give up politics after he failed to win the election in 1985.

73. Information on Agua Viva that follows was gathered on authors' extensive visit in June 1987.

74. When construction of Agua Viva's large church was under way in 1987, priests at the old Catholic Cathedral in downtown Quetzaltenango, a city of about two hundred thousand, said they were struggling to find enough money to support only two men who were working on the restoration of the church's baroque facade.

75. Interviews with authors, June 1987.

76. Jean Comaroff and John Comaroff, *Of Revelation and Revolution: Christianity, Colonialism, and Consciousness in South Africa,* Chicago: University of Chicago Press, 1991, p. 80.

77. Ibid., p. 81.

78. Ibid., p. 85.

79. Interview with authors, June 1987.

80. Ibid.

CHAPTER FIVE
Spiritual Warfare: The Case of the Philippines

1. Ramon Orosa, "A Voice in the Wilderness Speaks," *Ministry Digest*, November-December 1989, p. 2. A candidate in the 1992 Senate elections, Orosa is active in coordinating born-again crusades and conferences in the Philippines. He "received the Lord" in 1983, began a TV ministry in 1984, and established his church, Oro International Ministries, in 1987. Personal interview, Manila, 25 May 1992.

2. Ibid.

3. Quoted by Ramsey Clark in the Forword to Benjamin Pimentel, *Rebolusyon!: A Generation of Struggle in the Philippines*, NY: Monthly Review Press, 1991, p. 7.

4. Orosa, "Unveiling of His Glory," n.d., unpublished manuscript.

5. Siewert and Kenyon, *Mission Handbook*, p. 77.

6. Mgr. Bayani Valenzuela, "Update on Fundamentalist Groups in the Philippines Today," prepared by the Archdiocesan Office for Ecumenical and Interfaith Affairs, April 1990; "Fundamentalism: Twist of Faith," *IBON: Facts and Figures*, Vol. 14, No. 9, 15 May 1991, p. 2.

7. DAWN 2000 is an acronym for "Discipling A Whole Nation" which aims to plant a church in every *barangay* and people group in the Philippines by the year 2000.

8. "DAWN Research Report," prepared by Philippine Crusades Research, 5 November 1991.

9. "Catholic Guidelines on Fundamentalism: Hold Fast to What is Good," Manila: Catholic Bishops Conference of the Philippines, 1989, p. 11.

10. According to the report, this came after Vatican II and the Medellin Conference in 1968 when the Latin American Catholic bishops endorsed liberation theology. *Exploring the New Religious Movements in the Philippines*, Quezon City: Commission on Evangelism and Ecumenical Relations, National Council of Churches in the Philippines, 1989, p. 47.

11. Such syncretism can still be seen in the religious belief systems of many contemporary Filipinos. As sociologist Onofre Corpus writes: "Filipino folk Christianity reconciles in one system the rigid monotheism of Christian dogma alongside belief in a world of minor dieties that solicitously guard over dwellings, trees, rivers, straits, fields, and forests" (Onofre Corpuz, *The Philippines,* N.J.: Presidential, 1976, p. 5. See also Rebecca Asedillo and David Williams, eds., Rice in the Storm, NY: Friendship Press, 1989).

12. Asedillo and Williams, ed.; Stuart C. Miller, *Benevolent Assimilation*, New Haven: Yale University Press, 1982.

13. K. Enton Clymer, *Protestant Missionaries in the Philippines 1898–1916: An Inquiry into the American Colonial Mentality*, Chicago: University of Illinois Press, 1986, p. 72.

14. Quoted in Clymer, ibid., p. 154.

15. D. B. Schirmer and S. R. Shalom, eds. *The Philippines Reader: A History of Colonialism, Neocolonialism, Dictatorship, and Resistance*, Boston: South End Press, 1987, Ch. 3; R. Constantino and L. Constantino, *The Philippines: The Continuing Past*, Quezon City: Foundation for Nationalist Studies, 1987.

16. Constantino and Constantino, p. 70.

17. Schirmer and Shalom, *The Philippines Reader: A History of Colonialism, Neocolonialism, Dictatorship, and Resistance*, Boston: South End Press, 1987, Ch. 3; pp. 69–70.

18. Other "tigers" in the Pacific had per-capita incomes three to fifteen times that of the Philippines. Ramsey Clark in the Foreword to Pimentel, *Rebolusyon!*, p.9.

19. R. Pineda-Ofreneo, *The Philippines: Debt and Poverty*, Oxford: Oxfam, 1991; Asedillo and Williams, *Benevolent Assimilation*.

20. Schirmer and Shalom, *The Philippines Reader*, p. 126. Foreign domination of the Philippine economy was considerably strengthened during the martial-law years

(1972–1986), crippling the economy and ranking the Philippines the sixth most indebted country by 1989–1990 (Pineda-Ofreneo, p. 3). As the debt service increased (from 6.4 percent in 1965–72 to 17.1 percent in 1980–85 to 42 percent in 1986–89) health expenditures steadily declined, from 5.2 percent in 1965–72 to 3.2 percent in 1986–89 (p. 17). Debt service for 1990 totaled $4.719 billion. Nationally the ratio of doctors to inhabitants is 1:3000, way below the global standard of 1:1000 (p. 19). Only 15 percent of the population has a sanitary sewage system, and about 40 percent have no access to potable water. Seventy percent of the population is said to be malnourished, 22 percent to a serious degree (p. 20). The Presidential Commission on the Urban Poor estimated that at the end of 1988, there were four million squatters in metro Manila alone (Joseph Cortes, "Tackling the Squatters Problem," *Manila Times,* 28 May 1989).

21. The EDSA Event—as the February 1986 revolt against Marcos is often held much promise for democratic reform. Most now view this "revolution" with great cynicism, given that few of the changes that appeared possible actually occurred.

22. L. Bautista, *The Social Views of Evangelicals on Issues Related to the Marcos Rule 1972–1986*, master's thesis submitted to the College of Social Sciences and Philosophy, University of the Philippines, September 1991.

23. See Bautista, ibid.

24. Participating groups included ISACC, KONFES, InterVarsity Fellowship, the Faith Baptist Church, Diliman Bible Church, First Free Methodist Church, Greenshills Christian Fellowship.

25. F. Nicholas and J. de Leon, "Spiritual Renewal: The Philippines Experience," in *Exploring New Religious Movements*, p. 48.

26. Father Bayani Valenzuela ("Update on Fundamentalist Groups in the Philippines") conducted the study for the Archdiocesan Office for Ecumenical and Interfaith Affairs, p. 2. Also see "Fundamentalism: Twist of Faith."

27. "Philippine Council of Evangelical Churches, Inc.," pamphlet, n.d.

28. Valenzuela, "Update on Fundamentalist Groups."

29. Jun Vencer, "The Church and National Recovery," *Ministry Digest*, Vol. 1, No. 5, 1990, pp. 7–8.

30. Interview with Jun Vencer, Manila, 1 June 1992.

31. Interview with Ramon Orosa, Manila, June 1992.

32. Orosa, "A Voice," p. 2.

33. A theology student and pastor, Bautista argues that the development of relief organizations was primarily motivated by the availability of international funds (especially from The U.S.) rather than a fundamental concern for the poor. Nonetheless, the involvement of staff members deepened their understanding of poverty and gave them a new appreciation for the social implications of their faith. Bautista, pp. 91–92.

34. Butch Conde, "Touch of Glory," *Christian Journal*, August 1991, p. 8.

35. Vencer, "The Church," pp. 7–8.

36. J. Aquino, "Kulturang Coke at Relihiyong 'Born-Again'," *Kalinangan*, Vol. 1, No. 1, April 1981, pp. 8–9.

37. C. Peter Wagner, "Territorial Spirits," *Ministry Digest*, Vol. 1, No. 5, November/ December 1989, p. 42.

38. Ibid., p. 45.

39. Ibid., p. 47.

40. Excerpt from a TV address, "A Message to the Filipino Nation," by Villanueva in 1989, quoted in *Ministry Digest*, November/December 1989, p. 5.

41. Quoted in *Ministry Digest*, November/December 1989: 6.

42. Quoted in F. Conway and J. Siegelman, *Holy Terror: The Fundamentalist War on America's Freedom, Religion, Politics, and Our Private Lives,* NY: Dell Publishing, 1982, p. 172.

43. Daniel Tappeiner, "Prepare War! The Spirit's Call to Spiritual Warfare," *Ministry Digest*, November/December 42, 1989, p. 19.

44. Violeta B. Lopez-Gonzaga, *The Negrense: A Social History of an Elite Class,* Bacolod: Institute of Social Research, University of LaSalle, 1991.

45. Father O'Brien went on to say, however, that the landowners of Negros are more likely to be aligned with the conservative Catholic Opus Dei than with the Protestant fundamentalist groups (Interview, Bacolod, 1992).

46. Word for the World is a branch of the Church of God, Cleveland, Tennessee, and sister church of the Greenhills Christian Fellowship, a wealthy congregation in Makati, the business district of Manila. O'Dowd had been with the Swaggart ministries for five years. Word for the World holds English services in the morning, which draws people primarily from the middle classes, and an Illonggo language service in the afternoon, which draws people primarily from the lower classes. Most of the seven hundred members within the church's 120-mile ministry are from the lower classes: fishermen and plantation workers. The church has a hacienda outreach program called "Hacienda Harvest" which it highlights in their missions letters to U.S. donors.

47. Interview with Pastor Tom and Kaulei O'Dowd, Bacolod City, 31 May 1992.

48. Interview with Joberto Ramos, Bacolod, 29 May 1992.

49. McCollister, president of CCC's Christian Embassy.

50. Tom Marti, "Fundamentalist Sects and the Political Right," *Kalinangan*, Vol. 7, No. 1, 1987.

51. Peter Brock, "Fundamentalist Expansion," *WSCF Journal*, 1988, p. 4.

52. Interview with Pastor Tom and Kaulei O'Dowd, Bacolod, 31 May 1992.

53. Interview with Pastor Jose Rivera, 29 May 1992.

54. Interview with Father O'Brien; interview with Father R. Empestan, Diocesan Pastoral Center, Bacolod, 31 May 1992; see Niall O'Brien, *Island of Tears, Island of Hope: Living the Gospel in a Revolutionary Situation*, Maryknoll, NY: Orbis Books, 1993.

55. Miguel Colonel, *Pro-Democracy PEOPLE'S WAR*, Quezon City: Vanmarc Ventures, 1991, p. 523, Ch. 5.

56. Ibid., pp. 639–640.

57. Marti, "Fundamentalist Sects."

58. Waghelstein quoted in S. Miles, "Low Intensity Conflict: U.S. New Strategy in the Third World," reprinted by the Socio-Pastoral Institute (SPI), Special Issue, Series, n.d.; Col. J. W. Waghelstein, "Post-Vietnam Counterinsurgency Doctrine," *Military Review*, May 1985, p. 42.

59. Asedillo and Williams, p. 23. According to the *Road to Damascus* document

(which was based on two and a half years of international study in seven countries: the Philippines, Guatemala, South Korea, South Africa, Nicaragua, El Salvador, and Nambia), research reveals "an astonishing similarity of strategies, both in the structure and effects of the security systems in these countries.... LIC operates against both the population and the church."

60. Camba quoted in R. Alibutud, "Invasion of the Soul Snatchers," *Malaya*, Vol. 1, No. 3, 15 July 1990, p. 1.

61. See Marti, pp. 22–25; Sheila Coronel, "Right-Wing Evangelicals Take Part in Politics in the Name of God," *Kalinangan* Vol. 9, No. 2, 1989, pp. 39–42.

62. The military incorporated the vigilantes into its anti-communist campaigns in the 1940s. See Ramsey Clark et al., *Right-Wing Vigilantes and U.S. Involvement,* Manila: Philippine Alliance of Human Rights Advocates (PAHRA), 1987; "Vigilantes in the Philippines: A Threat to Democratic Rule," NY: Lawyers Committee for Human Rights, 1988. Some six hundred vigilante groups have been identified. They range in number from a few individuals to hundreds of members (A. De Guzman and T. Craige, Handbook on Militarization, Manila: Ecumenical Movement for Justice and Peace, 1990, p. 21). For a discussion about whether cultist vigilante groups are more violent than non-cultist ones, see Araceli Suzara, "Cultist Vigilantism in the Philippines" and David Kowalewski, "Rejoinder on Vigilantism in the Philippines," both in *Sociological Analysis*, Vol. 54, No. 3, Fall 1993, pp. 303–312; and David Kowalewski, "Cultism, insurgency, and vigilantism in the Philippines," *Sociological Analysis*, Vol. 52, 1991, pp. 241–253.

63. Interview with Commander Bagyo, Pulihans, Bacolod, 30 May 1992. Author had the impression of someone squeezed between the military and the New People's Army. "I believe in land reform, but I don't believe there's a chance of that." Hungry and poor, espousing a belief in God and his own invincibility, this man seemed less a cannibalistic murderer (his group had claimed responsibility for the decapitation of some of their victims and the eating of their brains) than a man fighting back, struggling to provide for himself and "his people" (a small farming community) with some pride and dignity intact.

64. "Sin Bats for Organization of Vigilante Groups," *Church Situationer*, Vol. 87, No. 6, June 1987, p. 93.

65. T. Costello, "An Analysis of the Filipino Church's Contribution to the Development of a Christian Political Ethic," unpublished paper, October 1989. In the two years after President Aquino came to power, 137 human rights violations against church workers were documented. Almost half of these cases were summary execution, shooting, or massacre. Many church workers have simply disappeared.

66. Editorial. "Right-Wing Vigilantes in Labor Repression," KMU International Department, Manila, 1987: 9.

67. A. Guillermo, "Comments," in The Religious Right and National Security Doctrine, *Tugon,* Vol. XI, No. 2, 1991, p. 230.

68. Suzara, "Cultist Vigilantism," p. 303.

69. Quoted in Asedillo and Williams, *Rice in the Storm*, p. vii.

70. De Guzman and Craige, *Handbook on Militarization,* pp. 13, 17–18.

71. Teresita Alo, Tito Craige, and Reinier ter Kuile, *The Iceberg and the Cross: Violence Against the Church*, Manila: Justice and Peace Commission, Association of Major Religious Superiors in the Philippines, 1990: 31; see also de Guzman and Craige; Peter Geremia, ed., *Church Persecution*, Quezon City: Claretian Publications, 1988.

72. E. Leogo, "Will Taiwan's Anti-Communist Strategy Be as Effective in the Philippines?" *Ang Tala*, September 1987, pp. 11, 17.

73. *CMF (Christian Military Fellowship) Philippines Newsletter*, n.d.

74. *Church Trends*, Manila: Church Data Center, 1990.

75. Representatives came from Korea (the largest delegation), Indonesia, Republic of China, Singapore, Australia, Japan, India, Malaysia, United Kingdom, the U.S., and the Philippines.

76. Cited in *CMF Newsletter*, January/February 1990, p. 5.

77. Interview with O'Brien.

78. F. T. Sabug, "The Religious Right in the Philippines: A Preliminary Study," in *The Religious Right and the National Security Doctrine*, Manila, Tugon, NCCP, 1991, p. 377.

79. Whitehall had made continual visits to the Philippines, as has the retired Major General John K. Singlaub, in concert with CAUSA. "Right-Wing Vigilantes and U.S. Involvement: Report of a Fact-Finding Mission to the Philippines May 20–30, 1987," Alliance of Human Rights Advocates (PAHRA), 1987, pp. 20–21.

80. Established since Tica began his ministry in the Philippines on July 9, 1974. "In some areas, they've dropped the name Baptist—in Mindinao Bataan you don't want to use my name—they'll kill you," he laughs. Interview with Gavino Tica, Manila, 1 June 1992.

81. Ibid.

82. Ibid.

83. These numbers are taken from an interview with Rev. Tica after service at the mother church, International Baptist Ministries in metro Manila, and seeing the livelihood program established at the same location.

84. Interview with Tica.

85. A military publication, "Value Formation," September 1987, p. 4.

86. Ibid.

87. Ibid., p. 18.

88. One U.S. missionary active in the DAWN 2000, Jim Van Meter, writes approvingly: "Almost fifty percent of the South Korean army are born-again Christians. A lot of exciting things are happening in Korea," *Making Missions Practical*, Davao City: Mindanao Challenge, 1990, p. 16.

89. Seminar held 13 August 1986 at the AGAPE Park Mission Guest House.

90. "Joshua for Christ: Bringing Good News to the Military," n.d., p. 2.

91. Author was unable to secure an interview with Almeda despite several attempts, but was able to meet his mother and talk with a young woman convert who was working full-time for him in exchange for room and board, Jesus Miracle Crusades (JMC), Manila, 24 May 1992. See also, *The Religious Right and National Security Doctrine*, pp. 372–373.

92. Interview with Celia Diaz-Laurel, Manila, 27 May 1992. *Groupwatch* reports

that CAUSA manuals were used for Special Operations Teams training; CAUSA held a National Security Conference in 1986 in the Philippines with ex-deputy CIA director Ray Cline and WACL president General Singlaub, CAUSA, p. 13.

93. Interview with Diaz-Laurel, 27 May 1992.

94. Vencer in "DAWN 2000: How many more churches to go?" n.d.

95. *Philippine Daily Globe* article, 14 July 1990, cited in "Fundamentalism: Twist of Faith," pp. 1–7.

96. Ibid., p. 4.

97. According to the head of InterVarsity Christian Fellowship in the Philippines, IVCF is active in two hundred universities, colleges, and high schools; he estimates that they have 2,000–3,000 committed members. Interview with George Capaque, Quezon City, 28 May 1992.

98. Interview with Bishop Ben Dominquez, Church of the Risen Lord at the University of the Philippines, Quezon City, 26 May 1992.

99. Interview with Tica.

100. Ibid.

101. "Catholic Guidelines on Fundamentalism," pp. 16, 20.

102. Ibid., pp. 10–11.

103. Ibid., p. 49.

104. Interview with Tica.

105. M. Maggay, "Comments," in *The Religious Right and National Security Doctrine*, Manila: Tugon, NCCP, 1991. p. 234.

106. Ibid., p. 235.

107. Ibid., p. 234.

108. Ibid., pp. 235–236.

109. "Documenting the Korean Missionary Surge," *MARC Newsletter,* Number 95-1, March 1995, p. 6.

CHAPTER SIX
South Korea: Modernization with a Vengeance, Evangelization with the Modern Edge

1. Peter L. Berger, "An East Asian Development Model?" in *In Search of an East Asian Development Model*, ed. Berger and Hsin-Huang Hsiao, New Brunswick: Transaction Books, 1988, p. 3.

2. Author's interview with missions' staff person, Yoido Full Gospel Church, June 1992.

3. Eileen V. Barker, "The Whole World in His Hand?" *Religion and the World Order*, ed. Roland Robertson and William R. Garrett, N.Y.: Paragon House, 1991, pp. 205–209.

4. See Martin Hart-Landsberg, *The Rush to Development: Economic Change and Political Struggle in South Korea*, NY: Monthly Review Press, 1993; and Walden F. Bello, *Dragons in Distress*, San Francisco: Institute for Food and Development Policy, 1990.

5. Christian Institute for the Study of Justice and Development, *Lost Victory*, Seoul: Minjungsa, 1988, p. 232.

6. Ibid., pp. 92 and 233; and *The Korean Situation 1991*, Seoul: Christian Institute, 1992, p. 94.

7. Ibid.

8. Donald N. Clark, ed., *The Kwangju Uprising*, Boulder: Westview, 1988.

9. Bello, *Dragons in Distress*.

10. Man Woo Lee, *The Odyssey of Korean Democracy*, NY: Prager, 1990, p. 4.

11. Hang Yul Rhee, "The Economic Problems of the Korean Political Economy," in *Political Change* in South Korea, ed. Ilpyong J. Kim and Young Whan Kihl, NY: Paragon House, 1988.

12. Pharis Harvey, "No Justice for Workers in Korea," *Democratic Left*, September-October 1990, p. 10; also see *The Korean Situation 1991*.

13. *Lost Victory*, pp. 241–243.

14. Ibid. p. 249.

15. Harvey, "No Justice," p. 10.

16. Man Woo Lee, *The Odyssey of Korean Democracy*.

17. Clark, *Kwangju Uprising*. After the Kwangju uprising of 1980, 37,000 journalists and teachers were sent to re-education camps.

18. Carter J. Eckert, et al., *Korea, Old and New*, Cambridge: Harvard, 1990, p. 183.

19. Song Kon-ho, "A History of the Christian Movement in Korea," *International Review of Missions*, v. 74, January 1985, p. 36.

20. Harold Hak-won Sunoo, *Korea: A History in Modern Times*, Seoul: Kunkuk University Press, 1970.

21. Kim Kwang-il and Mun Sang-hee, *New Religions in Korea*, Korea Christian Academy, East Asia Christian Conference, 1971, pp. 19–22; also see Felix Moos, *The Olive Tree Movement*, Seoul: Royal Asiatic Society, 1967; Shim Il Sup, "The New Religious Movements in the Korean Church," *International Review of Missions*, Jan. 1985.

22. Estimates of Protestant numbers range from David Martin's "over 20 percent" as of the early 1980s (Martin, *Tongues of Fire*, p. 143) to 25 percent–27 percent (and Catholics at 3.5 percent, Eckert, *Korea, Old and New*, p. 403) to almost 50 percent (Harvey Cox in 1994, *Fire from Heaven*, probably a bit too high).

23. David Kwang-sun Suh, "American Missionaries and a Hundred Years of Korean Protestantism," *International Review of Missions*, v. 74, 1985, p.10, shows growth from two hundred thousand Protestants in 1910 to three hundred seventy two thousand in 1930.

24. Song Kon-ho, "A History of the Christian Movement in Korea."

25. An Ch'angho, 1907, quoted in Kenneth M. Wells, *New God, New Nation*, Honolulu: University of Hawaii Press, 1990, p. 41.

26. Ibid., p. 39.

27. Kwang-sun Suh, "American Missionaries," p. 11. Also see footnote 21 in Chapter Two.

28. Song Kon-ho credits these conservative church practices with driving young people and nationalists away from Christianity during the 1910–1945 period; David Kwang-sun Suh, on the other hand, is more lenient with the missionaries, acknowledging the weakness of their apolitical stance but also stressing their good

works, especially their hospitals that served the poor.

29. Song Kon-ho contends that in the late 1940s the chances for a positive nationalist influence and for widespread progressive movement in the churches were compromised when Protestant pastors who had collaborated with the Japanese were allowed to return to prominent positions within the national denominations. A similar movement of personnel was allowed within the South Korean political and military realms in order to bolster anti-communist forces.

30. 1980 Religious Census of Korea, Ministry of Culture and Information, *Chosun Ilbo*, 16 May, 1981.

31. Kim Kwang-il, *New Religions in Korea*, p. 43.

32. Mun Sang-hee, "Fundamental Doctrines of the New Religions of Korea," in Kim Kwang-il and Mun Sang-hee *New Religions in Korea*, p. 26.

33. Ibid., pp. 26–27.

34. Ibid.

35. Author's interview with David Kwang-sun Suh and Reverend Park, head of the Christian Institute, in June 1992.

36. Lee Daniel Soonjung, *A Historical Study of the National Evangelization Movement of Korea*, Pasadena: doctoral dissertation, Fuller Theological Seminary, 1988, p. 208.

37. Ibid., p. 210. President Park tried to help lift Shin's sagging fortunes in 1975. Shin had prophesied a major oil find at a particular spot in South Korea; when nothing was found he lost momentum and credibility. By appearing at a news conference with an oil drum filled at that site—which was unfortunately not commercially exploitable, said Park—the President was apparently trying to demonstrate that Shin was not completely wrong.

38. Ibid., p. 209.

39. Jim Van Meter, "Making Missions Practical," p. 16.

40. Martin, *Tongues of Fire,* p. 143.

41. David Stoll, David Martin, Harvey Cox.

42. Martin, *Tongues of Fire,* p. 143.

43. Hadden and Shupe, *Televangelism*, p. 227.

44. Hadden, "The Globalization of American Televangelism," in *Religion and Global Order,* eds. Roland Robertson and William R. Garrett, N.Y. Paragon House, 1991, p. 229.

45. Jae Bum Lee, "Pentecostal type distinctives and Korean Protestant Church Growth," Ph.D. dissertation, Fuller Theological Seminary, Pasadena, 1986, p. 190.

46. Ibid., p. 258.

47. Ibid., p. 191.

48. Ibid., p. 256.

49. Paul Yonggi Cho, "How the World's Biggest Church Got That Way," *Christianity Today,* May 18, 1984, p. 53. Cho credits the quote to McGavran's book *Understanding Church Growth,* Grand Rapids; Eerdmans, 1970.

50. Ibid., pp. 52–53.

51. Ibid., p. 54.

52. From 1991 organizational chart of the church handed out to one of the authors, June 1992.

53. Cho, "How the World's Biggest Chruch...," p. 54.

54. Ibid., p. 60.

55. Jae Bum Lee, pp. 265–290.

56. Ibid., p. 279.

57. Peter Wagner, contributing the section on "Church Growth," *Dictionary of Pentecostal and Charismatic Movements*, p. 190. Other successful Baptists have been forced to leave the Southern Baptist denomination when their devotion to charismatic and Pentecostal elements became too public; in the United States, for instance, Jamie Buckingham, a prolific charismatic writer who now has his own large, independent church in Florida.

58. Jae Bum Lee, p. 286.

59. Ibid., p. 285.

60. Falwell's rejection of charismatic "gifts" at home does not necessarily affect his alliances abroad; in particular his alliance with Tica's "full-gospel" Baptist churches and military ministries in the Philippines (see Chapter five).

61. Jae Bum Lee, p. 213, referring to American charismatic writers such as Ladd and Kraft.

62. *The Dictionary of Pentecostal and Charismatic Movements*, p. 287.

63. Ibid.

64. George Marsden, *Reforming Fundamentalism.*

65. Yoido Church Mission documents, 1992.

66. Man Woo Lee, *The Odyssey of Korean Democracy,* p. 2.

67. Michael L. Mickler, *The Unification Church in America: A Bibliography and Research Guide,* NY: Garland, 1987, p. 10.

68. Sun Myung Moon, *Divine Principle*, NY: Holy Spirit Association, 1974, p. 530.

69. Mickler, p. 107.

70. Sun Myung Moon, *Divine Principle,* 1974, quoted in "The Last Civil Religion: Reverend Moon and the Unification Church," Thomas Robbins, Dick Anthony, Madeline Doucas, Thomas Curtis, in Irving Louis Horowitz, ed., *Science, Sin, and Scholarship,* Cambridge: MIT Press, 1978, pp. 61 and 64.

71. Eileen V. Barker, "The Whole World," p. 208.

72. Silvia Aliosa, "Setta di potere," *Panorama,* December 2, 1990, p. 98; *GroupWatch, Albuquerque: InterHemispheric Resource Center, 1990.*

73. Christopher Byron, "Seems Like Old Times," *New York,* 27 September, 1993, p. 22.

74. Ibid. Quoting Unification Church investigator Larry Zilliox Jr.

75. Marvin Harris, *America Now*, p. 150.

76. Frank Greve, "New Right Gets Millions from Moon," *Philadelphia Inquirer,* 20 December, 1987, p. 18A.

77. Ibid.

78. "Unification Church," *GroupWatch*, Albuquerque: The Resource Center, 1990.

79. Jon Lee Anderson and Scott Anderson, *Inside the League*, NY: Dodd, Mead, and Co., 1986, p. 125.

80. Fred Clarkson, "Heaven and Helms," *In These Times,* p. 5, September 13–19, 1989. Also mentioned in this article is the fact that Senator Jesse Helms made five speeches to American Leadership Conference events sponsored by CAUSA in 1988.

81. San Hun Lee, *The End of Communism,* NY: Unification Thought Institute, 1985; quoted in Mickler, p. 167.

82. Greve, "New Right," p. 18A.

83. Ibid. In 1986, the equally influential new right mobilizer Paul Weyrich commented on CBS television, "All Americans should be concerned because [Moon] opposes the constitutional system of goverment in the United States of America"; but only a year later, Weyrich was permitting Moon's groups to join his "Coalitions For America" and declining to comment about why he had a change of heart.

84. Ibid.

85. Richard L. Rubenstein and John K. Roth, eds., *The Politics of Latin American Liberation Theology,* Washington Institute, 1988, includes chapters by Roland Robertson, "Liberation Theology, Latin America, and Third World Underdevelopment" and W. E. Hewitt, "Myths and Realities of Liberation Theology: The Case of Basic Christian Communities in Brazil." Stoll cites these as he reviews the subject in *Rethinking Protestantism in Latin America,* Temple, 1993, and uses them to diminish the importance of liberation theology as a religion of "the people." Roland Robertson, for instance, downplays the importance of liberation theology as a religious movement. Open support for liberation theology is included in the form of an essay by Phillip Berryman.

86. In another New Era book, Donald W. Dayton, "Protestant Christian Missions to Korea as a Source of Unification Thought," *Religion in the Pacific Era,* NY: Paragon, 1985, p. 79, concludes that there has been "a common Protestant missionary culture that provided many threads that have been woven into the tapestry of Unification thought"; he finds strong influences of the Presbyterian and Methodist traditions, encompassing both premillennial dispensationalism and "world changing millennialism."

87. Chung Hwan Kwak, *Outline of the Principle, Level 4,* NY: Unification Church, 1980, p. 213.

88. Richard L. Rubenstein, "The Rational Society and the Future Religion," *The Search for Faith and Justice in the Twentieth Century,* ed. Gene G. James, NY: Paragon House 1987, p. 191. In an argument to prove this contention, Rubenstein points to the mass marriage of 4,000 performed by Rev. Moon at Madison Square Garden in 1982, "young men and women from every corner of the earth married outside of their inherited religious and tribal boundaries."

89. Anderson, *Inside The League,* p. 66.

90. Ibid.

91. Ibid. and author's interviews in Seoul, June 1992.

92. Christian Institute for the Study of Justice and Development, *Lost Victory,* p. 282.

93. Anderson, *Inside The League,* p. 149.

94. Anderson, *Inside The League,* p. 122.

95. For a description of the lack of success of the Unification Church as a U.S. religious organization, see Anson Shupe, "Sun Myung Moon's American Disappointment," *Christian Century,* August 22, 1990, pp. 764–766.

96. Eileen V. Barker, p. 215.

97. Roland Robertson and JoAnn Chirico, "Humanity, Globalization, and Worldwide Religious Resurgence: A Theoretical Exploration," *Sociological Analysis,* 1985, 46: 3, p. 238–9.

98. Robert Boettcher, *Gifts of Deceit,* NY: Holt, Rinehart, and Winston, 1980, pp. 39–40. This kind of political behavior has a long history of endorsement by the mainstream of U.S. political policy making; see, for instance, Samuel Huntington, in *Political Order in Changing Societies,* New Haven: Yale, 1968. Huntington approvingly describes Kim Jong Pil's almost single-handed efforts to set up an instant and legitimizing political party for dictator/President Park in 1963; he resigned from the KCIA and recruited twelve-hundred Army officers to fill all important posts, completely organizing the country's only political party, the Democratic Republican Party (still in power today, although partially democratized in the 1992 election of Kim Young Sam); within a few months, Kim Jong Pil had meticulously set the stage for Park to be elected "legitimately." Since Huntington thought Park's authoritarian rule was necessary and "modernizing," he judged that the new party was legitimate, too.

CHAPTER SEVEN
Christianity in Liberia

1. All the points discussed here can be found in more detail in Paul Gifford, *Christianity and Politics in Doe's Liberia,* Cambridge: Cambridge University Press, 1993.

2. *Guinness Book of Records 1990,* London: Guinness Publishing Company, 1989, p. 200.

3. Sanford J. Ungar, *Africa: The People and Politics of an Emerging Continent,* NY: Simon and Schuster, rev. ed. 1986, p. 94; Tuan Wreh, *The Love of Liberty…The Rule of President William V. S. Tubman in Liberia,* London: C. Hurst, 1976, p. 61.

4. The comparison was first made by Blaine Harden of the *Washington Post* on BBC's *Focus on Africa.*

5. For U.S. interests at the time of Doe's coup, see J. P. Chaudhuri, "Liberia under Military Rule 1980–1985," in *Liberia: Underdevelopment and Political Rule in a Peripheral Society,* ed. R. Kappel, et al., Hamburg: Institute fur Afrika-Kunde, 1986, pp. 52–55; D. Elsood Dunn and Byron Tarr, *Liberia: A National Polity in Transition,* London and Metuchen, NJ: Scarecrow Press, 1988, pp. 176–78.

6. Chester Crocker, U.S. assistant secretary of state for African affairs, alluded to the importance of Liberia's support in the United Nations "including on vital Middle East issues" in his January 23, 1986 "Statement before the Joint Session of the Subcommittees on Africa and on Human Rights and International Organizations of the House Foreign Affairs Committee," in *Liberia Forum,* 3/2, 1986, pp. 115–116.

7. Wreh, *Love of Liberty,* p. 123.

8. Ungar, *Africa,* p. 99.

9. Dunn and Tarr, *Liberia,* p. 191.

10. Doe reversed this procedure in October 1989 for $212 million in aid.

11. Dunn and Tarr, *Liberia,* p. 192.

12. For an extremely critical assessment of Israel's role in Doe's Liberia, see George Klay Kieh Jr., "An Analysis of Israeli Repenetration of Liberia," *LSJ,* XIV 2 (1989), pp. 117–129. Kieh argues that Doe, not Liberia, benefited from the Israeli link. He benefited from bribes from Israeli businesses and made full use of Israel's "technology of repression"; above all, it was Israeli "advisers" who foiled Quiwonkpa's 1985 coup (p. 126).

13. Chaudhuri, "Liberia under Military Rule," p. 57.

14. For aid to Liberia, see Lawyers' Committee for Human Rights, *A Promise Betrayed: A Report on Human Rights,* NY: Lawyers' Committee for Human Rights, 1986, p. 166.

15. For U.S. military aid to Liberia, its policies and objectives, see United States of America, *Congressional Presentation for Security Assistance Programs Fiscal Year 1990,* Washington, D.C., 1989, pp. 190–191.

16. Dunn and Tarr, *Liberia,* p. 178.

17. Patrick L. N. Seyon, "The Results of the 1985 Elections," *Liberian Studies Journal,* XIII, 2 (1988), p. 228.

18. Crocker, *Liberia Forum,* pp. 109–110. (See note 6 above.)

19. Ibid., p. 111.

20. Ibid., p. 116.

21. Ali Affum, "American Cure Fails Liberian Ills," All Africa Press Service release, 12 Dec. 1988.

22. *Daily Observer,* 25 May 1989, pp. 1 and 6. Note that Dynally gave at least equal space to the need for U.S. investments and strategic interests to be protected.

23. *Daily Observer,* 21 June 1989, pp. 1 and 6.

24. Dunn and Tarr, *Liberia,* p. 178. See also Hayden, "Many students…are asking whether the U.S. was interested in all of the people of Liberia or merely in maintaining a military leader in power so that the interests of the United States might be maintained" ("Liberia: Recent Developments and U.S. Foreign Policy: Testimony before the House of Representatives, 23 January 1986," *Liberia Forum,* 2/2(1986), p. 105).

25. *Europa Year Book 1988,* p. 1699.

26. "Too much training, too much equipment and too much power has been given to the Liberian army under the rubric of U.S.AID. The army is now not a protector of the people but a group of well-trained men who have almost absolute power to intimidate, arrest, beat and even execute Liberian citizens….Under Doe, thousands of Liberians [have been] killed by guns and bullets provided by the American taxpayer" (Hayden, p. 105.)

27. Seyon writes, "Liberia is now a textbook case of how the U.S. that preaches freedom, human rights and democracy can be the mainstay of a fascist, military dictatorship that is the very antithesis of what it preaches" ("The Results," p. 238). Byron Tarr writes: "Liberians learned to their sorrow that America has no commitment to any ideals but its interests, the range of which is narrow" ("Founding the Liberian

Action Party," *LSJ*, 15, 1 [1990], p. 35; see also p. 45, where he suggests that America's "preoccupation with the protection of its 'national interests' and investments (is) perhaps not uninfluenced by racism").

28. Chaudhuri, "Liberia under Military Rule," p. 47.

29. Merran Fraenkel, *Tribe and Class in Monrovia*, London: Oxford University Press, 1964, p. 158.

30. Amos J. Beyan, "The American Colonization Society and the Socio-Religious Characterization of Liberia: A Historical Survey 1822–1900," *Liberian Studies Journal*, 10,2 (1984–85), p. 5.

31. See Gifford, *Christianity and Politics*, pp. 73–83.

32. Both elements—the claim to be non-political, and the readiness to leave things exactly as they are—were illustrated on the same day by Stephen Olford speaking on ELWA. Preaching on Acts 16:9–15, he told the story of Lydia, and went on to draw as his message, "We are not interested in politics—just in doing what Paul did that day he changed Lydia's life." Yet earlier that morning, he had been preaching on another program. In the course of a standard evangelical sermon on obedience ("Trust and obey for there is no other way to happiness"), he stated, "All this superficial preaching around today is saying 'get with it'; (but) God is saying to us 'Get out of it'" ("Encounter" and "Calvary Church Hour" respectively, 23 July 1989).

33. *Footprints Today*, 16 September 1987, p. 3.

34. A few weeks later Doe urged Liberians "not to waste time on politics, but rather focus on the development of the country" (*Footprints Today*, 8 Oct 1987, p. 1).

35. He accused the Catholic Church's ELCM of wanting to "create chaos or confusion in the country" (*Daily Observer*, 23 June 1989, p. 1).

36. *Daily Observer*, 7 September 1989, p. 8.

37. *Herald*, 23–29 November 1989, p. 9.

38. *Daily Observer*, 12 August 1988, pp. 4 and 8.

39. *Herald*, 22–28 November 1989, p. 9.

40. *Daily Observer*, 21 April 1988, p. 3.

41. Ed Louis Cole's publications are available from Box 610588, Dallas, TX 75261, U.S.A. Billy Joe Daugherty's publications are available from Victory Christian Center, P.O. Box 470016, Tulsa, OK 74147, U.S.A.

42. See *Living Water Teaching*, Vol. 10, No. 9, p. 8.

43. Ibid.

44. Available from Billy Joe Daugherty's Victory Christian Center, P. O. Box 470016, Tulsa, OK 74147, and from Willie George Ministries, P.O. Box 639, Broken Arrow, OK 74013, respectively.

45. *Missiongram*, Vol. 10, No. 2, May 1989.

46. Letter dated 27 April 1989 and signed by Bethel pastor inviting people to launching ceremony on 5 May 1989 at Philadelphia Church, Monrovia.

47. Lester Sumrall, *Jerusalem: Where Empires Die*, Nashville, TN: Thomas Nelson, 1984, p. 121. Similarly, he argues that "(Britain's) decline began when its Parliament favored the Arabs over Israel" (Lester Sumrall, *I predict 2000 AD*, South Bend, IN: LeSEA Publishing, 1987, p. 78). This manipulation of Biblical texts to serve the national

interest reaches its limit in David Allen Lewis, *Magog 1982 Cancelled*, Harrison, AK: New Leaf Press, 1982, which argues that Russia would have invaded the oilfields of the Middle East in 1982 and thus begun the Third World War unless Israel had invaded Lebanon that year, thereby saving the United States. Thus dispensationalism is used to justify and applaud Israel's Lebanon invasion. This book ran through four printings in its first ten months.

For a detailed discussion of Christian Zionism, see: Ruth W. Mouly, *U.S.-Arab Relations: The Evangelical Dimension*, Washington, D.C.: National Council on U.S.-Arab Relations, 1985; Ruth W. Mouly, *The Religious Right and Israel: The Politics of Armageddon*, Chicago, IL: Midwest Research, 1985; Ronald R. Stockton, "Christian Zionism: Prophecy and Public Opinion," *The Middle East Journal*, Vol. 41, No. 2, Spring 1987, pp. 234–252; Dwight Wilson, *Armageddon Now! The Premillenarian Response to Russia and Israel Since 1917*, Grand Rapids, MI: Baker Book House, 1977; Hassan Haddad and Donald Wagner, *All in the Name of the Bible: Selected Essays on Israel and American Christian Fundamentalism*, Brattleboro, VT: Amana Books, 1986 (esp. appendixes A–H); Grace Halsell, *Prophecy and Politics: The Secret Alliance Between Israel and the U.S. Christian Right*, Chicago: Lawrence Hill, 1986; Grace Halsell, "Shrine Under Siege," *The Link*, Vol. 17, No. 3, August-September 1984, pp. 1–9; Grace Halsell, "Armageddon Theology," *Life and Peace Review*, Vol. 2, No. 2, 1988, pp. 7–10.

48. It may be that, of all African countries, Liberia was particularly susceptible to Christian Zionism because the "'back to Africa" movement made much of the parallels between the Jews in Egypt and enslaved blacks. See Yekutiel Gershoni, "Liberia and Israel: The Evolution of a Relationship," *LSJ*, 14,1(1989), esp. pp. 34–37.

49. Fraenkel, *Tribe and Class,* p. 155. Estimates of the numbers of Christians and Muslims in Liberia vary enormously. For example, Banks gives an estimate of 10 percent Christians and 10–20 percent Muslim (*Political Handbook*, p. 344); *Europa Year Book* 1988 gives 670,000 Muslims, which is nearly 30 percent of the population (p. 1708); Nya Kwiawon Taryor gives 5 percent Muslim, 15 percent Christian (*Justice, Justice: A Cry of My People: the Struggle for Economic Progress and Social Justice in Liberia*, Chicago: Strugglers' Community Press, 1985, p. 209); Dunn and Tarr, *Liberia,* give 15 percent Christian, 10 percent Muslim (p. 32). The Ministry of Education in Monrovia gave 50 percent Christian, 20 percent Muslim; many Muslim leaders claimed that Muslims numbered more than 50 percent of the population.

50. *Daily Observer*, 18 September 1989, p. 1.

51. *Herald* 1–7 June 1989, p. 7; *Herald*, 22–29 June 1989. p. 7; *Herald*, 13–19 July 1989, p. 7.

52. *Daily Observer*, 3 June 1988, pp. 4 and 6. One of the training center's team, reporting on the Liberia mission for U.S. supporters, writes of their new work in Tubmanburg: "Tubmanburg has experienced a great economic decline in the last decade. To make matters worse, approximately 50 percent of its population is of Moslem descent. (It is) a city that is economically and spiritually oppressed" (*Living Water Teaching*, p. 8).

53. *Daily Observer*, 3 June 1988, pp. 4, 6.

54. Constitution of Fellowship of Full Gospel Ministers, available from Box

10–4373, 1000 Monrovia 10.

55. Available from Change the World Ministries, Box 5838, Mission Hills, CA 91345, U.S.A.

56. Sanford J. Ungar, "The Roots of Estrangement," in *Estrangement: America and the World*, ed. Sanford J. Ungar, NY: OUP, 1985, pp. 5–7.

57. Lester Sumrall, *Jihad: the Holy War: the Destiny of Iran and the Moslem World*, Tulsa: Harrison House, 1980, p. 123.

58. Ibid., p. 128.

59. Ibid., p. 129.

60. Ibid.

61. Ibid., p. 126.

62. Ibid., p. 132.

63. Ibid., p. 131. Sumrall's reading of the Bible provides a single justification for both America's enmities and its allegiances: "Iran is destined to join the atheists—the communists of Russia—to come against Israel" (Ibid., p. 149). The ultimate limit of this U.S. evangelical crusade against Islam is found in a Chick tract titled *The Prophet*, which argues that Islam is a Catholic plot to create a new religion to provide a Messiah for the children of Ishmael; the Koran was written under the influence of Mohammad's Catholic advisers. Chick Publications (of Box 662, Chino, CA 91710) in 1987 produced 19 million such tracts and books.

64. *World Harvest*, September-October 1990, pp. 8–9.

65. *Daily Observer*, 5 September 1988, p. 3.

66. Ali Mazrui, "Uncle Sam's Hearing Aid," in Ungar, *The Roots of Estrangement*, pp. 189–191. Mazrui also contends that U.S. antipathy to Islam, an essentially non-white religion, has racial overtones and these racial attitudes are deep in the American character; conversely, the blind U.S. support for Israel is partly explained by the fact that Israel is white (Ibid., pp. 186–189).

67. Jean Marc Ela, *African Cry*, Maryknoll, NY: Orbis, 1986, p. 15.

CHAPTER EIGHT
The "New" Christianity in Africa: The Charismatic Explosion

1. Trinity Broadcasting Network Newsletter, January 1987.

2. We have noted before that "charismatic" and "neo-Pentecostal" are pretty much synonymous worldwide; charismatic is used throughout this chapter because it is the general term used in Africa, as opposed to the neo-Pentecostal label that predominates in Latin America in order to distinguish it from Catholic charismaticism.

3. Paul Pierson, "Non-Western Missions: the Great New Fact of our Time," in *New Frontiers in Mission*, ed. Patrick Sookhdeo, Exeter: The Paternoster Press, 1987, p. 11.

4. Bob Coote, "The Numbers Game in World Evangelization," *Evangelical Missions Quarterly*, 27: 2 (April 1991), pp. 118–127.

5. *Economist*, 21 August 1993, p. 14 (survey).

6. *Economist*, 22–26 January 1994, p. 53.

7. 24 Hours, BBC World Service, 8 Sept 1991.

8. Blaine Harden, *Africa, Dispatches from a Fragile Continent*, London: Harper Collins, 1991, p. 15. Harden balances this with a necessary positive note: "Africa's problems, as pervasive and ghastly as they seem, are not the final scorecard on a doomed continent. They are the preliminary readings from the world's messiest experiment in cultural and political change" (Ibid., p. 16).

9. E. G. J. Hanlon, *Mozambique: Who Calls the Shots?* London: James Currey, 1991.

10. The two indispensable source books for mission statistics are: John A Siewert and John A. Kenyon, *Mission Handbook: U.S./Canada Christian Ministries Overseas*, Monrovia CA: Marc, 13th ed. 1986, 14th ed. 1989, 15th ed 1993; and Patrick Johnstone, *Operation World*, Carlisle, OM Publishing, 3rd ed. 1978, 4th ed. 1986, and 5th ed. 1993. The latter gives the Protestant missionaries in Guinea as few in 1978, 27 in 1986, and 187 in 1993; the former gives the American missionaries as 60 in 1989, and 101 in 1993.

11. A good introduction to church growth thinking is C. Peter Wagner, Win Arn, and Elmer Towns, *Church Growth: State of the Art*, Wheaton IL: Tyndale, 1989, especially Wagner's article, "The Church Growth Movement after Thirty Years," pp 21–39. Those who suspect that this thinking takes the quantifying and computerizing approach to its extreme are likely to have their suspicions confirmed when Wagner speaks of his hope of developing "an instrument for measuring church quality (that will) be widely accepted internationally and interdenominationally. I hope that soon we will objectively be able to say that such-and-such a church at a given time is an 84 or a 69 or whatever on a scale of 100 in church quality" (Ibid., p. 35).

12. For example, the 14th and 15th editions of *Mission Handbook* change the basic category from "career" or "life" missionary to missionary for "more than four years."

13. One source even shows a decrease in activity: in 1989, of all the Protestant missionaries around the world 65 percent were North American, but by 1992 this percentage had fallen to 57 percent. Siewert and Kenyon, *Mission Handbook*, 14th ed., p. 576, and 15th ed., p. 76.

14. Siewert and Kenyon, *Mission Handbook*, 15th ed., p. 59.

15. Siewert and Kenyon, *Mission Handbook*, 15th ed., p 57. See Mark Robinson, ed., *Summer Missions Handbook 1990*, La Mirada, CA: Biola University, 1989; of the 99 mission agencies listed here, 27 have summer activities in Africa.

16. Siewert and Kenyon, *Mission Handbook*, 15th ed., *ad loc* and p. 73.

17. African Independent Churches, *Speaking for Ourselves: Members of African Independent Churches Report on their Pilot Study of the History and Theology of their Churches*, Braamfontein: Institute for Contextual Theology, 1985, p. 26.

18. *Revival Report*, 1/90E, p 11.

19. *Revival Report*, B/93E, p. 5. In February 1994, Bonnke claimed, 6,800 pastors attended his Fire Conference in Madras, India (*Revival Report Telegram*, 25 March 1994, p, 3).

20. *The Trumpet*, January 1989, pp. 19–21.

21. In 1993 the governments of Zambia and Kenya negotiated licenses with U.S.-based evangelical radio stations.

22. John Avancini's books were: *The Wealth of the Wicked: Yours for the Taking*, Hurst, TX: Avancini Ministries, 1986; *30-60-100 fold: Your Financial Harvest Released*, Hurst,

TX: Avancini Ministries, 1989; *Faith Extenders*, Hurst, TX: Avancini Ministries, 1988; *Powerful Principles of Increase Released in You*, Harrison House, 1989; *Stolen Property Returned*, Harrison House, 1984. Three of Sumrall's videos were also for sale.

23. Emmanuel Eni, *Delivered from the Powers of Darkness*, Ibadan: Scripture Union, 1987.

24. Kaniaki and Mukendi, *Snatched from Satan's Claws: An Amazing Deliverance by Christ*, Nairobi: Enkei Media Services, 1991.

25. Symons Onyango, *Set Free from Demons: a Testimony to the Power of God to Deliver the Demon Possessed*, Nairobi: Evangel, 1979.

26. Victoria Eto, *Exposition on Water Spirits*, Warri: Shalom Christian Mission, 1988.

27. Among the many other African treatments of demonology are: E. O. Omoobajesu, *My Experience in the Darkness of this World before Jesus Saved Me*, Agege (Lagos State): Omoobajesu World Outreach, n.d.; Zacharias Tanee Fomum, *Deliverance from Demons*, Yaounde (Cameroon): IGH (Box 6090 Yaounde), n.d.; Kaluy Abosi, *"Born Twice": From Demonism to Christianity*, Benin City: Joint Heirs Publications, 1990; John Cudjoe-Mensah, *Satan and his Tricks*, Kumasi: St Mary's, 1989; Sunday Adekola, *Understanding Demonology*, Ibadan: Scripture Union, 1993; Victoria Eto, *How I Served Satan Until Jesus Christ Delivered Me: A True Account of My Twenty-one Years Experience as an Agent of Darkness and of My Deliverance by the Powerful Arm of God in Christ Jesus*, Warri: Shalom Christian Mission, 1981; Heaven U. Heaven, *How to Cast Out Demons or Evil Spirits: A Practical Guide to Deliverance*, Lagos: Heaven and Blessings Books, 1985; Iyke Nathan Uzora, *Occult Grand Master Now in Christ*, Benin City: Osabu, 1993.

28. Frank E. Peretti, *This Present Darkness*, Wheaton: Crossway, 1986; Frank E. Peretti, *Piercing the Darkness*, West Chester: Crossway, 1989; Rebecca Brown, *He Came to Set the Captives Free*, Springdale, PA: Whitaker, 1989; Rebecca Brown, *Prepare for War*, Springdale, PA: Whitaker, 1990. Among the Western books and booklets on demons widely available in Africa are: Bill Subritsky, *Demons Defeated*, Chichester: Sovereign World, 1986; Lester Sumrall, *Three Habitations of Devils*, LeSea Publications, 1989; Stuart Gramenz, *Who Are God's Guerrillas?,* Chichester: Sovereign World, 1988; Stephen Bransford, *High Places*, Wheaton, IL: Crossway, 1991; Elbert Willis, *Exposing the Devil's Work*, Lafayette, LA: Fill the Gap Publications, n.d.; John Osteen, *Pulling Down Strongholds*, Houston: John Osteen Ministries, 1972; Frank Hammond and Ida Mae Hammond, *Pigs in the Parlor: A Practical Guide to Deliverance*, Kirkwood MO: Impact Books, 1973; Lester Sumrall, *Alien Entities: Beings from Beyond*, South Bend: Lesea, 1984, and the pamphlets of Kenneth Hagin and Gordon Lindsay.

29. *Step*, Vol. 13, No. 11, P. I.

30. I would suggest that an example of this would be Richmond Chiundiza, "High Level Powers in Zimbabwe," in *Territorial Spirits: Insights on Strategic Level Spiritual Warfare from Nineteen Christian Leaders,* ed. C. Peter Wagner, Chichester: Sovereign World, 1991, pp. 121–127. In this article the author, a Zimbabwean, takes two historical figures, Nehanda and Chaminuka, both heroes of the Shona resistance against white settlers in 1896, and can understand them only as powers in the charismatic demonic hierarchy. We can note also in this context that the fact that something as evangelical (in the traditional sense) as the Scripture Union can publish Eni's *Delivered*,

and that the evangelical Youth for Christ International can dedicate an issue of its magazine *Step* to Eni and Mukendi, is further evidence of the shift towards the charismatic in what were formerly strictly traditional "evangelical" circles.

31. Quoted in D. R. McConnell, *A Different Gospel: A Historical and Biblical Analysis of the Modern Faith Movement*, Peabody, MS: Hendrickson Publishers, 1988, p. 175.

32. See Paul Gifford, *Christianity and Politics in Doe's Liberia*, Cambridge: Cambridge University Press, 1993, pp. 168–169.

33. *Revival Report*, D/91E, p. 2.

34. G. J. O. Moshay, *Who is this Allah?*, Ibadan: Fireliners International, 1990.

35. Ibid., pp. 119, 163.

36. Interview, 7 March 1991.

37. *The Sword of the Spirit*, no. 47, 1991, pp. 8–9.

38. Quoted in *Today's Challenge* (Jos), no. 6, 1988, p. 26.

39. See also *Kenya Times*, 2 February 1992, p. 2.

40. *Kenya Times*, 24 February 1992, p. 1; see also *Daily Nation*, 24 February 1992, p. 1; *Standard*, 24 February 1992, p. 1; *Signpost*, March 1992, p. 1.

41. *Daily Nation*, 1 April 1993, p. 26.

42. *Financial Times*, 24 March 1993, p. 6.

43. Wilson Mamboleo, *Prayer that Touches the Heart of God*, Nairobi: Prayer and Word Publications, 1991, p. 45.

44. Interview, 9 February 1994.

CHAPTER NINE

Spreading the Word: Organizational Techniques, Theological Emphases, and Pastoral Power

1. While services appear spontaneous and unstructured, there indeed is a pattern. See Susan Rose, *Keeping Them Out of the Hands of Satan*, Critical Social Thought Series, London: Routledge & Kegan Paul, 1988 (Chapter 3) for a more detailed discussion of the orchestration of charismatic worship. Also see Harvey Cox, *Fire From Heaven*, Reading, MA: Addison-Wesley, 1995.

2. Linda Green, "Shifting Affiliations: Mayan Widows and Evangelicalism in Guatemala," in *Rethinking Protestantism in Latin America,* ed. Virginia Garrard-Burnett and David Stoll, Philadelphia: Temple University Press, 1993, p. 173.

3. Ibid., 1993, p. 174.

4. Emilio Willems, *Latin American Culture: An Anthropological Synthesis*, New York: Harper and Row, 1975, p. 369.

5. Frank Lechner, "Fundamentalism and Sociocultural Revitalization: On the Logic of Dedifferentiation," in *Differentiation Theory and Social Change*, ed. Jeffrey C. Alexander and Paul Colomy, NY: Columbia University Press, 1990, p. 99.

6. David Martin, *Tongues of Fire: The Explosion of Protestantism in Latin America*, Oxford: Basil Blackwell, 1990, Chapter 13 in particular.

7. Ibid., du Plessis quoted, p. 178.

8. Quentin Schultze, "Orality and Power in Latin American Pentecostalism," in

Coming of Age: Protestantism in Contemporary Latin America, ed. Daniel Miller, University Press of America, 1994, p. 72. Also see Walter Ong, *Orality and Literacy: The Technologizing of the Word,* NY: Methuen, 1982.

9. Emilio Willems, *Latin American Culture,* p. 368.

10. Andrew F. Walls, "World Christianity, the Missionary Movement, and the Ugly American," in *World Order and Religion,* ed. Wade Clark Roof, Albany: SUNY Press, 1990, p. 157.

11. Dana Roberts, "The Crisis of Missions," in *Earthen Vessels: American Evangelicals and Foreign Missions, 1880–1980,* ed. Joel A. Carpenter and Wilbert R. Shenk, Grand Rapids: Eerdmans, 1990, p. 30; 36,600 in 1988; by 1992, the categories of missionaries had changed somewhat, so the numbers cannot be accurately compared with 1985; 33,260 personnel serving over four years, 7,882 serving two to four years, 36,201 on brief stays (two weeks to two months), and 1,040 self-supporting "tentmakers." See *Mission Handbook,* ed. John Siewert and John Kenyon, p. 59. Also, there were 5,441 Catholic missionaries sent abroad from the U.S. in 1992. (*Mission Handbook 1993–95,* 15th ed., Monrovia, CA: MARC, 1993, p. 493.)

12. The fruitful issue of a 25-year program, Bold Mission Thrust, begun in 1976 and described in *MARC Newsletter,* December 1993, p. 5. Southern Baptists seem to be meeting their funding and personnel goals but not their projected number of new baptisms.

13. Walls, "World Christianity," p. 148.

14. From such sources as "Seven Hundred Plans to Evangelize the World," by David B. Barrett, World Evangelization Center, Richmond, and James W. Reapsome, Evangelical Missions Information Service, Wheaton. All numbers are problematic, of course, if for different reasons: another estimate, 333 million, purports to count all Pentecostals and charismatics, which include 63 million who are Catholics and an unknown number who continue to hold membership within the historical Protestant denominations. The Catholic numbers represent everyone who was ever baptized in infancy as a Catholic. Among Lutherans, 75 million, many are designated as being citizens of northern European countries that have a state church; Orthodox believers, mostly in Eastern Europe, are probably estimated generously to account for repression of religious activity under communist regimes. Among the more accurate numbers is probably the so-called "quasi-Christian" grouping, 20 million total, which includes small liberal groups such as the Unitarians, 300,000; and large "heretical" groups such as Mormons, 6.9 million, and Jehovah's Witnesses, 11.9 million, who have many similarities with the fundamentalists.

15. Stanley M. Burgess, Gary B. McGee, and Patrick H. Alexander, ed., *The Dictionary of Pentecostal and Charismatic Movements,* Grand Rapids: Zondervan, 1988, p. 909.

16. Siewert and Kenyon, ed., *Mission Handbook,* pp. 64 and 71.

17. David Stoll, *Fishers of Men or Founders of Empire?,* London: Zed, 1982.

18. A report from the NCC-USA suggests that "there appears to be a correlation between the place for which members feel a burden and parts of the world where the U.S. has particular interests"; other airlifts in 1986 took place in El Salvador, Guatemala, Costa Rica, Mexico, and South Africa; p. 300.

19. David Stoll, "Jesus is Lord of Guatemala," in *Accounting for Fundamentalism,* ed. Emmanuel Sivan and Gabriel Almond, Chicago: University of Chicago Press, 1994.

20. *Christianity Today,* April 26, 1993, p. 52.

21. David Stoll, *Fishers of Men or Founders of Empire?*; Sara Diamond, *Spiritual Welfare: The Politics of the Christian Right,* Boston: South End Press, 1989.

22. Marc Cooper, "God and Man in Colorado Springs," *The Nation,* 2 January, 1995, p. 9.

23. Much documentation and detail about the overtly political connections among the Christian right are provided by Diamond in *Spiritual Warfare.* While some investigators on the left have been attacked for constructing overly conspiratorial theories of fundamentalist influence in regard to U.S. foreign policy, Diamond's sources, information, and depth of research are generally sound. Her information concerning informal patterns of communication and cooperation between Christian relief groups and U.S. military figures, both active and retired, are right on the mark; for instance, the cooperation between Pat Robertson's Operation Blessing (providing material relief in Central America and elsewhere), the U.S. Navy bases, and other international relief agencies was nicely coordinated through the friendly contact between two retired Navy officers in San Diego (ex-Commander Tevelson, coordinating non-profit religious groups activities through Navy channels) and Virginia (ex-Capt. Warren, Operation Blessing director), pp. 223–241.

24. Ernest R. Sandeen, *The Roots of Fundamentalism: British and American Millenarianism, 1800–1930,* Chicago: University of Chicago Press, 1970, p. 163.

25. Margaret Lamberts Bendroth, *Fundamentalism and Gender, 1875 to the Present,* New Haven: Yale University Press, 1993, p. 10.

26. Andrew F. Walls, "The American Dimension in the Missionary Movement," in *Earthen Vessels: American Evangelicals and Foreign Missions, 1880–1980,* ed. Joel A. Carpenter and Wilbert R. Shenk, Grand Rapids: Eerdmans, 1990, p. 13.

27. Author's attendance at many revivals throughout Africa.

28. Ernest Sandeen, *The Roots of Fundamentalism;* Virginia Lieson Brereton, *Training God's Army,* Bloomington: University of Indiana Press, 1990.

29. Walls, "World Christianity," p. 155.

30. Ibid.

31. Cash surpluses from growing, industrializing economies have been key to Protestant evangelization. This is as true today for Korean missionary expansion abroad as it was for American or English efforts in previous eras. Members of the Philippine NCC are disturbed at the tendency of Korean missionaries to move into already established churches or new areas, offering financial support as long as the local congregations allow one or two Korean missionaries to be actively involved in the ministry. Interviews by one of the authors, Manila, June 1992.

32. Martin Riesebrodt, *Pious Passion: The emergence of modern fundamentalism in Iran and the United States,* Berkeley: University of California Press, 1993, p. 77, emphasis in the original.

33. Ibid., p. 79.

34. Walls, "World Christianity," p. 155.

35. "World-Shakers," *Word of Faith*, July 1994, p. 8.

36. See Paul Gifford, *To Save or Enslave*.

37. To illustrate further how the charismatic "Faith" networks operate, both Living Water churches were assisted financially by Kenneth Copeland of Fort Worth; and Copeland himself and Ray McCauley appear at Reinhard Bonnke's Fire Conferences.

38. The Living Water churches and Livets Ord are not even listed in the *Rhema Ministerial Association International Church Guide* of over one thousand approved churches in the U.S. and abroad that are headed by Rhema graduates; possibly this is because they set up their own Bible schools without permission or sanction from Tulsa. Listing appeared in *Word of Faith*, August 1994.

39. *Word of Life Newsletter*, 2 (1993), published by the Livets Ord Church in Uppsala. Simon Coleman has studied this church intensively and the Swedish reaction to this "global product." Those outside the church attack it as an insidious "Americanization" of Swedish culture. See Coleman, "Controversy and the Social Order: Responses to a Religious Group in Sweden." Ph.D. dissertation, Cambridge University, 1989.

40. Sumrall also provides financial aid for foreign charismatic churches, and in the early 1990s began ambitious relief efforts called "Operation Joseph" to Africa; in 1992, "Joseph" offered an entire hospital to the Maforga Christian Mission in war-ravaged Mozambique. David Sumrall, his nephew, heads another big church in Manila that has 13,000 members: "Communicating Faith," *Church Growth Manual*, Seoul: Church Growth International, Yoido Church, 1990, p. 190.

41. Don Stewart is even better known for his associated ministries: Mission of Hope (health centers), Feed My People (food distribution) and Children's Hope (schools). He contributed over $1 million of seeds to Liberia's "Green Revolution"; later he donated another shipment of seeds to Action Faith Ministries in Ghana, although in this case they were so old they were unusable. His fund-raising magazine bears the heading "the Most Effective Evangelical Relief Operation in the World," and the magazine itself, with its photos of distended bellies and emaciated limbs, is a potent fund-raising tool. It is noteworthy that the Philippine edition of this magazine is more openly given to the prosperity message than his American edition.

42. Reisebrodt, *Pious Passion*, p. 175.

43. Ibid.

44. Paul Yonggi Cho, "Successful Church Growth," *Church Growth Manual #3*, Seoul: Church Growth International, 1990, p. 32.

45. Walls, "World Christianity," p. 161.

46. From *Urkristendommen*, quoted in Nils Boch-Hoell, *The Pentecostal Movement*, New York: Humanities Press, 1964, p. 14; emphasis in the original.

47. *The Dictionary of Pentecostal and Charismatic Movements*, p. 611.

48. W. J. Hollenweger, *The Pentecostals*, Minneapolis: Augsburg, 1972, p. 485.

49. Richard Van Dijk, "Young Born-again Preachers in Post-independence Malawi: the Significance of an Extraneous Identity," p. 71, in *New Dimensions in African Christianity*, ed. Paul Gifford, Ibadan, Nigeria: SEFER Books, 1992, p. 71 .

50. Ibid.

51. C. Peter Wagner, "Third Wave," in *The Dictionary of Pentecostal and Charismatic*

Movements, p. 844. This de-emphasis on speaking in tongues probably assumes a context where the new fundamentalism is already well-established, such as South Korea, rather than a place like Malawi (discussed earlier) where young charismatics have used "speaking in tongues" as a way to establish some social space.

52. See Cindy Jacobs, *Possessing the Gates of the Enemy,* Grand Rapids: Chosen Books, 1991, including pp. 222, 234. This spiritual-warfare approach goes beyond the metaphorical: for instance, Jacobs claims that the major witch in Mar del Plata, Argentina, actually died the night the "Generals of Intercession" arrived in the city and began to pray at her; she could not stand up to the spiritual onslaught. Also see the Introduction by C. Peter Wagner of Fuller Theological Seminary, who sees this as the most erudite book of its kind and requires it as reading by all his divinity students.

53. Authors' Guatemalan research 1987–1990.

54. Jim Williams, "Church Growth and Goal-Setting," *Church Growth Manual,* No. 3, Seoul: Church Growth International, 1990, p. 235.

55. Martin, *Tongues of Fire.*

56. Stoll, *Fishers of Men or Founders of Empire?* pp. 112 and 316.

57. Christian Lalive D'Epinay, *Haven to the Masses: A Study of the Pentecostal Movement in Chile,* London: Lutterworth Press, 1969.

58. The 1990 figure was 14.4 million in 85,000 churches; the numbers submitted from the Brazilian Church, in December 31, 1993, were so much larger than the 1990 figure that the Division of Foreign Missions, USA, stated, "We were not comfortable publishing the results, so we are carrying forward the best previous estimate [1990] that we have available." These annual statistics were forwarded from the General Council of the Assemblies of God, USA, Springfield, MO, 1994. Of course, the irony of all this is that the Brazilian church, whether it outnumbers the U.S. Assemblies by 5 to 1, 7 to 1, or 9 to 1, does not care to be the object of a "mission" from the North or to be subject to U.S. rules for verification.

59. Hollenweger, *The Pentecostals,* p. 104.

60. Benedita da Silva, an Assembly of God member, was also nearly elected to the mayor's office in Rio de Janeiro. She has been lionized, deservedly (see Harvey Cox, *Fire from Heaven*), as an example of faith contributing to political activism; still, her victories and de Melo's period of progressive ecumenicism appear to be anomalies, perhaps fueled by the youth movements of the 1960s, the examples of Catholic base communities, and, in da Silva's case, by her association with the Workers' Party.

61. Paul Freston, "Brother Votes for Brother: The New Politics of Protestantism in Brazil," in *Rethinking Protestantism in Latin America,* ed. Virginia Garrard-Burnett and David Stoll.

62. Ibid., p. 75.

63. Rowan Ireland, *Kingdom Come: Religion and Politics in Brazil, Pittsburgh:* University of Pittsburgh Press, 1992, pp. 103–107.

64. Ibid., p. 99. See also Francisco Cartaxo Rolim's studies of Brazilian Pentecostalism (for instance, *Pentecostais no Brasil,* Petropolis: Vozes, 1980). Ireland distinguishes between the pastoral control over the members of many large churches and his own observation of how particular "creentes," especially individual members from certain

small congregations, are empowered by their inner feelings of faith to stand up to those in power (landowners, corrupt officials) at the local level.

65. Paul Freston, "Brother Votes for Brother," pp. 70–71.

66. Information supplied to the authors by their research assistant, Gloria, apropos her home church and others, 1987.

CHAPTER TEN
By Defining Enemies, Christian Fundamentalism Defines Itself: Anti-Islamic, Anti-Communist, Anti-Catholic, Anti-Feminist

1. Martin Riesebrodt, *Pious Passion*, p. 144.

2. Ibid.

3. *World Christian*, November-December 1993.

4. Another interesting note about the Urbana Conference pertains to the "globalizing" of Christian culture within the U.S.: fully 10 percent of participants were Korean-Americans, 25 percent were Asian-Americans. *Christianity Today*, 7 February 1994, p. 48.

5. "Muslim Mission Breakthrough," *Christianity Today*, 13 December 1993.

6. Audiocassette tapes supplied to Rose and Brouwer by an officer working in U.S. Marine Corps intelligence department during the Gulf War.

7. *MARC Newsletter*, January 1994, p. 4; Patrick Johnstone, *Operation World*, Grand Rapids: Zondervan, 1993. Note a sign of the multinational potential of Zondervan: the evangelical publisher was bought up in 1994 and is now a division of the Murdoch-owned media giant HarperCollins.

8. McCollister, president of CCC's Christian Embassy, quoted in *Sojourners Critique of CCC*, p. 10.

9. Paul Gifford, *Religious Right in Southern Africa*, Harare: Baobab, 1988, p. 42.

10. Sara Diamond, *Spiritual Warfare*, Boston: South End, 1989, p. 208. Diamond's scholarship concerning such connections is considerable; although some left-wing analyses of the spread of Protestantism have been fairly criticized for relying on conspiratorial suggestion, her assertions are well-documented and generally show open collaboration, and occasionally some conspiracy, between political and religious agents where it actually exists. Her emphasis is on the political agenda, not on why fundamentalism may actually take hold as a serious religious influence in different national contexts. Thus her occasional sarcasm may strike some readers as anti-religious, for example: "Adherents of the 'pre-tribulation rapture" theory are anxiously packing their spiritual bags as they await departure from the planet."

11. Jacobs, *Possessing the Gates of the Enemy*, pp. 58–59.

12. Paul Gifford, *Religious Right in Southern Africa*, p. 52.

13. Ibid. See the Balsiger report, p. 35.

14. *New Christian Movements in Africa and Madagascar*, Accra: SECAM, 1993; published also in *Catholic International*, January 1993, pp. 28–36. The French version was published in *La Documentation Catholique*, 15 November 1992, pp. 989–996.

15. In Guatemalan towns such as Chichicastenango, for instance, believers regularly burn offerings to the corn deities on the stone floor in the center of the main church.

16. Bruce Lawrence, *Defenders of God,* New York: Harper and Row, 1989, p. 100.

17. Jan Goodwin, *Price of Honor: Muslim Women Lift the Veil of Silence on the Islamic World,* NY: Little, Brown, and Co., 1994; and Margaret Lamberts Bendroth, *Fundamentalism and Gender, 1875 to the Present,* New Haven: Yale University Press, 1993.

18. Martin Riesebrodt, "The Comparative Study of Fundamentalism," Fundamentalism Project lecture, 30 October 1989, p. 11.

19. The first-tier male elite, those who control the major financial institutions and/or manage the corporate structures, are not so preoccupied with this kind of patriarchal restoration, perhaps because their prerogatives seem relatively unthreatened. In business they may find more qualified, and more profitable middle-management employees by opening up competition to women; or, they may want their own daughters to excel in the more prestigious professions. Furthermore, they may be able to depress male wages and undercut old definitions of skilled and unskilled employment (traditionally favorable to men over women, white over colored) by undermining the male solidarity present in professional organizations and labor organizations.

20. We say rhetorically, because in daily practice there is evidence of a significant amount of negotiation of gender roles within the family, and between family and work responsibilities (see Susan D. Rose, "Woman Warriors: the Negatation of Gender in a Charismatic Community," *Sociological Analysis,* Vol. 48, No. 3, 1987 and Susan D. Rose, "Conversations of Conversion: Interviewing American Evangelical Women," *International Journal of Oral History,* Vol. 8, No. 1, 1987.). As Judith Stacey concludes in *Brave New Families,* these marriages may represent a "patriarchy of the last gasp" (NY: Basic Books, 1991, pp. 41–174).

21. From the fundamentalist periodical *The King's Business,* 1919, p. 701, as quoted in Riesebrodt, *Pious Passion,* p. 57.

22. Bendroth, p. 17.

23. Ibid.

24. The scouts were calling for "REAL, live men—red-blooded and right-hearted men—BIG men; No Miss Nancy need apply" (Boy Scouts of America literature quoted in Jeffrey Hantover, "The Boy Scouts and the Validation of Masculinity," *Journal of Social Issues,* Vol. 34, No. 1, 1978, pp. 184–195.

25. Bendroth, p. 23.

26. Quoted in Bendroth, p. 24.

27. Ibid., p. 6.

28. See James Gibson, *Warrior Dreams,* NY: Hill and Wang, 1995.

29. Rose, *Keeping Them Out of the Hands of Satan,* p. xvii.

30. Ibid., p. xvii.

31. John S. Hawley, ed., "Hinduism, Sati, and its Defenders," *Fundamentalism and Gender,* Oxford: Oxford University Press, 1994, p. 101.

32. Ibid. Hindu fundamentalism concerns itself with maintaining caste status as well as gender status. Upper-class and middle-class Hindus mounted a right-wing ideological campaign after President Singh attempted to help the "scheduled" or "backward" castes in matters affecting political representation, admission to educational institutions, and hiring government employees. The 1990 decision to reserve 50

percent of jobs in government and education for "the oppressed classes" invited a "storm of devastating confrontations" orchestrated by the middle class.

33. Helen Hardacre, "Japanese New Religions: Profiles in Gender," *Fundamentalism and Gender*, Oxford: Oxford University Press, 1994, p. 126.

34. Ibid., p. 126. Risshokoseikai no longer permits women in leadership roles.

35. Ibid., p. 112. These are freedoms in the legal sense, compared with pre-World War II Japan: to marry without parental consent, have access to birth control, and initiate divorce proceedings.

36. Karen McCarthy Brown, "Fundamentalism and the Control of Women," *Fundamentalism and Gender*, Oxford: Oxford University Press, 1994, p. 197.

37. Riesebrodt, *Pious Passion,* p. 189.

38. Margaret Paloma, *The Assemblies of God at the Crossroad: Charisma and Institutional Dilemmas*, Knoxville: University of Tennessee Press, 1989.

39. Paul Yonggi Cho, "How the World's Largest Church Got That Way," *Christianity Today*, 19 May, 1984, pp. 50–51.

40. Elizabeth Brusco, *The Reformation of Machismo,* Austin: University of Texas Press, 1994.

41. Joseph Fichter, "Family and Religion Among the Moonies," in *Families and Religions*, ed. William V. D'Antonio and Joan Aldous, Beverly Hills: Sage, 1983, p. 299. As to organizational hierarchy, although there have been important women teachers in the church, national and state leaders "are selected from among the experienced males," p. 300.

42. Eileen Barker, "The Whole World in His Hand?" p. 203.

43. Sun Myung Moon, *Divine Principle*, NY: Holy Spirit Association, 1977, quoted in Fichter, p. 298.

44. Ibid., p. 295. Moon writes: "Fornication [is]…the principal cause of the downfall of numerous nations….We can never expect the ideal world to be established unless we can eradicate the source of this crime."

45. F. K. Flinn, "Christian Hermeneutics and Unification Theology," in *A Time For Consideration*, ed. M. Darrol Bryant and Herbert W. Richardson, New York: Edwin Mellen Press, 1978, p. 296.

46. Y.O. Kim, *Unification Theology*, New York: Holy Spirit Association, 1980, p. 76.

47. Bendroth, p. 23.

48. Gustav Niebuhr, "Promise Keepers," *New York Times*, August, 6, 1995, p. A1.

49. "Redemptoris Mater," in *Origins* 16, No. 43, April 9, 1987.

50. Andrew Greeley, in his nationally syndicated column, in *The Sentinel,* Carlisle, PA, June 10, 1994.

CHAPTER ELEVEN
The New Spirit of Protestantism and the Global Consumer

1. Peter L. Berger in the Foreword to David Martin, *Tongues of Fire*, p. ix. anticipates a "Second Internationale" of revolutionary bourgeois activity.

2. Ferdnand Braudel, *Capitalism and Civilization*, Volume Two, "The Wheels of

Commerce," NY: Harper and Row, 1982, pp. 578–580. Braudel especially recommends the multivolume Libri della Famiglia, by Leon Battisti Alberti, written in the early fifteenth century. Werner Sombart follows this lead in *Le Bourgeois* and other books, tying the great leap forward to the Renaissance rather than to the Reformation. Braudel rather effectively deals with the Weber-Sombart debate, taking them (and their generation of thinkers) to task for having a European "superiority complex."

3. Peter L. Berger, in Introduction to *In Search of an East Asian Development Model,* ed. Berger and Hsin-Huang Hsiao, New Brunswick: Transaction Books, 1987, p. 6.

4. Christopher Hill, *Change and Continuity in Seventeenth Century England*, Cambridge: Harvard University Press, 1975, p. 99.

5. Ibid., p. 91.

6. Ibid., quote from Thomas Taylor, p. 89.

7. Richard Hofstadter, *Anti-Intellectualism in American Life*, NY: Knopf, 1963; Susan D. Rose, *Keeping Them Out Of the Hands Of Satan*, New York, London: Routledge, 1988.

8. Martin Luther quoted in R. D. Tawney, *Protestantism and the Rise of Capitalism,* London: J. Murray, 1929, p. 101. Though Luther's rise to prominence was intimately connected to the egalitarian spirit of the Peasant Wars in the late fifteenth century, he became so disappointed in the rambunctiousness of the Peasant Leagues and their messianic defiance of aristocratic government that he deserted them and supported the princes.

9. Tawney, p. 117.

10. Protestants were not unique, of course. Catholics of the time were equally adept at punishing infidels in other parts of the world.

11. Concerning the "planting" of the Scots Irish in Ulster and then America, see Ned C. Landsman, *Scotland and Its First American Colony*, Princeton: Princeton University Press, 1985.

12. Martin Marty, *Righteous Empire*, NY: Dial Press, 1970; good treatment of the religious dynamic of Manifest Destiny.

13. Tawney, p. 267.

14. David Martin, *Tongues of Fire*; David Stoll, *Is Latin America Turning Protestant?;* and chapters by David Stoll and Virginia Garrard-Burnett in *Rethinking Protestantism in Latin America.*

15. Peter L. Berger, "America and the Myth of Inequality," in *Capitalism and Equality in America,* ed. Peter L. Berger, Lanham MD: Hamilton Press, 1987, pp. 13–14.

16. Berger, Foreword to Martin, *Tongues of Fire*, p. ix. Martin's research was supported by Berger's Institute for the Study of Economic Culture at Boston University.

17. We give credit to Peter Berger for clearly recognizing this: "Various theorists of modernization (for instance, Talcott Parsons) assumed that individualism...is inevitably and intrinsically linked to modernity. The East Asian experience, at the very least, makes this assumption less self-evident," *In Search of an East Asian Development Model*, p. 6.

18. Ibid., pp. 6–7.

19. Berger, *In Search of an East Asian Development Model*, Introduction, pp. 6–7. Berger refers to Robert Bellah's coinage of the term "bourgeois confucianism," and the

work done by S. G. Redding and associates at the University of Hong Kong. Again we credit Berger's intellectual energy and curiosity with uncovering what may be the very antithesis of his hypothesis; he finds that the power of "folk magic" is appealed to much more regularly than any formal Confucianism. Confucianist practice is too tainted by aristocratic pretensions and bureaucratic obeisance to appeal to many hardworking merchants and small-time entrepreneurs.

20. Elton M. Eenigenburg, "The Ordination of Women," *Christianity Today,* 27 April, 1959, pp. 15–16.

21. See remarks on Chile and Brazil in Chapter Nine. See anthropologist Graham Howe on Peru: "American-sponsored fundamentalist organizations in Latin America... provide an identifiable solution to a hegemonic dilemma," Graham Howe, "God Damn Yanquis: American Hegemony and Contemporary Latin American Christianity," in *World Order and Religion,* ed. Wade Clark Roof, Albany: State University of New York Press, 1991, p. 94.

Also, evangelicals in Peru were a key element in the election of President Fujimoro, and seemingly quite undisturbed by his "auto-golpe," the coup he successfully carried out against his own democratic government in order to gain more autocratic control of the political process. President Serrano of Guatemala, himself an evangelical, was inspired by the Peruvian's example, but failed to get the backing of the Armed Forces for his own auto-golpe and thus was deposed by his Congress.

22. Steve Chan, *East Asian Dynamism*, Boulder: Westview, 1990, p. 53.

23. Il Sa Kong, *Korea in the World Economy*, Washington: Institute for International Economics, 1993, p. 5. It is significant, as a measure of mainstream Americans' acceptance of this view, that moderates Peter G. Peterson and Bergsten, both former U.S. secretaries of commerce, are the principal officers of the Institute.

24. Many American experts say the same things themselves. Lawrence R. Klein, Nobel laureate in economics, said of South Korea, "I'm impressed...by the work ethic giving rise to high productivity, matched by a high propensity to save and a strong entrepreneurial spirit." His Preface to *Models of Development: South Korea and Taiwan,* ed. Lawrence J. Lau, San Francisco: Institute for Contemporary Economics, 1986.

25. Berger and Michael Novak, *Speaking to the Third World: Essays on Democracy and Development,* Washington, D.C.: American Enterprise Institute, 1985, p. 29. The cultivation of neoliberal and neoconservative intellectuals by corporate think tanks and corporate funding for university research have encouraged Berger, Novak, and many others to produce pro-capitalist tracts of a "boosterist" variety that sometimes resemble U.S. chamber of commerce literature. In this particular book, conservative Catholic intellectual Novak (who is employed by the American Enterprise Institute) joined Berger in celebrating the four East Asian "dragons" and their wonderous economic development; the book actually speaks very little to the issue of "democracy" made prominent in the title. Novak has written *The Catholic Ethic and the Spirit of Capitalism,* NY: Free Press, 1994, in order to demonstrate that Catholicism is a pro-capitalist religion. There is, of course, ample room within fundamentalist Americanism for Catholics to jump on board; Patrick Buchanan is one of the more outspoken right-wing Catholic politicians who have endeavored successfully to make a place for themselves

in the culture of the Americanist religious right; in 1993 he pronounced: "Our culture is superior because our religion is Christian, and that is the truth that makes us free."

26. See Samuel P. Huntington, *Political Order in Changing Societies*, Cambridge: Yale University Press, 1968, a conservative justification of dictatorship as being in the interests of American foreign policy; see Thomas B. Gold, *State and Society in the Taiwan Miracle*, Armonk, NY: M. S. Sharpe, 1986, for a less approving interpretation.

The anti-labor authoritarianism of the developmental state bears more than a passing resemblance to fascism: Charles Maier, in writing about "Economics of Fascism and Nazism," *Development, Democracy, and the Art of Trespassing*, ed. Alejandro Foxley, et al., South Bend: Notre Dame, 1986) reminds us that "the suppression of labor remained what these movements were about" and "the crucial premise of both movements: the destruction of the independent labor movement." Furthermore, he cautions that for all their draconian measures the economic results of Nazism and fascism were mediocre: "Their mixed performance remains as a warning not to justify future authoritarian regimes in terms of alleged economic results."

27. William H. Swatos, "Max Weber as 'Christian Sociologist,'" *Journal for the Scientific Study of Religion*, December 1991, p. 357. Weber's early versions of *The Protestant Ethic* were written with the explicit intent of influencing his colleagues in German Protestant political groups, the liberal democratic circles in which he was very active, to choose the English Puritan tradition over what he felt was the backward German pietistic pattern; he "pitted Calvinism against Lutheranism," for he faulted German Lutheran tradition for preventing the nation from duplicating English "political-economic revolution" and becoming an equal world power. Weber's enthusiasm for Calvinist values should not be construed as anti-German, however; he enthusiastically backed German entry into World War I, thinking it was the appropriate way to build up German capabilities to a world-class level.

28. Hill, *Change and Continuity*, p. 91.

29. Max Weber, *Protestant Ethic and the Spirit of Capitalism*, London: G. Allen Unwin, 1930.

30. Quoted in Benedict Anderson, *Language and Power*, Ithaca: Cornell University Press, 1990, p. 80. Anderson's book is itself worth reading for its description of charisma and irrationality in an authoritarian modern state, Indonesia.

31. Emilio Willems, *Followers of the New Faith*, Nashville: University of Tennessee Press, 1967.

32. Quoted in Rowan Ireland, *Kingdoms Come: Religion and Politics in Brazil*, Pitt Latin American Series, Pittsburgh: University of Pittsburgh Press, 1992, p. 99.

33. Kenneth M. Coleman et al., Aguilar, Sandoval, Steiganga, "Protestantism in El Salvador: Conventional Wisdom Versus the Survey Evidence," in Stoll and Garrard-Burnett, *Rethinking Protestantism in Latin America*, p. 132.

34. Linda Green, "Shifting Affiliations: Mayan Widows and Evangelicos in Guatemala," ibid., p. 162.

35. Bryan R. Roberts, *Organizing Strangers: Poor Families in Guatemala City*, Texas Pan American Series, Austin, TX: BooksDemand, 1973, p. 206.

36. Bryan R. Roberts, "Protestant Groups and Coping with Urban Life in Guatemala

City," *American Journal of Sociology*, May 1968, 73(6), p. 765. Roberts's study took place before the Protestant "boom," and before middle-class neo-Pentecostal churches developed and offered something different from Weberian rigor.

37. Robert F. Wearmouth, *Methodism and the Working Class Movement of England*, London: Epworth Press, 1937, p. 140.

38. See other references to Anthony F. C. Wallace, *Rockdale,* (NY: W. W. Norton, 1978) in Chapter Two. Also see Liston Pope, *Millhands and Preachers,* New Haven: Yale University Press, 1942.

39. Emilio Willems, *Followers of the New Faith*, Nashville: Vanderbilt University Press, 1967; Christian Lalive D'Epinay, *Haven of the Masses*, London: Lutterworth Press, 1969. See Liston Pope, *Millhands and Preachers*, New Haven: Yale University Press, 1942.

40. Thompson, p. 386.

41. Peter Fry, in *Manchester and Sao Paulo: Problems of Rapid Urban Growth*, ed. John D. Wirth and Robert L. Jones, Stanford: Stanford University Press, 1978.

42. Daniel H. Levine, *Popular Voices in Latin American Catholicism*, Princeton: Princeton University Press, 1992.

43. Max Weber, *Economy and Society*, Vol. I, Berkeley: University of California Press, 1968, p. 482.

44. Levine, p. 365.

45. Ibid., p. 359.

46. Ibid., p. 336.

47. Ibid., p. 361.

48. Ibid., p. 80.

49. Ibid., p. 361. Also see Penny Lernoux, *The People of God.*

50. Scott Mainwaring, "Grass-roots Catholic Groups," *The Progressive Church in Latin America,* ed. Mainwaring and Alexander Wilde, South Bend: University of Notre Dame Press, 1989, p. 175. He notes that the grass-roots socialist party in Brazil, the Workers Party (or "PT"), has become very powerful without being an extension of the Popular Church, but could not have come into being without base community support: "It is difficult to even imagine the existence of the PT had grass-roots church groups not existed. The PT was inspired by progressive Catholic ideas emphasizing popular participation, grass-roots democracy, popular organization and basic needs."

51. Christian Smith, *The Emergence of Liberation Theology: Radical Religion and Social Movement Theory*, Chicago: University of Chicago Press, 1991. Smith charts the historical emergence of a theology of liberation and its social and political engagement within and outside of the structure of the Latin American Catholic Church.

52. Grant Wacker, "Planning Ahead: The Enduring Appeal of Prophecy Belief," *Christian Century*, 19 January, 1994, p. 48.

53. Paul Boyer, *When Time Shall Be No More: Prophecy Belief in American Culture*, Cambridge: Harvard University Press, 1994.

54 Elda Susan Morran and Lawrence Schlemmer, *Fear for the Faithful*, Durban: Centre for Applied Social Sciences, University of Natal, 1984, p. 182.

55. Ibid., p. 171. Answers to their survey questions show that new Christians in

South Africa are markedly more distrustful of any analytic process than Christians in the older denominations.

56. Gary North, *Is the World Running Down?: A Dominionist Challenge*, 1988, quoted in James Moore, "Creationist Cosmos of Protestant Fundamentalism," in *Fundamentalisms and Society,* ed, Martin E. Marty and R. Scott Appleby, 1993, p. 66.

57. George Marsden, *Understanding Fundamentalism and Evangelicalism,* p. 120.

58. Norman Vincent Peale quoted in W. A. Swanberg, *Luce and His Empire,* NY: Scribner's, 1972, p. 105.

59. Anthony Giddens, *Modernity and Self-Identity: Self and Society in the Late Modern Age,* Stanford: Stanford University Press, 1991; see also Roy Baumeister, *Escaping the Self,* NY: Basic Books, 1991.

60. Ibid., p. 197.

61. Aril Edvardsen, "Multi-Level Evangelism," *Church Growth Manual* #3, Seoul: Church Growth International, 1990, p. 203.

62. Bruce Barton, *The Man Nobody Knows,* Indianapolis: Bobbs-Merrill, 1925, Introduction (no page number in original).

63. Leslie Gill, "Religious Mobility and the Many Words of God in La Paz, Bolivia," in Stoll and Burnett, *Rethinking Protestantism in Latin America,* p. 195.

64. Stephen Crook et al., *Postmodernization,* London: Sage, 1992, p. 228.

65. Stuart Ewan, "Marketing Dreams: The Political Elements of Style," in *Consumption, Identity, and Style,* ed. A. Tomlinson, London: Routledge, 1990, p. 52.

66. Frank J. Lechner, "Fundamentalism and Sociocultural Revitalization: On the Logic of Dedifferentiation," in *Differentiation Theory and Social Change,* ed. Jeffrey C. Alexander and Paul Colomy, NY: Columbia University Press, 1990, pp. 114–115.

67. Ibid., p. 104.

68. Stanley Johannesen, "The Holy Ghost and the Ordering of the World," *Religion and Global Order,* NY: Paragon, 1991, p. 119.

69. Ibid., p. 129.

70. Ibid., p. 130.

CHAPTER TWELVE
The Mystery of the Capitalist Ethic

1. From figures published by United Nations Development Programme, *Human Development Report—1992,* NY: Oxford University Press, 1992. For a drastic accounting of the increased poverty in the world in the 1980s, actually induced by capitalist expansion, i.e., structural adjustment programs and loans imposed by the World Bank, see Walden Bello, *Dark Victory,* London: Pluto Press and Food First, 1994. In Latin America alone the number of people living in poverty increased from 130 million to 180 million in ten years.

2. Berch Berberoglu, *The Political Economy of Development,* Albany: SUNY Press, 1992, pp. 8–30, cogently reviews the developmental arguments. Developmentalism originated in the United States through the transfer of Parson's sociological ideas of "modern" versus "traditional" societies; it was thought that modernizing factors must

penetrate traditional, "backward" societies through a "diffusion of principles" (a phrase of W. W. Rostow's) such as free markets, free enterprise, modern tax systems, and rationalization of the state.

Note the difference between the utter deprivation that is currently being imposed on the majorities in modernizing societies (previous footnote) and the previously widely accepted (though debatable) Kuznets syndrome, named for economist Simon Kuznets. He postulated that rapid economic growth would be accompanied by a period of greater inequality; however, this was usually understood to mean "relative" inequality, that lower and upper classes would both advance in terms of their standards of living, but at different rates.

3. Samuel Huntington, "The Clash of Civilizations," *Foreign Affairs*. While Huntington prepares his readers to be wary of the possibly dangerous Islamic bloc countries (and a rather improbable alliance of them with the Chinese), he does not completely demonize them or suggest trying to overwhelm them with Pax Americana.

4. J. Gordon Melton, "The Evangelical Thrust into Eastern Europe in the 1990s," paper presented at International Conference on New Religion and the New Europe, London School of Economics, 25–28 March, 1993. Melton continues to be the recipient of data from many sources.

5. Steven Erlanger, "Korean Missionaries Sow Christianity in Caucasus," *New York Times*, 22 April, 1995, p. 4.

Bibliography

Abosi, Kaluy. 1990. *"Born Twice": From Demonism to Christianity.* Benin City: Joint Heirs Publications.

Academy for Educational Development (AED). 1985. *Guatemala: Education Sector Assessment.* Guatemala City: AED.

Adams, Richard. 1970. *Crucifixion by Power: Essays on Guatemalan National Social Structure 1944–1966.* Austin: University of Texas.

Adekola, Sunday. 1993. *Understanding Demonology.* Ibadan: Scripture Union.

Affum, Ali. 1988. "American Cure Fails Liberian Ills." All Africa Press Service Release, 12 December.

African Independent Churches. 1985. *Speaking for Ourselves: Members of African Independent Churches Report on their Pilot Study of the History and Theology of their Churches.* Braamfontein: Institute for Contextual Theology.

Alejandria, Noel. 1989. "Cold War: Christian Soldiers." *Midweek,* 29 March.

Alibutud, Raul. 1990. "Invasion of the Soul Snatchers." *Malaya,* 15 July.

Aliosa, Silvia. 1990. "Setta di Potere." *Panorama,* December 2.

Alo, Teresita with Tito Craige and Reiner ter Kuile. 1990. *The Iceberg and the Cross: Violence Against the Church.* Manila: Justice and Peace Commission, Association of Major Religious Superiors.

Ammerman, Nancy. 1987. *Bible Believers: Fundamentalists in the Modern World.* New Brunswick, NJ: Rutgers University Press.

Anderson, Benedict. 1990. *Language and Power.* Ithaca: Cornell University Press.

Anderson, Gerald. 1969. *Studies in Philippine Church History.* Ithaca: Cornell University Press.

Anderson, Jon Lee, and Scott Anderson. 1986. *Inside the League.* NY: Dodd, Mead, and Co.

Anderson, Robert Mopes. 1979. *Vision of the Disinherited: The Making of Modern Pentecostalism,* NY: Oxford.

Anfuso, Joseph, and David Sczepanski. 1983. *Efrain Rios Montt: Servant or Dictator?* Ventura, CA: Vision House.

Annis, Sheldon. 1988. *God and Production in a Guatemalan Town.* Austin: University of Texas Press.

Anyon, Jean. 1983. "Intersections of Gender and Class: Accommodation and Resistance by Working Class and Affluent Females to Contradictory Sex-Role Ideologies." In *Gender, Class and Education,* edited by Stephen Walker and Len Barton. NY: Falmer Press.

315

Appleby, R. Scott, and Martin E. Marty. 1992. *The Glory and the Power.* Boston: Beacon Press.

Aquino, Jeremias. 1981. "Kulturang Coke at Relihiyong Born-Again." *Kalinangan* 1(1), April, 8–9.

Asedillo, Rebecca, and B. David Williams, eds. 1989. *Rice in the Storm.* NY: Friendship Press.

Avancini, John. 1984. *Stolen Property Returned.* Hurst, TX: Harrison House.

Avancini, John. 1986. *The Wealth of the Wicked: Yours for the Taking.* Hurst, TX: Avancini Ministries.

———. 1988. *Faith Extenders.* Hurst, TX: Avancini Ministries.

———. 1989. *Powerful Principles of Increase Released in You.* Hurst, TX: Harrison House.

———. 1989. *30-60-100fold: Your Financial Harvest Released.* Hurst, TX: Avancini Ministries.

Banks, Arthur. 1993. *Political Handbook of the World.* CSA Publications.

Barker, Eileen V. 1991. "The Whole World in His Hand?" In *Religion and the World Order.* edited by Roland Robertson and William R. Garrett. New York: Paragon House.

Barrett, David B. 1982. *World Christian Encyclopedia.* New York: Oxford University Press.

Barrett, David B., and James W. Reapsome. 1988. "Seven Hundred Plans to Evangelize the World." Richmond: World Evangelization Center; Wheaton: Evangelical Missions Information Service.

Barry, Tom. 1986. *Low Intensity Conflict: The Battlefield in Central America.* Albuquerque: The Resource Center.

———. 1989. *Guatemala: A Country Guide.* Albuquerque: The Inter-Hemispheric Education Resource Center.

Barry, Tom, and Deb Preusch. 1986. *The Central American Fact Book.* NY: Grove Press.

Barton, Bruce. 1925. *The Man Nobody Knows.* Indianapolis: Bobbs-Merrill.

Bastian, Jean Pierre. 1986. *Breve historia del protestantismo en América Latina.* Mexico City: Casa Unida de Publicaciones (CUPSA).

Baumeister, Roy. 1991. *Escaping the Self.* NY: Basic Books.

Bautista, Lorenzo. 1991. *The Social Views of Evangelicals on Issues Related to the Marcos Rule 1972–1986.* Master's thesis submitted to the College of Social Sciences and Philosophy, University of Philippines, September.

Baybay, Noel. 1992. Director of Development for Ecumenical Center for Justice and Peace and UCC pastor. Interview by author, Bacolod 1 June.

Bello, Walden F. 1990. *Dragons in Distress.* San Francisco: Institute for Food and Development Policy.

Bendroth, Margaret Lamberts. 1993. *Fundamentalism and Gender, 1875 to the Present.* New Haven: Yale University Press.

Berberian, Martha de. 1983. "Analisis de la educacion cristiana en Guatemala." Escuela de Teologia, Universidad Mariano Galvez de Guatemala.

Berberoglu, Berch. 1992. *The Political Economy of Development.* Albany: SUNY Press.

Berger, Peter L. 1967. *The Sacred Canopy*. Garden City, NY: Doubleday.

Berger, Peter L., and Michael Novak. 1985. *Speaking to the Third World: Essays on Democracy and Development*. Washington, D.C.: American Enterprise Institute.

Berger, Peter L., And Hsin-Huang Hsiao eds. 1987. *In Search of an East Asian Development Model*. New Brunswick: Transaction Books.

Berger, Peter L., ed. 1987. *Capitalism and Equality in America*. Lanham, MD: Hamilton Press.

Berger, Peter L. 1990. "Foreword" to David Martin, *Tongues of Fire*. Oxford: Basil Blackwell.

Bernal, Dick. 1992. "The Power of Faith," in *Church Growth Manual*, Spring.

Berryman, Philip. 1984. *The Religious Roots of Rebellion*. Maryknoll, NY: Orbis Books.

———. 1994. *Stubborn Hope: Religion, Politics, and Revolution in Central America*. Maryknoll, NY: Orbis Books.

Beyan, Amos J. 1984–85. "The American Colonisation Society and the Socio-Religious Characterisation of Liberia: A Historical Survey 1822–1900." *Liberian Studies Journal*. 10, 2, 5.

Birai, Umar M. 1993. "Islamic Tajdid and the Political Process in Nigeria." In *Fundamentalism and the State*, Vol. III, edited by Martin Marty and R. Scott Appleby. Chicago: University of Chicago Press.

Black, George. 1984. *Garrison Guatemala*. London: Zed Press.

———. 1988. *The Good Neighbor*. NY: Pantheon.

Bluestone, Barry, and Bennett Harrison. 1988. *The Great U-Turn*. NY: Basic Books.

Boch-Hoell, Nils. 1964. *The Pentecostal Movement*. NY: Humanities Press.

Boettcher, Robert. 1980. *Gifts of Deceit*. New York: Holt, Rinehart, and Winston.

Bondoc, Jarius. 1989. "What are Fundamentalists Really Up To?" *Philippine Free Press*. 25 February.

Boyer, Paul. 1994. *When Time Shall be no More: Prophecy Belief in American Culture*. Cambridge: Harvard University Press.

Bransford, Stephen. 1991. *High Places*. Wheaton, IL: Crossway.

Braudel, Fernand. 1982. *Civilization and Capitalism, 15th–18th Century; Volume 2: "The Wheels of Commerce."* NY: Harper and Row.

Brereton, Virginia Lieson. 1990. *Training God's Army: The American Bible School 1880–1940*. Bloomington: University of Indiana Press.

Brock, Peter. 1988. "Fundamentalist Expansion: An Historical Perspective." *WSCF Journal*, 4 April.

———. 1989. "Religious Revitalization and Politics" and "Fundamentalist Expansion." In *Exploring the New Religious Movements*.

Brouwer, Steve. 1992. *Conquest and Capitalism*. Carlisle: Big Picture Books.

———. 1992. *Sharing the Pie*. Carlisle: Big Picture Books.

Brouwer, Steve, and Susan D. Rose. 1990. "The Export of Fundamentalist Americanism: Evangelical Education in Guatemala." *Latin American Perspectives*. Vol. 17, No. 4.

Brown, Karen McCarthy. 1994. "Fundamentalism and the Control of Women." In *Fundamentalism and Gender,* edited by John S. Hawley. Oxford: Oxford University Press.

Brown, Rebecca. 1990. *Prepare for War.* Springdale, PA: Whitaker.

Bruce, Steve. 1993. "Fundamentalism, Ethnicity, and Enclave." In *Fundamentalism and the State,* edited by Martin Marty and Scott Appleby. Chicago: University of Chicago Press.

Brusco, Elizabeth. 1986. "The Household Basis of Evangelical Religion and the Reformation of Machismo in Colombia." Ph.D. dissertation Tulane University.

———. 1993. "The Reformation of Machismo: Asceticism and Masculinity among Colombian Evangelicals." In *Rethinking Protestantism in Latin America,* edited by Virginia Garrard-Burnett and David Stoll. Philadelphia: Temple University Press.

———. 1994. *The Reformation of Machismo.* Austin: University of Texas Press.

Burgess, Stanley M., Gary B. McGee, and Patrick H. Alexander. 1988. *The Dictionary of Pentecostal and Charismatic Movements.* Grand Rapids: Zondervan.

Byron, Christopher. 1993. "Seems Like Old Times." *New York,* 27 September.

Calder, Bruce. 1970. *Crecimiento y Cambio de la Iglesia Catolica Guatemalteca.* Guatemala City and Austin: Seminario de Integracion Social de Guatemala and University of Texas.

Capaque, George. 1992. General Secretary Inter-Varsity Christian Fellowship. Interview. Quezon City, 28 May.

Carino, Feliciano. 1992. General Secretary NCCP. Interview by author. Manila, 6 June.

Carmack, Robert, 1988. *Harvest of Violence: The Maya Indians and the Guatemalan Crisis.* Norman, OK: University of Oklahoma Press.

Carpenter, Joel A. and Wilbert R. Shenk, ed. 1990. *Earthen Vessels*: Evangelicals and Froeigh Missions, 1880–1980. Grand Rapids, MI: Eerdmans.

"Catholic Guidelines on Fundamentalism: Hold Fast to What is Good." 1989. Manila: Catholic Bishops Conference of the Philippines.

Chan, Steve. 1990. *East Asian Dynamism.* Boulder: Westview.

Chaudhuri, J. R. 1986. "Liberia Under Military Rule 1980–1985." In *Liberia: Underdevelopment and Political Rule in a Peripheral Society,* edited by R. Kappel et al. Hamburg: Institut für Afrika-Kunde.

Chiundiza, Richmond. 1991. "High Level Powers in Zimbabwe." In *Territorial Spirits: Insights on Strategic Level Spiritual Warfare from Nineteen Christian Leaders,* edited by C. Peter Wagner. Chichester: Sovereign World.

Cho, Paul Yonggi. 1992. "Mobilizing the Laity for World Evangelism," *Church Growth.* Spring.

Christian Institute for the Study of Justice and Development. 1988. *Lost Victory.* Seoul: Minjingsa.

———. 1991. *The Korean Situation.* Seoul: Minjungsa.

Church Growth Manual #3. 1990. Seoul: Church Growth International.

Church Trends. 1990. Church Data Center.

Clad, James. 1987. "The Soldiers of God." *Far Eastern Economic Review*, 12 March.

Clark, Donald N. 1988. *The Kwangju Uprising*. Boulder: Westview.

Clark, Ramsey et al. 1987. *Right-Wing Vigilantes and U.S. Involvement*. Manila: Philippine Alliance of Human Rights Advocates (PAHRA).

Clymer, Kenton. 1986. *Protestant Missionaries in the Philippines 1898–1916: An Inquiry Into the American Colonial Mentality*. Chicago: University of Illinois Press.

CMF Newsletter (Christian Military Fellowship). 1990. January-February.

Coleman, Kenneth M. et al. 1993. "Protestantism in El Salvador: Conventional Wisdom Versus the Survey Evidence." In *Rethinking Protestantism in Latin America,* edited by Virginia Garrard-Burnett and David Stoll. Philadelphia: Temple University Press.

Coleman, Simon. 1989. "Controversy and the Social Order: Responses to a Religious Group in Sweden." Ph.D. dissertation, Cambridge University.

Colonel, Miguel. 1991. *Pro-Democracy PEOPLE'S WAR*. Quezon City: Vanmarc Ventures.

Comaroff, Jean and John Comaroff. 1991. *Of Revelation and Revolution: Christianity, Colonialism, and Consciousness in South Africa*. Chicago: University of Chicago Press.

Comblin, Jose. 1979. *The Church and the National Security State*. Maryknoll, NY: Orbis.

Conde, Butch. 1991. "Touch of Glory," *Christian Journal*. August.

Connolly, S. J. 1992. *Religion, Law, and Power*. Oxford: Oxford University Press.

Constantino, Renato, and Letizia Constantino. 1987. *The Philippines: The Continuing Past*. Quezon City: Foundation for Nationalist Studies.

Constitution of Fellowship of Full Gospel Ministers. Box 10-4373, 1000 Monrovia 10.

Conway, Flo, and Jim Siegelman. 1982. *Holy Terror: The Fundamentalist War on America's Freedom, Religion, Politics, and Our Private Lives*. NY: Doubleday Publishing.

Cooper, Marc. 1995. "God and Man in Colorado Springs." *The Nation,* 2 January.

Coote, Bob. 1991. "The Numbers Game in World Evangelisation," *Evangelical Missions Quarterly* 27, 2 April, 118–127.

Copeland, Kenneth. 1974. *The Laws of Prosperity*. Fort Worth, TX: Kenneth Copeland Publications.

———. n.d. *God's Will is Prosperity*. Fort Worth, TX: Kenneth Copeland Publications.

Corado, José Adonias. 1990. Interview with author. 3 April.

Coronel, Sheila. 1989. "Right-Wing Evangelicals Take Part in Politics in the Name of God." *Kalinangan* 9(2), 39–42.

Corpuz, Onofre. 1976. *The Philippines*. NJ: Presidential.

Costello, T. 1989. "An Analysis of the Filipino Church's Contribution to the Development of a Christian Political Ethic." Unpublished paper.

Cox, Harvey. 1995. *Fire From Heaven*. NY: Addison-Wesley.

Crocker, Chester. 1986. "Statement Before the Joint Session of the Subcommittees on Africa and on Human Rights and International Organizations of the House Foreign Affairs Committee," *Liberia Forum* 3/2, 115–116.

Crook, Stephen, Jan Pukulski, and Malcolm Waters. 1992. *Postmodernization*. London: Sage.

Cudjoe-Mensah, John. 1989. *Satan and his Tricks*. Kumasi: St. Mary's.

Dayton, Donald W. 1985. "Protestant Christian Missions to Korea as a Source of Unification Thought." *Religion in the Pacific Era*. NY: Paragon House.

———. 1987. *The Theological Roots of Pentecostalism*. Metuchen, NJ: Scarecrow Press.

D'Epinay, Christian Lalive. 1969. *Haven to the Masses: A Study of the Pentecostal Movement in Chile*. London: Lutterworth Press.

DeGolyer, James. 1985. "Unlearning the Ways of the World." *Radiance*, 13 May.

De Guzman, Arnel, and Tito Craige. 1990. *Handbook on Militarization*. Manila: Ecumenical Movement for Justice and Peace.

Deiros, Pablo A. 1991. "Protestant Fundamentalism in Latin America." In *Fundamentalisms Observed*, edited by Martin E. Marty and R. Scott Appleby. Chicago: University of Chicago Press.

"Diagnostico de la Educacion Guatemalteca." 1985. Guatemala City: Ministerio de Educacion, Oficina de Planeamiento Integral de Educacion.

Diamond, Sara. 1989. *Spiritual Warfare: The Politics of the Christian Right*. Boston: South End Press.

Diaz-Laurel, Celia. 1992. President of CAUSA, Philippines, and wife of former Vice president Laurel. Interview with author. Manila, 27 May.

Directorio de Iglesias, Organizaciones y Ministerios del Morimiento Protestante Guatemala. Guatemala City: Instituto Internacional de Evangelizacion a Fondo [IINDEF] y Servicio Evangelizador para America Latina [SEPAL].

Dodson, Michael, and Laura O'Shaughnessy. 1990. *Nicaragua's Other Revolution*. Albany: State University of New York Press.

Dominquez, Bishop Ben. 1992. Church of the Risen Lord at University of the Philippines. Interview with author. Quezon City, 26 May.

Dorfman, Ariel. 1984. *How to Read Donald Duck*. New York: International General.

Duarte, Anibal F. 1989. "Radiofonia Religiosa en Guatemala." Licenciado en Ciencias de la Communicacion thesis. Universidad de San Carlos de Guatemala.

Dulles, John Foster. 1939. *War, Peace and Change*. NY: Harper.

Dunn, D. Elsood, and Byron Tarr. 1988. *Liberia: A National Polity in Transition*. London and Metuchen, NJ: Scarecrow Press.

Echevaria, Ricardo. 1990. Interview with author. 2 April.

Eckert, Carter J. et al. 1990. *Korea, Old and New*. Cambridge: Harvard University Press.

Einigenburg, Elton M. 1959. "The Ordination of Women," *Christianity Today*, 27 April.

Ela, Jean Marc. 1986. *African Cry*. Maryknoll, NY: Orbis.

Empestan, Father Romeo. 1992. Diocesan Pastoral Center. Interview with author. Bacolod, 31 May.

Engelhardt, Tom. 1995. *The End of Victory Culture: Cold War America and the Disillusioning of a Generation*. NY: Basic Books.

Eni, Emmanuel. 1987. *Delivered from the Powers of Darkness*. Ibadan: Scripture Union.

Erlanger, Steven. 1995. "Korean Missionaries Sow Christianity in the Caucasus." *New York Times*. 22 April, p. 4A.

"Escuela del futuro' y el proyecto neoconservador." 1991. *Infopress Centro Americana*, 21 de Marzo, 3–5.

Eto, Victoria. 1981. *How I Served Satan Until Jesus Christ Delivered Me: A True Account of My Twenty-one Years Experience as an Agent of Darkness and of My Deliverance by the Powerful Arm of God in Christ Jesus*. Warri: Shalom Christian Mission.

———. 1988. *Exposition on Water Spirits*. Warri: Shalom Christian Mission.

Europa Year Book 1988. 1989. London: Europa Publications, Omnigraphics Ltd.

"Evangelicals' Manila Visit to Prop up Pro-bases Sentiment?." 1990. *The Manila Times*, 18 May, 5.

Exploring the New Religious Movements in the Philippines. 1989. Quezon City: Commission on Evangelism and Ecumenical Relations, National Council of Churches, Philippines.

Ewan, Stuart. 1990. "Marketing Dreams: the Political Elements of Style." In *Consumption, Identity, and Style*, edited by A. Tomlinson. London: Routledge.

Falwell, Jerry. 1980. *Listen America*. NY: Bantam Books.

Fichter, Joseph. 1983. "Family and Religion Among the Moonies." In *Families and Religions*, edited by William V. D'Antonio and Joan Aldous. Beverly Hills: Sage.

Flinn, F. K. 1978. "Unification Hermeneutics and Christian Theology." In *A Time for Consideration*, edited by M. Darrol Bryant and Herbert W. Richardson. NY: Edwin Mellon Press.

Flores, Ding. 1992. Socio-Pastoral Center. Interview with author. Bacolod, 29 May.

"Focus on Africa." BBC program with Blaine Harden.

Fomum, Zacharias Tanee. n.d. *Deliverance From Demons*. Yaounde, Cameroon: IGH.

Foxley, Alejandro et al, ed. 1986. *Development, Democracy, and the Art of Trespassing*. South Bend: Notre Dame.

Fraenkel, Merran. 1964. *Tribe and Class in Monrovia*. London: Oxford University Press.

Fry, Peter. 1978. "Two Religious Movements: Protestantism and Umbanda." In *Manchester and Sao Paulo*, edited by J. D. Wirth and R. L. Jones. Stanford: Stanford University Press.

"Fundamentalism: Twist of Faith." 1991. *IBON: Facts and Figures* 14(9), 15 May, 1–7.

Garrard-Burnett, Virginia. 1989. "Jerusalem under Siege: Protestantism in Rural Guatemala, 1960–1987." Paper presented at the Latin American Studies Association, 15 September.

Garrard-Burnett, Virginia, and David Stoll, ed. 1993. *Rethinking Protestantism in Latin America*. Philadelphia: Temple University Press.

Gellner, Ernest. 1981. *Muslim Society*. Cambridge: Cambridge University Press.

———. 1988. *Plow, Sword, and Book: the Structure of Human History*. Chicago: University of Chicago Press.

———. 1992. *Postmodernism, Reason, and Religion*. London: Routledge.

Gershoni, Yekutiel. 1989. "Liberia and Israel: The Evolution of a Relationship." *Liberian Studies Journal*. 14, 1.

Gibson, James. 1995. *Warrior Dreams*. NY: Hill and Wang.

Giddens, Anthony. 1991. *Modernity and Self Identity: Self and Society in the Late Modern Age.* Stanford: Stanford University Press.

Gifford, Paul. 1988. *The Religious Right in South Africa.* Harare: Baobab.

———. 1990. *To Save or Enslave.* Harare: EDICESA (Ecumenical Documentation and Information Centre of Eastern and Southern Africa).

———. 1992. *New Dimensions in African Christianity.* Ibadan, Nigeria: SEFER Books.

———. 1993. *Christianity and Politics in Doe's Liberia.* Cambridge: Cambridge University Press.

Glazier, Stephen D., ed. 1980. *Perspectives on Pentecostalism: Case Studies from the Caribbean and Latin America.* Washington, D.C.: University Press of America.

Gold, Thomas B. 1986. *State and Society in the Taiwan Miracle.* Armonk: M. S. Sharpe.

Goodwin, Jan. 1994. *Muslim Women Lift the Veil of Silence on the Islamic World.* NY: Little, Brown, and Co.

Gordon, Linda. 1988. *Heroes of Their Own Lives: The Politics and History of Family Violence.* NY: Viking.

Gould, Stephen J. 1981. *Mismeasure of Man,* NY: W. W. Norton & Co.

Gramenz, Stuart. 1988. *Who are God's Guerrillas?* Chichester: Sovereign World.

Green, Linda. 1993. "Shifting Affiliations: Mayan Widows and Evangelicos in Guatemala." In *Rethinking Protestantism in Latin America,* edited by Virginia Garrard-Burnett and David Stoll. Philadelphia: Temple University Press.

Greve, Frank. 1987. "New Right Gets Millions from Moon." *Philadelphia Inquirer,* 20 December.

Greven, Philip. 1977. *The Protestant Temperament: Patterns of Child-Rearing, Religious Experience, and the Self in Early America.* NY: Alfred A. Knopf.

Groupwatch. 1990. "The Unification Church." Albuquerque: the InterHemispheric Resource Center.

Gruson, Lindsey. 1991. "Right-Wing Protestant Elected President of Guatemala," *New York Times,* 8 January, A3.

Guatemala 1986: The Year of Promises. 1987. Guatemala City: Infopress Centroamericana.

Guillermo, Alice. 1991. "Comments" in *The Religious Right and National Security Doctrine.* Tugon, XI(2), 230.

Guinness Book of Records 1990. 1989. London: Guinness Publishing Co.

Haddad, Hassan and Donald Wagner. 1986. *All in the Name of the Bible: Selected Essays on Israel and American Christian Fundamentalism.* Brattleboro, VT: Amana Books.

Hadden, Jeffrey K. 1978. *Televangelism.* NY: Knopf.

Hadden, Jeffrey K. 1991. "The Globalization of Televangelism. In *Religion and the Global Order,* edited by Roland Robertson and William R. Garrett. New York: Paragon House.

Hadden, Jeffrey K.and Shupe, Anson. 1988. *Televangelism, Power, and Politics on God's Frontier.* NY: Henry Holt.

Hagin, Kenneth. 1980. "How to Write Your Ticket with God." Tulsa, OK: Faith Library Publications, 5.

————. 1993. *The Word of Faith*, August.

Halévy, Elie. 1927. *A History of the English People 1830–1841*. London: T. Fisher Unwin.

Hall, Verna M. 1966. *The Christian History of the Constitution of the United States*. San Francisco: The Foundation for American Christian Education.

Halsell, Grace. 1984. "Shrine Under Siege," *The Link*, Vol. 17, No. 3, August-September.

————. 1986. *Prophecy and Politics: The Secret Alliance Between Israel and the US Christian Right*. Chicago: Lawrence Hill.

————. 1988. "Armageddon Theology," *Life and Peace Review*, Vol. 2, No. 2.

Hammond, Frank, and Ida Mae Hammond. 1973. *Pigs in the Parlor: A Practical Guide to Deliverance*. Kirkwood Missouri: Impact Books.

Handy, Jim. 1984. *Gift of the Devil*. Boston: South End Press.

Hanlon, E. G. J. 1991. *Mozambique: Who Calls the Shots?* London: James Currey.

Hantover, Jeffrey. 1978. "The Boy Scouts and the Validation of Masculinity." *Journal of Social Issues*. Vol. 34, No. 1.

Harbury, Jennifer. 1994. *Bridge of Courage*. Monroe, Maine: Common Courage Press.

Hardacre, Helen. 1994. "Japanese New Religions: Profiles in Gender." In *Fundamentalism and Gender,* edited by John S. Hawley. Oxford: Oxford University Press.

Harden, Blaine. 1991. *Africa, Dispatches from a Fragile Continent*. London: Harper Collins.

Harrell, David Edwin. 1975. *All Things are Possible: The Healing and Charismatic Revivals in Modern America*. Bloomington: University of Indiana Press.

————. 1985. *Oral Roberts: An American Life*. Bloomington: University of Indiana Press.

————. 1987. *Pat Robertson: A Personal, Religious, and Political Portrait*. San Francisco: Harper and Row.

Harris, Marvin. 1981. *America Now*. NY: Simon and Schuster.

Hart Landsberg, Martin. 1993. *The Rush to Development: Economic Change and Political Struggle in South Korea*. NY: Monthly Review Press.

Harvey, Pharis. 1990. "No Justice for Workers in Korea," *Democratic Left,* September-October.

Hawley, John S. 1994. "Hinduism, Sati, and its Defenders." In *Fundamentalism and Gender,* edited by John S. Hawley. Oxford: Oxford University Press.

————. ed. 1994. *Fundamentalism and Gender.* Oxford: Oxford University Press.

Hayden. 1986. "Liberia: Recent Developments and US Foreign Policy: Testimony Before the House of Representatives," *Liberia Forum*, 23 January, 2/2.

Heaven U. Heaven. 1985. *How to Cast out Demons or Evil Spirits: A Practical Guide to Deliverance*. Lagos: Heaven and Blessings Books.

Henares, Hilarion. "Who Are Considered Right-wing Christians?" 1989. *Philippine Daily Inquirer*, 8 September, 1.

Hill, Christopher. 1961. *The Century of Revolution*. Edinburgh: Thomas Nelson and Sons.

————. 1975. *Change and Continuity in Seventeenth Century England*. Cambridge: Harvard University Press.

Hobsbawm, Eric. 1969. *Industry and Empire*. Harmondsworth: Penguin.

Hofstadter, Richard. 1963. *Anti-Intellectualism in American Life*. NY: Knopf.

———. 1965. *Social Darwinism in American Thought.* NY: Braziller.

Hollenweger, Walter. 1972. *The Pentecostals.* Minneapolis: Augsburg.

———. 1986. "After Twenty Years' Research on Pentecostalism." *International Review of Mission,* 75.

Horowitz, Irving. 1981. "The Last Civil Religion: Reverend Moon and the Unification Church," in *In God We Trust,* edited by Thomas Robbins et al. New Brunswick: Transaction.

"How the World's Largest Church Got That Way," *Christianity Today,* 18 May, 1984, 53.

Howe, Graham. 1991." God Damn Yanquis: American Hegemony and Contemporary Latin American Christianity." In *World Order and Religion,* edited by Wade Clark Roof. Albany: SUNY Press.

Hunter, James Davison. 1983. *American Evangelicalism,* New Brunswick: Rutgers University Press.

Huntington, Deborah. 1984. *The Salvation Brokers: Conservative Evangelicals in Central America,* NACLA Report on the Americas 18, No. 1.

Huntington, Samuel P. 1968. *Political Order in Changing Societies.* New Haven: Yale University Press.

———. 1995. "The Clash of Civilizations," *Foreign Policy,* Summer.

Ireland, Rowan. 1992. *Kingdoms Come: Religion and Politics in Brazil.* Pittsburgh: University of Pittsburgh Press, Pitt Latin Series.

Jacobs, Cindy. 1991. *Possessing the Gates of the Enemy.* Grand Rapids: Chosen Books.

Jehle, Paul W. 1982. *Go Ye Therefore...and Teach.* Plymouth, MA: Plymouth Rock Foundation.

———. 1985. *The Principle Approach to Political Involvement.* Buzzards Bay, MA: Heritage Institute Ministries.

Jeter, Stan. 1990. Project Light coordinator, interview with author. Guatemala City, 3 April.

Johannesen, Stanley. 1991. "The Holy Ghost and the Ordering of the World." In *Religion and the Global Order,* edited by Roland Robertson and William R. Garrett. New York: Paragon.

Johnstone, Patrick. 1978. *Operation World.* 3rd ed. Carlisle, PA: OM Publishing.

———. 1986. *Operation World.* 4th ed. Carlisle, PA: OM Publishing.

———. 1993. *Operation World.* 5th ed. Carlisle, PA: OM Publishing.

Jonas, Suzanne. 1991. *The Battle for Guatemala.* Boulder, CO: Westview.

Jonas, Suzanne, and David Tobias. 1974. *Guatemala.* Berkeley: North American Congress on Latin America (NACLA).

Jones, Maldwyn A. 1991. "The Scots Irish in British America." In *Strangers in the Realm,* edited by Bernard Bailyn and Philip D. Morgan. Chapel Hill: University of North Carolina Press.

"Joshua for Christ: Bringing Good News to the Military." n.d. *Maiden Issue* 2.

Kaniaki and Mukendi. 1991. *Snatched from Satan's Claws: An Amazing Deliverance by Christ.* Nairobi: Enkei Media Services.

Kearney, Michael. 1986. "Religion, Ideology, and Revolution in Latin America." *Latin American Perspectives.* 13 (Summer), 3–12.

Kieh, George Klay, Jr. 1989. "An Analysis of Israeli Repenetration of Liberia," *Liberian Studies Journal.* XIV 2, pp. 117–129.

Kim, Kwang-il and Mun Sang-hee. 1971. *New Religions in Korea.* Korea Christian Academy, East Asia Christian Conference.

Kim, Y. O. 1980. *Unification Theology.* NY: Holy Spirit Association.

Kong, Il Sa. 1993. *Korea in the World Economy.* Washington, D.C.: Institute for International Economics.

Korean Council of Churches, ed. 1990. *Korean Church.* Seoul: Christian Institute of Justice and Development.

Kowalewski, David 1993. "Rejoinder on Vigilantism in the Philippines." *Sociology of Religion.* 54(3) Fall, 309–312.

Krueger, Chris, and Kjell Enge. 1985. "Security and Development in the Guatemalan Highlands." Washington, D.C.: Washington Office on Latin America. August.

Kuznets, Simon Smith. 1979. *Growth, Population, Income Distribution.* NY: W. W. Norton.

Kuran, Timur. 1993. ""Fundamentalists and the Economy" and "The Economic Impact of Islamic Fundamentalism." In *Fundamentalisms and the State.* Vol. III, edited by Martin Marty and R. Scott Appleby. Chicago: University of Chicago Press.

Kwak, Chun Hwan. 1980. *Outline of the Principle, Level 4.* New York: Unification Church.

Lalive D'Epinay, Christian. 1969. *Haven of the Masses.* London: Lutterworth Press.

Lamban, Sonny "Popoy." 1992. Gen. Secretary Ecumenical Movement for Justice and Peace (EMJP). Interview with author. Bacolod, 28 May.

Landsman, Ned C. 1985. *Scotland and its First American Colony.* Princeton: Princeton University Press.

Larmer, Bruce. 1989. "Guatemala: Evangelical Spurt Meets Spiritual Needs and Political Goals," *Christian Science Monitor,* 9–15 March, 1.

Latin American Evangelical Center for Pastoral Studies (CELEP). Survey.

Lau, Lawrence J., ed. 1986. *Models of Development: South Korea and Taiwan.* San Francisco: Institute for Contemporary Economics.

Lawrence, Bruce. 1989. *Defenders of God.* NY: Harper and Row.

Lawyers' Committee for Human Rights. 1986. *A Promise Betrayed: A Report on Human Rights.* NY: Lawyers' Committee for Human Rights.

Lechner, Frank. 1990. "Fundamentalism and Sociocultural Revitalization: On the Logic of Dedifferentiation." In *Differentiation Theory and Social Change,* edited by Jeffrey C. Alexander and Paul Colomy. NY: Columbia University Press.

Lee, Daniel Soonjung.1988. *A Historical Study of the National Evangelization Movement of Korea.* Pasadena: Doctoral dissertation, Fuller Theology Seminary.

Lee, Jae Bum. 1986. "Pentecostal type distinctives and Korean Protestant Church Growth." Ph.D. dissertation. Fuller Theological School, Pasadena, California.

Lee, Man Woo. 1990. *The Oddyssey of Korean Democracy.* NY: Praeger.

Lee, San hun. 1985. *The End of Communism.* NY: Unification Thought Institute.

Lernoux, Penny. 1988. "The Fundamentalist Surge in Latin America." *Christian Century* 20 (January).

——. 1989. *People of God: The Struggle for World Catholicism*. NY: Viking Penguin.

Levine, Daniel H. 1992. *Popular Voices in Latin American Catholicism*. Princeton: Princeton University Press.

——. ed. 1986. *Religion and Political Conflict in Latin America*. Chapel Hill: University of North Carolina Press.

Lewis, David Allen. 1982. *Magog 1982 Cancelled*. Harrison, AK: New Leaf Press.

Liebman, Robert C., and Robert Wuthnow ed. 1983. *The New Christian Right*. NY: Aldine.

Lindsey, Hal. 1970. *The Late Great Planet Earth*. Grand Rapids: Zondervan.

Lloret, Julian. n.d. "The Gospel in the Mayan Culture of Guatemala," *Dialogo Hermanidad Maya*, 7(3).

Lopez, Jorge H. 1990. Interview with author, 3 April.

Lopez-Gonzaga, Voileta B. 1991. *The Negrense: A Social History of an Elite Class*. Bacolod: Institute of Social Research, University of La Salle.

"Lumen 2000." 1988. *L'Actualité Religieuse*, March.

Lynch, Colum. 1989. "Catholics, Evangelicals Tangle Amid Latin Turmoil." *San Francisco Chronicle*, 10 May, 4.

Madrid, A. Edmundo. 1990. Interview with author, Guatemala City, 3 April.

Maggay, Melba. 1991. "Comments." In *The Religious Right and National Security Doctrine*. Manila: Tugon, NCCP.

Mainwaring, Scott. 1986. *The Catholic Church and Politics in Brazil, 1916–1985*. Stanford: Stanford University Press.

——. 1989. "Grass-roots Catholic Groups." In *Progressive Church in Latin America,* edited by Mainwaring and Alexander Wilde. South Bend: University of Notre Dame Press.

Mamboleo, Wilson. 1991. *Prayer that Touches the Heart of God*. Nairobi: Prayer and Word Publications.

Manz, Beatriz. 1988. *Refugees of a Hidden War: The Aftermath of Counterinsurgency in Guatemala*. Albany: State University of New York.

MARC Newsletter. 1993. December, 5.

Marsden, George. 1991. *Understanding Evangelicalism and Fundamentalism*. Grand Rapids: Eerdmans.

——. 1987. *Reforming Fundamentalism: The Fuller Seminary*, Grand Rapids: Eerdmans.

Marshall, Ruth. 1992. "Pentecostalism in Southern Nigeria." In *New Dimensions in African Christianity,* edited by Paul Gifford. Ibadan, Nigeria: SEFER.

Marti, Tom. 1987. "Fundamentalist Sects and the Political Right." *Kalinangan* 7(1), 22–25

——. 1989. "Doctrine and Strategy: Low Intensity Conflict." Manila: Socio-Pastoral Institute.

Martin, David. 1990. *Tongues of Fire: The Explosion of Protestantism in Latin America*. Oxford: Basil Blackwell.

Marty, Martin E. 1970. *Righteous Empire*. NY: Dial Press.

Marty, Martin E., and R. Scott Appleby, eds. 1993. *Fundamentalisms and the State. Vol. III*. Chicago: University of Chicago Press.

———. 1993. *Fundamentalisms and Society: Reclaiming the Sciences, the Family, and Education. Vol. II*. Chicago: University of Chicago Press.

———. 1991. *Fundamentalisms Observed. Vol. I*. Chicago: University of Chicago Press.

"Massive Extrajudicial Executions in Rural Areas Under the Government of General Efrain Rios Montt." 1982. *Amnesty International*.

Mayer, Ann Elizabeth. 1993. "The Fundamentalist Impact on Law, Politics, and Constitutions in Iran, Pakistan, and the Sudan," in *Fundamentalisms and the State*, edited by Martin Marty and R. Scott Appleby. Chicago: University of Chicago Press.

McConnell, D. R. 1988. *A Different Gospel: A Historical and Biblical Analysis of the Modern Faith Movement*. Peabody, MS: Hendrickson Publishers.

McGavran, Donald. 1970. *Understanding Church Growth*. Grand Rapids: Eerdmans.

McLoughlin, W. 1978. *Revivals, Awakenings, and Reform*. Chicago: University of Chicago Press.

Melton, J. Gordon, ed. 1987. *Encyclopedia of American Religions*. Detroit: Gale Research.

———. 1993. "The Evangelical Thrust into Eastern Europe in the 1990s." Paper presented at International Conference on New Religion and the New Europe, Ondon School of Economics, 25–28 March.

Mickler, Michael L. 1987. *The Unification Church in America: A Bibliography and Research Guide*. NY: Garland.

Miguez Bonino, Jose. 1970. "Protestantism's Contribution to Latin America." *Lutheran Quarterly*, 22, 92–98.

———. 1975. *Doing Theology in a Revolutionary Situation*. Philadelphia: Fortress Press.

Miles, Sarah. n.d. "Low-Intensity Conflict: US New Strategy in the Third World," reprinted by Socio-Pastoral Institute (SPI). Special Issue, Series 5.

Miller, Stuart C. 1982. *Benevolent Assimilation*. New Haven: Yale University Press.

Missiongram. 1989. Vol. 10, No. 2.

Moon, Sun Myung. 1974. *Divine Principle*. NY: Holy Spirit Association.

Moore, James. 1993. "The Creationist Cosmos of Protestant Fundamentalism." In *Fundamentalism and Society*, edited by R. Scott Appleby and Martin E. Marty. Chicago: University of Chicago Press.

Moran, Elda Susan, and Lawrence Schlemmer. 1984. *Faith for the Fearful*. Durbin, South Africa: Center for Applied Social Science, University of Natal.

Moshay, G. J. O. 1990. *Who is this Allah?* Ibadan: Fireliners International.

Mouly, Ruth W. 1985. *The Religious Right and Israel: The Politics of Armageddon*. Chicago: Midwest Research.

———. 1985. *US-Arab Relations: The Evangelical Dimension*. Washington, D.C.: National Council on US-Arab Relations.

Moyers, Bill. 1987. "God and Politics"—Part I, Public Broadcasting System, 8 December. (Film).

Nasaw, David. 1979. *Schooled to Order: A Social History of Public Schooling in the United States*. Oxford: Oxford University Press.

Neibuhr, H. Richard. 1951. *Christ and Culture*. NY: Harper and Row.

New Christian Movements in Africa. 1993. Accra: SECAM.

Nicholas, Fort and Jojo de Leon. 1989. "Spiritual Renewal: The Philippine Experience." In *Exploring the New Religious Movements* in the Philippines. Auezon City: National Council of Churches in the Philippines.

Nida, Eugene A. 1969. *Communication of the Gospel in Latin America*. Cuernavaca, Mexico: Directorio de Publicaciones CIDOC.

Niebuhr, Gustav. 1987. "Poor, Rich Alike Stay Tuned to TV Preachers." *Atlanta Constitution*, 2 March, 6A.

———. 1995. "Promise Keepers." *New York Times*, 6 August 1A.

Novak, Michael. 1994. *The Catholic Ethic and the Spirit of Capitalism*. NY: Free Press.

O'Brien, Niall. 1992. Interview with author, Bacolod, June.

———. 1993. *Island of Tears, Island of Hope: Living the Gospel in A Revolutionary Situation*. Maryknoll, NY: Orbis Books.

O'Dowd, Tom and Kaulei Dowd. 1992. Interview with author. Bacolod, 31 May.

Omoobajesu, E.O. n.d. *My Experience in the Darkness of this World before Jesus Saved Me*. Agege (Lagos State): Omoobajesu World Outreach.

"On Their Own: A Preliminary Study of Youth Gangs in Guatemala City." 1988. *Cuadernos de Investigación*, No. 4, Guatemala City: AVANCSO, 40–44.

Ong, Walter. 1982. *Orality and Literacy: The Technologizing of the Word*. NY: Methuen.

Onyango, Symons. 1979. *Set Free from Demons: A Testimony to the Power of God to Deliver the Demon Possessed*. Nairobi: Evangel.

Orosa, Ramon. 1989. "A Voice in the Wilderness Speaks." *Ministry Digest*, November-December, 2.

———. 1992. Interview. Manila, 1 June.

———. n.d. "Unveiling of His Glory." Unpublished manuscript.

Osteen, John. 1972. *Pulling Down Strongholds*. Houston: John Osteen Ministries.

Our Family: The Magazines of the New Apostolic Church. 1993. Vol. 5, No. 7, July, 12.

Paloma, Margaret. 1989. *The Assemblies of God at the Crossroad: Charisma and Institutional Dilemmas*. Knoxville: University of Tennessee Press.

Pangilinan, Noel, and Merpu Roa. 1990. "Protestants Worry over Fundamentalist Drive." *Philippine Daily Globe*, 3 May, 7.

———. 1990. "RP clergy braces for 'invasion' by US fundamentalists." *Philippine Daily Globe*, 21 April, 18.

Peretti, Frank E. 1986. *This Present Darkness*. Wheaton IL: Crossway.

———. 1989. *Piercing the Darkness*. Wheaton IL: Crossway.

"Philippine Council of Evangelical Churches, Inc." Pamphlet.

Pierson, Paul. 1987. "Non-Western Missions: The Great New Fact of Our Time." In *New Frontiers in Mission*, edited by Patrick Sookhdeo. Exeter: The Paternoster Press.

Pimentel, Benjamin. 1991. *Rebolusyon!: A Generation of Struggle in the Philippines*. NY: Monthly Review Press.

Pineda-Ofreneo, Rosalinda. 1991. *The Philippines: Debt and Poverty*. Oxford: Oxfam.

Platt, Anthony. 1977. *The Child Savers*. Chicago: University of Chicago Press.

"Politica Institucional Hacia el Desplazado Interno en Guatemala." 1990. Cuadernos de Investigación No. 6. Guatemala City: AVANSCO, January.

Pope, Liston. *Millhands and Preachers*. New Haven: Yale University Press, 1942.

Prince, Derek. n.d. *Our Debt to Israel*. Fort Lauderdale, FL: Derek Prince Ministries.

Ramos, Joberto. 1992. Interview with author. Bacolod, 29 May.

National Council of Churches of the Philippines. 1991.*The Religious Right and National Security Doctrine*. Tugon: Manila.

"Retrato de Guatemala." 1988. Guatemala City: Equipo Sepal con Alianza Evangelica, Vision Mundial, Cruzada Estudiantil y Profesional para Cristo, December, 2.

Rhee, Hang Yul. "The Economic Problems of the Korean Political Economy," in *Political Change in South Korea,* edited by Ilplhong J. Kim and Young Whan Kihl. NY: Paragon House.

Riesebrodt, Martin. 1989. "The Comparative Study of Fundamentalism." Fundamentalism Project Lecture, University of Chicago, 30 October.

———. 1993. *Pious Passion: the emergence of modern fundamentalism in Iran and the United States*. Berkeley: University of California Press.

Rifkin, Jeremy (with Ted Howard). 1979. *The Emerging Order: God in an Age of Scarcity*, NY: Putnam.

"Right-Wing Vigilantes and U.S. Involvement: Report of a U.S. Fact-Finding Mission to the Philippines May 20–30, 1987." 1987. Manila: Philippine Alliance of Human Rights Advocates (PAHRA).

Rivera, Pastor Jose. 1992. Maranatha. Interview with author. Bacolod City, 29 May.

The Road To Damascus: Kairos and Conversion. 1989. Skotaville: Braamfontein, July, 23.

Robbins, Thomas. 1978. "The Last Civil Religion." with Dick Anthony, Madeline Doucas, Thomas Curtis. *Science, Sin, and Scholarship,* edited by Irving Horowitz. Cambridge: MIT Press.

Robert, Dana L. 1990. "The Crisis of Missions." in *Earthen Vessels: American Evangelicals and Foreign Missions, 1880–1980*, edited by Joel A. Carpenter and Wilbert R. Shenk. Grand Rapids: Eerdmans.

Roberts, Bryan. 1968. "Protestant Groups and Coping with Urban Life in Guatemala City." *American Journal of Sociology*, 73(6), May.

———. 1973. *Organizing Strangers: Poor Families in Guatemala City.* Austin: BooksDemand.

Robertson, Pat. 1986. *America's Date with Destiny*. Nashville, TN: Nelson.

———. 1987. *The Secret Kingdom*. San Francisco: Harper and Row.

———. 1991. *The New World Order.* Dallas: Word Publishing.

Robertson, Roland, and JoAnn Chirico. 1985. "Humanity, Globalization, and World-wide Religious Resurgence: A Theoretical Exploration." *Sociological Analysis* Vol. 46:3.

Robinson, Mark. 1989. *Summer Missions Handbook 1990*. La Mirada, CA: Biola University.

Rolim, Fernando Cartaxo. 1985. *Pentecostals No Brasil*. Petropolis Vozes.

Roof, Wade Clark, ed. 1991. *World Order and Religion*. Albany: SUNY Press.

Rose, Susan D. 1987. "Conversations of Conversion: Interviewing American Evangelical Women." *International Journal of Oral History*, Vol. 8, No. 1: 28–40.

———. 1987. "Woman Warriors: The Negotiation of Gender in a Charismatic Community." *Sociological Analysis*. Vol. 48: No. 3: 245–258.

———. 1988. *Keeping Them Out of the Hands of Satan*. Critical Social Thought Series edited by Michael Apple. London: Routledge & Kegan Paul.

———. 1993. "Christian Fundamentalism and Education in the United States." *Fundamentalisms and Society*, edited by Martin E. Marty and R. Scott Appleby. Chicago: University of Chicago.

———. 1996. "The Politics of Philippine Fundamentalism." In Questioning the Secular State, edited by David Westerlund. In press: Hurst.

Rose, Susan D. and Stephen Brouwer. 1987. "The Reproduction of Secular Worlds in Sacred Institutions: A Critique of Christian Schools." *Issues in Education* 4 (Fall), No 2, 136–150.

Rose, Susan D. and Quentin Schultz. 1993. "An Awakening in Guatemala." In *Fundamentalisms and Society*, edited by Martin E. Marty and R. Scott Appleby. Chicago: University of Chicago Press.

Rostow, W. W. 1991. *The Stages of Economic Growth: A Non-Communist Manifesto*. Cambridge: Cambridge University Press.

Rubenstein, Richard L. 1987. "The Rational Society and the Future of Religion." In *The Search for Faith and Justice in the Twentieth Century,* edited by Gene G. James. New York: Paragon House.

Rubenstein, Richard L., and John K. Roth, ed. 1988. *The Politics of Latin American Liberation Theology*. Washington: Washington Institute.

Rushdoony, Rousas John. 1991. *The Roots of Reconstruction*. Vallecito, CA: Ross House Books.

Ryrie, Charles C. 1981. *The Best is Yet to Come*. Chicago: Moody Press.

Sabug, Fructuoso T. 1991. "The Religious Right in the Philippines: A Preliminary Study." In *The Religious Right and The National Security State*. Manila: Tugon, NCCP.

Salazar, Stuart. 1990. Interview with author, 22 March.

Sandeen, Ernest R. 1970. *The Roots of Fundamentalism: British and American Millenarianism, 1800–1930*. Chicago: University of Chicago Press.

Scannone, Juan Carlos. 1977. "Popular Culture: Pastoral and Theological Considerations." *Lumen Vitae*, 32, 159–174.

Schirmer, Daniel B., and Stephen R. Shalom, ed. 1987. *The Philippines Reader: A History of Colonialism, Neocolonialism, Dictatorship, and Resistance*. Boston: South End Press.

Schultze, Quentin J. 1990. *AEM*. Grand Rapids, MI: Zondervan/Academic.

———. 1994. "Orality and Power in Latin American Pentecostalism." In *Coming of Age: Protestantism in Contemporary Latin America*, edited by Daniel Miller. NY: University Press of America.

Seyon, Patrick L. N. 1988. "The Results of the 1985 Elections," *Liberian Studies Journal*, XIII, 2.

Shupe, Anson. 1990. "Sun Myung Moon's American Disappointment," *Christian Century,* 22 August.

Siewert, John, and John Kenyon, ed. 1986. *Mission Handbook*. 13th ed. Monrovia, CA: MARC.

———. 1989. *Mission Handbook*. 14th ed. Monrovia, CA: MARC.

———. 1993. *Mission Handbook 1993–95*. 15th ed. Monrovia, CA: MARC.

Signpost. 1992. March, 1.

Simons, Marlise. 1982. "Latin America's New Gospel," *New York Times Magazine,* 7 November.

Slater, Rosalie. 1965. *Teaching and Learning America's Christian History*. San Francisco: The Foundation for American Christian Education.

Smith, Dennis. 1988. "The Impact of Religious Programming in the Electronic Media on the Active Christian Population in Central America." *Latin American Pastoral Issues*, 15 (July), 76–77.

———. 1990. "The Gospel According to the United States: Evangelical Broadcasting in Central America," *American Evangelicals and the Mass Media*, edited by Quentin Schultze. Grand Rapids, MI: Zondervan/Academie.

———. 1991. *The Emergence of Liberation Theology: Radical Religion and Social Movement Theory.* Chicago: University of Chicago Press.

Smith, Dennis. n.d. "Guatemala in Numbers" (manuscript), 1.

———. 1990. Interview with author. March.

Smith, Steve. 1990. Interview with author. Guatemala City, 3 April.

"Something More Than A CIA Conspiracy" 1989. In the *Faith and Ideology Series*. Manila, Socio-Pastoral Institute, C4.

Song Kon-ho. 1985. "A History of the Christian Movement in Korea." *International Review of Missions,* Volume 74, January.

Soonjung, Lee Daniel. 1988. *A Historical Study of the National Evangelization Movement of Korea*. Dissertation, Fuller Theology School.

Stacey, Judith. 1991. *Brave New Families*. NY: Basic Books.

Standard. 1992. 24 February, 1.

Step. Vol 13, No 11, I.

Stockton, Ronald R. 1987. "Christian Zionism: Prophecy and Public Opinion." *The Middle East Journal*. Vol. 41, No. 2, Spring.

Stoll, David. 1982. *Fishers of Men or Founders of Empire?* London: Zed Press.

———. 1990. *Is Latin America Turning Protestant? The Politics of Evangelical Growth*. Berkeley: University of California Press.

———. 1994. "Jesus is Lord of Guatemala: The Prospects for Evangelical Reform in a Death Squad State." In *Accounting for Fundamentalism*, edited by Emmanuel Sivan and Gabriel Almond. Chicago: University of Chicago Press.

Stoll, David and Virginia Garrard-Burnett, ed. 1993. *Rethinking Protestantism in Latin America*. Philadelphia: Temple University Press.

Subritsky, Bill. 1986. *Demons Defeated.* Chichester: Sovereign World.

Suh, David Kwang-sun. 1985. "American Missionaries and a Hundred Years of Korean Protestantism," *International Review of Missions,* Vol. 74.

Suh, Kim Kyong. 1985. "The Explosive Growth of the Korean Church Today," *International Review of Mission,* Vol. 74, January.

Sumrall, Lester. 1980. *Jihad: The Holy War: The Destiny of Iran and the Moslem World.* Tulsa: Harrison House.

———. 1984. *Alien Entities: Beings from Beyond.* South Bend, IN: Lesea.

———. 1984. *Jerusalem: Where Empires Die.* Nashville, TN: Thomas Nelson.

———. 1987. *I Predict 2000 AD.* South Bend, IN: Lesea Publishing.

———. 1989. *Three Habitations of Devils.* LeSea Publications.

———. 1990. "Communicating Faith." In *Church Growth Manual #3.* Seoul: Church Growth International, 173–194.

Sunoo, Harold Hak-won.1970. *Korea: A History in Modern Times.* Seoul: Kunkuk University Press.

Suzara, Araceli. 1993. "Cultist Vigilantism in the Philippines," Sociology of Religion 54 (3) Fall, 303–308.

Swatos, William H. 1991. "Max Weber as 'Christian Sociologist'." *Journal for the Scientific Study of Religion.* December.

The Sword of the Spirit. 1991. No. 47.

Synan, Vinson. 1971. *The Holiness Pentecostal Movement in the United States.* Grand Rapids: Eerdmans.

———. 1992. *The Spirit Said: "Grow."* Monrovia, CA: MARC.

Takaki, Ronald. 1993. *A Different Mirror.* Boston: Little Brown and Company.

Tanee, Zacharias Foomum. n.d. *Deliverance from Demons.* Yaounde (Cameroon): IGH (Box 6090 Yaounde).

Tangeman, Mike. "'Evangelización 2000' and 'Lumen 2000': Their Impacts on the Catholic Faith in the Developing World." Unpublished manuscript.

Tappeiner, Daniel. 1989: "Prepare War! The Spirit's Call to Spiritual Warfare." *Ministry Digest.* November/December, 42, Fall, 303–308.

Tarr, Byron. 1990. "Founding the Liberian Action Party," *Liberian Studies Journal,* 15, 1.

Taryor, Nya Kwiawon. 1985. *Justice, Justice: A Cry of My People: The Struggle for Economic Progress and Social Justice in Liberia.* Chicago: Strugglers' Community Press.

Tawney, R. D. 1929. *Protestantism and the Rise of Capitalism.* London: J. Murray.

Taylor, Clyde W. and Wade T. Coggins. 1961. *Protestant Missions in Latin America: A Statistical Survey.* Washington, D.C.: Evangelical Foreign Missions Association, vii.

Thomas, George. 1989. *Revivalism and Cultural Change.* Chicago: University of Chicago Press.

Thompson, Edward P. 1968. *The Making of the English Working Class.* Harmondsworth: Penguin.

Tibi, Bassam. 1993. "The Worldview of Sunni Arab Fundamentalists: Attitudes Toward Modern Science and Technology." In *Fundamentalisms and Society,* edited by

Martin E. Marty and R. Scott Appleby. Chicago: University of Chicago Press.

Tica, Gavino. 1993. Interview with author. Manila. 1 June.

Tiplas, 1992. Bishop, Philippines Independent Church. Interview with author. Bacolod, 29 May.

Today's Challenge (Jos). 1988. No. 6, 26.

Torres, Fernando. 1989. "La fe via satélite." *Solidaridad*, June.

Toulouse, Mark. 1985. *The Transformation of John Foster Dulles*. Macon: Mercer University Press.

Toville, Ariel 1992. Bishop, Church of the Latter Day Saints. Interview with author. Bacolod, 31 May.

The Trumpet. 1989. January.

24 Hours. 1991. BBC World Service, 8 September.

Ungar, Sanford J. 1985. "The Roots of Estrangement." In *Estrangement: America and the World*. edited by Sanford J. Unger. NY: Oxford University Press.

———. 1986. *Africa: The People and Politics of an Emerging Continent*. Rev. ed. NY: Simon and Schuster.

"U.S. Evangelist's Expensive Nicaraguan Campaign Encounters Rocky Ground." 1990. *CEPAD Report*. March-April, 5–7.

United States of America. 1989. *Congressional Presentation for Security Assistance Programmes Fiscal Year 1990*. Washington, D.C.

United Nations Development Programme. 1992. *Human Development Report—1992*. NY: Oxford University Press.

Uzora, Iyke Nathan. 1993. *Occult Grand Master Now in Christ*. Benin City, Osabu.

Valenzuela, Monsignor Bayani. 1990. "Update on Fundamentalist Groups in the Philippines Today." Prepared by the Archdiocesan Office for Ecumenical and Interfaith Affairs, April.

———. 1992. Interview with author. Quezon, 2 June.

"Value Formation." 1987. *Ang Tala*, September, 4, 18.

Van Meter, Jim. 1990. *Making Missions Practical*. Davao City: Mindanao Challenge.

Vencer, Jun. 1990. "The Church and National Recovery." *Ministry Digest*. 1(5), 7–8.

———. 1992. Interview with author. Manila, 1 June.

Vigilantism in Negros. 1988. Bacolod: Task Force Detainees of the Philippines.

Villanueva, Brother Eddie. 1989. Excerpt from TV on address on December 4, "A Message to the Filipino Nation." *Ministry Digest*. November/December, 5–6.

Wacker, Grant. 1994. "Planning Ahead: The Enduring Appeal of Prophecy Belief." *Christian Century*. 19 January, 48.

Waghelstein, Col. John W. 1985. "Post-Vietnam Counterinsurgency Doctrine," *Military Review*, May, 42.

Wagner, C. Peter. 1989. "Territorial Spirits." *Ministry Digest*, November/December, 42.

Wagner, C. Peter, Win Arn, and Elmer Towns. 1989. *Church Growth: State of the Art*. Wheaton, IL: Tyndale.

Waldrop, Rick. 1987. Interview with author. Guatemala City, July.

Wallace, Anthony. 1978. *Rockdale*. NY: W. W. Norton and Co.

Wallerstein, Immanuel. 1983. *Historical Capitalism*. London: Verso.

Wallis, Jim. 1986. "A Wolf in Sheep's Clothing: the Political Right Invades the Evangelical Fold." *Sojourners,* May.

Wallis, Jim, and Wes Michaelson. 1976. "Building Up the Common Life." *Sojourners.* April.

Walls, A. F. 1990. "The American Dimension in the Missionary Movement." In *Earthen Vessels: American Evangelicals and Foreign Missions,* edited by Joel A. Carpenter and Wilbert R. Shook. Grand Rapids: Eerdmans.

———. "World Christianity, the Missionary Movement, and the Ugly American." In *World Order and Religion*, edited by Wade Clark Roof. Albany: SUNY Press.

Walvoord, John F. 1967. *The Nations in Prophecy*. Grand Rapids, MI: Zondervan.

Wearmouth, Robert F. 1937. *Methodism and the Working Class Movement of England.* London: Epworth Press.

Weber, Max. 1930. *Protestant Ethic and the Spirit of Capitalism*. London: G. Allen Unwin.

———. 1968. *Economy and Society, Volume I.* Berkeley: University of California Press.

Weinstein, James. 1968. *The Corporate Ideal in the Liberal State: 1900–1918*. Boston: Beacon Press.

Wells, Kenneth. 1990. *New God, New Nation: Protestants and Self-Reconstruction Nationalism in Korea*. Honolulu: University of Hawaii Press.

Wert, Maria C., and Robert L. Stevenson. 1988. "Global Television Flow to Latin America." *Journalism Quarterly*. 65 (Spring), 182–185.

White, Robert. 1982. "The Church and Communication in Latin America: Thirty Years to Search for Patterns." *Communication Socialist Yearbook*. Indore, India: Sat Prachar Press, 98.

Williams, Jim. 1990. "Church Growth and Goal-Setting." *Church Growth Manual #3.* Seoul: Church Growth International.

Willems, Emilio. 1967. *Followers of the New Faith*. Nashville: Vanderbilt University Press.

———. 1975. *Latin American Culture: An Anthropological Synthesis*. NY: Harper and Row.

Willis, Elbert. n.d. *Exposing the Devil's Work*. Lafayette, LA: Fill the Gap Publications.

Wilson, Dwight. 1977. *Armageddon Now! The Premillenarian Response to Russia and Israel Since 1917*. Grand Rapids, MI: Baker Book House.

1988. Wilson, Everett. "The Central American Evangelicals," *International Review of Missions*, 77, January.

Wimber, John. *Signs and Wonders and Church Growth*. Placentia, CA: Vineyard Missions International.

World Harvest. 1990. September-October, 8–9.

"World Shakers." 1994. *Word of Faith*, July.

Wreh, Tuan. 1976. *The Love of Liberty…The Rule of President William V. S. Tubman in Liberia*. London: C. Hurst.

Wright, Gavin. 1990. "The Origins of American Industrial Success, 1879–1940," *American Economic Review*, September.

Wuthnow, Robert. 1983. "Cultural Crises." In *Crises in the World System,* edited by Albert Bergesen.

———. 1993. "Pious Materialism: How Americans View Faith and Money." *Christian Century.* 3 March.

Zapata A., Virgilio. 1982. *Historia de la iglesia evangélica en Guatemala.* Guatemala City: Genesis Publicidad.

———. 1987. Interview with author, Guatemala City. June.

Index